Relying on personal interviews with senior officials in a dozen countries and never-before-released classified information, *Bridled Ambition: Why Countries Constrain Their Nuclear Capabilities* explains how and why nine countries—South Africa, Argentina, Brazil, Ukraine, Belarus, Kazakhstan, India, Pakistan, and North Korea—have capped, curtailed, or rolled back their nuclear weapons programs during the past few years.

Their motivations varied. In the successors of the Soviet Union, for example, the end of the cold war eliminated the initial reason the weapons had been put in place, and new political, economic, and military uncertainties made it dangerous to maintain them. In South Africa, the anticipated transition to majority rule would put nuclear weapons in the hands of a longstanding, untrusted opposition.

But in general, Reiss suggests, nuclear weapons may have come to be viewed as expensive and dangerous anachronisms.

Reiss details the histories of the debates and politics of these nuclear programs. His account draws on interviews with more than 150 officials, on documentary evidence, and on journalistic accounts. In addition to the information brought forward on politics within the affected countries, *Bridled Ambition* includes information on the efforts and influence of U.S. diplomacy on these processes.

Bridled Ambition

Bridled Ambition

Why Countries Constrain Their Nuclear Capabilities

Mitchell Reiss

W/ *Published by The Woodrow Wilson Center Press*
Distributed by The Johns Hopkins University Press

Woodrow Wilson Center Special Studies

The Woodrow Wilson Center Press
Editorial Offices
370 L'Enfant Promenade, S.W.
Suite 704
Washington, D.C. 20024-2518 U.S.A.
telephone 202-287-3000, ext. 218

Distributed by
The Johns Hopkins University Press
Hampden Station
Baltimore, Maryland 21211
order department telephone 1-800-537-5487

Cover design by Meadows and Wiser Graphic Design, Washington, D.C.

Printed in the United States of America

♾Printed on acid-free paper.

Library of Congress Cataloging-in-Publication Data

Reiss, Mitchell.
Bridled ambition : why countries constrain their nuclear capabilities / by
    Mitchell Reiss.
        p.   cm.—(Woodrow Wilson Center special studies)
    Includes bibliographical references and index.
        ISBN 0-943875-72-2 (cloth) : $45.00.—ISBN 0-943875-71-4 (pbk.) : $16.95
        1. Nuclear weapons—Government policy—Case studies.   2. Nuclear
    nonproliferation—Case studies.   I. Title.   II. Series.
    U264.R45   1995
    355.02′17—dc20
                                                                        95-2646
                                                                          CIP

To Elisabeth

The Woodrow Wilson International Center for Scholars

The Center is the living memorial of the United States of America to the nation's twenty-eighth president, Woodrow Wilson. The Congress established the Woodrow Wilson Center in 1968 as an international institute for advanced study, "symbolizing and strengthening the fruitful relationship between the world of learning and the world of public affairs." The Center opened in 1970 under its own board of trustees.

Woodrow Wilson Center Special Studies

The work of the Center's Fellows, Guest Scholars, and staff—and presentations and discussions at the Center's conferences, seminars, and colloquia—often deserve timely circulation as contributions to public understanding of issues of national and international importance. The Woodrow Wilson Center Special Studies series makes such materials available by the Woodrow Wilson Center Press to interested scholars, practitioners, and other readers. In all its activities, the Woodrow Wilson Center is a nonprofit, nonpartisan organization, supported financially by annual appropriations from the Congress, and by the contributions of foundations, corporations, and individuals. Conclusions or opinions expressed in Center publications and programs are those of the authors and speakers and do not necessarily reflect the views of the Center staff, Fellows, trustees, advisory groups, or any individuals or organizations that provide financial support to the Center.

Contents

Chapter 1

Introduction

The end of the cold war has forced the United States to rethink the tenets that have guided American foreign policy for the past five decades. Government officials and foreign policy pundits alike have struggled to fashion a unified field theory that sets out a comprehensive U.S. approach to a radically changed, and still changing, international environment. Attempts to map a clear path forward, from President George Bush's "new world order" to National Security Adviser Anthony Lake's "democratic enlargement" to former Secretary of State James Baker's "selective engagement," have emphasized different and sometimes contradictory national interests.

All of these competing strategic approaches, however, share one essential priority: preventing the spread of nuclear weapons. This concern is not new. Since the early days of the Manhattan Project, Washington has tried to thwart the nuclear ambitions of other countries, but the intensity of these efforts has fluctuated over time. With the end of the cold war, fears that many countries might build the bomb have revived. Reflecting this renewed apprehension, President Bill Clinton has repeatedly stressed that nuclear proliferation poses the single greatest threat to U.S. security and international peace in the 1990s.

Yet recent expressions of proliferation anxiety have ignored many positive developments during the past few years. Coinciding with the thaw and then the end of the cold war, several countries that possessed robust nuclear weapons programs or harbored nuclear aspirations have slowed, halted, or even reversed their activities. This book examines eight of these countries—South Africa, Argentina, Brazil, Ukraine, Belarus, Kazakhstan, India, and Pakistan—and explores the reasons for their nuclear restraint.

The book also analyzes a ninth country: North Korea. When I began my research in late 1992, it appeared that Pyongyang had curtailed its nuclear program and abandoned the pursuit of nuclear weapons; in other words, North Korea was another nonproliferation success story.

1

But in February 1993, North Korea rejected a formal request by the International Atomic Energy Agency (IAEA) to inspect two nuclear waste sites, and two months later Pyongyang threatened to leave the nuclear Nonproliferation Treaty (NPT). Although it eventually remained an NPT member, Pyongyang refused to fully abide by its nonproliferation obligations. By 1994, the U.S. intelligence community believed that Pyongyang had separated enough bomb-grade plutonium to build one or two nuclear devices.

During much of the time that I conducted my research, North Korea seemed the odd man out in this study. Yet even though the country thumbed its nose at the rest of the world and played a risky game of nuclear brinkmanship, closer examination revealed that Pyongyang had deliberately refrained from taking certain steps: breaking unambiguously with the NPT, denying complete access to IAEA inspectors, or reprocessing nuclear fuel since 1992. Certainly, no one would have praised North Korea's behavior during the past few years, but it could have been much worse. Why it was not seemed worth examining. An even more compelling reason for including the country in this study was provided in October 1994 when the United States and North Korea arrived at an Agreed Framework that, if fully honored, promised to resolve the nuclear dispute in the next ten to twelve years.

Many of the nonproliferation developments in these countries were not predicted; some challenged conventional wisdom and overturned expectations. They certainly were not inevitable.

So why did they occur?

Many factors swayed policy in each of these countries, all of which were influenced unequally and sporadically. The demise of the Soviet Union and the end of the superpower competition influenced the entire international system, upsetting old relationships, forging new ones, and creating overnight three sovereign states with nuclear weapons stationed on their territories. For some countries, new uncertainties provided new incentives for acquiring nuclear arms.

But for most others, the end of the cold war reinforced an antinuclear taboo that has gained strength as the nuclear age has unfolded. That thirty thousand nuclear weapons could not preserve the Soviet Union, and may even have hastened its collapse, raised new questions about the value of nuclear arms. Recent reductions in the nuclear arsenals of Moscow and Washington lowered the status usually associated with these weapons and strengthened the perception that they are little more than elaborate and expensive anachronisms. Other arms control and disarmament steps, notably the moratoria on nuclear testing by four nuclear weapon states, further contributed to delegitimizing this type of military force.

A fuller accounting of the "hidden" costs of the nuclear competition has reinforced this devaluation. The enormous economic sacrifice of the Soviet-American nuclear arms race includes the opportunity costs of having talented scientists, engineers, and technicians devote their professional careers to expanding the nuclear stockpile and the costs of the significant environmental damage from the nuclear weapons complexes. Nor has the expense of the arms race ended with the cold war; nuclear weapons dismantlement and environmental cleanup costs furnish a bitter nuclear legacy for future generations. In the United States, estimates for environmental remediation range from $30 billion to $100 billion. Given the strained financial conditions of Russia and the other newly independent states, it is unlikely that funds will be made available to adequately repair the even more widespread environmental damage from the Soviet nuclear weapons complex. All of these developments increase the perception that the coin of the realm in the twenty-first century will be economic, not military, power.

Traditional diplomatic haggling played a far more direct role in the decisions of many of these countries. The United States, and others, used a mixture of carrots and sticks to move countries away from the nuclear threshold. To an unprecedented degree, financial incentives rewarded restraint. For North Korea, Ukraine, Kazakhstan, and Belarus, for example, it literally became profitable to renounce nuclear weapons or constrain nuclear activities.

Unrelated to the tectonic shifts at the international and regional levels, prosaic local concerns also influenced nuclear decision making. Economic costs were crucial in at least two countries, and an inevitable change in government was determinative in another. In all these countries, political personalities and the quality of leadership, both good and bad, influenced nuclear decisions.

Understanding how each of these states came to restrain or abandon its nuclear aspirations is not only valuable in its own right. Since the past is not a "wilderness of single instances," in the words of the English poet Lord Tennyson, the nuclear decisions taken by all of these countries have common factors that can inform future nonproliferation policies. It is not enough to mourn nonproliferation failures. We need to understand past successes in order to apply their lessons in the future.

Future proliferation problems may even involve a few of the countries in this study, since many of the "success stories" examined here remain unfinished. Nonproliferation backsliding may yet occur; political commitments can be renounced, and legal obligations can be broken. Nuclear recidivism is a possibility, with North Korea the most likely candidate.

Any discussion of a subject as complex as nonproliferation contains its own priorities and assumptions and hence its own limitations. This book devotes special attention to the U.S. role in all of these developments. To be sure, the United States was not the only actor—and at times, not even the most important one—in the nuclear decisions of the nine countries. Yet even critics of U.S. nonproliferation policy would agree that Washington played a useful, and sometimes indispensable, role in cajoling, convincing, or coercing these countries to relinquish their nuclear ambitions. A key question, therefore, is how Washington influenced these decisions or why it fell short in the attempt.

This book does not attempt a comprehensive review of proliferation developments around the globe. Other countries, such as Iraq, Israel, South Korea, and Taiwan, could have been included but were not. Iraq was not examined because the reasons for the country's denuclearization are plain: its defeat in the Persian Gulf war led to the mandatory inspections and dismantlement activities imposed by the United Nations. In Israel's case, there is simply not enough progress to report at this time. Although Israel has recently discussed its nuclear weapons program with the United States, there has been no apparent change in its nuclear posture. South Korea and Taiwan, in response to great American pressure, abandoned their nuclear ambitions during the 1970s, which predates the focus of this study.[1]

A book that depends as heavily as this one does on personal interviews must recognize the hazards of writing contemporary history. Foremost among them is that recollections of those interviewed always present the possibility of bias, selective memory, or outright falsehoods. That I talked with many individuals personally responsible for developing and implementing the nuclear policies under discussion only multiplies incentives for self-aggrandizement and misrepresentation. "Vanity," the novelist Joseph Conrad warned, "plays lurid tricks with our memory."

Certain precautions have been taken to counter flawed memories and attempts to rewrite history. Information from personal interviews has been checked against the written record of government reports, official statements, scholarly articles, and newspaper accounts or was confirmed by at least one other person. In addition, most interviews were conducted off the record, in the hope that with anonymity would come greater honesty and candor. By and large, this method seems to have worked well.

A wit once remarked that there are only two types of foreign policy: "muddle through" and "screw up." This skeptical comment suggests that the task of constructing policies whose wisdom and shrewdness are confirmed over time is not just a mystery but a mirage. The histories of all countries are littered with good intentions and not-so-good results. Fainthearted leaders, uncooperative allies, cunning adversaries, malicious domestic critics, and faulty implementation can frustrate even the most thoughtful designs. Samuel Johnson, that keen observer of eighteenth-century life, was not far wrong when he wrote, "The history of mankind is little else than a narrative of designs, which have failed, and hopes that have been disappointed." Sometimes things go right, however, if only by accident or luck. Loose change does not always roll away when dropped, taxicabs are not always off duty when hailed in the rain, and the breakfast toast does not always land on the floor jam-side down.

Yet serendipity and good fortune do not deserve all the credit for the rare happy successes. Things sometimes do work as planned. Countries, and their leaders, are not passive bystanders in the unfolding historical drama; they are not always at the mercy of vast impersonal forces beyond their control. Wise decisions on issues of great national importance can be conceived and implemented successfully. Beyond muddling through and screwing up, there is a third way: getting it right.

Regarding nuclear weapons, many of the countries in this book "got it right." In most cases they succeeded not immediately, perhaps, but eventually; in some cases, not completely but partially; and in a few cases, not always of their own free will. In this last group, other countries got it right, by successfully convincing, compelling, or coercing these states to abandon or curb their nuclear weapons programs.

Although these developments undoubtedly contributed to international peace and stability, their larger significance may simply be the examples they offer: eloquent testimony that the nuclear age is man-made and can, perhaps, be ended by man. These events remind the world, especially the United States and the other nuclear weapon states, that nuclear arsenals are not permanent fixtures on the international landscape. Although nuclear know-how can never be disinvented, policies can be reversed, weapons labs can be shut down, and nuclear arms can be dismantled and destroyed. By doing the unthinkable, these countries force us to reexamine our devoutly held assumptions about the importance of nuclear weapons and their place in international affairs.

Note

[1]For an examination of Iraq's nuclear program and the UN inspection and dismantlement programs, see Peter D. Zimmerman, "Iraq's Nuclear Achievements: Components, Sources, and Stature," *CRS Report for Congress*, Library of Congress, February 18, 1993; IAEA, "IAEA Inspections and Iraq's Nuclear Capabilities" (Vienna: IAEA, 1992); Hans Blix, "Verification and Iraq," and Rolf Ekeus, "Iraq and Nonproliferation," *Washington Quarterly* 15, no. 4 (Autumn 1992): 57–65, 67–73.

According to one news report, the United States has held secret discussions with Israel on constraining its nuclear program. See Seymour Hersh, "Israel May Give Up Nuclear Edge," *Los Angeles Times*, February 2, 1993.

For an examination of the South Korean case, see Mitchell Reiss, *Without the Bomb: The Politics of Nuclear Nonproliferation* (New York: Columbia University Press, 1988), pp. 78–108. For an examination of the Taiwanese case, see Joseph Yager, "Taiwan," in Joseph Yager, ed., *Nonproliferation and U.S. Foreign Policy* (Washington, D.C.: Brookings, 1980), pp. 66–81.

Chapter 2

South Africa: "Castles in the Air"

On Wednesday, March 24, 1993, before a special joint session of the South African parliament and a national radio audience, President F. W. de Klerk disclosed, "At one stage South Africa did develop a limited nuclear deterrent capability . . . of seven nuclear fission devices." He explained, "Early in 1990, final effect was given to decisions that all the nuclear devices should be dismantled and destroyed." According to de Klerk, "all the hardware and design information was destroyed" by the time South Africa signed the NPT in July 1991.[1]

De Klerk's announcement shocked the world, including the staff of the American Embassy in South Africa and U.S. government analysts who had long charted South Africa's nuclear program.[2] De Klerk provided official confirmation of what many had long suspected: that South Africa had surreptitiously acquired a small nuclear arsenal. But no one would have predicted that after building these devices, South Africa would become the first and only example of nuclear "rollback," voluntarily and unilaterally dismantling its nuclear arsenal.

South Africa's Nuclear Program

In his parliamentary speech, de Klerk emphasized his hope that "this chapter of the past [could] be closed and that a new one of international cooperation and trust [could] be opened." But South Africa's suspicious nuclear past cast a long shadow. Despite his claims that "South Africa's hands" were "clean" and that the country was "concealing nothing," the president's announcement resurrected old questions about the country's nuclear activities and raised new ones about the original motives behind South Africa's decision to build nuclear weapons.

BUILDING THE CAPABILITY: 1970–79

On July 20, 1970, Prime Minister John Vorster informed parliament that government scientists had developed a "unique" process for en-

7

riching uranium. Vorster repeatedly emphasized that this technology, the product of almost ten years of secret research, would be used only for peaceful purposes.[3] Left unsaid was that this new capability could also make South Africa the world's next nuclear weapon state.

In March 1971, the minister of mines, Carel de Wet, approved "preliminary investigations" into the feasibility of producing nuclear explosives. These investigations were limited to theoretical calculations, however; no serious development was carried out at this stage. For example, only three engineers were assigned to study implosion technology and ballistics research related to gun-type devices.[4]

A nuclear device required the capability either to enrich uranium or reprocess spent fuel to obtain plutonium. That same year, construction of a small-scale "pilot" enrichment plant began at Valindaba, next to the headquarters of the Atomic Energy Corporation (AEC) at Pelindaba, located outside of Pretoria.[5] In 1974, the AEC reported to Prime Minister Vorster that it could build a nuclear explosive device. Vorster authorized development of nuclear explosives and approved funding for a testing site.[6]

The pilot enrichment plant, named the Y Plant, first produced a small quantity of highly enriched uranium (HEU) in January 1978. During the remainder of that year and most of the next, the Y Plant continued to produce enriched uranium hexafluoride. This material was later converted to uranium metal at a facility at Pelindaba. It was enriched to only 80 percent U-235—far short of the 90-plus percent enrichment levels preferred by weapons designers.[7] South Africa's first workable nuclear device was fitted with this not-quite-weapons-grade HEU in November 1979.[8]

During this period, South Africa did not lack motivation to build nuclear weapons. The regime's peculiar policy of racial separateness, known as *apartheid*, had long aroused international criticism. But a series of setbacks during the 1970s shattered domestic tranquility and severely eroded the strategic position of the white laager. In 1974, the Caetano regime in Lisbon fell, triggering the devolution of Portugal's colonial holdings in southern Africa and the removal of a white *cordon sanitaire* around South Africa. The January 1975 Alvor Accords outlining a peaceful transition in Angola broke down almost immediately as three rival liberation movements made a grab for power. In October, South Africa's failed intervention in the ensuing Angolan civil war resulted in the new Luanda government's open hostility toward Pretoria and the introduction of fifty thousand Cuban troops.[9] And on South Africa's northeastern border, a pro-Soviet, Marxist-Leninist regime assumed power in Mozambique.

Inside South Africa, the June 1976 Soweto riots and the death of the black consciousness leader Steven Biko while in police detention the following year resulted in further international censure. This ostracism spilled over to nuclear matters as the United States refused to export enriched uranium for the Safari-1 research reactor, even though South Africa had already paid for the fuel.[10] The IAEA, which South Africa had helped found, kicked its former patron off the Board of Governors in June 1977. That same year, the United States, Britain, France, Canada, and West Germany formed a "Contact Group" to push Pretoria's withdrawal from Namibia and manage that country's transition to independence.[11] In addition, the United Nations (UN) Security Council mandated the voluntary arms embargo against South Africa that had existed since 1963.

Pretoria viewed this constellation of economic, political, and military pressures against the country as a conspiratorial "total onslaught" by the forces of international communism, orchestrated by Moscow. As the 1977 Ministry of Defense *White Paper* warned, "We are today involved in a war, whether we wish to accept it or not." This challenge to the country's existence could be countered only by a "Total National Strategy"—a comprehensive plan for "state mobilization and coordination of all South Africa's resources to meet the threat of 'total war.' "[12] To sustain the country's military involvement in Angola and Namibia and to suppress domestic unrest and terrorism inside its borders, Pretoria doubled the size of its armed forces and tripled the defense budget during the latter half of the decade.

Believing that it would receive no outside assistance should it be attacked, South Africa also decided to accelerate the nuclear program. In 1977, Vorster convened his senior officials to discuss the future of the program and instructed them to draft a document outlining the country's nuclear course, which he formally approved in April 1978. That October, Prime Minister P. W. Botha appointed an "Action Committee" to recommend future plans for producing nuclear devices. The committee delivered its first recommendations in July 1979, proposing the manufacture of seven weapons.[13]

THE KALAHARI TEST SITE

To ensure that all its time, effort, and money were not wasted, Pretoria planned a test of its first nuclear device, just as all previous nuclear weapon states had done. In 1974, it began construction of a nuclear test site at the Vastrap military base in the Kalahari desert. The world's mild response to India's testing of a nuclear explosive in May

1974 had encouraged South Africa to believe that testing a nuclear device "would not lead to excessive international reaction."[14] Three test shafts were drilled. One hit unfavorable geological conditions and flooded, but the other two were completed.

Pretoria chose not to bury the electronic monitoring equipment, power generators, and associated facilities because it did not anticipate that its activities would be observed. Further, according to J. W. de Villiers, a weapons designer who later became president and then chairman of the board of the AEC, it was simply "too damn expensive to go underground completely."[15]

By 1977, the AEC had assembled all the nonnuclear components of a nuclear device, although the Y Plant had not yet produced any HEU for the core. The AEC planned a fully instrumented "cold test" using a depleted uranium "pit" to show the behavior of uranium metal under the conditions expected when exploding a nuclear weapon.[16] According to the original plans, the AEC intended to conduct a "true" nuclear test using an HEU pit the following year.[17]

On July 30, 1977, a Soviet satellite passing over South Africa spotted the distinctive configuration of a nuclear test site in the Kalahari desert. On August 6, a second Soviet satellite made four more passes.[18] Moscow immediately alerted Washington that South Africa was preparing to conduct a nuclear test. The United States redirected its satellites to independently confirm this information, and it then told Pretoria that a nuclear explosion would have severe repercussions. Paris, Bonn, and London issued similar warnings.[19] In response, South Africa sealed the shafts with concrete slabs, abandoned the site, and "put the entire testing program on ice, on the shelf."[20]

THE MYSTERY DOUBLE FLASH

Two years later, a second suspicious event in southern Africa attracted international attention. On September 22, 1979, a U.S. Vela satellite's optical sensors registered a double-peaked signature, characteristic of a nuclear explosion, over the South Indian Ocean.[21] Speculation soon centered on South Africa, which denied knowledge of the event.

To investigate the matter, the administration of President Jimmy Carter convened a panel of distinguished scientists under the chairmanship of MIT Professor Jack Ruina. The Ruina panel's final report, released in July 1980, submitted that the Vela signal was "possibly a consequence of the impact of a small meteoroid on the satellite" but was "probably not from a nuclear explosion."[22] Two other studies by the Defense Intelligence Agency and the Naval Research Laboratory, however, determined that a nuclear explosion equivalent to less than three thousand tons of TNT had occurred. A December 1979 National Intelligence Estimate (NIE), released in 1990 under the Freedom of Information Act, concluded, "On the basis of available information, we cannot determine with certainty the nature and origin of the event."[23] However, the NIE contended that Israel had both technical and military incentives to test low-yield battlefield nuclear weapons, small tactical nuclear warheads, or a fission trigger for a thermonuclear device.[24] While downplaying the likelihood that Pretoria was responsible for the test, the NIE hinted at South African collaboration; the South African Navy had declared the Simonstown naval base on the southern tip of the country off-limits, and a naval search-and-rescue team had suddenly been placed on alert at the time of the alleged test.[25]

As of 1995, the American intelligence community had not arrived at an official consensus on the mystery flash. Unofficially, the widespread view in the U.S. government was that the Vela satellite had detected the test of a low-yield nuclear bomb and that Israel alone was responsible.[26]

BUILDING THE BOMB: 1980–89

In August 1979, operations at the Y Plant halted when a massive chemical reaction contaminated the facility. The plant resumed limited operations eight months later, but not until July 1981 was it capable of producing more highly enriched uranium.[27] By the time the Y Plant stopped enriching uranium in 1989, South Africa had doubled its annual output to roughly 100 kilograms—enough material for two crude nuclear devices a year.[28]

Despite the problems at the Y Plant, by November 1979 South Africa had acquired sufficient HEU for a gun-type device.[29] The AEC assembled the first device, including the enriched uranium core, to see if everything fitted properly. The device was then disassembled and handed over to Armscor, the state-owned arms manufacturing corporation, for safekeeping. The two halves of the first device were stored in separate high-security vaults.[30] This precaution was repeated for all the devices; not one was ever stored in assembled form.[31]

The second nuclear device was manufactured in April 1982, and the arsenal increased roughly every year and a half until it numbered six weapons by the late 1980s. Earlier models were upgraded as South Africa improved reliability over the years. A seventh device was planned but was only partially constructed when the program ended in 1989.[32]

Each nuclear weapon weighed about one ton, was 1.8 meters long, and was nearly sixty-five centimeters in diameter. Four primitive gun-type designs were used, all similar to the "Little Boy" atomic bomb that the United States had dropped on Hiroshima. Each contained about fifty-five kilograms of highly enriched uranium.[33] In contrast to the process followed in the United States, in South Africa the people entrusted with designing the weapons did not consult those responsible for using them—the South African Defense Force. Consequently, operational considerations in the design phase, such as the size and weight of the devices, were ignored.[34] Theoretical calculations estimated the yield at ten to eighteen kilotons, but some estimates were as low as five kilotons. As de Villiers admitted, without a test the AEC "just didn't know the yield."[35]

There was no question, though, about whether the devices would work. South Africa's nuclear weapons were very rich in HEU, containing almost twice the amount of enriched uranium typically used for a gun-type nuclear device. The constraints on the program effectively required this; the international uproar over the 1977 Kalahari incident had ruled out a nuclear test. Pretoria wanted to engineer redundancy to ensure that the devices would perform correctly without testing.[36] Had South Africa adopted more sophisticated implosion designs and been willing to tolerate a greater degree of risk, its nuclear arsenal could have been twice as large.

COMMAND AND CONTROL

All nuclear weapon states want to maintain tight command and control over nuclear weapons, and South Africa was no exception. This task presents serious challenges, including both how to avert a decapitating first strike by an adversary and how to prevent unauthorized or accidental use.[37]

Traditionally, to prevent a nuclear arsenal from being destroyed in a surprise "bolt from the blue" first strike, countries hide or bury sensitive command and communications posts, harden missile silos, take measures to preserve the national leadership, and disperse the nuclear weapons. South Africa did none of these things; it never had any "worst case" nuclear planning.[38] The country's secret nuclear policy ensured that other African states remained uncertain of Pretoria's actual nuclear capability. None had the surveillance and intelligence resources to pinpoint an exact location, and even if they had possessed this information, the other African states could not have projected sufficient military power into the heart of South Africa to destroy the entire nuclear inventory.

But Pretoria still needed to guard against unauthorized or accidental use. Here South Africa followed a more conventional path, employing coded locking devices (better known as permissive action links, or PALs), strict monitoring of personnel, and "two-man" rules dictating that at every stage in storing, maintaining, deploying, and using these devices, at least two people were to work in tandem.

The subcritical halves of each device were housed in different vaults, with the nonnuclear components of the weapon stored with one of the halves. Releasing the contents of each vault required two access codes, knowledge of at least three combinations for mechanical and electronic locks, and written approval from the president. Assembly required a third code. The heads of the AEC, Armscor, and the South African Defense Force were the only individuals entrusted with these three codes. Fully arming the device required inserting and turning a "key." This last step could not be performed without a fourth code, held solely by the president. To arm each device demanded a total of seven people working cooperatively.[39]

REVISITING KALAHARI

In 1988, South Africa revisited the Kalahari site.[40] According to atomic energy officials, "The site was being examined not for nuclear weapons development reasons, but as a precaution in case South Africa needed to test."[41] President P. W. Botha had wanted to know how long it would take to prepare for a nuclear test. To obtain this information, Armscor needed to check the condition of one of the test shafts. In June and July it cast a concrete floor around the site and during September and October erected a hangar twenty meters high and one hundred meters long. If the project was discovered, the cover story was that the facility was for vehicle storage and repair. Technicians pumped the water out of the shaft and lowered a specially designed probe. The shaft was intact and could still be used if necessary; test preparations would take a week or two.[42]

If Botha had merely wanted to check the readiness of the test site, the timing was curious. It came a full three years after a 1985 strategy review, when such a question might typically have been raised. But revisiting Kalahari was curious for another reason. The South Africans knew that since at least 1977, U.S. and Soviet satellites had routinely observed the site. Yet during this second visit, South Africa cast a concrete hangar floor and constructed a new building over the old test holes; such conspicuous activity was sure to be detected. Indeed, U.S. intelligence picked up activity at the test site but concluded that Pretoria was not going to conduct a nuclear test.[43]

In fact, Pretoria had returned to the Kalahari site to send a political signal to Washington and Moscow as part of the diplomatic endgame in southern Africa. In March 1988, South Africa had joined the United States and Angola in negotiations over Namibian independence and the withdrawal of Cuban forces from Angola. Meanwhile, Cuban leader Fidel Castro had escalated the stakes in late 1987 and early 1988 with a major influx of Cuban troops, which parried with South African Defense Force and Unita soldiers around the southern Angolan town of Cuito Cuanavale. In early June 1988, Castro warned Pretoria that it risked a "serious defeat" and implied that his forces might cross the border into northern Namibia.[44]

It appears that Castro's threat provoked President Botha to respond in a far more potent manner—he ordered test preparations at the Kalahari site that same month. In August, Pretoria formally agreed to a cease-fire and to removing all its forces from Angola by the end of the month. However, it took three more months to settle on a withdrawal schedule for the Cuban troops. During these strenuous negotiations, Pretoria constructed the hangar and prepared the test hole. South Africa's leaders likely concluded that such activity would reinforce their bargaining position by quietly signaling to the United States and the Soviet Union the potential costs of failing to get the Cuban issue resolved. The timing also explains why the United States and the Soviet Union did not publicly reveal the activity at Kalahari, in marked contrast to 1977, when their satellites had first noticed test preparations. Given the amount of time and effort the United States had invested in southern Africa and the delicate stage of the negotiations, neither Washington nor Moscow had any interest in publicizing Pretoria's nuclear activities. On December 22, 1988, South Africa, Cuba, and Angola formally agreed to Namibia's independence and to a timetable for withdrawing the Cuban forces.

In late 1989, the testing site was completely abandoned. In June 1993, under IAEA supervision, South Africa filled in the two shafts.

THE COST OF THE NUCLEAR PROGRAM

During its lifetime, the nuclear weapons program employed about one thousand people. Fewer than ten scientists knew the details of the entire project, which used over twenty different code names. Only a handful of key government officials were fully informed.[45]

South Africa claimed that the total cost of the nuclear program over ten years was R 680 million (about U.S.$200 million). Even if this dollar figure does not account for the rand's steady depreciation during the decade or include the historical cost of the Y Plant (which amounted to R 200 million or about U.S.$60 million),[46] or the R 145 million spent by Armscor (about U.S.$44 million),[47] or the nuclear program's operational costs, Pretoria was able to build a nuclear weapons arsenal relatively cheaply—for $300 million to perhaps $600 million, an amount equal to 1 or 2 percent of South Africa's defense budget during this period. The African National Congress (ANC) and other experts who have studied the South African nuclear program dispute these figures, arguing that costs approached the amount spent by the United States during World War II and were perhaps as much as R 8 billion (or almost U.S.$2.5 billion).[48] Yet cost comparisons with the wartime Manhattan Project and its $2 billion price tag are misleading. The United States investigated every possible way to obtain the special nuclear material for bombs. South Africa, on the other hand, had a dedicated program that developed and used only one method for enriching uranium and thus would have been an order of magnitude less expensive.

The Nuclear Strategy

South Africa's nuclear strategy consisted of three gradually escalating phases. Strategic uncertainty characterized phase 1: the government would neither confirm nor deny whether it possessed a nuclear weapons capability. If the country was threatened militarily, phase 2 required that South Africa would quietly reveal its nuclear capability to leading Western governments, principally the United States. This phase of the strategy aimed to provoke Washington, which would be so disturbed at the potential use of nuclear weapons in the region, and so sensitive to the implications for its global nonproliferation agenda, that it would intervene on South Africa's behalf before the country was overrun.

Should phase 2 fail to rouse the United States or the international community, phase 3 raised the stakes. As a last resort, South Africa would reveal its nuclear arsenal, either by an official announcement or by an underground nuclear test. According to an individual who claims to have read the Afrikaans-language document defining the country's nuclear strategy, South Africa would conduct *two* underground nuclear tests to try to persuade the United States to intervene on its behalf. If this did not work, a third nuclear test would be conducted over the Atlantic Ocean by toss-dropping a bomb from a Buccaneer or Mirage jet.[49] The purpose of the third test would be to demonstrate Pretoria's capability for delivering nuclear bombs to targets in southern Africa. Again, Pretoria thought these steps would prove its capability and demonstrate its resolve to use the remainder of the nuclear arsenal against its adversaries. As before, the intention was to compel the United States to intervene politically on its behalf.

South Africa alleged that, according to its strategy, it never intended to use the nuclear devices in an offensive way and that senior advisers fully recognized that such use would bring about international retaliation on a massive scale. According to senior atomic energy officials, "South Africa never had any idea of waging a nuclear war."[50]

In practice, the strategy never advanced beyond phase 1. As long as there was no overt military threat, South Africa maintained its policy of nuclear uncertainty. Pretoria believed that such an approach, wisely and discreetly employed, would prevent war rather than cause it.[51] According to Waldo Stumpf, the current CEO of the AEC: "The strategy was never to use the weapons. Consequently, these were just devices and not weapons in the true sense of the word."[52]

However, the South African military undertook steps to develop a target list and delivery capabilities to support the possible use of nuclear weapons. According to a former chief of South African military intelligence, the military drew up a list of targets in all the regional states. To be sure, this was normal contingency planning and not done solely for the nuclear weapons program, but it could have been used for this purpose if deterrence had failed.

Further, South Africa's interest in thermonuclear weapons was at odds with a strict adherence to the nuclear deterrent strategy. In his March 1993 speech, de Klerk stated that the country had not manufactured any thermonuclear weapons. Although this statement was accurate, the AEC had conducted preliminary studies on thermonuclear explosives until September 1985, when battlefield reversals in Angola prompted a strategy review that deemed such a capability unnecessary for the country's limited deterrent strategy.[53] At this review, the government also reconfirmed its decision to limit nuclear weapons production to seven gun-type devices.[54] According to Stumpf, the Kalahari site was revisited in 1988 to ensure that phase 3 of the strategy—an underground nuclear test—could be conducted if needed.[55] Finally, the overall deterrent strategy was reconfirmed. Pretoria would preserve its ambiguous nuclear posture.

Reversing Course

South Africa required five years to build its first nuclear device and a total of sixteen years to construct its six-weapon arsenal. Ending the program, however, took less than twenty-four months.

DISMANTLING THE PROGRAM

On September 14, 1989, F. W. de Klerk was elected state president. De Klerk had been aware of the country's nuclear weapons program since the late 1970s, when he had served as minister of mines. Immediately on taking office, he received a briefing from de Villiers and others on the status of the program. De Klerk then instructed an "Experts Committee" of senior officials of the AEC, Armscor, and the South African Defense Force to evaluate the pros and cons of dismantling the nuclear devices and joining the NPT as a nonnuclear weapon state.[56]

Specifically, de Klerk ordered the committee to examine all aspects of denuclearization, including dismantlement of the nuclear devices, safe storage of the enriched uranium, and destruction of all the hardware and design and manufacturing information. De Klerk also wanted a timetable setting out how quickly the country could join the NPT and sign a safeguards agreement with the IAEA.[57] Even before receiving this charge, senior members of the committee had known that de Klerk wanted to dismantle the nuclear arsenal. Some of these members later claimed that they had also favored dismantlement at this time.[58]

The Experts Committee completed its deliberations a month later and in November presented both a formal recommendation to disassemble the arsenal and an outline of the dismantlement procedures. De Klerk and his cabinet approved the plan. As a first step, the AEC ordered that the Y Plant be shut down by February 1, 1990.[59]

In late February, de Klerk requested a comprehensive planning and feasibility study to determine the best procedures for dismantling the nuclear devices.[60] To oversee dismantlement efforts, the president chose Waldo Stumpf. It is likely that Stumpf was selected not simply because of his position as head of the AEC but also because of his known opposition to the nuclear weapons program.[61] As an added precaution, de Klerk selected as the project's independent auditor Wynand Mouton, a retired nuclear physicist and university president whom de Klerk, then minister of education, had met in the mid-1980s.[62]

Mouton's primary responsibility was to guard against any diversion of bomb materials by disgruntled personnel who might seek to blackmail the government in an attempt to preserve the apartheid system.[63] Over the next five months he spent much of his time judging the trustworthiness of the scientists and technicians responsible for dismantlement.[64]

By July 1990, the dismantlement study was completed. It presented two options. One option called for first destroying one-half of each of the six devices before destroying the remaining halves; this would be the speediest way to eliminate the arsenal. The second option called for dismantling one entire device at a time, until all six were destroyed; this would allow South Africa to retain a nuclear deterrent until the last weapon was eliminated. Mouton presented both options, along with his personal recommendation to take the slower route, to de Klerk. According to Mouton, some personnel opposed the decision to eliminate the country's nuclear arsenal. Although he believed that this attitude stemmed more from professional pride than partisan politics (they balked at destroying devices they had devoted years to creating), it posed unnecessary risks. Mouton believed a slower approach would help acclimate the dismantlement team to the reality of the president's decision. De Klerk accepted Mouton's recommendation.[65] In this manner, the dismantlement approach that was selected became a metaphor for the gradual political and psychological reorientation of white South Africans to the coming of black majority rule.[66] The entire dismantlement process, including destruction of all the nonnuclear weapons components, was accomplished ahead of schedule, in early July 1991.

In approximately twenty trips over four nights, the dismantled nuclear materials and components were transferred in the trunks of Toyota sedans to the AEC for storage and safekeeping.[67] Mouton's final report to de Klerk certified that on the basis of what he had seen, the weight of the nuclear cores closely approximated the weight of the enriched uranium at the end of the dismantlement process. He did not certify that all of South Africa's weapons-grade uranium was accounted for.[68]

Even with the dismantlement of the nuclear devices, the arsenal could be reconstituted quickly if the program's blueprints were preserved. To prevent this, the more than twelve thousand technical documents used for designing the Y Plant and building the nuclear weapons were retrieved and compiled; this effort took over a year to complete. Files were kept in a steel cage at the dismantlement center.[69] According to South African officials, all the technical documents, drawings, design information, computer software, and data associated with the nuclear weapons program were recovered and destroyed.[70]

But some records relating to the nuclear program were saved. These included de Klerk's original dismantlement order, the operating and production records for both the Y Plant and a larger enrichment plant (known as the Z Plant),[71] and Mouton's final report. Mouton sent copies of his report to the president and to the heads of Armscor, Advena (the organization that actually dismantled the weapons), and the AEC.[72] Of potentially greater significance, Wally Grant, the "father" of South Africa's uranium enrichment process and in retirement the science adviser to the proapartheid Afrikaner People's Front (Volksfront), claimed to have documented the entire history of the nuclear weapons program, which he said he was preserving for future generations.[73]

South Africa formally joined the NPT on July 10, 1991. Not all the pieces of the nuclear cores had been melted down and reshaped by this time; this step was accomplished by the time Pretoria signed a safeguards agreement with the IAEA eight weeks later, on September 16, 1991.[74] That same month, South Africa resumed its seat at the IAEA General Conference for the first time in twelve years.

Given that no other country had ever abolished a stockpile of nuclear weapons, South Africa made special efforts to eliminate suspicions that it had secretly squirreled away nuclear weapons or material. It voluntarily opened all production records of the Y Plant, told IAEA inspectors that they could "go anywhere, anytime," furnished documentation on nuclear imports and exports, provided the IAEA with dismantling and accountancy records, and offered to accept any special safeguards arrangements deemed necessary.[75] The enriched uranium, in different chemical forms and at various enrichment levels, was stored in specially designed vaults at Pelindaba, where it was inspected at least once a month by the IAEA.[76]

REASONS FOR DISMANTLEMENT

Why did South Africa reverse course and voluntarily destroy a program in which it had invested so much time, effort, money, and scientific talent? The decision to dismantle South Africa's nuclear weapons bears much of F. W. de Klerk's personal imprint.

The most obvious reason for de Klerk's decision was that the factors motivating South Africa to acquire nuclear weapons in the first place had largely or wholly disappeared by the late 1980s. Within the region, a cease-fire on the northern border of Namibia was agreed in August 1988, and South Africa, Angola, and Cuba had signed a tripartite agreement in December 1988 for a phased withdrawal of all the Cuban troops from Angola. The following April, the UN Security Council implemented resolution 435/1978, which paved the way for an independent Namibia. Although the Berlin Wall did not fall until one month after de Klerk's initial dismantlement decision, by this time it was already clear that the Soviet Union's influence in southern Africa was waning and that the Soviet-American superpower rivalry had lessened considerably. As de Klerk stated in his March 1993 speech, "During 1989 the global political situation changed dramatically. . . . The Cold War had come to an end." In sum, the threat of total onslaught had abated.

Bureaucratic personalities also played a role. That the two founding members of the country's nuclear weapons program, Wally Grant and A. J. A. "Ampie" Roux, had both retired from the AEC by this time undoubtedly eased the dismantlement decision. Their drive and determination had propelled South Africa on its uranium enrichment program, and they were instrumental in persuading the government to actively develop nuclear weapons. By September 1989, others closely associated with the program, such as Prime Minister P. W. Botha and Magnus Malan, chief of the defense force, had either left government or lost influence. In addition, senior officials at the AEC seriously questioned the value of the nuclear stockpile and supported the dismantlement decision.[77]

In the absence of the old rationale for acquisition, a new rationale for elimination presented itself. De Klerk's strategy, first outlined to the country at the opening of parliament in February 1990, envisioned South Africa reentering the community of nations by abolishing apartheid, entering into a new political dialogue with the country's black majority, and abandoning attempts to destabilize countries in the region.[78] His nuclear policy was part of this larger strategy to normalize South Africa's relations with the rest of the world, especially in southern Africa, where, in de Klerk's words, Pretoria could make a "significant contribution . . . toward peace, stability and progress."

Another, more cynical motivation was the prospect of an ANC-led government with nuclear arms. For the white regime, the specter of Nelson Mandela with nuclear weapons concentrated the mind wonderfully. Even the possibility of a black government inheriting nuclear technology or any undeclared nuclear material was unsettling, given the traditional support for the ANC by Libya and the Palestine Liberation Organization.

To many South African officials, the removal of these external threats rendered the country's nuclear deterrent superfluous. In fact, it had become a liability.[79] It prevented improved relations with the West, especially the United States. It stood as a barrier to joining the NPT, which would grant Pretoria valuable access to peaceful nuclear technology and international cooperation on nuclear energy matters and would ensure that foreign customers (i.e., Germany and France) could continue to purchase South African uranium.[80] South Africa could use its nuclear expertise to win favorable publicity and goodwill in other African countries, help shape a treaty declaring the African continent a nuclear-weapon-free zone, and eventually regain its seat on the IAEA Board of Governors.

With the end of the cold war, the changed regional environment (especially the removal of the Cuban forces from Angola), and the certainty that a black government would assume power in South Africa at some future point, how much credit does de Klerk deserve for dismantling the nuclear weapons program? Was his decision really a Hobson's choice, that is, no choice at all? In other words, was the decision to reverse the nuclear weapons program inevitable?

To say that this decision would have been taken at some point in time ignores the fact that it was taken at this *precise* moment in South Africa's history. Although the white government may have had to abandon the nuclear weapons program at some point, it did not have to do so in 1989. With the removal of the Cuban forces from Angola, the regional security environment markedly favored South Africa. By 1989, South Africa arguably was stronger than at any other time since the early 1970s. Although international sanctions remained in force, South Africa no longer attracted the world's interest as it had in the 1970s and early 1980s; the dramatic events unfolding in eastern Europe and the Soviet Union now captured international attention. The country's depressed economy created some hardship, but most of this fell on the black majority; the whites could have survived comfortably for many more years. The benefits of NPT membership had existed previously and would exist in the future. So why did de Klerk move forward in 1989?

De Klerk's Afrikaner background and conservative political beliefs gave no indication that he would usher in a new period of race relations in South Africa.[81] His true motives may never be known. Yet it seems likely that de Klerk possessed that rarest combination of politi-

cal attributes—a vision for his country and the courage to implement
it. De Klerk's strategy called for a gradual transition from white to majority rule, a process that he may even have hoped to control and
dominate. The alternative was an increasingly brutal repression of the
black population and a descent into greater domestic violence and
chaos. De Klerk saw the implications if South Africa stuck to its present course and decided to take another path.

Even so, the dismantlement decision may have been more of a
close-run thing than realized. Timing and leadership were essential.
The external threat to South Africa had evaporated, thereby discount-
ing the chief rationale for the nuclear weapons program. The internal
threat had increased, but it was widely conceded that nuclear
weapons were completely unsuitable for quelling domestic unrest. Although other members of the government were willing to go along
with de Klerk's decision, no one had made this recommendation in
the past. Whether anyone was likely to suggest it in the foreseeable future was unclear; as majority rule appeared more likely, some may
have done so. But it was de Klerk who immediately seized on the
opening produced by his election victory to dismantle the program.
"If he had waited, he never would have gotten cabinet approval," said
one senior South African official, "since opposition to giving up the
program in the defense community was great."[82]

REASONS FOR DISCLOSURE

Having decided to dismantle the nuclear weapons program, why
didn't de Klerk immediately trumpet this deed to the world to garner
international acclaim? Why did he wait until March 1993 to reveal details of the nuclear program?

To be sure, South Africa was under no legal obligation to disclose
any of its nuclear activities before the time it joined the NPT. Further,
the IAEA required only that Pretoria declare all of its existing nuclear
facilities; there was no duty to announce any previous programs or
plans.

During 1989 and 1990, white South Africa was undergoing a pro-
found political upheaval.[83] Public announcement of the dismantlement decision at that time would have enraged the Conservative
Party and extraparliamentary white extremists. Even in March 1993,
opposition party members interrupted de Klerk's announcement to
angrily accuse him of jeopardizing the country's national security. At
the very least, publicity would have made the negotiated political
transformation to black majority rule more difficult. If the decision
had been publicized before July 1991, the dismantlement effort might

have been stopped or even reversed. Thus de Klerk's reticence was understandable; he had demonstrated boldness in choosing to dismantle the nuclear program, but he was not reckless.

Second, in the wake of the Persian Gulf war, South Africa watched as teams of international inspectors canvassed Iraq and demolished the facilities involved in its nuclear, chemical, biological, and ballistic missile programs. Pretoria feared similar treatment. Any public revelation during 1991 would closely link the two countries in the eyes of the world, despite the fact that South Africa, unlike Iraq, had not violated the NPT, to which it was not a party during its nuclear buildup.

Finally, South Africa wanted to collect as much favorable publicity as possible by its accession to the NPT. Disclosure in July 1991 about the country's cloudy nuclear past would have overshadowed the face Pretoria wanted to show the world—its commitment to nonnuclear status.

Toward the end of 1992, however, international press attention on South Africa's nuclear past increasingly forced the government's hand. In October, the widely respected industry journal *Nuclear Fuel* identified "Building 5000" at Pelindaba as the site where the first nuclear weapon had been assembled. Two months later, the ANC convened an international news conference to demand that the government come clean about its past nuclear activities and stop lying. (The impetus behind the conference came from a young, American-trained scientist, Roger Jardine, who had just started working at the ANC's Shell House headquarters.) At this press conference, the ANC demanded that the government "admit the full extent of its nuclear weapons program and weapons-grade uranium stockpile now." Further stonewalling would damage the sensitive power-sharing negotiations then under way. "To continue to act clandestinely and give ambiguous answers on nuclear matters," the ANC claimed, "undermines the important process of building the confidence of all South Africans in the process of democratizing our country."[84]

In fact, earlier that year Stumpf had recommended that de Klerk reveal the history of the nuclear weapons program. The president demurred, saying that the timing was not right. Stumpf tried a second time in January 1993. This time de Klerk agreed.[85]

De Klerk did not make the announcement immediately, however, since he could not decide whether to destroy all the policy papers detailing the nuclear weapons program. Once he made up his mind, documents had to be collected from senior cabinet members, defense officials, and atomic energy personnel. The last records were not destroyed until March 24, 1993, the day de Klerk addressed parliament. Remembering that Iran had pieced together shredded classified information seized from the U.S. Embassy in Teheran in November 1979, Pretoria first shredded and then burned these papers.[86]

In his speech, de Klerk acknowledged that international pressure had influenced the timing of disclosure: "Such allegations . . . are beginning to take on the dimensions of a campaign." After de Klerk's revelations, Jardine proudly declared that the ANC had accomplished in six months what the world had been trying to force Pretoria to do for decades. "We smoked them out."[87]

De Klerk had specific reasons for revealing the existence and destruction of the nuclear stockpile. He hoped to convince a still skeptical international community, in particular the United States, that South Africa had nothing to hide in connection with its past nuclear activities. Two months earlier, Washington had obliquely criticized South Africa's nuclear behavior.[88] Pretoria wanted to be forthcoming and cooperative, especially with the newly installed Clinton administration. "I sincerely trust," said de Klerk, "that this unprecedented act, namely the voluntary dismantling of a nuclear deterrent capability, and the voluntary revelation of all relevant information, will confirm the government's effort to assure transparency."

In addition, de Klerk wanted to assure the international community that South Africa's nonproliferation commitments under the NPT and to the IAEA were sound. South Africa was eager to share in the benefits of peaceful nuclear technology. With its substantial uranium deposits and an experimental laser enrichment technology still under development, it also hoped to become a major player in international nuclear commerce. As de Klerk noted, any residual suspicions would be bad for business.

De Klerk's speech elicited favorable responses from foreign governments. The sole exception was Japan, which expressed its regret that Pretoria had built the nuclear devices in the first place.[89]

Conclusions: "Castles in the Air"

A popular maxim states that if something is worth doing, it is worth doing well. South Africa's nuclear weapons program offers a variation on this theme—just because something can be done does not necessarily mean that it should be done.

UNANSWERED QUESTIONS

There has not yet been, and may never be, an official history of the South African nuclear weapons program. Despite a remarkable degree of transparency and unprecedented cooperation with the IAEA since 1991, some questions linger.

Has South Africa hidden any nuclear devices in the country? A November 1993 National Intelligence Estimate reportedly assigned a very low probability to the prospect that South Africa was keeping a "bomb in the basement" but concluded that there will never be 100 percent certainty.[90] A 1993 Russian intelligence report was more definite: "The Republic of South Africa does not have any nuclear weapons."[91] Perhaps the most convincing testimony was provided by a former chief of South African military intelligence, now a member of a right-wing Afrikaner organization, who lamented, "Regrettably, we have given away everything."[92]

If there are no bombs left, could there be a secret cache of highly enriched uranium somewhere in the country? South Africa cannot give precise figures for the amount of enriched uranium it produced during the 1970s and 1980s. This does not indicate Pretoria's malevolence—South Africa's nuclear program was less concerned with maintaining strict accounting procedures than with operating the Y Plant to maximize output, just as was the United States at its uranium enrichment facilities.[93] In retrospect both de Villiers and Stumpf acknowledged, "It might have been a mistake on our side to dismantle the devices before the IAEA could inspect."[94]

The November 1993 U.S. intelligence assessment also could not determine with certainty if South Africa had declared all of its enriched uranium to the IAEA and placed it under safeguards at Pelindaba. A complete accounting of South Africa's enriched uranium inventory may never be known.

Did South Africa's nuclear weapons program receive any foreign assistance? Understandably, South Africa has always insisted that its nuclear program was the product of its own labors and has vehemently denied all allegations of overseas help. Additionally, Pretoria claimed that all personnel working on the bomb project were South African nationals born in South Africa, with no other citizenship.

Yet there have long been rumors of Pretoria's cooperation with foreign governments, in particular with Israel and Germany. The 1979 National Intelligence Estimate on the South Indian Ocean double flash stated, "Israelis have not only participated in certain South African research activities over the last few years, but they have also offered and transferred various sorts of advanced nonnuclear weapons technology to South Africa."[95] According to one British news report, atomic scientists from Israel were stationed in South Africa from the beginning of the nuclear program,[96] and there have been other stories of Israelis at the Kalahari test site.[97] Another report claimed that during Prime Minister Vorster's visit to Israel in April 1976, Israeli Defense Minister Moshe Dayan won a commitment "for a series of joint Israeli–South African [nuclear] tests in South Africa."[98] From this meeting allegedly came other secret nuclear deals, including the export to Israel of fifty tons of "yellowcake," the commercial form of uranium concentrate. In September 1991, after joining the NPT, South Africa informed the IAEA of this shipment and stated that it had notified the IAEA of all other exports of nuclear material.[99]

What South Africa had not told the IAEA, however, was that in return for the yellowcake, Israel reportedly supplied thirty grams of tritium, which can be used to boost the yield of nuclear bombs. The tritium was code-named "Teeblare" (tea leaves) and was delivered over a twelve-month period to South Africa in tiny capsules of only two and a half grams at a time.[100] The AEC acknowledged in May 1993 that it had imported tritium from unspecified overseas sources for commercial purposes, such as glow-in-the-dark safety signs.[101] A more alarming development was disclosed by the deputy chief of mission at the South African Embassy in Washington, who admitted in early 1993 not only that Israel and South Africa had entered into nuclear and conventional weapons cooperation agreements but also that some of the nuclear agreements were still in force.[102]

Numerous reports have also claimed that South Africa's enrichment program benefited from West German assistance, specifically that its "vortex-tube" enrichment process derived from a similar process previously invented in West Germany by Ernst Becker. Pretoria has consistently claimed that its process was wholly indigenous and has denied that it received assistance from any other country.[103] The two processes have some features in common,[104] although it appears that the extent of cooperation has been exaggerated.

Did the Vela satellite detect a South African nuclear test in September 1979? South Africa had the capability to build a nuclear weapon at this time. It had manufactured the nonnuclear components for its cold test at Kalahari in 1977, and the IAEA confirmed that the Y Plant had yielded its first bomb-grade material in January 1978.

However, the low yield (less than three kilotons) of the September 1979 explosion and the absence of measurable fallout (if it was a fission device) suggest a sophisticated nuclear device that would have been difficult for South Africa's weapons designers to achieve in a maiden test. Each of its six nuclear devices was modeled on the Hiroshima bomb and had an estimated yield of ten to eighteen kilotons. It is doubtful that South Africa could have produced the type of small-yield nuclear device that fit the characteristics of the September 1979 event. As Stumpf conceded, "We were not that good."[105] If South Africa had this technical capability, it is unclear why it would then have chosen to build six bulkier, less sophisticated, and more expensive (in terms of using enriched uranium) weapons for its nuclear arsenal.[106] And it is also unclear why South Africa would breach its obligations under the Partial Test Ban Treaty when it could have carried out a test underground at a site already prepared in the Kalahari.[107]

When did South Africa first decide to embark on a nuclear weapons program? Numerous South African officials have claimed that Prime Minister Vorster's 1974 authorization to develop a nuclear explosive was limited to peaceful purposes; the decision to militarize the program was not taken until 1978. On the other hand de Klerk, in his March 1993 speech, placed the decision to develop the country's limited nuclear deterrent capability "as early as 1974." Further, during a South African television interview immediately following the president's revelations, and again two weeks later at an international conference in Harare, Zimbabwe, Stumpf stated that the nuclear weapons program had started in 1974.[108]

The difference in dates has serious implications for understanding Pretoria's motivations to acquire nuclear weapons. Although South Africa's regional and international situation had deteriorated by 1974, the Cubans had not yet been airlifted to Angola, nor could a Cuban presence have even been anticipated. The United Nations' mandatory arms embargo was still three years off. A decision to acquire nuclear weapons at this time would suggest that South Africa had incentives other than its immediate security needs. If the decision was taken in 1978, however, this could be seen as a countermeasure to increasingly unfavorable regional developments, especially the fifty thousand Cuban troops backed by Warsaw Pact military advisers who collectively threatened South Africa's interests in neighboring Namibia.

A Solomonic judgment is that even if South Africa had decided in 1974 to develop nuclear explosives only for peaceful purposes, everyone associated with this decision would have known that developing a peaceful nuclear explosive was virtually indistinguishable from developing a first-generation nuclear weapon. To have the one meant also to have the other.

LESSONS

The South African case provides an interesting commentary on different aspects of the international nonproliferation regime: the unintended consequences of international isolation; the lessons of Pretoria's nuclear program for would-be proliferators; the influence of U.S. diplomacy; and the usefulness of nuclear weapons.

South Africa's international isolation influenced every element of its nuclear program. This ostracism intensified the government's laager mentality, which played a large part in the initial decision to develop nuclear weapons. At the same time, this isolation reinforced senior officials' parochial worldview, which inevitably influenced nuclear decision making. Few leaders had traveled extensively outside of the country and fewer still beyond southern Africa to Europe or the United States. The bureaucracy shared and reinforced these views. The Foreign Ministry, which might have been expected to add a more cosmopolitan understanding to government decisions, was not consulted on the decision to either initiate or terminate the nuclear weapons program.

This air of unreality was demonstrated most noticeably by the country's nuclear strategy, which was less a rigorous strategy than wishful thinking. As one senior government official remarked, "It now seems like building castles in the air to think that the nuclear strategy would have worked as planned."[109]

This strategy reflected a seat-of-the-pants approach to security issues, an approach that ultimately rested on assumptions that went not only unchallenged but wholly unexamined. The ostensible security rationale for the nuclear weapons program was the threat of "total onslaught" confronting the country in the mid-1970s. Yet the former chief of South African military intelligence during this period, General H. D. E. V. du Toit, discounted this danger: "I don't think we ever thought it was feasible for anyone to attack us from the north." As for the Soviet threat, he said, "The Communist bogey was set up at every stage—but we had no one in the military who read, spoke, or studied Russian." It was "silly to set the Soviets up as the force behind the total onslaught."[110] The Foreign Ministry also lacked any Soviet expertise. Further, as part of the peculiar ad hoc decision-making process that seemed the norm rather than the exception in the South African government, communication and policy coordination among government departments and ministries were sporadic at best.[111] Until 1985, the military did not even have a policy planning staff.

The success of South Africa's nuclear strategy depended on Pretoria's ability to manipulate Washington's behavior—to compel the United States to intervene politically or militarily on Pretoria's behalf. Yet relations were so strained between the two countries that it is impossible to believe that any American administration would have rushed to extricate the white regime from imminent extinction—and relations only worsened during the 1980s. Given U.S. domestic politics, it is unlikely that Washington could have aided South Africa even if it had somehow wanted to. Moreover, how could Pretoria have expected U.S. armed forces, with a significant percentage of black Americans, to rescue the white regime? As one expert commentator has noted, "Only in the event of a direct Soviet invasion of South Africa (and only if that was seen as threatening an important U.S. strategic interest) was the nuclear test tactic likely to have succeeded—and in such a case it would probably have proved unnecessary."[112] Actual use of nuclear weapons against Soviet forces was unthinkable, since such a step would have provoked overwhelming retaliation. The use of nuclear weapons against any other adversary would have been unnecessary because of South Africa's superior conventional forces. In any case, no other country in southern Africa would have been able to project military power to South Africa's borders; the few north-south rail links and roads could easily have been interdicted.

That nuclear bombs were developed without an overwhelming strategic rationale suggests the presence of other motivations. In South Africa's case, the nuclear scientists played a key role. The president of the Atomic Energy Corporation, Ampie Roux, decided in the early 1960s that the country should create a uranium enrichment industry, and he gained the backing of Prime Minister H. F. Vorwoerd. Wally Grant headed this secret effort, which resulted in the vortex-tube enrichment method. In 1968, Roux and Grant urged the new prime minister, John Vorster, to fund construction of a pilot enrichment plant; Vorster and his cabinet initially balked at the idea. Roux and Grant persisted and the following year obtained government approval.[113] This facility became the Y Plant, which enriched the uranium for South Africa's bombs. According to General du Toit, Roux later urged Vorster to use this enrichment capability to develop nuclear weapons.[114] With the capability already in place, the subsequent decision to build nuclear weapons was made that much easier.

The half-baked nature of South Africa's nuclear strategy may thus be explained by the fact that it was developed ex post facto. It provided some semblance of intellectual justification for a decision that the atomic energy officials and a few government officials had already decided to make.

This haphazard approach was also evidenced by the less-than-rigorous way in which South Africa determined the size of its nuclear arsenal. According to de Villiers and Stumpf: "This was a government decision, a political decision. The thinking was that we needed one for a test, two if the first test did not work, and so then the number rose to three. It was thought prudent to double this number, and that is how we arrived at six. The arsenal depended on the amount of HEU. There could have been four, there could have been nine. It just turned out to be six."[115]

Are there any lessons the international community can derive from South Africa's nuclear experience? In his March 1993 address, de Klerk voiced his hope that South Africa's initiative would "inspire other countries to take the same steps," in other words, to roll back their nuclear weapons programs. This is unlikely, at least for the foreseeable future. India, Pakistan, and Israel are the only countries with ambiguous nuclear postures analogous to South Africa's stance during the 1970s and 1980s. The domestic, regional, and international objectives of these three states—and the roles played by their unannounced nuclear weapons capabilities—differ markedly from those of South Africa.[116]

But the South African experience offers other, darker lessons that bode ill for preventing the spread of nuclear weapons. South Africa's nuclear program indicates that acquiring nuclear weapons may be both cheaper and quicker than generally assumed. Spread over a decade, the $300–$600 million price tag of Pretoria's arsenal is well within the reach of many countries in the developing world. Factoring in the program's "benefits" reduces this cost even further.[117] Key among them was the emotional comfort purchased by the nuclear program. Speaking for those members of the white regime who knew of the nuclear weapons program, or even simply suspected its existence, Stumpf explained the psychological benefit: "It is like an insurance policy. I have bought myself peace of mind."[118]

The nonproliferation implications of the activities of Roux and Grant are also worrying. Substitutes can be fashioned for the security and status that some countries believe are ensured with nuclear weapons. Traditionally, these substitutes have assumed the form of bilateral or multilateral security guarantees, closer state-to-state cooperation, or impressive economic accomplishments. But there are few nonproliferation buttons to push when a leading scientist or bureaucrat decides that his country should have nuclear weapons. These "nuclear myth makers" will be far less receptive to outside inducements or pressures.[119] If a key incentive to building bombs is a combination of personal ambition and professional pride, it will be much more difficult for the international community to dissuade countries from going nuclear.

Even as rudimentary and inexpensive a nuclear program as South

Africa's, however, can be sensitive to costs. Notably, Soviet and American satellites spotted the 1977 preparations in the Kalahari because the expense of burying all the equipment proved prohibitive to South Africa. The resulting international commotion convinced Pretoria that it could not afford the political price of testing a device, subsequently hobbling South Africa's nuclear weapons development. To be sure, the international reaction did not prevent development. But South Africa's six nuclear weapons took longer to build, were less sophisticated, and were less efficient in their use of HEU than would have been the case if Pretoria had been able to test its weapons designs. Thus, raising the costs of nuclear weapons acquisition—both political and financial costs—may have real, and unanticipated, nonproliferation benefits.

South Africa's relatively rapid development of nuclear weapons offers a cautionary tale. From breaking ground on the Y Plant to fabricating a workable nuclear device took eight years. Even more impressive, South Africa needed only five years once the government had decided to build a nuclear explosive. This compares favorably with the French and Chinese nuclear programs. At the very least, the international community will have to employ better intelligence-gathering capabilities and react faster to nascent nuclear programs if it wants to prevent countries from acquiring nuclear weapons in the future.

The South African case also illustrates what might be termed the indivisibility of the nonproliferation regime. Although every nuclear weapons program will have its own unique characteristics, countries observe, react to, and are influenced by developments in other parts of the world. The lack of public international outrage after India's nuclear test in May 1974, and the absence of any kind of immediate punishment or concrete penalties, led South Africa to believe that it too could test a nuclear device without being censured. This was a major reason for Pretoria's surprise at the diplomatic reaction when the Kalahari test site was discovered in August 1977.

The Kalahari incident also reveals a nonproliferation paradox. U.S. outrage when the test site was first discovered must have reinforced Pretoria's belief that Washington placed a high value on South Africa's *not* conducting a nuclear test. The white regime could thus be forgiven for believing (even if incorrectly) that in the event of a military threat to the country, the United States would intervene to prevent South Africa from testing one of its nuclear devices. This formed the basis for Pretoria's nuclear strategy, which was developed immediately after the 1977 Kalahari incident. On the other hand, if the United

States and the Soviet Union had ignored an imminent South African test, and if Pretoria had proceeded, the example would have damaged nonproliferation efforts around the world.

Perhaps the most interesting question surrounding South Africa's nuclear weapons program is whether it could have been prevented in the first place. Since 1968, when South Africa refused to join the NPT, every U.S. administration had urged South Africa to formally renounce its nuclear ambitions by signing the treaty and placing all its nuclear facilities under international safeguards. Donald Sole, the South African ambassador to Washington from 1977 to 1982, wrote, "The U.S.—more than any other country—applied pressures on South Africa to accede to the NPT."[120]

But what role did Washington play in getting South Africa to reverse its nuclear program? De Villiers bluntly exclaimed, "None!"[121] Stumpf replied: "We found pressure from the U.S. counterproductive. It kept us out of the NPT longer."[122] A less partisan and more balanced assessment suggests that U.S. diplomatic pressure on South Africa was never great enough to force Pretoria to surrender the bomb and join the NPT (although by dissuading Pretoria from actually testing a nuclear device, Washington helped to keep the nuclear program covert). Mistrust on both sides prevented closer ties. For Washington, Pretoria's policy of apartheid made an improved relationship, or much of any relationship at all, politically impossible. For its part South Africa, remembering its maddening experience with nuclear supplies during the 1970s and its assessment that Congress would never tolerate closer U.S.–South African links, doubted that the United States could ever be a reliable partner.

In the end the realization—first by de Klerk and eventually by other South African officials—that nuclear weapons actively prevented Pretoria from achieving its larger objectives led the government to dismantle its nuclear arsenal. Indeed, as de Klerk remarked in March 1993, "A nuclear deterrent had become not only superfluous, but in fact an obstacle to the development of South Africa's international relations." Only by relinquishing its nuclear bombs could South Africa reenter the community of nations and begin to pursue its true national interests.

Chronology

JULY 20, 1970 Prime Minister John Vorster informs parliament that South Africa has developed a "unique" process for enriching uranium.

MARCH 1971 Carel de Wet, minister of mines, approves "preliminary investigations" into the feasibility of producing nuclear explosives; work on a pilot enrichment facility, called the Y plant, begins this year.

1974 The AEC reports to Prime Minister Vorster that it can build a nuclear device; Vorster authorizes development of nuclear explosives and approves funds for a test site.

1975 The Alvor Accords, outlining a peaceful transition in Angola, break down almost immediately as three rival liberation movements make a power grab; South Africa's failed intervention in the ensuing Angolan civil war results in the new Luanda government's open hostility and the introduction of fifty thousand Cuban troops; a pro-Soviet, Marxist-Leninist regime assumes power in Mozambique.

1977 Ministry of Defense *White Paper* warns, "We are today involved in a war, whether we wish to accept it or not"; the paper outlines a "Total National Strategy."

Prime Minister Vorster convenes his senior officials to discuss the future of the nuclear program.

The AEC assembles all the nonnuclear components of a nuclear device.

South Africa is kicked off the Board of Governors of the IAEA.

The United States, Britain, France, Canada, and West Germany form a "Contact Group" to pressure Pretoria into withdrawing from Namibia and to manage that country's transition to independence.

The UN Security Council mandates the voluntary arms embargo against South Africa that has existed since 1963.

JULY 30 A Soviet Cosmos 922 satellite makes two passes over South Africa and spots a nuclear test site in the Kalahari desert; the United States later independently confirms this information and South Africa is then pressured to abandon its "cold test."

JANUARY 1978 The Y Plant produces the first small amounts of highly enriched uranium (HEU).

APRIL Vorster formally approves his senior officials' document that articulates the country's nuclear strategy.

OCTOBER Components of the first workable nuclear device are completed; Prime Minister P. W. Botha appoints an "Action Committee" to recommend future plans for the production of nuclear devices.

JULY 1979 The Action Committee proposes a nuclear arsenal of seven devices.

SEPTEMBER 22 A U.S. Vela satellite registers a double-peaked signature, characteristic of a nuclear explosion.

NOVEMBER Completed components of the first workable gun-type nuclear device are fitted with 80 percent enriched U-235.

APRIL 1982 The second nuclear device is manufactured.

1985 South Africa reexamines its nuclear strategy and decides not to pursue hydrogen weapons.

JUNE–OCTOBER 1988 South Africa revisits the Kalahari nuclear test site and erects a hangar, twenty meters high and one hundred meters long, over the test hole.

DECEMBER 22 Angola, Cuba, and South Africa formally agree on Namibia's independence and on a schedule for Cuban troops to withdraw from Angola.

SEPTEMBER 1989 F. W. de Klerk is elected president, decides to terminate the nuclear program, and establishes an "Experts Committee" to outline procedures for dismantling the country's nuclear capabilities; HEU production at the Y Plant is halted; South Africa's nuclear inventory stands at six weapons, with a seventh device partially constructed.

FEBRUARY 1, 1990 The Y Plant is formally shut down.

JULY South Africa begins to dismantle its nuclear weapons and destroy the hardware and design information.

JULY 10, 1991 South Africa joins the NPT.

SEPTEMBER South Africa and the IAEA sign a comprehensive safeguards agreement, which enters into force the following month.

MARCH 24, 1993 President de Klerk discloses, "At one stage South Africa did develop a limited nuclear deterrent capability . . . of seven nuclear fission devices."

Notes

[1]For the text of de Klerk's speech, see Joint Publications Research Service, *Proliferation Issues* (hereafter referred to as JPRS-TND), 93-009 (March 29, 1993), pp. 1–3.

[2]U.S. government officials claim that Washington knew of South Africa's nuclear weapons program and the size of its stockpile. U.S. government officials, personal interviews, Cape Town and Pretoria, May 1993, Washington, D.C., 1993 and 1994. What is unclear is *precisely* what the U.S. intelligence community knew and when it knew this.

[3]*Debates,* House of Assembly, Parliament, South Africa, vol. 29, col. 55–58, July 20, 1970; see also A. R. Newby-Fraser, *Chain Reaction: Twenty Years of Nuclear Research and Development in South Africa* (Pretoria: Atomic Energy Board, 1979), pp. 91–95. The nuclear program was aided by the return from overseas of at least six leading nuclear scientists in the early 1970s; among this group was the former director of the Harwell nuclear laboratory in Britain.

[4]J. W. de Villiers, personal correspondence, August 24, 1993. "In the gun-assembly technique, a propellant charge propels two or more subcritical masses into a single supercritical mass inside a high-strength gun-barrel-like container." U.S. Congress, Office of Technology Assessment, *Technologies Underlying Weapons of Mass Destruction,* OTA-BP-ISC-115 (Washington, D.C.: USGPO, 1993), p. 174.

[5]The organization entrusted with atomic energy development in South Africa was called the Atomic Energy Board (AEB) until July 1, 1982, when its name was changed to the Atomic Energy Corporation (AEC). For the sake of simplicity and consistency, this organization is referred to here as the AEC.

[6]De Villiers, personal correspondence, August 24, 1993.

[7]Waldo Stumpf, paper provided to the author, November 16, 1993 (hereafter cited as Stumpf November 16, 1993, paper).

[8]Stumpf November 16, 1993, paper. Enriched uranium from the first bomb was later recycled to increase the enrichment level to weapons-grade, which in turn increased the probability that the nuclear device would explode with the expected yield. Under IAEA definitions, low-enriched uranium is uranium that consists of less than 20 percent U-235; highly enriched uranium is uranium that consists of 20 percent or more U-235. "Weapons-grade" or "bomb-grade" uranium generally refers to uranium that consists of 90 percent or more U-235.

[9]See John Marcum, *The Angolan Civil War,* vol. 2 (Cambridge: MIT Press, 1978).

[10]See Donald B. Sole, "The Rise of Nuclear Sanctions against South Africa," *American Review* (Autumn 1986), pp. 2–8.

[11]Earlier in the decade, the International Court of Justice had rescinded South Africa's mandate for South West Africa/Namibia and assigned "direct responsibility" for the territory to the United Nations.

[12]See Republic of South Africa, *White Paper on Defense, 1977* (Simonstown: South African Navy, 1977).

[13]De Villiers, personal correspondence, August 24, 1993. The committee also

recommended that the development and manufacture of nuclear devices be transferred to Armscor, the South African arms manufacturing corporation. The atomic energy program would still supply the HEU, develop nuclear technology, and conduct the necessary theoretical work. During this time, South Africa revised its form of government; it was now led by a state president, not a prime minister.

[14]De Villiers, personal correspondence, August 24, 1993.

[15]J. W. de Villiers and Waldo Stumpf, joint interview, Pelindaba, May 25, 1993 (hereafter cited as de Villiers and Stumpf joint interview).

[16]Stumpf November 16, 1993, paper. Depleted uranium contains less than 0.72 percent U-235.

[17]De Villiers and Stumpf joint interview. Also, Stumpf November 16, 1993, paper.

[18]See J. Yeld, "N-Secrets Were Unveiled," Argus (Cape Town), March 25, 1993.

[19]New York Times, August 21, 1977; International Herald Tribune, August 29, 1977. France reportedly threatened to cancel its construction of the two Koeburg power stations in South Africa if Pretoria conducted a nuclear test. See David Albright, "South Africa's Secret Nuclear Weapons," ISIS Report 1, no. 4 (May 1994): 7. A South African naval officer, Commodore Dieter Gerhardt, working undercover for the Soviet Union, may have provided Moscow with the information on the Kalahari test site.

After the discovery of the Kalahari site, Prime Minister Vorster personally assured President Jimmy Carter that South Africa did not have any plans to build nuclear weapons. Vorster's personal involvement in planning the nuclear weapons program with his senior advisers during 1977–78 belied these assurances. For a fuller discussion of the Kalahari incident, see South Africa's Plan and Capability in the Nuclear Field (New York: United Nations, 1981), pp. 29–31; J. D. L. Moore, South Africa and Nuclear Proliferation (New York: St. Martin's Press, 1987), pp. 111–15.

[20]De Villiers and Stumpf joint interview.

[21]This information did not become public until a month after the flash occurred. See New York Times, October 26, 1979. If a nuclear explosion caused the flash, it was detected only because of favorable atmospheric conditions; the satellite's sensors could not penetrate cloud cover.

[22]Executive Office of the President, Office of Science and Technology Policy, "Ad Hoc Panel Report on the September 22 Event," p. 2. See also South Africa's Plan and Capability, pp. 31–33.

[23]Director of Central Intelligence, The 22 September 1979 Event, Interagency Intelligence Memorandum, December 1979, p. 1. The language used here deserves careful parsing. The NIE did not say that it could not determine the nature or the origin of the September 22 event. In other words, the NIE could have determined that a nuclear test had occurred but not which country was responsible.

National Intelligence Estimates are the responsibility of the National Intelligence Council, which relies on the various entities that compose the intelligence community, entities including the CIA, the Defense Intelligence Agency, the State, Energy, and Defense Departments, the National Security Agency, and the weapons laboratories.

[24]Ibid., p. 9.

[25]Ibid., p. 8. See also Albright, "South Africa's Secret Nuclear Weapons," p. 18.

[26]Personal interviews, Washington, D.C., 1993 and 1994. Seymour Hersh has

claimed, "The warhead tested that Saturday morning was a low-yield nuclear artillery shell that had been standardized for use by the Israeli Defense Forces." *The Samson Option: Israel's Nuclear Arsenal and American Foreign Policy* (New York: Random House, 1991), pp. 271ff. See also Moore, *South Africa and Nuclear Proliferation*, pp. 115–18; James Adams, *The Unnatural Alliance: Israel and South Africa* (London: Quartet Books, 1984), pp. 187–96.

[27]Stumpf November 16, 1993, paper. The IAEA confirmed that the Y Plant ceased operations during this period. See *Report on the Completeness of the Inventory of South Africa's Nuclear Installations and Material*, attached to IAEA Document Gov/2609, September 3, 1992, p. 5 (hereafter cited as IAEA Inventory Report). Three months earlier, in April 1981, Pretoria had alerted the world that it could build nuclear weapons when it publicly revealed that it had enriched uranium to 45 percent U-235 for its Safari research reactor.

[28]Wynand Mouton, personal interview, Johannesburg, May 25, 1993.

[29]Stumpf November 16, 1993, paper.

[30]SAPA (Johannesburg), March 26, 1993, reported in JPRS-TND-93-010 (April 16, 1993), p. 4.

[31]De Villiers and Stumpf joint interview.

[32]SABC TV 1 Network interview with Waldo Stumpf and Pik Botha, reported in JPRS-TND-93-009 (March 29, 1993), p. 6.

[33]De Villiers and Stumpf joint interview; SAPA, March 26, 1993, reported in JPRS-TND-93-010 (April 16, 1993), p. 4. The dimensions of the nuclear devices were confirmed by a knowledgeable U.S. government official, personal interview, Washington, D.C., 1993. For a general discussion of the devices, see Albright, "A Curious Conversion," *Bulletin of the Atomic Scientists* (June 1993), pp. 8–11.

[34]De Villiers and Stumpf joint interview.

[35]Ibid.

[36]To be sure, it is not necessary to test a gun-type device to be confident that it will detonate. For example, the gun-type device the United States dropped on Hiroshima was not tested beforehand.

[37]For a discussion of command and control issues, see Bruce Blair, *The Logic of Accidental Nuclear War* (Washington, D.C.: Brookings Institution, 1993); Peter Douglas Feaver, *Guarding the Guardians: Civilian Control of Nuclear Weapons in the United States* (Ithaca, N.Y.: Cornell University Press, 1992); Feaver, "Command and Control in Emerging Nuclear Nations," *International Security* 17, no. 3 (Winter 1992–93): 160–87; Paul Bracken, *The Command and Control of Nuclear Forces* (New Haven: Yale University Press, 1983).

[38]De Villiers and Stumpf joint interview.

[39]Stumpf November 16, 1993, paper; de Villiers and Stumpf joint interview; Mouton, personal interview, Johannesburg, May 25, 1993.

[40]U.S. government officials, personal interviews, Washington, D.C., May 1993 and 1994; presentation by Stumpf at the Program for Promoting Nuclear Nonproliferation (PPNN) Workshop, Harare, Zimbabwe, April 2–4, 1993, p. 1. At Harare, John Simpson reduced Stumpf's oral presentation to writing and then showed him the transcript, which Stumpf approved after a few minor revisions. Page references are to this document, which is hereafter cited as the Harare Report. See also Don Henning, personal correspondence, May 20, 1994. Henning is in charge of corporate communications for Armscor.

[41]De Villiers and Stumpf joint interview.

[42]Armscor, personal correspondence, June 1993. "We knew that the holes were filled with water and that this water would have to be pumped out before the inspections could take place. It was feared that water pumped out close to the hangar could be observed by spy satellites. Water was therefore pumped into tanker vehicles, which delivered the water to tanks erected on another part of the Vastrap test range." Henning, personal correspondence, May 20, 1994.

[43]U.S. government officials, personal interviews, November 21, 1993, and May 18, 1994. The officials were surprised that information on the renewed activity at Kalahari had not been leaked to the press at the time.

[44]Chester Crocker, *High Noon in Southern Africa: Making Peace in a Rough Neighborhood* (New York: Norton, 1992), pp. 363–72; see also Helmoed-Romer Heitman, *War in Angola: The Final South African Phase* (Gibraltar: Ashanti, 1990), pp. 295–302.

[45]De Villiers and Stumpf joint interview. Informed officials included the Ministers of Mines, Defense, and Finance, the Chief of the Defense Force, the CEO of the AEC, and the Chairman of Armscor. De Villiers, personal correspondence, August 24, 1993. Ambassador Donald Sole claimed that he was not told of the nuclear weapons program until 1988, although he had served as a member of the AEC board since the early 1980s. Donald Sole, personal interview, Cape Town, May 27, 1993.

[46]Presentation by Waldo Stumpf, Carnegie Endowment for International Peace, Washington, D.C., November 16, 1993; Stumpf November 16, 1993, paper.

[47]Armscor, personal correspondence, June 1993.

[48]See, for example, Stephen Laufer and Arthur Gavshon, "The Real Reasons for SA's Nukes," *Weekly Mail* (Johannesburg), March 26–April 1, 1993, pp. 3, 5, reported in JPRS-TND-93-009 (March 29, 1993), p. 9; Michael Cherry, "A Double Flash at Ground Zero," *Leadership* 12, no. 2 (1993); Michael Hamlyn, "ANC Calls on Pretoria to Come Clean on Bomb Costs," *Times* (London), March 27, 1993; Office of Economic Research, *South Africa's Nuclear Options and Decision Making Structures,* Interagency Intelligence Memorandum, February 6, 1978 (released under the Freedom of Information Act, July 10, 1990).

[49]One retired South African general claimed in 1993 that the military had fabricated "mock" nuclear weapons and tested their aerodynamics by placing bomb casings under the wings of Buccaneer bombers. General Tienie Groenewald, personal interview, Pretoria, June 1, 1993. Groenewald also claimed that South Africa miniaturized nuclear devices for ballistic missiles, but this has been denied by all the other South African officials I interviewed. South Africa originally intended to use only the Buccaneer to deliver nuclear bombs, but its age raised questions over how long it might remain in service. Consequently, South Africa developed plans for modifying the Mirage fighter, but the necessary hardware for carrying a bomb was reportedly never acquired. I am indebted to David Albright for this information.

[50]De Villiers and Stumpf joint interview. In a November 1993 interview, one individual who claimed to have read a document discussing the country's nuclear strategy stated that it was silent on any actual military use of nuclear weapons, but he claimed that "it was obvious" that the nuclear arsenal would be used in extremis against military forces threatening South Africa.

[51]De Villiers, personal correspondence, August 24, 1993; Stumpf November 16, 1993, paper.

[52]SABC TV 1 Network interview with Waldo Stumpf and Pik Botha, p. 5. When asked to explain the difference between a weapon and a device, Stumpf replied, "A device would typically be a device which one would only use for purposes of demonstrations and which would not be used for offensive purposes."

[53]De Villiers and Stumpf joint interview. The AEC reported to President P. W. Botha at this strategy review that the country had the capability to develop thermonuclear weapons. Albright has reported that "implosion development and theoretical work on more advanced devices continued" after the 1985 review. Albright, "South Africa's Secret Nuclear Weapons," p. 13.

It is probable that developments in Angola spurred General Jan Geldenhuys, then chief of the Defense Force, to establish in 1985 a policy planning committee for the military. Helmoed-Romer Heitman, personal interview, Cape Town, May 27, 1993.

In a report released in 1993, Moscow alleged that South Africa had worked on hydrogen bomb designs. In early 1993, the Foreign Broadcast Information Service issued a draft translation of a report by Ye. Primakov: *A New Challenge after the "Cold War": Proliferation of Weapons of Mass Destruction* (Moscow: Foreign Intelligence Service of the Russian Federation, 1993), reprinted by Joint Publications Research Service, undated, p. 73. Primakov was director of the Russian Federation's Foreign Intelligence Service, the successor to the KGB. His report analyzed sixteen countries, including the Republic of South Africa. This report is hereafter cited as the Primakov Report.

[54]Stumpf November 16, 1993, paper; de Villiers, personal correspondence, August 24, 1993.

[55]Stumpf November 16, 1993, paper.

[56]Ibid.

[57]Ibid.

[58]De Villiers, personal interview, Washington, D.C., July 21, 1993.

[59]Ibid. In fact, HEU production stopped at the Y plant in 1989. A primary concern during this period was how to reassign the facility's 150 technicians to prevent them from emigrating with their nuclear knowledge to other countries.

[60]De Villiers and Stumpf joint interview.

[61]At a seminar on South Africa's nuclear program at the Carnegie Endowment for International Peace on November 16, 1993, Stumpf said, "I always had my doubts about the wisdom of the [nuclear weapons] program." Stumpf's long-standing opposition to the nuclear weapons program has been corroborated by American officials.

[62]Mouton was well-known to key South African officials. He was a college classmate of J. W. de Villiers's, a former chairman of the South African Broadcasting Company, a former president of the University of the Orange Free State, and a former member of the Armaments Board (the predecessor to Armscor). Mouton, personal interview, Johannesburg, May 25, 1993.

[63]R. Jeffrey Smith, "South Africa's 16-Year Secret: The Nuclear Bomb," *Washington Post*, May 12, 1993. Smith claimed, "Two workers had to be severed from the [dismantlement] program and kept under continuous surveillance when they threatened to abscond with the bomb materials." Mouton would not confirm the accuracy of this story to me. Mouton, personal interview, Johannesburg, May 25, 1993.

[64]Mouton, personal interview, Johannesburg, May 25, 1993.

[65]Ibid.

[66]I am indebted to Mark Bellamy for this metaphor. To be sure, the change in attitudes among many white South Africans on matters of race evolved slowly over many years.

Before the two subcritical halves of the final device were melted, Mouton again briefed de Klerk to ensure that the president was absolutely certain of his decision to eliminate the nuclear arsenal. De Klerk told him to complete the job. Mouton, personal interview, Johannesburg, May 25, 1993. The main technical problem that arose during this period occurred when the sole vacuum-induction furnace used to melt the enriched uranium metal cracked, causing a delay.

[67]Mouton, personal interview, Johannesburg, May 25, 1993. Stumpf November 16, 1993, paper. See also, Smith, *Washington Post*, May 12, 1993. U.S. government officials do not believe that all nonnuclear components were destroyed. Personal interview, Washington, D.C., 1994.

[68]Mouton was concerned with kilogram, not gram, discrepancies. When the "before" and "after" weights did not match, Mouton not only asked the technicians for an explanation but personally checked the IAEA's guidelines to determine if the explanation was plausible. According to Mouton, losses were within "acceptable limits." Mouton, personal interview, Johannesburg, May 25, 1993.

[69]Ibid. Mouton periodically requested random documents from the steel cage to determine the accuracy of the filing system and to satisfy himself that it operated properly.

[70]See SABC TV 1 Network interview with Waldo Stumpf, March 25, 1993, reported in JPRS-TND-93-010 (April 16, 1993), p. 4; Armscor, personal correspondence, June 1993. But according to a member of an IAEA inspection team investigating South Africa's nuclear complex in 1991, the IAEA found nuclear design documents and nonnuclear components for nuclear weapons that had not been destroyed. Personal interview, Washington D.C., December 15, 1994.

[71]"At the request of the [IAEA inspection] team the historical operating and accounting records of those South African facilities selected by the team were audited by Agency inspectors during their inspection of these facilities." IAEA Inventory Report, p. 1. See also R. Jeffrey Smith, "S. Africa's Nuclear File to Be Age-Tested," *Washington Post*, May 13, 1993.

[72]De Villiers, personal interview, Washington, D.C., July 21, 1993. A copy of Mouton's report was shown to the IAEA but as of January 1994 had not been shown to the African National Congress, despite repeated requests.

[73]See *Weekly Mail* (Johannesburg), March 26–April 1, 1993, p. 5, reported in JPRS-TND-93-010 (April 16, 1993), p. 7. Grant's successor at the Y Plant, Anthony Jackson, said he would not be surprised if Grant had taken the project's technical documents with him when he retired as chief executive officer of the AEC in 1987. Personal interview, Pelindaba, May 25, 1993. Grant now lives on his farm in the eastern Transvaal, where I called him when visiting South Africa in May 1993. He was unwilling to talk about the nuclear program either over the telephone or in person, stating that his government security oath still prevented him from discussing classified matters.

[74]Jeremy Shearer, personal interview, Washington, D.C., July 21, 1993. Shearer was a senior South African foreign service officer responsible for nuclear matters. South Africa submitted a report to the IAEA on October 30, 1991, with an initial inventory of South Africa's nuclear material and facilities as of September 30, 1991.

[75]Harare Report, p. 4. The offer to "go anywhere, anytime" was used by IAEA inspectors to visit the Kalahari test site to ensure that it was no longer operational. Regarding the information on nuclear commerce, it should be mentioned that South Africa deleted the names of suppliers and customers on the export and import documents it shared with the IAEA.

[76]Harare Report, p. 3.

[77]De Villiers, personal correspondence, August 24, 1993; presentation by Stumpf, Carnegie Endowment for International Peace, November 16, 1993.

[78]See de Klerk's "new dispensation" speech, in Foreign Broadcast Information Service (FBIS)-AFR-023, February 2, 1990, pp. 5–11.

[79]Stumpf November 16, 1993, paper; de Villiers, personal correspondence, August 24, 1993.

[80]I am indebted to David Fischer for bringing this point to my attention. See also Fischer, *Stopping the Spread of Nuclear Weapons: The Past and the Prospects* (London: Routledge, 1992), pp. 215–16.

[81]On de Klerk's personal background and political career, see David Ottaway, *Chained Together: Mandela, De Klerk, and the Struggle to Remake South Africa* (New York: Random House, 1993), pp. 52–71.

[82]Quoted in Mark Hibbs, "South Africa's Secret Nuclear Program: The Dismantling," *Nuclear Fuel,* May 24, 1993, p. 10.

[83]For a good discussion of political developments in South Africa at this time, see Marina Ottaway, *South Africa: The Struggle for a New Order* (Washington, D.C.: Brookings Institution, 1993).

[84]Quoted in David Albright and Mark Hibbs, "South Africa: The ANC and the Atom Bomb," *Bulletin of the Atomic Scientists* 49 (April 1993): 33.

[85]Presentation by Stumpf, Carnegie Endowment for International Peace, November 16, 1993.

[86]South African government official, personal interview, Johannesburg, May 1993.

[87]Roger Jardine, personal interview, Johannesburg, May 26, 1993.

[88]In mid-January 1993, the U.S. Arms Control and Disarmament Agency issued a report to Congress on compliance with international arms control treaties. Without further explanation, the report stated, "The United States has serious questions about South Africa's compliance with its Article II and III obligations [under the NPT]." See U.S. Arms Control and Disarmament Agency, "Adherence to and Compliance with Arms Control Agreements and the President's Report to Congress on Soviet Noncompliance with Arms Control Agreements," January 14, 1993, p. 18; see also Steve Coll and Paul Taylor, "Tracking S. Africa's Elusive A-Program," *Washington Post*, March 18, 1993. Article 2 of the NPT requires nonnuclear parties not to receive nuclear explosive devices, not to manufacture nuclear explosive devices, and not to seek or receive any assistance in the manufacture of nuclear explosive devices. Article 3 requires nonnuclear parties to accept comprehensive safeguards on all their nuclear activities and nuclear material, such as HEU, and forbids all parties to export such material to any nonnuclear weapon state or to export any nuclear technology for producing such material, unless this material is subject to safeguards.

[89]Shearer, personal interview, Pretoria, May 25, 1993. A week before de Klerk's appearance before parliament, the Foreign Ministry had instructed South Africa's

embassies around the world to schedule a meeting with their respective host governments on the morning of March 24. They were not told why. The text of de Klerk's speech was faxed to them only twenty-four hours beforehand.

[90]U.S. government officials, personal interviews, Washington, D.C., 1993 and 1994.

[91]Primakov Report, p. 73.

[92]General Groenewald, personal interview, Pretoria, June 1, 1993. See also Richard Ellis, "Honest . . . I Gave Up the Bomb!" *Sunday Times,* March 28, 1993.

[93]IAEA, GOV/2609, September 3, 1992, p. 6; de Villiers statement before IAEA Board of Governors, September 16, 1992, printed in GOV/OR.788, November 6, 1992. See also Harare Report, pp. 3–4. Albright suggests that the South African declaration to the IAEA of its uranium enrichment operations and the IAEA's estimate of that declaration "are within one significant quantity, or the equivalent of 25 kilograms of weapon-grade uranium." Albright, "South Africa's Secret Nuclear Weapons," p. 3.

[94]De Villiers and Stumpf joint interview. David Fischer has remarked that the IAEA would have had severe constitutional and practical problems in monitoring the dismantlement process. Personal correspondence, April 25, 1994.

[95]*The 22 September 1979 Event,* p. 10.

[96]Ellis, "Honest . . . I Gave Up the Bomb!"

[97]Mark Stansfield, *Sunday Star* (Johannesburg), reported in JPRS-TND-93-010 (April 16, 1993), p. 8.

[98]Hersh, *The Samson Option,* p. 265; see also Albright, "South Africa's Secret Nuclear Weapons," p. 5.

[99]IAEA Inventory Report, p. 7.

[100]Des Blow, "Nuke Bombshell," *City Press* (Johannesburg), March 28, 1993, reported in JPRS-TND-93-010 (April 16, 1993), pp. 2–3; Hibbs, "South Africa's Secret Nuclear Program," p. 11; see also Des Blow, "Nuke Bombshell: Govt to Get Rhoodie Awakening," *City Press,* April 18, 1993. Eschel Rhoodie, who worked in the Ministry of Information in the Vorster cabinet, referred to the tritium matter and the South African–Israeli relationship in his book, *The Real Information Scandal* (Pretoria: Orbis, 1983).

[101]Hibbs, "South Africa's Secret Nuclear Program," p. 11.

[102]Errol de Montille, personal interview, Washington, D.C., April 7, 1993.

[103]See Zdenek Cervenka and Barbara Rogers, *The Nuclear Axis: Secret Collaboration between West Germany and South Africa* (London: Julian Friedman, 1978), esp. pp. 51–103; for a rebuttal by the Federal Republic of Germany, see *Fact v. Fiction: A Rebuttal of the Charges of Alleged Cooperation between the Federal Republic of Germany and South Africa in the Nuclear and Military Fields* (Bonn: Press and Information Office of the Federal Government, 1978). See also Sole, "The Rise of Nuclear Sanctions against South Africa," pp. 5–6; Donald B. Sole, "This Above All," unpublished autobiography, Embassy of South Africa, Washington, D.C., pp. 323–31.

[104]See Allan S. Krass, Peter Boksma, Boelie Elzen, and Wim A. Smit, *Uranium Enrichment and Nuclear Weapons Proliferation* (London and New York: Taylor and Francis, 1983), p. 20.

[105]Presentation at the Carnegie Endowment for International Peace, November 16, 1993.

[106]In addition, if this was a South African nuclear test, it is curious that General

Magnus Malan, then chief of South Africa's defense force, was not in South Africa or at least at the test observation point during such an important event; he was reported to be touring South America at the time. See *The 22 September 1979 Event*, p. 8.

[107]David Fischer, personal correspondence, April 25, 1994.

[108]SABC TV 1 Network interview with Waldo Stumpf and Pik Botha, p. 5.

[109]Shearer, personal interview, Pretoria, May 25, 1993.

[110]General H. D. E. V. du Toit, personal interview, Pretoria, May 24, 1993.

[111]The chief interdepartmental mechanism was the State Security Council (SCC), which met infrequently. Telephone conversation with Rod Fisk, April 1994. Fisk served in the South African Foreign Ministry with responsibility for nuclear matters. For an understanding of how the SCC operated, as well as other aspects of South Africa's foreign policy decision making, see Deon Geldenhuys, *The Diplomacy of Isolation: South African Foreign Policy Making* (Johannesburg: Macmillan, 1984).

[112]David Fischer, "South Africa," in Mitchell Reiss and Robert S. Litwak, eds., *Nuclear Proliferation after the Cold War* (Washington, D.C.: Woodrow Wilson Center Press, 1994), p. 216.

[113]Newby-Fraser, *Chain Reaction*, pp. 101–2.

[114]Du Toit, personal interview, Pretoria, May 24, 1993.

[115]De Villiers and Stumpf joint interview. Of course, it could also have turned out to be seven, which was the number of devices Pretoria had originally selected for its nuclear stockpile but did not have time to manufacture.

[116]The nuclear programs of these three countries are examined in Reiss and Litwak, *Nuclear Proliferation after the Cold War*, in the chapters by Brahma Chellaney (India), Ali T. Sheikh (Pakistan), and Shai Feldman (Israel).

[117]South African officials have claimed that a benefit of nuclear weapons was their cost-effectiveness when compared with the high price of conventional weapons, such as jet fighter aircraft. This argument is far-fetched, since there was no real trade-off. Pretoria could not have acquired modern combat aircraft on the international arms market and could not have itself developed this technology. Moreover, nuclear weapons are traditionally complements to, and not substitutes for, conventional weapons, so it is likely that the nuclear arsenal would have been an *added* defense expenditure if Pretoria could have purchased or acquired jet fighters. On the debit side of the ledger, the nuclear weapons program siphoned off many of the country's most talented scientists and engineers. The loss to South Africa's industrial productivity must be recognized when toting up the benefits and liabilities of the nuclear weapons program.

[118]Presentation at the Carnegie Endowment for International Peace, November 16, 1993.

[119]The term "nuclear myth makers" was coined by Peter R. Lavoy. See Lavoy, "Nuclear Myths and the Causes of Nuclear Proliferation," in Zachary S. Davis and Benjamin Frankel, eds., *The Proliferation Puzzle: Why Nuclear Weapons Spread (and What Results)* (London: Frank Cass, 1993), pp. 192–212.

[120]Donald B. Sole, "South Africa and the Nonproliferation Treaty," *American Review* (1993), p. 5.

[121]Personal interview, Washington, D.C., July 21, 1993.

[122]Presentation at the Carnegie Endowment for International Peace, November 16, 1993.

Chapter 3

Argentina and Brazil: Rivals, Not Enemies

On November 28, 1990, Presidents Carlos Saul Menem of Argentina and Fernando Collor de Mello of Brazil met at the border town of Foz de Iguazú. Overlooking spectacular waterfalls, the two leaders signed a historic agreement in which their countries pledged to establish a bilateral nuclear inspection system, open all their nuclear installations to the IAEA, and revise and then fully implement the Treaty of Tlatelolco, which establishes a nuclear-weapon-free zone (NWFZ) across Latin America.[1]

It had taken over a decade to reach this point. During this period, the process of Argentine-Brazilian nuclear cooperation had been interrupted by war, opposed by influential military factions, stymied by senior nuclear energy officials, and hampered by suspicions of nuclear weapons programs. Yet Buenos Aires and Brasilia had managed to overcome these obstacles. They had allayed their joint concerns, formalized their mutual obligations, and attenuated their hostility to the nonproliferation regime. Their efforts in the nuclear field would subsequently be devoted solely to peaceful purposes. This collaborative nuclear effort was unprecedented.

Argentina

During the 1970s and much of the 1980s, Argentina was one of a handful of countries suspected of wanting to acquire nuclear weapons. Foreign observers cited numerous motives for an Argentine bomb program: to win status and prestige; to vault over other South American countries, especially Brazil (and thus fulfill the traditional Argentine desire for "exceptionalism"); to secure popular approval for illegitimate military regimes; to maintain a technological and scientific lead over its neighbors; and perhaps most important, to hedge against the possibility of a Brazilian nuclear bomb.

The country's ambitious plans in the nuclear energy field during this period reinforced the impression that it maintained an interest in developing a nuclear option. The direction of Argentina's nuclear program, which selected technologies that could produce bomb-grade materials, raised doubts about the country's nuclear intentions. Its avoidance of international safeguards on sensitive technologies, its lack of public accountability, and the refusal by Buenos Aires to ratify and fully implement the Treaty of Tlatelolco or join the NPT reinforced these fears.

Nuclear Capabilities

The history of the Argentine nuclear energy program—the oldest and most sophisticated in Latin America—is one of slow but steady progress, marked largely by stability, professionalism, and the quest for energy independence.[2] Under its National Atomic Energy Commission (CNEA), Argentina became the first country in South America to produce a fission chain reaction, reprocess spent fuel to extract plutonium, enrich uranium, manufacture fuel elements, and export a nuclear reactor.[3]

In the 1960s Argentina purchased from West Germany the Atucha I heavy-water power reactor and in 1973 contracted with Canada for a second heavy-water power reactor at Embalse to provide electricity to Córdoba, the country's third-largest city. However, after Ottawa discovered that India had used a Canadian-supplied reactor to produce the plutonium for its May 1974 "peaceful nuclear explosion," it insisted on renegotiating the safeguards applicable to Embalse.[4] Partially because of the delays caused by these negotiations, the reactor came on-line three years behind schedule, in March 1983, and at five times the initial price.

Earlier, in March 1976, the newly installed military regime led by General Jorge Videla had placed Navy Captain Carlos Castro Madero as president of CNEA. Castro Madero soon announced plans for a third nuclear power plant, Atucha II, and a commercial heavy-water plant that would eliminate the need for overseas suppliers for the Atucha I and Embalse plants.

By the time Buenos Aires began to entertain bids for the Atucha II facility and the heavy-water plant, the nuclear supplier countries (e.g., West Germany and Canada) had decided to require comprehensive safeguards as a condition of purchase. However, Bonn indicated that it would insist on full-scope safeguards only if it won both bids; Buenos Aires took the hint and split the order, awarding the reactor contract to West Germany and the heavy-water plant contract to Sulzer Brothers, a Swiss firm. Atomic Energy of Canada, Limited, which had far greater experience than its competitors and offered to supply both the power station and the heavy-water plant at significantly lower cost, lost out apparently because it demanded full-scope safeguards.[5]

In 1978, Argentina decided to build a spent-fuel reprocessing plant at Ezeiza, near Buenos Aires. The Ezeiza plant was subject to international safeguards only when it reprocessed safeguarded spent fuel (which was the only type of spent fuel Argentina had at the time because all of its nuclear reactors were safeguarded). CNEA claimed that the facility was needed to recycle plutonium for reuse in Atucha I, to use for breeder reactor fuel, and to provide the full range of fuel services to potential nuclear customers, which was essential for Argentina to enter the nuclear export market.[6] Left unsaid was that, when completed, the reprocessing facility would also be able to extract enough plutonium for one or two nuclear weapons per year.

At this same time, motivated partially by the U.S. announcement in July 1974 that it would no longer fill contract orders to supply enriched uranium for Argentina's research reactors and by Brazil's 1975 nuclear deal with West Germany, Buenos Aires clandestinely constructed a gaseous diffusion uranium enrichment facility at Pilçaniyeu.[7] The Pilçaniyeu plant, which was not subject to IAEA safeguards, could produce low-enriched uranium for Argentina's research reactors and could potentially service the overseas research reactor market. In principle, it could also produce highly enriched uranium suitable for nuclear bombs.

Argentina undertook elaborate precautions to keep construction of the Pilçaniyeu plant secret: it developed the technology itself, and few CNEA personnel knew all facets of the project.[8] Argentine officials claimed that the primary reason for this secrecy was to prevent a cut-off of Canadian assistance to the Embalse power plant, which was still under construction, but Buenos Aires may also have been wary of provoking Washington. In fact, the United States knew of the Pilçaniyeu facility and had observed the site by satellite but could only guess at the installation's function; Washington thought it might be a second reprocessing plant.[9]

On November 10, 1983, Castro Madero announced, "Argentina has successfully demonstrated the technology for the enrichment of uranium."[10] It now had a capability matched by only nine other countries in the world. Theoretically, the plant could enrich enough weapons-grade uranium for four to six nuclear bombs per year.[11] In an attempt to dispel international suspicion and disapproval, Argentine scientists claimed that Pilçaniyeu was designed to enrich uranium to only 20 percent U-235 and would have to be reconfigured before it could produce highly enriched uranium suitable for nuclear bombs. Argentina also informed other countries, including Brazil and the United States, a few days in advance of the announcement.[12]

One purpose behind the Pilçaniyeu announcement was to restore national pride and regain international prestige after the 1982 Falklands-Malvinas war.[13] All sectors of Argentine society, including the nuclear program, had suffered the repercussions of the ignominious defeat inflicted by Britain.[14] London's use of nuclear-powered submarines and rumors of the presence of nuclear-armed British vessels spurred increased calls for an Argentine nuclear bomb after the war. In response, Castro Madero commissioned a CNEA study to explore nuclear propulsion for naval subs. CNEA duly completed the nuclear propulsion study, but the issue faded from view.[15]

The war's direct impact on the nuclear program was far less important than its indirect impact through the changes it wrought in Argentine society. A discredited military returned to the barracks and permitted the country's first popular election, in 1983. Newly elected president Raúl Alfonsín removed Castro Madero, replaced him with a civilian, Alberto Constantini, made CNEA accountable to a council of ministers within the Foreign Ministry, and cut CNEA's budget by 40 percent during his first year in office. At his first presidential news conference, on January 15, 1984, Alfonsín declared, "Argentina is committed exclusively to the peaceful use of nuclear energy."[16]

However, Argentina still refused to renounce its right to conduct peaceful nuclear explosions or to codify its nonnuclear weapon status by joining the NPT or ratifying the Treaty of Tlatelolco. By the mid-1980s many observers thought that Argentina was only a few years away from acquiring a nuclear weapons capability. With the construction of its Pilçaniyeu and Ezeiza plants outside of international safeguards, Buenos Aires had preserved its ability to produce enough enriched uranium and plutonium for several nuclear bombs per year.[17]

Brazil

Like Argentina, Brazil was eyed by the international community during the 1970s and 1980s as a potential nuclear weapon state. These suspicions were spurred by Brazil's competition with Argentina to be the first to go nuclear, as well as by its desire for regional leadership and international status commensurate with the country's geographic size, population, and natural resources. The scale and ambition of Brazil's 1975 nuclear deal with West Germany, which included the transfer of sensitive technologies that could produce bomb material, increased these concerns, as did a secret nuclear program controlled by the military. Also, the navy's interest in enriched uranium for submarine propulsion, the lack of legislative oversight, Brasilia's refusal to join the NPT or accept full-scope safeguards, its assertion of the right to conduct peaceful nuclear explosions, and its refusal to bring fully into force the terms of the Treaty of Tlatelolco all fueled these fears.

NUCLEAR CAPABILITIES

Until the early 1970s, Brazil had a modest nuclear program, which included the 1971 purchase of a turnkey power station, named Angra I, from Westinghouse. The country first aroused serious proliferation concern with its June 1975 "nuclear deal of the century" with West Germany.[18] The agreement represented the largest transfer of nuclear technology to a developing country, encompassing all aspects of the nuclear fuel cycle, from uranium exploration to nuclear waste storage.[19] The multibillion-dollar deal included the sale of two 1,250-megawatt reactors, with an option for six additional reactors. Its two most sensitive aspects involved construction of an industrial-scale uranium enrichment plant in Brazil, with aerodynamic jet-nozzle technology then being developed by West Germany, and a pilot plant facility that could reprocess spent fuel to extract plutonium.[20] Bonn assumed the entire financial risk of the first two nuclear reactors—Angra II and III—through concessionary financing.

As a condition of the agreement, the regime of Army General Ernesto Geisel accepted rigorous international inspections. Since these inspections were not comprehensive, however, they did not prohibit Brazil from producing bomb material in facilities outside of the agreement with West Germany, nor did they force Brazil to renounce its interest in nuclear explosives.[21]

Brazil had many motives for such a grandiose scheme. First, it saw technological autonomy as an important component of its national security; technology would spur economic development, which in turn would enhance the overall security of the state. In the context of the nuclear deal, technology transferred from West Germany would permit Brazil to escape the discriminatory system of export controls imposed by the international nonproliferation regime. Further, because it imported 80 percent of its oil, Brazil believed that it needed energy security, especially after the Organization of Petroleum Exporting Countries (OPEC) 1973 oil "shock." An indigenous enrichment capability would eliminate Brazil's dependence on the United States, whose reliability had been questioned when it suspended the signing of future enrichment contracts in July 1974. Nationalism played a role too. By the mid-1970s, Argentina's nuclear program far outpaced Brazil's. The nuclear deal with West Germany would allow Brasilia to leapfrog Buenos Aires at one go. It would also reinforce Brazil's claims to regional leadership.[22]

These motivations did not silence Brazilian critics of the deal. They argued that the country had contracted for an unproven enrichment technology and that the project was far too expensive, ambitious, and technically challenging for Brazil's slender scientific and engineering resources. Further, they claimed that the deal seemed to favor commercial German interests over Brazilian needs and inadequately considered environmental and safety factors.[23] Many also suspected that the underlying motivation behind the Geisel regime's purchase of the entire nuclear fuel cycle was to provide the country with the capability to build nuclear weapons.

THE SECRET "PARALLEL PROGRAM"

Among the domestic critics of the nuclear agreement with West Germany were members of Brazil's military. The first signs of disapproval were aired by a junior naval officer, Othon Luis Pinheiro da Silva, who portrayed the safeguards regime as onerous and intrusive; he also doubted the viability of the unproven jet-nozzle technology. At the request of the navy minister, Pinheiro da Silva subsequently formed a small group at the Research Institute on Nuclear Engineering (IPEN) in São Paulo to master the ability to enrich uranium independently from the German deal and international safeguards.[24] The navy had an institutional interest in small nuclear reactors for submarine propulsion, and one of its goals was to produce 6-to-7 percent U-235, which would not be useful for nuclear weapons but could serve as reactor fuel for submarines.[25] But this enrichment capability would also permit Brazil to produce weapons-grade uranium. The military referred to its covert nuclear activities as the "autonomous program," which later became more generally known as the "parallel program." The effort went forward in secret to prevent the West Germans from cutting off Brazil's access to nuclear technology and to stifle domestic critics.[26]

In 1982 Rex Nazaré Alves became head of the National Nuclear Energy Commission (CNEN). Nazaré Alves had close ties to the military, especially the army, and he personally energized the clandestine project in his capacity as its "coordinator."[27] Each branch of the armed services had a piece of the action—and each had its own program to develop nuclear weapons.[28]

Widespread publicity on the parallel program came in August 1986, when the newspaper *Folha de São Paulo* exposed what it claimed was a nuclear test site at an air force training ground at Serro de Cachimbo in the state of Pará, the heart of the Amazon. According to José Goldemberg, a longtime critic of Brazil's nuclear policies who served as science adviser to President Collor, the Cachimbo site was the brainchild of Brigadier General Hugo de Oliveira Piva. Toward the end of the regime of General João Figueiredo, Piva promised the general that he could conduct a nuclear explosion.[29] In 1984–85, the air force dug a hole at Cachimbo as part of its "Projeto Solimoes," named after a river in the Amazon. The hole was less than a meter in diameter and approximately 280 meters deep, with concrete and lead-lined underground galleries. These dimensions correspond to the holes dug for the U.S. "Project Plowshares" peaceful nuclear tests in Nevada during the 1950s and 1960s.[30]

When the story broke, Brasilia immediately denied that Cachimbo was a nuclear test site or that the country had a nuclear weapons program; rather, it explained that the hole had been part of a mineral exploration project.[31] The armed forces disavowed that the site was even connected to the parallel program, claiming that it was merely a hole for testing equipment and materials for an "aerospace capability."[32] Domestic critics of the parallel program and foreign experts doubted the official explanations—they accurately pegged Cachimbo as a nuclear test site developed as part of an off-the-shelf military program.[33] Consensus prevailed on only one point: Brazil did not possess the special nuclear material needed for a nuclear test at this time.[34] It did not even have the nonnuclear components for a "cold" test.[35]

But Brasilia's activities in the nuclear field promised to provide bomb-grade material in the foreseeable future. The military, with CNEN's support, had created a clandestine program that was designed to produce highly enriched uranium or weapons-grade plutonium outside of IAEA safeguards. President José Sarney confirmed these suspicions when he proclaimed in September 1987 that the navy's IPEN facility had conducted the successful laboratory-scale enrichment of uranium.[36] Further, Brazil refused to renounce its right to conduct peaceful nuclear explosions (PNEs) or to codify its nonnuclear weapon status by joining the NPT or fully implementing the

Treaty of Tlatelolco. By the mid-1980s, some knowledgeable observers had concluded that Brazil was committed to developing nuclear weapons by the early 1990s.[37]

Nuclear Rapprochement

Argentina and Brazil both faced significant disincentives to acquiring nuclear weapons during the 1970s and 1980s. For Buenos Aires, provoking an unwinnable arms race with a much larger and wealthier Brazil made little sense. As one particularly farsighted Argentine strategist recognized in the mid-1970s, an arms race with Brazil would involve "enormous cost at a time when both peoples need[ed] to apply all their resources to projects that will assure their socioeconomic, spiritual, and cultural progress."[38] Nuclear weapons were simply incapable of furthering this type of development.

This logic also applied to Brazil, although it was in a better financial position to fund a full-scale nuclear weapon effort. Yet because Brazil enjoyed comparative advantages over Argentina in wealth, size, and political stability, it was not in Brazil's interest to launch a nuclear arms race that could diminish this edge.[39] Moreover, there was no real conflict between the two countries. Their last war had ended in 1828; Brazil and Argentina had never seen each other as enemies and certainly never envisioned a nuclear war with one another.

Yet obstacles to bilateral cooperation also existed. Although never adversaries, Buenos Aires and Brasilia displayed a culture of competition, which was especially prevalent in southern Brazil. Important elements of the military regimes in both countries opposed cooperation in the nuclear sphere. Suspicion and mistrust, especially in such a sensitive area, played a role, as did the fact that their nuclear programs were not synchronous—Brazil was always trying to catch up with Argentina.

No single factor can fully explain the evolution of Argentine-Brazilian nuclear relations. Numerous incentives differently influenced this process as it unfolded: a common position during negotiations in the mid-1960s on the Tlatelolco Treaty; a shared hostility to the international nonproliferation regime that led to the formation of an "anti-NPT axis"; the advent in the mid-1980s of civilian governments that wanted to wrest control over nuclear programs from the military; presidential leadership; and eventually a greater mutual appreciation, on both sides, of the political and commercial benefits of joining the nonproliferation regime and the corresponding liabilities of maintaining a nationalistic nuclear stance.

EARLY EFFORTS

Relations between Argentina and Brazil during the 1970s foundered on competition over exploiting the fertile Rio de la Plata basin, which covers one-sixth of Latin America. The most divisive issue concerned construction of an enormous hydroelectric dam at Itaipu on the Paraná River, whose Brazilian headwaters empty into Argentina. The October 1979 Rio de la Plata agreement (among Argentina, Brazil, and Paraguay) resolved the dispute over water resources, put an end to a tradition of zero-sum competition, and set the stage for a dramatic improvement in bilateral relations.[40]

With this thorny issue out of the way, the two military regimes gravitated closer to one another in response to common pressures. By the end of the 1970s, the nuclear programs in both countries had encountered multiple technical and financial obstacles, in no small part due to a technology denial strategy adopted by the nuclear supplier countries.[41] The two countries resented a discriminatory nonproliferation regime that did not recognize their sovereign right to nuclear technology, which each viewed as essential for economic development and national security. A common adversary—the international nonproliferation regime—moved them toward a defiant diplomatic posture. Regional collaboration, not competition, became a means to surmount the hurdles erected by the nonproliferation regime. This anti-NPT axis permitted them to coordinate their nuclear efforts and strengthen their resistance to the restrictive export policies of the nuclear suppliers.[42]

The personal commitment of Brazil's military leader, João Figueiredo, to improving relations with Argentina propelled this process forward. In May 1980 Figueiredo visited Buenos Aires; he was the first Brazilian president to do so in forty years. And, for the first time, nuclear matters were on the agenda. An agreement reached by the two countries highlighted their joint opposition to the NPT regime: "The parties will pursue talks concerning situations of mutual interest which arise on the international scene in relation to the application of nuclear energy for peaceful purposes with a view to coordinating their positions when this is desirable."[43] The two national nuclear commissions reached agreement on a wide range of joint research projects, which included research and development on experimental and power reactors, exchange of nuclear materials, uranium prospecting, and the manufacture of fuel elements.[44]

Personal relationships at the working level also facilitated cooperative efforts. Argentine and Brazilian nuclear officials knew each other from international conferences, IAEA meetings, and bilateral exchanges. Even before formal bilateral exchanges, many Argentine nuclear scientists and technicians who had left the CNEA in the mid-1970s—due to political litmus tests imposed by the Perónists, poor leadership, low salaries, and deteriorating working conditions—had gone to work in Brazil.

Finally, nuclear cooperation was helped by Argentina's reaction to the West Germany–Brazil nuclear deal. Buenos Aires had not publicly criticized the deal when it was first unveiled, even though the Paraná River dispute had strained bilateral relations at the time. In fact, Argentine civilian officials and military officers had defended Brazil's right to acquire nuclear technology. This quiet support reinforced Argentina's common cause with Brazil against the hierarchy of the global nonproliferation regime. Further, it testified to Argentina's view that the regime threatened its economic development and national security more than did the potential nuclear ambitions of its neighbor.[45]

The agreements of May 1980 marked the first important, if small, steps toward broader nuclear cooperation. Although it produced few tangible results, this opening strengthened personal relationships, reduced suspicions and misunderstandings, and built trust.

CIVILIAN GOVERNMENTS AND THE INSTITUTIONALIZATION OF COOPERATION

Implementation of the May 1980 agreement fell somewhat short of initial expectations. Political and economic difficulties in both countries distracted the attention of the governments, which were preoccupied with managing the complex transition from military to civilian rule. In addition, two events raised potential obstacles to further cooperation. Argentina's 1982 seizure of the Falklands-Malvinas Islands, coupled with its poor showing in the ensuing conflict with Britain, sowed doubts in Brazil about the wisdom of dealing with an erratic military regime. And the following year, Brazil was caught off guard by the announcement of the Pilçaniyeu enrichment facility, which revived old doubts about Argentina's reliability.[46]

The election of civilian presidents in both countries in the mid-1980s infused the bilateral relationship with renewed momentum. In Argentina, military defeat led to the election of Radical Civic Union candidate Raúl Alfonsín as president on October 30, 1983. In Brazil, economic mismanagement on a colossal scale forced the military to abdicate power to the civilians.[47] In February 1985, president-elect

Tancredo Neves met Alfonsín, and the two leaders promised to revive nuclear cooperation and, more important, to permit mutual inspections of each other's nuclear installations.

Alfonsín and José Sarney, who assumed the presidency after Neves's untimely death, met at Foz de Iguazú later that year, in November 1985. Greater engagement characterized this new beginning. The "Declaration of Iguazú" outlined broad goals: "the creation of mechanisms that could ensure the higher interests of peace, security, and the development of the region." It reemphasized the mutual commitment to develop nuclear energy for exclusively peaceful purposes, promote close cooperation in the nuclear field, and coordinate activities to surmount increasing obstacles to obtaining nuclear equipment and materials.[48]

The most concrete achievement at Iguazú was the creation of a joint working group, with representatives from the respective nuclear bureaucracies and industries. This working group had three subgroups to deal with technical cooperation, foreign policy coordination, and the legal and technical aspects of nuclear cooperation.[49] Lodging the working groups in the foreign ministries—the institutions most sensitive to international nonproliferation pressures and most committed to bilateral collaboration—significantly accelerated efforts. Spawning new bureaucracies with substantive expertise institutionalized bilateral nuclear cooperation. As one of their first acts, they agreed that mutual inspections would be conducted without IAEA assistance and that no information would be shared with the agency.[50]

Also starting in 1985, each country's head of state paid an annual visit to the other and on each occasion issued a joint statement on nuclear cooperation. These declarations were more than window-dressing; they demonstrated unprecedented high-level political support for the process. In December 1986, Brazil allowed Argentine nuclear officials to visit IPEN, where the navy secretly conducted research on both uranium enrichment and reprocessing outside of IAEA safeguards.[51] This visit paved the way for Sarney's reciprocal visit to Pilçaniyeu in July 1987. Two months later, Sarney announced that IPEN had enriched uranium. As a reflection of their new friendship, Sarney had sent a personal letter to Alfonsín with this news before his public announcement in Brazil.[52]

Disarray in both countries' nuclear programs during the latter half of the 1980s also facilitated nuclear rapprochement. Ambitious plans for mastering the nuclear fuel cycle and acquiring the capability to produce weapons-grade nuclear material had fallen on hard times. Alfonsín and Sarney had slashed the budgets. The political influence of the armed forces in each country was at its lowest in decades. Reciprocal visits to nuclear installations raised confidence that the other was not building nuclear bombs.

Argentina's nuclear program was characterized by cost overruns, safety hazards, and inefficiencies. Maintenance problems at the Atucha I and Embalse power reactors required intermittent shutdowns. In March 1990, Buenos Aires suspended work indefinitely on the Ezeiza reprocessing plant; the Atucha II power station remained unfinished. Plans to build four 600-megawatt power reactors and a complete nuclear fuel cycle by 1997 had been abandoned long ago.

The Pilçaniyeu facility, whose existence had been disclosed amid much fanfare in 1983, had experienced severe technical and funding problems that were well known to Brazilian officials. According to one American scientist who visited the facility a number of times: "It's a piece of crap now [1994], and back in 1983 it was probably an even bigger piece of crap. It will probably never produce weapons-grade uranium."[53]

Brazilian President Sarney had inherited in March 1985 a peaceful nuclear energy program in shambles and a covert autonomous nuclear program led by the armed forces. From the start, Angra I had experienced severe technical difficulties that worsened over time. Maintenance problems had shut it down more than twenty times since 1982, prompting the plant's derogatory nicknames of "lightning bug," "fire-fly," and "glow worm." The 1975 nuclear deal with West Germany had turned into a fiasco. Sarney's predecessor, President João Figueiredo, had already reduced CNEN's budget and phased out much of the original deal with West Germany. Because the jet-nozzle enrichment method was not fully developed, the Germans had "sold Brazil a technology they didn't have."[54] Construction of the Angra II and III power stations was already well over budget and behind schedule; financial constraints in mid-decade forced Brazil to cancel the planned purchase of additional nuclear reactors from West Germany. Work on Angra II stalled in 1988 yet still cost Brazil over $350 million a year; its estimated total cost of $5.3 billion made it one of the world's most expensive nuclear reactors.[55]

The parallel program was not in much better shape. The Aramar uranium enrichment facility outside São Paulo caused the greatest international unease, yet it had produced only minute amounts of 3-to-4 percent U-235. IPEN's ultracentrifuge facility was no more productive.[56] Construction of the reprocessing facility at Resende was indefinitely postponed. These difficulties tempered Argentina's reaction when revelations about the scope and character of Brazil's clandestine nuclear activities began to emerge during the late 1980s.

The original incentive for bilateral cooperation—shared hostility to the international nonproliferation regime—had not disappeared with the advent of civilian administrations. To mollify foreign critics of their nuclear policies, Alfonsín repeated to Sarney at their first meeting in 1985 the suggestion that they create a bilateral inspection system. Alfonsín had another motive as well. Such a system would further diminish the military's influence over the nuclear program. It would symbolize, both domestically and internationally, that he was in full control of Argentina's nuclear program and, by extension, of the military and the country.[57]

For Brazil, this was a case of too much, too soon, and it politely rejected the offer. Nazaré Alves and members of the military opposed the nuclear cooperation policy, which was being driven by the Foreign Ministry and a small host of advisers attached to Sarney's office.[58] Each of the three branches of the armed services was committed to developing a nuclear weapons option, which obviously could not be revealed to Argentine inspectors. Inspections would not only jeopardize their nuclear ambitions but also raise questions about the wisdom of the military's costly strategy to invest in reprocessing and uranium enrichment technology in the first place.

Nonetheless, the nuclear rapprochement continued. By March 1988, Argentina had reportedly visited all operating nuclear facilities not under IAEA safeguards (although it is doubtful that it gained access to the army's secret facility outside Rio de Janeiro, which housed a subcritical nuclear assembly).[59] The declaration at Iperó, Brazil, the following month transformed the joint working group into the Argentine-Brazilian Permanent Committee on Nuclear Affairs. Meeting every four months, this committee became the standard channel for bilateral nuclear discourse and action.

The diplomatic process that started with the "Declaration of Iguazú" led to greater interaction on a broad range of issues, especially commercial relations. In late 1985, the two sides announced the Argentine-Brazilian Integration and Cooperation Program (PICAB), which facilitated Argentina's reintegration into the regional and international community after the Falklands-Malvinas war. For Brazil, increased access to Argentine markets offered a way to revive its own economy. The 1986 Act for Argentine-Brazilian Integration, which emphasized trade issues, formalized and expanded the original Foz de Iguazú commitments. These steps led, by the end of the decade, to the

Southern Cone Common Market ("Mercosur").[60] By this time, the nuclear rapprochement had become one element in a larger effort to promote economic integration in the region.[61]

ALIGNING NUCLEAR POLICY WITH NATIONAL OBJECTIVES

The two countries had come a long way since their initial tentative steps in 1980. But although Argentina and Brazil had successfully reassured each other of their peaceful intentions in the nuclear field, they had not yet convinced the rest of the world of their bona fides. They needed to find a way to dispel the mistrust that had grown over the years. This would not be a simple task, though, for two countries that in the past had ignored the suspicions of the international community. It would require nothing less than a fundamental transformation in Argentina's and Brazil's traditional thinking about their nuclear energy programs and, more generally, about the price of sovereignty, the true nature of status, and how best each country could achieve its national aspirations.

Iguazú Falls, 1990.   New personalities in both countries brought new energy to the cooperative effort. In June 1989, the Perónist candidate, Carlos Menem, became president of Argentina. Menem, who had not invested any of his personal prestige in a nuclear program that was draining financial resources and aggravating relations with the United States, nonetheless surprised experts by his accommodating stance toward nuclear cooperation with Brazil.[62] He reaffirmed Argentina's support for the nuclear rapprochement during his first presidential summit with Sarney in August 1989.

The following March, the dynamic Fernando Collor became Brazil's president. Collor, who strongly opposed nuclear weapons, moved to establish strict civilian control over all nuclear activities.[63] First, Collor fired Nazaré Alves. Next, in a move both substantive and symbolic, he brought into his administration an outspoken critic of both the official and the parallel nuclear programs, José Goldemberg. Shortly after taking office, Collor reviewed a classified, fifty-page document, which had been prepared by the outgoing Sarney administration, on the secret parallel program. The new president called in the heads of the army, navy, and air force and told them he was going to shut the program down.[64]

Collor also demonstrated a flair for showmanship, which effectively reassured domestic and international audiences that the nuclear program was under firm civilian control. In summer 1990, after press reports resurfaced about the Cachimbo nuclear test site, he ordered the army, navy, and air force ministers to join him on board the presidential jet to visit the site. When faced with the evidence, the three military officers denied any knowledge of the Cachimbo program, reportedly enraging Collor.[65] Collor revisited Cachimbo a few days later, this time with a planeload of press in tow. He dropped a shovelful of lime in the hole and then sealed it. In September, Collor addressed the UN General Assembly, where he renounced Brazil's hitherto sacrosanct right to conduct a PNE, thereby removing an official rationale for the parallel program and an important symbol of Brazil's hostility toward the international nonproliferation regime.[66] Three months later, a special fact-finding commission set up by the Brazilian parliament released a report detailing the parallel program's illicit activities.[67]

Collor's commitment to nuclear transparency placed bilateral cooperation on a fast track. On November 28, 1990, he and Menem signed the landmark Joint Declaration of Common Nuclear Policy at Iguazú. Both countries pledged to use nuclear energy only for peaceful purposes, create a formal system of bilateral inspections, forsake the right to conduct peaceful nuclear explosions, and adhere jointly to a revised Treaty of Tlatelolco.

The biggest surprise at Iguazú was that both countries agreed to accept IAEA safeguards on all their nuclear activities, including their reprocessing and uranium enrichment facilities. At an international conference the year before in Montevideo, Uruguay, Argentine and Brazilian participants had dismissed the need for *any* type of safeguards and had asserted instead that an informal set of reciprocal confidence-building measures (CBMs) was sufficient. A Brazilian Foreign Ministry official argued that such inspections were unnecessary because "no control mechanism could effectively replace the intimate contacts that were then taking place at the technical and political levels."[68]

By 1990, this attitude had changed. Given each country's ability to produce nuclear material, reciprocal visits to sensitive facilities did not reveal either the quantity of nuclear material produced or how such material was used. Both Argentina and Brazil clearly understood that although the bilateral effort established mutual confidence, the international community required a verification scheme consistent with traditional nonproliferation arrangements.

What accounted for the policy shift? Central to this phase of the nuclear rapprochement were the similar political agendas and personalities of Presidents Menem and Collor. Each possessed superb political skills to match an outsized ego. Both wanted to create roles on the international stage for their countries and, not incidentally, for themselves. Menem and Collor saw as the main objectives for their administrations the revitalization of their economies and the integration of their countries into the larger world community.

To do this, Menem first had to address outstanding differences with the United States.[69] The colorful phrase of Argentine Foreign Minister Guido Di Tella captured this attitude: Argentina wanted relations with the United States as intimate as *"relaciones carnales."* To reorient Argentina's foreign policy, Menem withdrew from the Non-Aligned Movement, reestablished ties with Britain, and in 1990 announced the suspension of the Condor II ballistic missile program, which had been strongly opposed by Washington.[70] The following year Buenos Aires contributed two navy frigates to the U.S.-led effort in the Persian Gulf war; this marked the first time in Argentina's history that it had allied itself with the United States in a military conflict.[71] In these tasks, Menem was aided by a small coterie of advisers in the Foreign Ministry who opposed Argentina's traditional isolation, recognized the trend toward democracy and open markets in Latin America, realized that the international political environment had changed after the cold war, and favored "new thinking" on security, economic, and political issues.[72]

Brasilia did not feel the need to align itself so closely with Washington. But Collor understood that he could not keep his country indefinitely outside the international nonproliferation regime without paying a heavy political and economic price imposed by the most powerful and advanced industrialized countries. No matter how discriminatory or unfair, the nuclear suppliers, particularly Germany and the United States, would continue to deny access to advanced technologies and exert intense pressure on Argentina and Brazil to accept comprehensive international safeguards on their nuclear programs. Rigid opposition to the nonproliferation regime would jeopardize Collor's ambitious plans for economic development.[73]

Guadalajara, Mexico.   Building on their November 1990 meeting, Argentina and Brazil codified the Foz de Iguazú pledges in Guadalajara, Mexico, on July 18, 1991, in front of twenty-three heads of state from Latin America, Spain, and Portugal. Both parties explicitly ruled out the testing, use, manufacture, production, or acquisition of any explosive nuclear device. However, the agreement permitted the use of nuclear energy for submarine propulsion, reflecting Brazil's ongoing quest in this area. In the event of "serious noncompliance" by a party, the other party could terminate or suspend the accord and notify the UN secretary general and the Organization of American States.

The Guadalajara Accord established the Joint System of Accounting and Control of Nuclear Materials (SCCC), whose purpose was to verify that no nuclear materials were diverted for military purposes. To implement this control system, the accord created the Brazilian-Argentine Agency for Accounting and Control of Nuclear Materials (ABACC), which was modeled on the multipartite inspection system set up by the European Atomic Energy Community (Euratom).[74] Headquartered in Rio de Janeiro, ABACC periodically draws on sixty officials from the nuclear establishments in Argentina and Brazil to conduct its inspections. It began operations in July 1992 and initially monitored those nuclear installations in Argentina and Brazil not under IAEA safeguards.

The Quadripartite Agreement.   In December 1991, Presidents Collor and Menem flew to Vienna to sign the Quadripartite Agreement among Brazil, Argentina, ABACC, and the IAEA. As part of its "Basic Undertakings," the agreement stipulated that safeguards would apply "on all nuclear material in all nuclear activities within their territories . . . for the exclusive purpose of verifying that such material is not diverted to nuclear weapons or other nuclear explosive devices."[75] In February 1992, the Menem government submitted the agreement to Congress, where both houses consented to ratification within six months.

Brazil's ratification of the agreement was more contentious and was hampered by a leadership vacuum. After a rousing first eighteen months as president, Collor increasingly devoted his time and attention to battling a bribery scandal that eventually forced him from office in late December 1992. He was replaced by his vice president, Itamar Franco, who had no political agenda and no real following in Congress.

Brazil's Chamber of Deputies (the lower house) approved the Quadripartite Agreement in September 1993, but the Senate expressed two main objections. First, its members proved reluctant to shelve the country's long-standing opposition to the IAEA and full-scope inspections. Whether because of fears of industrial espionage (especially regarding the ultracentrifuge enrichment technology), because of still-secret activities under the parallel program, or because of hostility to this erosion of Brazil's sovereignty, important elements of the military, certain CNEN officials, the scientific community involved in the parallel program, and nationalist political leaders joined together to fight IAEA inspections.[76]

A second, larger concern was the IAEA's right to "special inspections." Considering this issue in the aftermath of the Persian Gulf war, Brazilian deputies understood that revelations about Iraq's clandestine nuclear weapons program had introduced new rigor into IAEA inspection procedures, ensuring that post-Iraq safeguards would be marked by greater intrusiveness and zeal.[77] To ensure that the IAEA would not capriciously inspect any facility it wanted to see, Congress sought advance notification of IAEA visits and the reasons behind any allegations of proscribed nuclear activity.

Congress also raised a host of additional questions, complaints, and reservations about the entire inspection process. One controversial issue related to "subsidiary arrangements," that is, how the IAEA's general inspection procedures, especially the timing of inspections, would apply in practice to particular nuclear installations. Said Deputy Marcelo Barbieri, "Inspections can be requested in such a way as to open up to outsiders' eyes the technology that is being used."[78]

Given these concerns, why did the Senate eventually ratify the Quadripartite Agreement? Quiet diplomacy by the IAEA, a prior change in Germany's nuclear policy, and a concerted effort by the Brazilian executive branch all helped to sway the vote.

An August 1993 visit by Hans Blix, the IAEA director general, and Bruno Pellaud, deputy director general for safeguards, was instrumental in soothing much of the congressional irritation at the proposed safeguards regime and in debunking many of the more outrageous claims made by critics of the Quadripartite Agreement. Blix acknowledged Brazil's concerns with protecting proprietary information and explained that Germany, Japan, and other countries had similar reservations. He noted that the IAEA had met these concerns in the past and could meet them again. On the subject of special inspections, Blix insisted that the IAEA did not view Brazil as a rogue state and that therefore there was no reason why it would be treated like Iraq or North Korea. He also explained that submitting to the IAEA the blueprints and design information on nuclear facilities under construction was necessary for effective safeguards, which would reduce the time spent on-site by inspectors. Finally, Blix defused the hostility toward the IAEA by personally promising that agency personnel would cooperate fully with ABACC and CNEN officials.[79]

The role played by Germany in the Quadripartite Agreement has been little noted but was crucial. When the 1975 nuclear deal came up for extension in spring 1990, Bonn decided to renew it, even though it had reportedly known since 1987 that Brazil, in violation of the 1975 agreement, had transferred to the parallel program scientists who had trained in the official nuclear program.[80] In response to a number of embarrassing scandals involving exports of sensitive technology during the 1980s, however, and under intense pressure from the United States, West Germany announced at the NPT Review Conference in August 1990 that it had revised its nuclear policy. Henceforth, Bonn would require full-scope safeguards as a condition for future nuclear exports, and all nuclear deals would have to be renegotiated by 1995 to conform with this new policy. In other words, Brazil could accept full-scope safeguards and extend its nuclear cooperation with Germany, or it could refuse IAEA safeguards and have Bonn terminate all such cooperation.

In early October 1993, German Foreign Minister Klaus Kinkel visited Brazil, where he "requested" that Brasilia ratify the Quadripartite Agreement as soon as possible. According to one participant at these meetings, he reiterated the conditions for further German nuclear cooperation but did not use any theatrics or pressure tactics. There was no need. Brazil's finance minister, Fernando Henrique Cardoso, and foreign minister, Celso Amorim, were well aware of the August 1995 deadline. They also knew that Bonn held all the high cards.[81] Angra II, which was over 80 percent complete, and Angra III, which had not yet been canceled, depended overwhelmingly on German technology. At the time of Kinkel's visit, Brazil was negotiating with Germany for an additional $750 million in financial support to complete the Angra II reactor; the two sides also planned to discuss future financing for the Angra III plant.[82] Another item on the agenda was the possibility of gaining a permanent seat at the United Nations should the Security Council's membership be expanded.[83] Brasilia wanted Bonn's support, which Germany may have conditioned on passage of the Quadripartite Agreement.

Without strong presidential leadership, other government actors used their influence to ensure passage of the agreement. The Foreign and Finance Ministries strongly favored the Quadripartite Agreement. After the Kinkel visit, Amorim and Cardoso tried to deflect the impression that the country was responding to a German diktat. They announced to the local press that Brazil would not succumb to German pressure to join the NPT, neglecting to mention that Bonn had not discussed this subject but rather Brasilia's adherence to the Quadripartite Agreement.

The Strategic Affairs Secretariat (SAS) (analogous to the National Security Council in the United States) also worked hard to overcome parliamentary opposition and inertia. A pivotal figure was Admiral Mario Cesar Flores, who had served as the navy minister in the Collor government and whom Franco had asked to head the SAS. Along with Collor and Franco, Cesar Flores had concluded that accepting IAEA safeguards would benefit the country by accelerating technology transfers for economic development. He had also been reassured that full-scope safeguards would not imperil the navy's submarine reactor project. Not only did Flores instruct those military officers and government officials who opposed the Quadripartite Agreement to hand in their resignations, but he also had the institutional clout to make this threat credible.[84]

In early February 1994, only days before the Senate vote on the Quadripartite Agreement, CNEN President Marcio Costa and other CNEN officials publicly endorsed the agreement. Marcio Costa declared that only by allowing full-scope safeguards would Brazil avoid retaliation from the nuclear supplier countries, specifically citing Germany's threat to cut off technology transfers.[85] On February 9, 1994, the Senate ratified the agreement.[86] IAEA safeguards would now cover all the nuclear activities of both Argentina and Brazil.

The Treaty of Tlatelolco. The 1967 Treaty for the Prohibition of Nuclear Weapons in Latin America, also known as the Treaty of Tlatelolco, called for a nuclear-weapon-free zone (NWFZ) in Latin America. Parties to the agreement pledged to use nuclear energy exclusively for peaceful purposes; the testing, use, manufacture, acquisition, storage, or deployment of nuclear weapons was forbidden.[87]

Argentina signed the treaty in 1967 but did not ratify it at the time. Buenos Aires had never viewed Tlatelolco as enshrining a "discriminatory" arrangement, however, and was apparently prepared to ratify the treaty in 1978. According to a senior Argentine diplomat, under the regime of General Videla all three military services approved a policy paper recommending ratification of the Tlatelolco Treaty. Videla planned to announce the government's intention during his visit to Washington, but perhaps in reaction to the Carter administration's criticism of the junta's human rights abuses, the announcement never came. The 1983 elections ushered in the Alfonsín government and a new Congress, which consisted of parliamentarians opposed to Tlatelolco. Ratification was delayed for a decade.[88]

Brazil signed the treaty in 1967 and ratified it the following year but refused to waive the entry-into-force provisions contained in Article 28. The treaty's handling of peaceful nuclear explosions proved a sticking point. It stated that countries "may carry out explosions of nuclear devices for peaceful purposes—including explosions which involve devices similar to those used in nuclear weapons," but the treaty conditioned this use on the device's ability to release its energy in a controlled manner, which is impossible in a nuclear explosion. Nonetheless, Brazil insisted on retaining the option to test a peaceful nuclear explosion.[89]

As nuclear cooperation between the two countries evolved during the 1980s, opposition to Tlatelolco slowly thawed. The breakthrough came at the November 1990 Foz de Iguazú summit, where Menem and Collor pledged to work together to amend and then fully implement the treaty. In February 1992 Argentina and Brazil, joined by Chile, proposed amendments to Tlatelolco.

The revised treaty included the following amendments: (1) countries were no longer required to submit reports to the Organization of American States; (2) special reports on nuclear activities could be requested only in the case of an "extraordinary event or circumstance," by the general secretary of Tlatelolco's organizational body, the Agency for the Prohibition of Nuclear Weapons in Latin America (OPANAL); (3) only the IAEA was granted authority to conduct special inspections; and (4) OPANAL's general secretary could no longer transmit information from special inspections to the UN secretary general and the Organization of American States. These amendments provided Argentina and especially Brazil, which had long criticized the treaty, political cover for ratification, elevated the role of the IAEA, and ensured greater confidentiality of proprietary information by limiting OPANAL's investigative functions and eliminating "challenge" inspections. In August 1992, the amendments were approved at an OPANAL general conference.[90] Argentina ratified the amended Tlatelolco Treaty in January 1994, and Brazil followed suit four months later. By 1995, only three other countries had done so: Mexico, Chile, and Belize.[91]

The Treaty of Tlatelolco had the attraction of being a regional arrangement in which Brazil and Argentina had long played a role. The NPT, on the other hand, was the centerpiece of the international nonproliferation regime and symbolized, more than any other arrangement, the discrimination and dominance of the nuclear weapon states and nuclear supplier countries. In the frequently repeated phrase of Argentine diplomats, the treaty was described as "disarming the unarmed."[92] As of late 1994, Argentina had not ratified the NPT, but it had actually accepted more onerous nonproliferation obligations.[93] On February 10, 1995, Argentina formally joined the NPT.

Brazil is not expected to ratify the NPT anytime soon, although it accepted virtually the same obligations under the Quadripartite Agreement, including the right of the IAEA to conduct special inspections. In addition to the NPT's symbolism, more parochial motives explain Brazil's rejection of the NPT. In an ironic twist, members of the Brazilian nuclear energy community opposed both the Quadripartite Agreement and the NPT because ratification would *facilitate* the transfer of nuclear technology from the West—and throw out of work many technicians and engineers, who would be unable to find other jobs. The Brazilian Nuclear Energy Association, with one thousand nuclear professionals and the support of five nuclear companies, implored President Franco not to ratify the IAEA safeguards agreement.[94] Those most hardened in opposition were plant managers concerned about their employees.[95] Members of the military working on nuclear projects expressed similar fears.[96] They did not voice reservations about the ABACC inspection system, on the other hand, because it did not open the door to imported nuclear technologies and thus did not entail the prospect of imminent unemployment.[97]

Conclusion: How Useful a Precedent?

The story of the Argentine-Brazilian nuclear rapprochement would have been more dramatic if both countries had actually acquired nuclear weapons or even if they had developed legitimate nuclear weapon options. Such was not the case. Despite heavy investments in uranium enrichment and spent-fuel reprocessing capabilities, neither Buenos Aires nor Brasilia ever had the technical wherewithal to produce material for nuclear bombs.

Argentina's Ezeiza reprocessing plant, which could have separated enough plutonium for approximately one nuclear device per year, never became operational. The Pilçaniyeu uranium enrichment plant offered the most likely path to a nuclear weapons capability, yet it too ran into technical and financial difficulties. Argentina was able to enrich only *very* small amounts of 20 percent U-235.[98]

Likewise, Brazil was never in a position to develop a nuclear explosive device. Despite spending almost half a billion dollars on the parallel program, the military never overcame the technical hurdles to produce weapons-grade material suitable for nuclear bombs.[99] The military never even produced the 6-to-7 percent U-235 for its proposed submarine reactors, a far cry from the 90-plus percent U-235 preferred for nuclear weapons.[100] IPEN's laboratory-scale reprocessing facility stopped operating, and the Resende reprocessing plant never left the drawing board.

The debilitated state of Argentina's and Brazil's nuclear programs, and the absence of nuclear weapons or even the legitimate capability to manufacture nuclear weapons, provided fertile ground for nuclear cooperation, especially during the latter half of the 1980s and into the 1990s. The success of the nuclear suppliers in denying advanced technologies had contributed to this disorder in the Argentine and Brazilian nuclear programs. The nuclear suppliers' restrictions on nuclear commerce forced Argentina and Brazil to either develop advanced technologies indigenously or go without. This technology-denial strategy increased the amount of time needed to complete projects and raised their costs, which, together with the harsh economic recession in Latin America in the early to mid-1980s, severely strained budgets for nuclear activities. The examples of Argentina and Brazil strongly suggest that export controls can make a significant difference in preventing countries from increasing their nuclear competence.

Had either or both of these programs produced weapons-grade material, or even been fully functioning, mutual suspicions and mistrust would have made establishing a bilateral nuclear dialogue far more troublesome. Even though South Africa has demonstrated that a country can reverse course, getting two countries to dismantle, in tandem, advanced nuclear programs, perhaps with nuclear devices, would have presented new and even more complex challenges.

The motivations of Argentina and Brazil for their joint effort in the nuclear field changed over time, passing generally through three phases. Initially, starting with the May 1980 Buenos Aires summit, the two banded together in an anti-NPT axis to fight the inequities of the international nonproliferation regime. But the goals shifted with the appearance of civilian governments in both countries; now the new leaders were concerned with exerting greater control over the nuclear programs that the military had influenced, in Argentina's case, or had partially hijacked, in Brazil's case. These civilian leaders also sought greater economic integration, which gradually became the engine that pulled the two countries closer together, in commercial and nuclear matters. The third phase was in many ways the most complex as Argentina and Brazil reevaluated and then adjusted previous nuclear policies to align them with broader foreign policy objectives. During this period, which coincided with the end of the cold war, both countries developed a greater appreciation of the benefits of joining the nonproliferation regime, as well as a greater understanding of the penalties for remaining outside of it.

Nuclear rapprochement benefited both countries, in ways that each could not have accomplished alone. Domestically, Buenos Aires and Brasilia asserted and consolidated civilian control over the nuclear programs. Bilaterally, they increased economic cooperation and reduced mistrust and suspicion, thus increasing their own security as well as that of the rest of Latin America. They foreclosed a potential nuclear arms race that would have diverted attention, energy, and money from more urgent domestic problems.

The Latin American example strongly suggests that resolution, or at least amelioration, of outstanding political disagreements must precede cooperation in the nuclear sphere. The neuralgic Rio de la Plata dispute had to be settled amicably before the two parties could make real progress in the nuclear sphere, just as Brazilian concerns over Argentine behavior leading up to and during the Falklands-Malvinas war needed to subside before the nuclear dialogue could get back on track. This suggests an important parallel elsewhere: that nuclear arms control measures between India and Pakistan, or even the implementation of meaningful confidence-building measures, will be extraordinarily difficult, if not impossible, as long as the two sides cannot resolve their dispute over Kashmir. The same reasoning applies to the prospects for arms control agreements in the Middle East between Israel and its Arab neighbors; the pace of progress in this area will be tied to the overall peace process.

Moreover, the Latin American example indicates that nuclear cooperation operates best within a larger, supportive bilateral framework. As the Argentine diplomat Julio Carasales has commented on the Argentine-Brazilian case, the nuclear field was just one part of a broad range of cooperative efforts; the aim was economic and social integration, not simply an incremental increase in common security. Mutual trust usually will not exist in isolation. To expect a constructive dialogue on nuclear issues when other aspects of the relationship, even nonmilitary ones, are troubled is highly improbable and perhaps quixotic.[101]

Numerous commentators in the United States, Brazil, and Argentina have stressed that the transformation of both countries to functioning democracies was the key to Argentine and Brazilian nuclear rapprochement. The historical record does not support such a single overarching reason. Nuclear cooperation started in 1980, when military regimes ruled both countries. How far military governments would have traveled down this path can only be speculated. What is clear is that the advent of civilian governments in mid-decade deepened and accelerated this process. Even so, by the end of the decade, the civilian governments of Alfonsín and Sarney blanched at the idea of a comprehensive inspection regime. Other factors had to emerge—*different* leaders—to force Argentina and Brazil to realign their nuclear policies.

It is questionable whether democratic governments are even a necessary condition for bilateral nuclear cooperation. For example, the long record of Soviet-American nuclear arms control agreements, starting with the 1963 "Hot Line" agreement, testifies that a representative form of government is not essential for reducing suspicion and increasing mutual confidence through arms control and confidence-building measures. The most substantive arms control measure to date between India and Pakistan—their pledge not to attack each other's nuclear installations—was initiated by Pakistan's military ruler, General Mohammed Zia ul-Haq.

More important than the nature of the regime is the quality of political leadership, which needs to include a strong grasp of a country's strengths and weaknesses, a vision for its future, and a strategy to achieve it. Arguably, some of these qualities impelled General Figueiredo to venture to Buenos Aires in May 1980 to begin a nuclear dialogue, a step his civilian counterparts in Argentina had not taken before 1976. More recently, the difference between how quickly and painlessly Argentina ratified the Quadripartite Agreement and the almost three years it took Brazil can be attributed to the difference in leaders. The political savvy of Carlos Menem expedited the process, whereas Fernando Collor, mired in a political scandal that would eventually unseat him, was politically paralyzed.

Such political leadership may be necessary to smooth over the domestic implications of a surprising finding from the Brazilian case: nonproliferation may cost jobs, since imports of sophisticated nuclear technology can make domestic workers redundant. An effective nonproliferation policy should address this issue, whether by targeting assistance programs or by founding science and technology centers, as Washington has done for Moscow and Kiev.

The case of Argentina and Brazil also raises the question of whether regional or subregional initiatives have a greater chance of success at constraining nuclear ambitions among local rivals than do global initiatives. The answer is, it depends. Politically, it may be easier for some countries to undertake bilateral or regional initiatives than to join the NPT. Regional arrangements grant states much greater control over the pace and scope of nuclear cooperation. The Quadripartite

Agreement, for example, allowed Argentina and Brazil to address the safeguards issue together to avoid the risk that one would accept more onerous obligations than the other. If necessary, steps can be decelerated and even reversed, with little of the global criticism this would invite in an international agreement.

The merit of regional approaches extends beyond merely substituting for a global regime. They provide a useful safety net should the international regime weaken or collapse. The Quadripartite Agreement, involving ABACC and IAEA safeguards, and the Tlatelolco Treaty ensure that Latin America will enjoy a nuclear-free future regardless of the outcome at the NPT review and extension conference in spring 1995.

Given the often inflated perceptions by U.S. analysts of Washington's influence in the world, especially in the nuclear realm, the circumscribed role played by the United States in Argentina's and Brazil's nuclear evolutions is especially noteworthy. States other than the United States may be more effective in lobbying certain countries. Indeed, in some cases, the United States is best left out of the process altogether. According to an American official who negotiated nuclear matters with Brazil, whenever Washington raised the nuclear issue, it risked being held hostage to the entire bilateral agenda, and the countries then started "talking about orange juice and intellectual property." Washington should therefore welcome nonproliferation "burden-sharing" with allies that have the same nonproliferation goals.

In the case of Brazil, U.S. officials admit that American pressure had little or no influence.[102] Although Collor had adopted a new nuclear policy for Brazil in 1990, one that embraced the Quadripartite Agreement, his ouster two years later slowed the momentum toward full-scope safeguards. At this time, it was Germany's leverage that ensured Brazil's ratification of the Quadripartite Agreement—a case in which the tail ended up wagging the dog.[103] This dependence assumed a more critical nonproliferation dimension when Germany altered its nonproliferation policy in 1990. Foreign Minister Kinkel's October 1993 visit usefully reminded Brazil of the 1995 deadline for terminating all technical cooperation and financial assistance in the nuclear field.[104]

In the case of Argentina, U.S. and German pressure was constant but was not decisive in the country's nuclear about-face. The Menem government's overall foreign policy goal was to integrate Argentina into the world economy, and this required better relations with Washington. The change in nuclear policy is best seen as one element of a much larger and more comprehensive policy shift.[105]

LESSONS

The Argentine-Brazilian nuclear rapprochement is a remarkable success story. Undeniably, it is an important contribution to Latin American security and, more generally, to the international nonproliferation regime. But how useful a model is it for other regions? Can its great success be applied to South Asia (India and Pakistan), Northeast Asia (North Korea and South Korea), and the Middle East (Israel and its regional adversaries)?

The law of unintended consequences provides a partial answer to this question. What had started in 1980 as an Argentine-Brazilian coalition to resist the NPT regime had led, by 1990, to a very different destination. The original rationale for nuclear cooperation not only never contemplated that the two countries would end up with full-scope IAEA safeguards but was designed to prevent precisely this outcome. If Buenos Aires and Brasilia had been told in 1980, 1985, or perhaps even as late as 1989 that they would agree to comprehensive inspections by November 1990, this message would have been disbelieved or, worse, would have halted their nuclear rapprochement.

Argentina and Brazil may thus serve as a cautionary tale to those countries that do not want to accept full-scope safeguards or join the NPT. Looking at the Latin American example, other countries may draw the conclusion that they cannot afford to place even small constraints on their nuclear activities for fear that such action may lead inexorably to an unintended and undesirable result. An arrangement hailed by many as a model for other countries may ironically thwart even gradual, incremental steps toward nonproliferation.

It seems far more likely, however, that the cooperative path that Argentina and Brazil jointly charted will offer a positive and constructive guide, if not a precise model, for other regions. Their example demonstrates how two countries can successfully cooperate on controversial, sensitive, and highly politicized issues, to their mutual benefit.

Chronology

OCTOBER 1979 La Plata River Agreement is signed by Argentina, Brazil, and Paraguay.

May 1980 Argentina and Brazil sign an agreement to promote nuclear fuel-cycle cooperation.

APRIL–JUNE 1982 Britain defeats Argentina in dispute over Falklands-Malvinas Islands.

NOVEMBER 1983 Argentina publicly reveals the Pilçaniyeu uranium enrichment plant.

Raúl Alfonsín becomes president of Argentina, cuts CNEA's budget, and replaces Carlos Castro Madero.

FEBRUARY 1985 Alfonsín and Tancredo Neves agree in principle to greater Argentine-Brazilian nuclear cooperation, including mutual inspections.

NOVEMBER 30 Alfonsín and José Sarney meet at Foz de Iguazú and sign the Joint Declaration on Nuclear Policy, which creates the Joint Working Group on Nuclear Policy under the respective foreign ministries.

JULY 1986 The Foz de Iguazú agreement is formalized in Buenos Aires with the Act for Argentine-Brazilian Integration.

JULY 1987 Sarney visits the unsafeguarded Pilçaniyeu plant and inaugurates reciprocal presidential visits to nuclear facilities.

SEPTEMBER Sarney announces that IPEN has enriched uranium; he gives Argentina prior notice.

APRIL 1988 Iperó Joint Declaration on Nuclear Policy calls for mutual nuclear transparency, reserves the right to conduct PNEs, and establishes the Permanent Committee on Nuclear Affairs.

Alfonsín visits the Aramar uranium enrichment facility.

JULY 1989 Carlos Saul Menem assumes the Argentine presidency.

MARCH 1990 Fernando Collor becomes Brazil's president.

SEPTEMBER Collor "closes" the Cachimbo site, then renounces, before the UN General Assembly, Brazil's right to conduct PNEs.

NOVEMBER 28 The foundation for the Quadripartite Agreement is laid at Foz de Iguazú, where Argentina and Brazil pledge to establish a bilateral inspection system and agency, to accept comprehensive IAEA safeguards, and to revise and fully implement the Tlatelolco Treaty.

July 18 1991 Brazil and Argentina sign the Guadalajara Accord for the exclusive use of nuclear energy for peaceful purposes; this document creates a bilateral inspection system (SCCC) and an agency to administer it (ABACC).

DECEMBER 13 Argentina, Brazil, ABACC, and the IAEA sign the Quadripartite Agreement; the IAEA assumes responsibility for applying full-scope safeguards in Brazil and Argentina.

FEBRUARY 14, 1992 Collor and Menem propose amendments to the Tlatelolco Treaty.

JULY ABACC begins operations.

AUGUST Argentina ratifies the Quadripartite Agreement.

OPANAL General Conference approves the amendments to the Tlatelolco Treaty.

MARCH 1993 The Argentine Senate approves the Tlatelolco amendments.

SEPTEMBER 22 The Brazil Chamber of Deputies approves the Quadripartite Agreement and the Tlatelolco amendments.

NOVEMBER 10 The Argentine Chamber of Deputies approves the Tlatelolco amendments.

JANUARY 18, 1994 Argentina and Chile fully implement the revised Tlatelolco Treaty.

FEBRUARY 9 The Brazil Senate ratifies the Quadripartite Agreement.

MARCH The Quadripartite Agreement enters into force.

MAY 30 Brazil fully implements the revised Tlatelolco Treaty.

FEBRUARY 10, 1995 Argentina joins the NPT.

Notes

[1]There is a Foz de Iguazú on the Argentine side of the waterfalls and a Foz do Iguaçu on the Brazilian side of the waterfalls. For consistency, the Argentine spelling will be used in this chapter.

[2]See Emanuel Adler, *The Power of Ideology: The Quest for Technological Autonomy in Argentina and Brazil* (Berkeley: University of California Press, 1987), pp. 280–303. Argentina's earliest experience in the nuclear field ended in international embarrassment. In 1950, President Juan Perón appointed Ronald Richter, an Austrian scientist who had worked on fusion research in Nazi Germany, as director of a research center on Huemul Island, San Carlos de Bariloche, in southern Argentina. In February 1951, Richter claimed that he had performed a controlled fusion reaction in the laboratory. Argentine scientists exposed Richter as a fraud in late 1952, and he was fired. See Mario Mariscotti, *El secreto atómico de Huemul: Crónica del origen de la energía atómica en la Argentina*, 2d ed. (Buenos Aires: Sudamericana Planeta, 1987); see also Carlos Castro Madero and Esteban A. Takacs, *Politica Nuclear Argentina* (Buenos Aires: El Ateneo, 1991), pp. 51–52; Daniel Poneman, *Nuclear Power in the Developing World* (London: Allen and Unwin, 1982), pp. 68–70.

[3]Since 1967, the CNEA's official policy has been complete independence in the nuclear fuel cycle. See Daniel Poneman, "Argentina," in Jed C. Snyder and Samuel F. Wells, Jr., eds., *Limiting Nuclear Proliferation* (Cambridge, Mass.: Ballinger, 1985), p. 100. CNEA stands for Comisión Nacional de Energía Atómica. For more comprehensive surveys of Argentina's nuclear energy program, see Castro Madero and Takacs, *Politica Nuclear Argentina*; Adler, *The Power of Ideology*; Poneman, *Nuclear Power in the Developing World*, pp. 68–83.

[4]These enhanced safeguards included a ban on reexporting any materials produced at Embalse without Canada's permission and a prohibition on the use of Canadian technology or materials for manufacturing any explosive nuclear device. See Poneman, *Nuclear Power in the Developing World*, p. 77. In addition, Argentina's runaway inflation and currency devaluations during this period forced Canada to insist on renegotiating the financing for the Embalse power station, causing further construction delays.

[5]Argentina refused subsequent German requests for more extensive safeguards. See Rodney W. Jones, "Next Steps after INFCE: U.S. International Nuclear and Nonproliferation Policy," Center for Strategic and International Studies, Washington, D.C., March 1980, pp. 276–80; Poneman, *Nuclear Power in the Developing World*, pp. 79–80; see also William H. Courtney, "Nuclear Choices for Friendly Rivals," in Joseph A. Yager, ed., *Nonproliferation and U.S. Foreign Policy* (Washington, D.C.: Brookings, 1980), pp. 247–49.

[6]Poneman, "Argentina," p. 103. In 1969, CNEA had designed and constructed an unsafeguarded, laboratory-scale reprocessing facility that extracted very small amounts of plutonium. This facility was decommissioned in 1973.

[7]Other motivations may also have played a role. The CNEA viewed this facility as a technological challenge during a still-bullish period of Argentina's nuclear program. U.S. diplomat, personal interview, Bariloche, Argentina, April 20, 1994. Under IAEA definitions, low-enriched uranium is uranium that consists of less than 20 percent U-235; highly enriched uranium is uranium that consists of 20 per-

cent or more U-235. "Weapons-grade" or "bomb-grade" uranium generally refers to uranium that consists of 90 percent or more U-235.

[8]David Albright, "Bomb Potential for South America," *Bulletin of the Atomic Scientists* 45, no. 4 (May 1989): 19.

[9]U.S. government official, personal interview, Bariloche, Argentina, April 20, 1994. Even if Washington suspected that Argentina was building a reprocessing plant and not a uranium enrichment plant, it is curious why it apparently did not inform Ottawa or, if it did, why Ottawa did not take any action.

[10]Quoted in Daniel Poneman, *Argentina: Democracy on Trial* (New York: Paragon House, 1987), p. 179; see also Castro Madero and Takacs, *Politica Nuclear Argentina*, pp. 86–88. Interestingly, Castro Madero did not state that Argentina had actually enriched any uranium.

[11]Leonard S. Spector with Jacqueline R. Smith, *Nuclear Ambitions: The Spread of Nuclear Weapons, 1989–1990* (Boulder, Colo.: Westview, 1990), pp. 228, 388, 391.

[12]Retired State Department official, personal interview, Washington, D.C., May 25, 1994. According to this official, during a visit to Argentina in the early 1980s Castro Madero showed the country's nuclear facilities to Lewis Dunn, assistant director of the U.S. Arms Control and Disarmament Agency, and Richard Kennedy, ambassador-at-large for nonproliferation, with the single exception of the Pilçaniyeu uranium enrichment plant. Castro Madero later apologized to Kennedy for this omission.

[13]Other factors also influenced the timing of the Pilçaniyeu disclosure. Coming just before Raúl Alfonsín's presidential inauguration, it was viewed by his Radical Party supporters as a way to pressure the civilian regime to retain Castro Madero as the head of CNEA, keep military personnel involved in nuclear matters, and win support for the entire nuclear program. In fact, Castro Madero had briefed Alfonsín before the November 10 announcement, but Alfonsín reportedly thought it was just a ploy to ingratiate himself with his prospective boss. Richard Kessler, personal interview, Buenos Aires, April 23, 1994. Kessler reported on Latin American nuclear developments for *Nucleonics Week* during the 1970s and 1980s. Argentina may also have derived some added gratification from the announcement because Washington, which had supported Britain during the war, opposed unsafeguarded reprocessing facilities. U.S. government official, personal interview, Bariloche, Argentina, April 20, 1994.

[14]Britain refers to the disputed islands as the Falklands and Argentina as Las Malvinas. For a carefully balanced and thorough account of the war, see Lawrence Freedman and Virginia Gamba-Stonehouse, *Signals of War: The Falklands Conflict of 1982* (Princeton, N.J.: Princeton University Press, 1991); see also Joseph Tulchin, "The Malvinas War of 1982: An Inevitable Conflict That Never Should Have Occurred," *Latin American Research Review* 22, no. 3 (Fall 1987): 123–41; Fritz Hoffman and Olga M. Hoffman, *Malvinas/Falklands, 1493–1982: Sovereignty in Dispute* (Boulder, Colo.: Westview, 1984). For treatment of the conflict by Argentine authors, see Nicanor Costa Mendez, *Malvinas: Esta Es la Historia* (Buenos Aires: Editorial Sudamericana, 1993); Armando Alonso Pineiro, *Historia de la Guerra de Malvinas* (Buenos Aires: Planeta, 1992); Carlos Augusto Landaburu, *La Guerra de las Malvinas* (Buenos Aires: Circulo Militar, 1989).

[15]Although Castro Madero's motives in commissioning the nuclear propulsion study are unclear, it seems likely that he intended it to *deflect* interest in developing

nuclear weapons. According to some accounts, Castro Madero thought that pursuit of a nuclear option would destroy the country's nuclear energy program and thus his life's work. Indeed, immediately after the 1982 war, Castro Madero had restated Argentina's intention not to develop nuclear weapons. John Redick, personal conversation, April 1994; Julio Carasales, personal interview, Bariloche, Argentina, April 19, 1994. Carasales is a career Argentine diplomat with expertise in nuclear matters. A discussion of this episode can be found in Poneman, "Argentina," pp. 94, 110–11; see also Julio C. Carasales, Carlos Castro Madero, and José M. Cohen, *Argentina y el Submarino de Propulsión Nuclear: Posibilidades y Dificultades* (n.p.: Servicio de Hidrografia Naval, Atres Graficas, 1992).

16Quoted in Poneman, *Argentina*, p. 186. Constantini resigned in April 1987 in protest over cuts in CNEA's budget.

17See Leonard S. Spector, *Nuclear Proliferation Today* (New York: Vintage, 1984), pp. 197, 204–5, 218.

18The phrase "nuclear deal of the century" comes from Edward Wonder, "Nuclear Commerce and Nuclear Proliferation: Germany and Brazil, 1975," *Orbis* 21, no. 2 (Summer 1977): 277–306.

Angra I was supposed to generate electricity in 1977, but technical difficulties postponed start-up operations and prevented it from meeting its generating capacity of 626 megawatts. See David J. Myers, "Brazil's Reluctant Pursuit of the Nuclear Option," *Orbis* 27, no. 4 (Winter 1984): 898–99; *O Globo* (Rio de Janeiro), reported in Joint Publications Research Service, *Proliferation Issues* (hereafter cited as JPRS-TND), 92-038 (October 21, 1992), p. 6.

For an overview of Brazil's nuclear policy from the 1950s to the 1990s by a Brazilian scholar, see Paulo Wrobel, "A Politica Nuclear Brasileira," in *Sessenta Anos de Politica Externa Brasileira* (manuscript prepared for the Ministry of Foreign Affairs/University of São Paulo, 1992); see also Renato de Biasi, *A Energia Nuclear no Brasil* (Rio de Janeiro: Biblioteca do Exercito Editora, 1979); Spector with Smith, *Nuclear Ambitions*, pp. 242–63; Adler, *The Power of Ideology*, pp. 303–26.

19The text of the June 27, 1975, "Agreement Concerning Cooperation in the Field of the Peaceful Use of Nuclear Energy," along with the IAEA safeguarding arrangements, can be found in a Brazilian government publication, *O Programa Nuclear Brasileiro* (Brasilia, 1977), pp. 29–51. For a critical examination of this deal, see Norman Gall, "Atoms for Brazil, Dangers for All," *Foreign Policy*, no. 23 (Summer 1976), pp. 155–201; Wonder, "Nuclear Commerce and Nuclear Proliferation," pp. 277–306.

20The Brazilian uranium enrichment plant was intended to follow the construction of a pilot plant in West Germany, which was promised by 1981. Brasilia had requested that Bonn provide the new ultracentrifuge technology being used to construct the joint German-Dutch-British Urenco enrichment facilities, but the Dutch vetoed this request. A description of the jet-nozzle technique to enrich uranium can be found in Gall, "Atoms for Brazil, Dangers for All," p. 171.

Brazil's interest in reprocessing technology seems curious. According to Comissão Nacional de Energia Nuclear (CNEN) senior officials interviewed in 1994, Brazil believed it was important to master this technology for handling and storing spent fuel, especially if the country might one day operate eight nuclear power stations. Laercio Antonio Vinhas and Roberto Fulfaro, personal interview, Rio de Janeiro, April 28, 1994. Vinhas and Fulfaro are directors of nuclear safety and of research and development, respectively, at CNEN. According to a U.S. government official in Brasilia, national pride, the Brazilian military's desire for advanced technology, and its preference for keeping all options open also influenced the decision to purchase a reprocessing plant. Personal interview, April 26, 1994.

[21]The 1975 agreement prohibited Brazil from building any nuclear facilities with knowledge or expertise derived from its cooperation with West Germany; the agreement also contained a twenty-year prohibition against the Brazilian development or use of the same or similar technologies or processes outside of safeguards as those being transferred by West Germany. For example, this meant that Brazil was proscribed from indigenously developing a reprocessing facility unless it was placed under safeguards. See David Fischer and Paul Szasz, *Safeguarding the Atom: A Critical Appraisal* (London: Taylor and Francis, 1985), pp. 38–39.

[22]For analyses that regional competition primarily motivated the 1975 deal, see Gall, "Atoms for Brazil, Dangers for All"; Wonder, "Nuclear Commerce and Nuclear Proliferation," and especially Myers, "Brazil's Reluctant Pursuit of the Nuclear Option," p. 881. Paulo Wrobel argues that this explanation is too simplistic. Wrobel, "Brazil, the Nonproliferation Treaty, and Latin America as a Nuclear-Weapon-Free Zone" (Ph.D. diss., King's College, University of London, 1991), chapter 5. On the importance of prestige and national pride as motivating factors in Brazil's nuclear program, see Jean Krasno, "The Role of Belief Systems in Shaping Nuclear Weapons Policy Preference and Thinking in Brazil" (Ph.D. diss., City University of New York, 1994). On Brazil's motivations generally, see Myers, "Brazil," in Snyder and Wells, *Limiting Nuclear Proliferation*, pp. 123–25.

[23]See Wrobel, "Brazil," chapter 5. Brazil established a holding company, Nuclebras, to manage the many elements of the deal with West Germany. In 1978, the president of Nuclebras, Nogueira Batista, admitted that the cost of the deal now appeared closer to $15 billion; critics alleged that it would cost twice that amount. *Nucleonics Week* 19 (November 2, 1978): 11–12. See also José Goldemberg, *Energia nuclear no Brasil* (São Paulo: Editôra Hucitec, 1978).

The U.S. reaction to the German-Brazil nuclear deal was immediate and intense. A *New York Times* editorial exclaimed that the agreement was "a reckless move that could set off a nuclear arms race in Latin America, trigger the nuclear arming of a half-dozen nations elsewhere and endanger the security of the United States and the world as a whole." *New York Times*, June 13, 1975. Injured pride may also have played a part—the West German deal with Brazil signaled the end of American dominance in the nuclear energy field. See Paul L. Joskow, "The International Nuclear Industry Today: The End of the American Monopoly," *Foreign Affairs* 54 (July 1976): 788–803; Michael J. Brenner, *Nuclear Power and Nonproliferation: The Remaking of U.S. Policy* (Cambridge: Cambridge University Press, 1981). According to José Goldemberg, Washington's strident opposition to the deal in both Bonn and Brasilia backfired by galvanizing domestic support for the deal in Brazil. Personal interview, Princeton, New Jersey, July 8, 1994; see also Allen L. Hammond, "Brazil's Nuclear Program: Carter's Nonproliferation Policy Backfires," *Science* (February 18, 1977), pp. 657–59; Robert Wesson, *The United States and Brazil: Limits of Influence* (New York: Praeger, 1981), pp. 75–89.

Goldemberg, a professor of physics and later rector of the University of São Paulo, achieved a reputation in Brazil during the 1970s and 1980s as an eloquent and expert critic of the country's nuclear activities. President Collor asked Goldemberg to serve in his government first as secretary of science and technology in the Office of the President, then as minister of education, and simultaneously, for a short period of time, as acting minister of the environment. Although never officially responsible for nuclear energy policy, Goldemberg was able, through his personal relationship with Collor, to exert great influence over the country's nuclear activities.

[24]Wrobel, "Brazil," chapter 5. IPEN stands for Instituto des Pesquisas Energeticas e Nucleares.

[25]Britain's use of nuclear-powered submarines during the 1982 Falklands-Malvinas war—the HMS *Conqueror* sank Argentina's only cruiser, the *General Belgrano*, and kept the remainder of the Argentine fleet bottled up in port for most of the war—impressed the Brazilian navy. Brazil also gained a general impression of the importance of advanced technology in modern warfare. See Wrobel, "Brazil," introduction and chapter 5. The United States and Britain use 90-plus percent U-235 for their nuclear submarine reactors.

There was no thought that Brazil would actually develop nuclear weapons for these submarines. In the early 1980s, Brazil contracted with West German companies to acquire the know-how to construct conventional submarines in Brazil. Two submarines would be built in West Germany, with the participation of Brazilian scientists, engineers, and technicians; it was hoped that this would then enable Brazil to later build additional submarines with its own resources. Wrobel, "Brazil," chapter 5; *Gazeta Mercantil* (São Paulo), July 30, 1991, reported in JPRS-TND-91-014 (September 12, 1991), p. 10. For a discussion of nuclear-propelled submarines, see Paul L. Leventhal and Sharon Tanzer, *Averting a Latin American Nuclear Arms Race* (New York: St. Martin's Press, 1992), pp. 29–34; Spector with Smith, *Nuclear Ambitions*, pp. 49–55.

[26]According to a retired State Department official who worked on nuclear matters, Washington was aware of the existence of the parallel program virtually from its inception. Personal interview, Washington, D.C., May 25, 1994. But it is unclear what Washington knew, when it knew it, and whether it shared any of this information with Bonn. According to Rex Nazaré Alves, the program proceeded in secret because the Brazilian press and those opposed to nuclear energy would have irresponsibly whipped up public fears. Personal interview, Rio de Janeiro, April 29, 1994. Nazaré Alves served as head of CNEN from September 1982 to March 1990, when Fernando Collor became president.

[27]Nazaré Alves, personal interview, Rio de Janeiro, April 29, 1994. Goldemberg has described Nazaré Alves as "extremely subservient to the army" during his tenure at CNEN. Personal interview, Princeton, New Jersey, July 8, 1994.

[28]Goldemberg, personal interview, Princeton, New Jersey, July 8, 1994. The navy ran the Aramar ultracentrifuge enrichment project outside São Paulo. The air force performed laser enrichment research at the nearby Center for Aerospace Technology. The army had a jet-nozzle enrichment facility at Resende and a highly secret natural uranium, graphite-moderated reactor project outside of Rio designed to produce plutonium. The jet-nozzle enrichment facility violated the terms of Brazil's 1975 nuclear agreement with West Germany.

The plutonium production reactor was based on the model developed at Hanford, Washington, during the Manhattan Project; Brazilian scientists and engineers copied this model from the open literature. Goldemberg, personal interview, Princeton, New Jersey, July 8, 1994; see also David Albright, Frans Berkhout, and William Walker, *World Inventory of Plutonium and Highly Enriched Uranium, 1992* (New York: Oxford University Press, 1993), pp. 184–85.

Each branch of the armed services in Brazil has its own ministry, thereby complicating defense planning and coordination. The armed services have successfully opposed efforts to consolidate the branches under a single defense ministry. This institutional arrangement hampered civilian oversight of the military's nuclear activities. CNEN's activities, and those of the parallel program, were outside the president's purview; Nazaré Alves reported directly to the Ministry of Mines and Energy.

[29]Goldemberg, personal interview, Princeton, New Jersey, July 8, 1994.

[30]Antonio Rubens Britto de Castro, Norberto Majlis, Luiz Pinguelli Rosa, and Fernando de Souza Barros, "Brazil's Nuclear Shakeup: Military Still in Control," *Bulletin of the Atomic Scientists* 45, no. 4 (May 1989): 24.

The dimensions of the hole come from Nazaré Alves, who stated that the military dug only one hole at Cachimbo and that no other holes were dug at other military bases. Personal interview, Rio de Janeiro, April 29, 1994. This contradicts Brazilian National Congress, "Final Report of the Parliamentary Commission to Inquire into the Parallel Program" (December 14, 1990), which stated that two holes were dug at Cachimbo. Goldemberg has stated that he does not know how many holes were dug. Personal interview, Princeton, New Jersey, July 8, 1994.

[31]Spector with Smith, *Nuclear Ambitions*, pp. 245–46.

[32]See Richard House, "Brazil Steps Back from Race to Build Nuclear Weapons," *Washington Post*, August 28, 1986. In April 1994, Nazaré Alves stated that Cachimbo was part of a project to locate a suitable site for nuclear waste. He noted that the government "tried to identify large places to put nuclear waste" from the power station, Angra I. Every time CNEN announced a potential site, however, public protests prevented the government from proceeding. A hole was therefore dug on a military base to avoid these protests. Also, Nazaré Alves asked how Cachimbo could have been a nuclear test site if the military hit water. Personal interview, Rio de Janeiro, April 29, 1994.

When serving in the Collor administration, Goldemberg was told by the head of Brazil's internal security organization that its investigations had yielded no records referencing the Cachimbo site or any of the parallel program's activities. Goldemberg suspects that Nazaré Alves had these documents destroyed or hidden. Personal interview, Princeton, New Jersey, July 8, 1994.

[33]U.S. government official, personal interview, Brasilia, April 26, 1994; Fernando de Souza Barros, personal interview, Rio de Janeiro, April 29, 1994. Souza Barros is professor of physics at the Federal University of Rio de Janeiro and served on the Brazilian Physical Society's Commission for the Nuclear Question.

[34]Laercio Antonio Vinhas, personal interview, Rio de Janeiro, April 28, 1994; Souza Barros, personal interview, Rio de Janeiro, April 29, 1994; U.S. diplomat, personal interview, Brasilia, April 26, 1994; Goldemberg, personal interview, Princeton, New Jersey, July 8, 1994.

[35]Goldemberg, personal interview, Princeton, New Jersey, July 8, 1994.

[36]*International Herald Tribune,* September 7, 1987.

[37]See, for example, Myers, "Brazil's Reluctant Pursuit of the Nuclear Option," p. 905; Spector, *Nuclear Proliferation Today*, pp. 235–36, 266–68.

[38]Juan E. Guglialmelli, "The Brazilian-German Nuclear Deal: A View from Argentina," *Survival* 18, no. 4 (July/August 1976): 165. See also Jonathan Kandell, "Argentines Assay Their Atom Potential," *New York Times*, April 2, 1975.

Guglialmelli was prescient in thinking that Argentina ought to "negotiate with Brazil . . . an agreement for information, consultation, and eventual technical cooperation in the nuclear field." He noted, "Among other things, that agreement should erect effective and reciprocal safeguards against the possible construction of nuclear devices, even if these may be intended for peaceful purposes." "The Brazilian-German Nuclear Deal," p. 165. At the time, General Guglialmelli was director of the Argentine Institute of Strategic Studies and International Relations and one of Argentina's foremost strategic thinkers.

[39]See Jack Child, *Geopolitics and Conflict in South America: Quarrels among Neighbors* (New York: Praeger, 1985), p. 102; more generally, see also Virginia Gamba-Stonehouse, *Strategy in the Southern Oceans: A South American View* (London: Pinter, 1989).

[40]See "Argentina-Brazil-Paraguay: Agreement on Parana River Projects," October 19, 1979, 19 I.L.M. 615 (1979).

[41]By not joining the NPT or allowing full-scope IAEA safeguards, Argentina and Brazil had attracted the wrath of the industrialized northern countries that controlled access to advanced technologies. According to one Brazilian scholar, "Both nations began to coordinate and exchange ideas on the best way to resist the pressures constantly exerted by the nuclear states to join the regime." Wrobel, "Brazil," chapter 5.

[42]See Wrobel, "Brazil," where he uses the phrase "anti-NPT axis," chapter 5; Paulo Wrobel, "Brazil-Argentina Nuclear Relations: An Interpretation" (draft paper prepared for the Rockefeller Foundation, October 1993, copy provided to the author by John Redick), pp. 12–14.

[43]The full text of the May 18, 1980, agreement can be found in Foreign Broadcast Information Service (FBIS), *Nuclear Development and Proliferation*, no. 49 (June 25, 1980), pp. 4–16. See John Redick, "The Tlatelolco Regime and Nonproliferation in Latin America," *International Organization* 35, no. 1 (Winter 1981): 130–31; idem, "Latin America's Emerging Nonproliferation Consensus," *Arms Control Today* 24, no. 2 (March 1994): 3–4.

[44]As a result of the May 1980 meeting, Argentina leased uranium concentrate to Brazil and sold zircalloy tubing for nuclear fuel elements; Brazil supplied Argentina with a portion of the pressure vessel for its Atucha II nuclear power generator. Spector with Smith, *Nuclear Ambitions*, pp. 388–89.

[45]Wrobel, "Brazil," chapter 5; Wrobel, "Brazil-Argentina Nuclear Relations," p. 18.

[46]Carasales, in Leventhal and Tanzer, *Nuclear Arms Race*, p. 53; Bradley Graham, "Brazil, Argentina Forge Closer Ties," *Washington Post*, April 17, 1986.

[47]In 1982, Brazil was nearly insolvent, with foreign exchange reserves approaching zero, GDP growth at 1.1 percent, inflation running at 100 percent per year, and the real possibility of default to international lenders. On Brazil's economic adversity during this period, see Ronald M. Schneider, *"Order and Progress": A Political History of Brazil* (Boulder, Colo.: Westview, 1991), pp. 295–97; Albert Fishlow, "A Tale of Two Presidents: The Political Economy of Crisis Management"; Edmar L. Bacha and Pedro S. Malan, "Brazil's Debt: From the Miracle to the Fund," in Alfred Stepan, ed., *Democratizing Brazil: Problems of Transition and Consolidation* (New York: Oxford University Press, 1989), pp. 83–119, 120–40.

[48]See Carasales, in Leventhal and Tanzer, *Nuclear Arms Race*, p. 53. The formal

title of the declaration was the "Argentine-Brazilian Joint Declaration on Nuclear Policy."

[49]Ibid., p. 54. Argentina's Foreign Ministry created an entirely new Division of Nuclear Policy and Disarmament in response to the commitment undertaken at Foz de Iguazú.

[50]Richard Kessler, "Argentina and Brazil Will Not Provide the IAEA with Information," *Nucleonics Week*, March 2, 1986.

[51]Richard Kessler, "Sarney Visit to Pilçaniyeu Was Key to Reciprocal Inspections," *Nucleonics Week*, July 23, 1987. This reprocessing activity may have violated the terms of Brazil's 1975 nuclear deal with West Germany.

[52]Wrobel, "Brazil," chapter 5.

[53]U.S. government official, personal interview, Bariloche, Argentina, April 20, 1994.

[54]Oskar Klingl, personal interview, Brasilia, April 26, 1994. Klingl was chief of staff at the Brazilian Ministry of Science and Technology at the time of this interview.

[55]*O Estado de São Paulo,* October 17, 1993, reported in JPRS-TND-93-035 (November 10, 1993), p. 25.

[56]Vinhas and Fulfaro, personal interview, Rio de Janeiro, April 28, 1994. The sign at the entrance to the Aramar complex reads: "Brazil cannot be colonized through technological dependence."

[57]Wrobel, "Brazil," chapter 5.

[58]Retired U.S. ambassador, personal interview, Washington, D.C., May 25, 1994; Goldemberg, personal interview, Princeton, New Jersey, July 8, 1994. According to Goldemberg, the army was more resistant than the air force and the navy to external supervision of their nuclear activities.

[59]The military planned to build a plutonium production center at this site using a natural uranium/graphite-moderated nuclear reactor, but this never occurred. The existence of this subcritical unit was publicly revealed in 1991.

[60]"Mercosur" in Spanish stands for Mercado Comun del Sur; the Portuguese version is "Mercosul," which stands for Mercado Comum do Sul. The Treaty of Asunción, signed on March 26, 1991, formally created Mercosur. In addition to Argentina and Brazil, it now includes Uruguay and Paraguay. It came into force on January 1, 1995, with gradually lower tariff barriers theoretically leading to free trade. See James Brooke, "Brazil's Horizons Widening with New Common Market," *New York Times,* January 4, 1995.

[61]Placing this development in historical context, the Argentine diplomat Julio Carasales termed the Mercosur concept "the most important political-economic phenomenon to take place in South America in recent times." Carasales, in Leventhal and Tanzer, *Nuclear Arms Race,* p. 9. In October 1989, Carasales commented, "The integration of two great South American countries is becoming irreversible." Ibid., p. 50.

[62]For expressions of concern about the nuclear path Menem would pursue on taking office, see Richard Kessler, "Peronists Seek `Nuclear Greatness,'" *Bulletin of the Atomic Scientists* 45, no. 4 (May 1989): 13–15.

[63]On Collor's personal opposition to nuclear weapons: Goldemberg, personal interview, Princeton, New Jersey, July 8, 1994. According to Goldemberg, Collor's

father witnessed a U.S. nuclear test in the Pacific during the 1950s, and his subsequent opposition to nuclear weapons shaped his son's thinking.

In his effort to exert greater civilian control over nuclear activities, Collor was helped by some changes that predated his presidency. A 1988 organizational change already ensured greater civilian control by having CNEN report directly to the president's office. In addition, revelations of a clandestine nuclear program, the Cachimbo site, and a secret slush fund in European bank accounts for purchases of nuclear technology had persuaded Congress to add a clause limiting the country's nuclear ambitions when it revised the constitution in 1988. The Brazilian Society for the Advancement of Science collected the signatures of sixty thousand scientists in support of strong language that included banning the construction of nuclear devices, and the society sent this petition to Congress. Congress rejected this language in favor of a provision that stipulated, "All nuclear activities in the national territory will only be permitted if for peaceful purposes and if approved by Congress." This formulation was interpreted as permitting peaceful nuclear explosions.

[64]David Albright, "Brazil Comes in from the Cold," *Arms Control Today* (December 1990), p. 13. Collor also suspended work on Angra II and Angra III in July 1991. As of April 1994, senior CNEN officials believed that Angra II would not be completed. Vinhas and Fulfaro, personal interview, Rio de Janeiro, April 28, 1994.

[65]Goldemberg, personal interview, Princeton, New Jersey, July 8, 1994.

[66]Collor's speech before the United Nations came one month after West Germany's announcement at the 1990 NPT Review Conference that it would insist on comprehensive safeguards as a condition of nuclear cooperation. Nazaré Alves became visibly agitated when recounting Collor's "grandstanding" at Cachimbo, which he believed embarrassed the nuclear program, the military, and the country for the president's self-aggrandizement. Personal interview, Rio de Janeiro, April 29, 1994.

For an examination of Brazil's official and parallel nuclear programs, see Frederico Fullgraf, *A Bomba Pacífica: O Brasil e outros Cenários da Corrida Nuclear* (São Paulo: Editora Brasiliense, 1988); Luiz Pinguelli Rosa, Fernando de Souza Barros, and Suzana Ribeiro Barreiros, *A Política Nuclear no Brasil* (São Paulo: Greenpeace, 1991); Luiz Pinguelli Rosa, *A Política Nuclear e os caminhos das Armas Atômicas* (Rio de Janeiro: Jorge Zahar Editor, 1985); Spector with Smith, *Nuclear Ambitions*, pp. 242–63. For a speculative and somewhat sensationalist treatment that views the parallel program as an attempt to acquire nuclear weapons, see Tania Malheiros, *Brasil, A Bomba Oculta: O Programa Nuclear Brasileiro* (Rio de Janeiro: Gryphus, 1993). Nazaré Alves bluntly assessed this book: "Don't rely on this." Personal interview, Rio de Janeiro, April 29, 1994.

[67]See Brazilian National Congress, "Final Report of the Parliamentary Commission to Inquire into the Parallel Program."

[68]Carasales, in Leventhal and Tanzer, *Nuclear Arms Race*, p. 59. American participants at this conference explained the shortcomings of reciprocal inspections of sensitive facilities and stated that such inspections would not be sufficient to win the confidence of the United States and the other nuclear suppliers. American participants have subsequently heralded this conference as influential in revising Argentine and Brazilian thinking on IAEA safeguards. Goldemberg, who also attended this conference, said it had "no influence" on Brazil's nuclear policy. Personal interview, Princeton, New Jersey, July 8, 1994.

[69]In response to Western pressure, Menem's attitude was pragmatic: "I'd rather

govern the last country in the First World than the first country in the Third World." Menem's predecessor, Alfonsín, took a different tack, reportedly saying on one occasion in response to U.S. pressure, "I may break, but I will not bend."

[70]As a reaction to the Falklands-Malvinas war, the Argentine Air Force in 1984 began developing, with Egypt and Iraq, a medium-range ballistic missile, the Condor II. This missile was a clone of the U.S. Pershing II missile. The 1987 Intermediate-range Nuclear Forces (INF) Treaty outlawed this type of missile for the United States and the Soviet Union. A Soviet delegation had visited Argentina after Moscow had signed the INF Treaty and demanded that it terminate the Condor II program. U.S. diplomat, personal interview, Bariloche, Argentina, April 20, 1994.

The original Argentine rationale for the Condor II project was to develop a missile that could hit the Malvinas (approximately four hundred nautical miles from Argentine military bases). After years of pressure from the United States, the project was finally terminated in 1993. Two recent books by Argentine authors on the Condor program are Eduardo Barcelona and Julio Villalonga, *Relaciones Carnales: La Verdadera Historia de la Contruccion y Destruccion del Missil* (Buenos Aires: Planeta, 1992), translated in JPRS-TND-92-011-L (December 28, 1992); Daniel Santoro, *Operation Condor-2: The Secret History of the Missile Menem Dismantled*, translated in JPRS-TND-92-009-L (October 16, 1992). See also Janne E. Nolan, *Trappings of Power: Ballistic Missiles in the Third World* (Washington, D.C.: Brookings, 1991); Spector with Smith, *Nuclear Ambitions*, pp. 229–31; the articles by Nathaniel C. Nash in *New York Times*, May 13, 1991, August 19, 1992, and March 7, 1993; JPRS-TND-93-007-L (August 19, 1993), pp. 6–7; JPRS-TND-93-027 (August 26, 1993), p. 15.

The Condor II program and Argentina's nonproliferation commitments are linked in two ways. The demise of the missile program and the end of Argentina's independent nuclear stance evidenced both civilian control over the military and Argentina's susceptibility to international pressure.

[71]I am indebted to Virginia Gamba for this point.

[72]According to Enrique de la Torre, this small group was supported by Menem but was opposed by the majority of the Foreign Ministry, the military, the nuclear establishment, and the rest of the government. Personal interview, Bariloche, Argentina, April 20, 1994. De la Torre is director of international security and nuclear affairs in the Argentine Foreign Ministry.

De la Torre and his colleagues tried to promote a fresh vision of Latin American security, one that downplayed military force and emphasized economic cooperation, based on the Conference on Security and Cooperation in Europe (CSCE) model. Once the Argentine government adopted the idea of cooperative security, neighbors had to be persuaded. This idea competed against (1) a traditional balance-of-power concept, usually associated with Chile, in which constant tension among states constantly necessitated a large standing army, and (2) the idea of a North-South struggle, usually associated with Brazil, in which the military was needed to protect the country's sovereignty against encroachment from the industrialized North (i.e., the United States). De la Torre, personal interview, Bariloche, Argentina, April 20, 1994. To promote the CSCE model, Argentina sponsored an international conference in 1993 on Latin American confidence-building measures.

[73]See Julio Carasales, "Background and History of Argentina-Brazil Nuclear Nonproliferation Progress" (draft paper prepared for the Rockefeller Foundation, April 1994, copy provided to the author by John Redick), pp. 29–30.

[74]See "Agreement between the Argentine Republic and the Federative Republic

of Brazil for the Exclusively Peaceful Use of Nuclear Energy." The text of the agreement is reprinted as INFCIRC/395 (November 26, 1991) and in JPRS-TND-91-014 (September 12, 1991), pp. 6–9. The annex sets out the basic procedures of the SCCC.

Argentine and Brazilian officials are uncertain who deserves credit for thinking up the idea of ABACC. Personal interviews, Bariloche, Buenos Aires, Brasilia, Rio de Janeiro, April and May 1994.

75"Agreement between the Republic of Argentina, the Federative Republic of Brazil, the Brazilian-Argentine Agency for Accounting and Control of Nuclear Materials and the International Atomic Energy Agency for the Application of Safeguards," p. 2. This is the standard language used in INFCIRC/153, which is the model safeguards agreement for all nonnuclear weapon state parties to the NPT.

After ratification of the Quadripartite Agreement, ABACC expanded its activities to safeguard all nuclear installations in collaboration with the IAEA. ABACC inspects the Aramar and Pilçaniyeu facilities every other month, and it is expected that the IAEA will stick to the same schedule. ABACC hopes to expand its responsibilities in the future to cover other Latin American countries, such as Chile, Uruguay, and Paraguay. Areas where ABACC and the IAEA may coordinate activities include sharing, maintaining, and storing equipment and analyzing inspection data. Jorge Coll, personal interview, Rio de Janeiro, April 28, 1994. At the time of this interview, Coll, an Argentine, was ABACC's secretary.

ABACC officials argue that its inspectors may be more rigorous than their IAEA counterparts because of better training and greater motivation. ABACC employs people familiar with the specific types of installations to be inspected and tries to promote a "peaceful competition" among the two national nuclear establishments on safeguards measures and inspections. Senior ABACC official, personal interview, Rio de Janeiro, April 28, 1994.

The United States has also played a constructive role by training Argentine and Brazilian personnel for ABACC inspections. U.S. government official, personal interview, Bariloche, Argentina, April 19, 1994. This assistance was expanded and formalized by an April 1994 agreement between the U.S. Department of Energy and ABACC under which the United States will provide information, equipment, personnel, and funding to assist in improving ABACC's verification techniques and procedures. See "Agreement between the United States Department of Energy and the Brazilian-Argentine Agency for Accounting and Control of Nuclear Materials Concerning Research and Development in Nuclear Material Control, Accountancy, Verification, and Advance Containment and Surveillance Technologies," Bariloche, April 18, 1994, copy in author's possession.

76See Gazeta Mercantil (São Paulo), July 30, 1991, reported in JPRS-TND-91-014 (September 12, 1991), p. 11. The day after these complaints appeared, CNEN President José Luis de Santana Carvalho stated, "[IAEA inspections] will not be intrusive, i.e., they will not penetrate into areas where there are industrial-commercial secrets." He added, "We will preserve the secrets of all the advances which, using our own resources, we have developed for peaceful purposes." Gazeta Mercantil, July 31, 1991, reported in JPRS-TND-91-014 (September 12, 1991), p. 11.

ABACC could not legally exist, and the Quadripartite Agreement could not be signed, until the Guadalajara Treaty was ratified. The Brazilian Congress was pressured to expedite this process, but the resulting resentment contributed to delaying the vote on ratification of the Quadripartite Agreement.

77Stelson Ponce de Azevedo, personal interview, Brasilia, April 26, 1994. Ponce de Azevedo was the legislative assistant for foreign policy issues for Senator Dirceu Carneiro, who was chairman of the Senate Foreign Relations Committee. Two CNEN officials also confirmed congressional concern about special inspections. Vinhas and Fulfaro, personal interview, Rio de Janeiro, April 28, 1994.

[78]*Gazeta Mercantil,* June 25, 1993, reported in JPRS-TND-93-024 (July 27, 1993), p. 14. Subsidiary arrangements are outlined in Articles 37 and 38 of the Quadripartite Agreement. A more subtle argument than the fear of revealing proprietary secrets was that other countries would learn Brazil's level of technological sophistication and then withhold the necessary technology; in this way, the country's economic development would be strangled. Ponce de Azevedo, personal interview, Brasilia, April 26, 1994.

[79]U.S. government official, personal interview, Brasilia, April 26, 1994. The IAEA reportedly had reservations about ABACC because it remembered its past differences with Euratom over safeguards. Coll, personal interview, Rio de Janeiro, April 28, 1994. For a summary of the disagreements between the IAEA and Euratom, see Fischer and Szasz, *Safeguarding the Atom,* pp. 70–73.

[80]See Spector with Smith, *Nuclear Ambitions,* pp. 252–54; Alexander Kelle, "Germany," in Harald Müller, ed., *European Nonproliferation Policy: 1988–1992* (Brussels: European Interuniversity Press, 1993), p. 127 n.

[81]German diplomat, personal interview, Brasilia, April 26, 1994; this account was corroborated by a U.S. government official, personal interview, Brasilia, April 26, 1994. See also *Gazeta Mercantil,* October 8, 1993, reported in JPRS-TND-93-037 (December 8, 1993), pp. 31–32; JPRS-TND-93-034 (October 27, 1993), pp. 23–24.

[82]The negotiations at this time centered on Brazil's request that the German government redirect funds originally allocated to Angra III to complete the Angra II power station. See *Jornal do Brasil,* October 6, 1993, reported in JPRS-TND-93-009-L (November 9, 1993), pp. 15–16.

[83]U.S. government official, personal interview, Brasilia, April 26, 1994.

[84]U.S. government officials, personal interviews, Brasilia, April 26, 1994. According to Goldemberg, Flores was also very influential with members of Congress. Personal interview, Princeton, New Jersey, July 8, 1994. Flores commented at this time, "Either Brazil modernizes and internationalizes or loses its place in the world and in history." Quoted in José Goldemberg and Harold A. Feiveson, "Denuclearization in Argentina and Brazil," *Arms Control Today* 24, no. 2 (March 1994): 13.

[85]Reported in JPRS-TND-94-010 (May 5, 1994), p. 10. This article also included reports of other influential Brazilian scientists who advocated Senate approval of the Quadripartite Agreement.

[86]Congress could only approve or disapprove the Quadripartite Agreement; any amendments to the agreement required the approval of the other parties. But the Senate did attach a condition that it be notified before any change in the subsidiary arrangements.

[87]Brazil proposed a nuclear-weapon-free zone for Latin America in September 1962, a month before the Cuban Missile Crisis. Tlatelolco is the name of the Mexico City suburb where the treaty was signed.

On the formation of the Tlatelolco Treaty, see Alfonso Garcia Robles, *El Tratado de Tlatelolco: Genesis, Alcance y Propositos de la Proscripcion de Armas Nucleares en America Latina* (Mexico City: El Collegio de Mexico, 1967); John Redick, "The Politics of Denuclearization: A Study of the Treaty for the Prohibition of Nuclear

Weapons in Latin America" (Ph.D. diss., University of Virginia, 1970); Mónica Serrano, "The Latin American Nuclear-Weapons-Free Zone Established under the 1967 Treaty of Tlatelolco" (D.Phil. diss., Oxford University, 1990).

[88]Carlos Ortiz de Rozas, personal interview, Buenos Aires, April 22, 1994. In the late 1970s, Ortiz de Rozas was the head of the Foreign Ministry's Interministerial Committee on Disarmament, which had responsibility for coordinating the positions of the relevant ministries and agencies on all disarmament subjects. He had prepared the policy paper on Tlatelolco ratification, circulating it to the three military branches. Ortiz de Rozas later served as Argentina's ambassador to the Conference on Disarmament, the United Nations, and the United States.

Carasales has written that ratification was delayed because Argentina wanted some form of political compensation for taking this step and because it was reluctant to accept IAEA safeguards for a Tlatelolco regime, a hesitance that was tied to the government's desire to keep open the option to conduct a peaceful nuclear explosion. Carasales, "Background and History," p. 22.

[89]When Brazil signed the treaty in 1967, its signature was accompanied by a note stating that its interpretation of Article 18 permitted parties to conduct peaceful nuclear explosions. Wrobel, "Brazil," chapter 4. When the United Kingdom, the United States, and the USSR ratified Additional Protocol II, they all rejected Article 18 as incompatible with Articles 1 and 5, which effectively ruled out PNEs.

[90]The amendments were negotiated with Mexico, which consulted with the other parties to the treaty. An OPANAL General Conference unanimously approved the amendments on August 26, 1992. The amendments can be found in OPANAL, GC/PV/E/73 and CG/385 and in INFCIRC/411 (July 12, 1993). OPANAL stands for Organismo para la Proscription de Armas Nucleares na America Latina. The rest of the treaty text can be found in U.S. Arms Control and Disarmament Agency, *Arms Control and Disarmament Agreements: Texts and Histories of the Negotiations* (Washington, D.C.: USGPO, 1990), pp. 68–88.

[91]Information on Tlatelolco membership was provided to the author by the U.S. Arms Control and Disarmament Agency. Each prior party to Tlatelolco, including those parties to Additional Protocols I and II, must review the latest version of the treaty, in accordance with its constitutional procedures, before it fully enters into force for that party. However, under Article 18 of the Vienna Convention on the Law of Treaties, "A state is obliged to refrain from acts which would defeat the object and purpose of a treaty when: it has signed the treaty . . . until it shall have made its intentions clear not to become a party to the treaty; or it has expressed its consent to be bound by the treaty, pending the entry into force of the treaty and provided that such entry into force is not unduly delayed." As of January 1995, St. Lucia and St. Kitts-Nevis have never ratified any version of the treaty; Cuba and Guyana have neither signed nor ratified any version of the treaty.

Article 28(4) of the Tlatelolco Treaty stipulates that the appearance of a new nuclear power after the entry into force of the treaty for all the parties may cause the treaty to be suspended until the new power ratifies Additional Protocol II. According to John Redick, after New Delhi's 1974 PNE, OPANAL requested that India sign Additional Protocol II. New Delhi refused. Personal conversation, April 1994.

[92]See, for example, Julio Carasales, *El Desarme de los Desarmados: Argentina y el Tratado de No Proliferacion de Armas Nucleares* (Buenos Aires: Pleamar, 1987).

Carasales later came to support NPT membership for Argentina; to his chagrin, the arguments in his 1987 book were used by Argentine opponents of the NPT.

[93]Both the Quadripartite Agreement and the NPT required full-scope safeguards. But for nuclear exports, Argentina's obligations as a member of the Nuclear Suppliers Group, which it joined in 1994, were broader than the obligations under Article 3(2) of the NPT.

[94]See *O Estado de São Paulo,* November 6, 1992, reported in JPRS-TND-92-045 (December 7, 1992), pp. 10–11.

[95]U.S. government official, personal interview, Bariloche, Argentina, April 19, 1994.

[96]Goldemberg, personal interview, Princeton, New Jersey, July 8, 1994.

[97]See *Gazeta Mercantil* (São Paulo), July 31, 1991, reported in JPRS-TND-91-014 (September 12, 1991), pp. 11–12.

[98]Kessler, personal interview, Buenos Aires, April 23, 1994; U.S. government official, personal interview, Washington, D.C., May 26, 1994.

This raises the interesting question of where Argentina obtained the low-enriched uranium needed to fuel the indigenously manufactured research reactor it sold to Algeria in the late 1980s. During the 1980s, Argentina had imported 20 percent U-235 from the Soviet Union and China. Despite Argentina's claims to the contrary, the Pilçaniyeu facility had not produced the necessary amounts of enriched uranium for the Algerian reactor, so Buenos Aires used the imported nuclear material instead. U.S. government official, personal interview, Washington, D.C., May 26, 1994.

[99]The official government cost figure for the parallel program from its inception in 1975 through mid-1991 is $440 million. *Gazeta Mercantil* (São Paulo), August 15, 1991, reported in JPRS-TND-91-014 (September 12, 1991), p. 15. Many observers believe this underestimates the true cost of the program. For revelations of slush funds and secret bank accounts to pay for the parallel program, see *Jornal do Brasil* (Rio de Janeiro), August 4, 1991, reported in JPRS-TND-91-009-L (August 21, 1991), pp. 1–5.

[100]In April 1989, it was announced that the Aramar enrichment plant had produced some uranium enriched to 20 percent U-235. See *O Globo,* April 9, 1989, reported in JPRS-TND-89-008 (April 25, 1989), p. 13. According to a U.S. government official who closely followed Brazil's nuclear activities, Brazil has no 20 percent U-235 that he knows about. Personal interview, Brasilia, April 26, 1994. This was also affirmed by Goldemberg, personal interview, Princeton, New Jersey, July 8, 1994.

In 1994, CNEN officials confessed that the small nuclear reactor program was best viewed as a fifteen- to twenty-year effort. More skeptical observers thought that the program would die a slow death over the next decade. Vinhas, personal interview, Rio de Janeiro, April 28, 1994. On the eventual demise of the submarine propulsion program, a U.S. diplomat in Brasilia predicted, "It will be a military decision; the civilians will not force them to do it." Personal interview, Brasilia, April 26, 1994.

[101]Carasales, "Background and History," pp. 33–34.

[102]Nor can Washington claim indirect credit, since it was *not* using Bonn as its proxy with Brazil; Germany had its own motivations. U.S. government official, personal interview, Bariloche, Argentina, April 20, 1994.

[103]Gall had much earlier sensed that German financing for the 1975 nuclear deal would confer future leverage: "[The deal] also means, for the future, an important source of potential leverage for financial as well as technological restrictions on nuclear proliferation." See "Atoms for Brazil, Dangers for All," p. 197.

[104]A German diplomat in Brazil downplayed the significance of Foreign Minister Kinkel's visit in October 1993; if it had never occurred, Brazil would have ratified the Quadripartite Agreement anyway. According to this official, it was not one meeting but rather a series of meetings over time, in both Brazil and Germany and at different levels, that resulted in the Brazilian ratification of the Quadripartite Agreement. Personal interview, Brasilia, April 26, 1994. This may be true, but his claim merely emphasizes the larger point: without the 1990 revision in Germany's nonproliferation policy and with Collor out of power, all the meetings in the world may not have persuaded Brasilia to ratify the Quadripartite Agreement.

[105]Carasales, personal interview, Bariloche, Argentina, April 19, 1994. Significantly, though, Washington rewarded Buenos Aires for ratifying the Quadripartite Agreement. In December 1993, Washington signed a technology cooperation agreement that permitted Buenos Aires to purchase advanced computer equipment, nuclear technology, and aeronautical guidance systems; the deal itself symbolized American confidence in Argentina. Two months later, the United States approved the sale to Argentina of thirty-six A-4M Skyhawk jets with advanced radar technology, despite British objections. The following month the U.S. Department of Energy entered into a nuclear cooperation agreement with CNEA. Argentina was also invited to join the Missile Technology Control Regime in November 1993 and to become a full member of the Nuclear Suppliers Group in 1994; Argentina was the lone South American and Third World country to belong to both of these nonproliferation arrangements.

Chapter 4

The Former Soviet Union: Managing the Nuclear Inheritance

A brief phone call from KGB Chairman Vladimir Kryuchkov to Boris Yeltsin's office at the Russian parliament building in the early morning hours of Wednesday, August 21, 1991, signaled that the attempted putsch by hard-line Communists had failed. In the aftermath, it became clear that the Communist Party would no longer rule the Soviet Union. Far less clear was whether there would be a Soviet Union to rule at all. As uncertainty mounted over whether the country would hold together or splinter into fifteen constituent parts, concern also increased over the future of the Soviet Union's massive and far-flung nuclear arsenal. As the USSR slowly descended into disorder and chaos, the question of who maintained control of the nuclear archipelago—the thirty thousand tactical and strategic nuclear weapons spread throughout the country—assumed greater urgency.

The straw that broke the Soviet Union's frail back was Ukraine's nationwide December 1 referendum, in which more than 90 percent of the Ukrainian people voted for independence. A few days later, former Communist Party apparatchik and ideology chief Leonid Kravchuk became the first president of Ukraine. With the Soviet Union's demise clearly in sight, Yeltsin, who had spent the period since August trying to devise a way to remove his nemesis, Mikhail Gorbachev, and to consolidate his own position as leader of the Russian Federation, now administered the coup de grace. At his initiative, the leaders of the three Slavic republics met the following weekend at Belovezhskaya Pushcha, a hunting resort between Minsk and Brest. On December 8, Yeltsin, Kravchuk, and Byelorussia's Stanislav Shushkevich announced the formation of the Commonwealth of Independent States (CIS). The categorical language of the founding CIS declaration took Washington by surprise and sounded the death knell of the Soviet Union. The parties concluded, "The USSR, as a subject of international law and geopolitical reality, is ceasing its existence."

Kazakhstan and four other Central Asian republics opted to join the CIS the following week.

The two CIS summits later that month, at Alma Ata and Minsk, solidified the Commonwealth's framework and outlined its organizational authority. The primary business of both these meetings was how best to handle the Soviet nuclear inheritance—the tactical and strategic nuclear weapons that remained on the territories of Ukraine, Kazakhstan, and Belarus (formerly Byelorussia). Russia drafted the summit declarations, which, not surprisingly, envisioned that Moscow would be the sole beneficiary of the nuclear stockpile and that Ukraine, Kazakhstan, and Belarus would join the NPT as nonnuclear weapon states.

The events of December 1991 set in motion a denuclearization process that continues to this day. The story of how the tactical nuclear weapons were eventually removed from Ukraine, Kazakhstan, and Belarus, and of how these three countries pledged to remove the strategic nuclear warheads, is complex. It is really three separate stories, since the circumstances of denuclearization efforts in Ukraine, Kazakhstan, and Belarus differ in important details. They involve secret diplomacy, false starts, threats, incompetence, political courage and cowardice, and broken promises. However, certain themes are present in all three cases. Each of the countries tried to use the nuclear weapons stationed on its territory to win monetary compensation and to enhance its national security and international prestige. To these ends, each played the nuclear card—though differently and with varying degrees of skill.

Finally, although there has been great success in gathering many of these weapons back into Russia, this is still an unfinished story. All the tactical nuclear weapons have been shipped to Russia; Ukraine, Kazakhstan, and Belarus have joined the NPT. But the commitments of the three non-Russian republics to return all the strategic nuclear warheads will not be completely implemented for several years. By the beginning of 1995, over twelve hundred strategic nuclear warheads remained in Ukraine, over five hundred nuclear warheads remained in Kazakhstan, and over thirty nuclear warheads remained in Belarus. Pledges have yet to fully become deeds.

Ukraine: The Nuclear Hedgehog

Ukraine's long and troubled history with Russia, as much as contemporary relations between Kiev and Moscow, influenced the denuclearization issue. For many Russians, their imperialist interpretation of the past is based on Kievan Rus (a loose-knit political entity founded in the late tenth century around Kiev), which subsequently gave way to the Muscovite Principality and then Russia. Beginning in the mid-seventeenth century, what is today Ukraine came under increasing Russian protection and then tsarist domination. The disintegration of the Russian empire in 1917 allowed the "little Russians" (*malorosy*) a short-lived and miserable stab at self-determination. By early 1919, Ukraine was engulfed in chaos. A combination of internal weakness (especially inexperienced leadership and lack of military preparedness) and external enemies (Poland, the White Volunteer Army, and the Bolsheviks) blocked Ukraine's attempt to preserve independence. Foreign powers did not come to Kiev's aid. A Bolshevik military force invaded Ukraine later that year and quickly defeated the Ukrainian and White armies; it took a further two years for the Bolsheviks to subdue and control the countryside.

A relatively enlightened period of Communist rule in Ukraine during the 1920s, characterized by the New Economic Policy and a cultural renaissance, gave way at the end of the decade to Stalin's forced collectivization policy designed to crush the Ukrainian peasantry and national identity. An artificial famine in 1932–33 killed between three and seven million people.[1] The other source of Ukrainian nationalism—the intelligentsia—were liquidated by Stalin as part of the "great terror" campaign.[2]

Fifty years later, the Soviet Union's handling of the Chernobyl nuclear power plant explosion in April 1986 represented all the worst aspects of Soviet rule in Ukraine: overcentralized control, secrecy, and no Ukrainian say in its own affairs.[3] When independence finally came to Ukraine in 1991, old hatreds, along with a Russian mind-set that continued to see Ukraine as an indivisible part of Russia, contaminated Ukrainian-Russian relations and vastly complicated the task of removing the tactical and strategic nuclear weapons from Ukrainian soil.

AFTER THE AUGUST COUP

The Ukrainian Supreme Soviet proclaimed independence on August 24, 1991. Since the Soviet Union still existed, the precise meaning of this declaration was uncertain. For the West, the question of who was actually in charge had serious implications for international security. The world's third-largest nuclear arsenal—approximately 1,800 strategic nuclear warheads, 560 air-launched cruise missiles, and 4,000 tactical nuclear weapons—remained on the territory of a state whose leadership the United States hardly knew.

Many of the strategic nuclear weapons were aimed at the United States. The failed August coup had scrambled U.S. calculations and forced the United States to devise a new strategy toward a crumbling Soviet Union.[4] During the fall, the Bush administration discussed how best to ensure that there was only one beneficiary of the Soviet nuclear legacy.[5] Of paramount importance was preventing the creation of three new nuclear weapon states and any "leakage" of nuclear warheads, technology, or expertise from any of the former Soviet republics to certain countries like Iran and Libya—the "loose nukes" and "brain drain" problems.

There was broad agreement on the objective: U.S. strategic interests demanded an economically and militarily strong Ukraine, as well as good Ukrainian-Russian relations. But there was strong disagreement over the best way to get there. Voices largely based in the Pentagon wanted to focus less exclusively on the nuclear issue and instead construct a broader dialogue with Ukraine; in this way, Washington and Kiev would first establish mutual trust and a positive relationship, and the surrender of the nuclear weapons to Russia would follow. Conversely, if Kiev doubted Washington's good faith, any commitments to denuclearize would be much more difficult to fulfill. The alternative view, expressed generally by the State Department, wanted first to "lock in" Kiev's denuclearization pledges. Only if Ukraine lived up to its commitments would the United States then extend political and economic support. President Bush's personal friendship with Gorbachev (especially when contrasted with his unfamiliarity with Kravchuk) played an important role. Not wanting to do anything that might weaken Gorbachev's precarious position, and perhaps sensing the eagerness of Ukrainian officials for American approval, the Bush administration concluded that it should withhold diplomatic recognition and other benefits until Kiev returned the nuclear weapons to Russia.[6]

The United States anticipated that a nonnuclear Ukraine would be fairly easy to achieve. The Chernobyl disaster had created a widespread "nuclear allergy" that grew only more virulent when the negligent engineering, haphazard evacuation, and shoddy cleanup gradually became known. On July 16, 1990, the Ukrainian parliament, or Rada, passed a declaration of state sovereignty. This statement solemnly proclaimed the country's intention to become a permanently neutral state, take no part in military blocs, and adhere to three nonnuclear principles: "not to accept, not to produce, and not to acquire nuclear weapons." Although the 1990 declaration was meant as an anti-Soviet, anti-Chernobyl statement, the Rada reiterated its nonnuclear pledge two months after the August 1991 coup attempt. In high-level conversations with Ukraine that fall, the United States focused on Kiev's adherence to the limits of the Conventional Forces in Europe (CFE) treaty, reflecting Washington's concern with conventional weapons as much as with nuclear weapons.

THE KEY MONTH: DECEMBER 1991

With the imminent demise of the Soviet Union, the military was the only remaining Soviet institution that could still operate across all the republics; it moved quickly into the vacuum caused by the collapse of the Communist Party apparatus and Soviet political institutions. With self-preservation as a professional fighting force as its primary concern, it viewed the CIS structure as the best means of guaranteeing continued command and control over the Soviet nuclear arsenal.

On December 21, the CIS members met in Alma Ata, Kazakhstan. The meeting was organized and its agenda driven by its largest member, Russia, and it reflected the priorities and concerns of the Russian military. The key document at this summit was the "Agreement on Joint Measures on Nuclear Arms." Ukraine, Kazakhstan, and Belarus pledged to help withdraw the tactical nuclear weapons on their territories by July 1, 1992. This date had not been negotiated but had been set in advance by the Russian military in accordance with its logistical calculations for removing the weapons. Ukraine also agreed to join the NPT as a nonnuclear weapon state and place IAEA safeguards on all its nuclear activities. Nine days later, at the CIS summit in Minsk, Ukraine agreed that nuclear weapons on its soil were under the joint command of the Combined Strategic Forces Command, and it promised to dismantle the strategic nuclear weapons by the end of 1994. This timetable too had been dictated by the Russian military.[7]

For Ukraine, December marked the first, heady days of independence.[8] Unlike the isolation of 1917–20, immediate and widespread international recognition greeted Ukraine in 1991. This romantic period was the culmination of the independence movement, which had been led by poets and intellectuals such as Dmytro Pavlychko, Bogdan Horyn, Ivan Drach, and Vyacheslav Chornovil (all of whom became influential Rada members). Unfortunately, the personal attributes that permitted these men to overcome years of official repression were not the ones best suited to address the formidable domestic and international challenges ahead.

REMOVAL OF THE TACTICAL NUCLEAR WEAPONS

Moscow began withdrawing the estimated four thousand tactical nuclear weapons from Ukraine immediately after the Minsk summit. By February 23, 1992, the first group of weapons had been removed from Ukraine. The Russian military's schedule provided for a hiatus of a few weeks before the next round of withdrawals would start. During this break, Kravchuk announced, on March 12, that he would "suspend" further withdrawals.[9] As a strictly legal matter, Kiev was within its rights. The Alma Ata Agreement on Joint Measures on Nuclear Arms had never been ratified by the Rada and therefore was never binding on Ukraine.[10] Somewhat inconsistently, Kiev alleged that Moscow was not living up to its commitments under the terms of the agreement because the withdrawal and destruction of weapons were not being jointly monitored, leaving Kiev with doubts over whether they were actually being destroyed. (In fact, a backlog at the dismantlement centers had caused delays.)[11] Ukrainian officials feared that if left undestroyed, these weapons might one day be used against Ukraine.

Kravchuk's announcement immediately preceded the March 20 meeting of CIS members, which Kiev was hosting; the timing may have been designed to gain negotiating leverage with Moscow on other issues, such as the fate of the Black Sea Fleet and the resumption of oil and gas supplies. (Ukraine depended on Russia for 90 percent of its natural gas and 50 percent of its oil.) The two countries were unable to resolve the nuclear dispute at the CIS summit. According to Kravchuk, "[Dismantlement] must be done so that the shipment of nuclear weapons does not strengthen one country and weaken another."[12]

Domestic politics, driven by fear and mistrust of Russia, was the overriding motive behind Kravchuk's suspension announcement. On February 6, Kravchuk had announced in Kiev that half of the tactical nuclear weapons in Ukraine had already been withdrawn. This alerted the Rada, whose more nationalist members started openly criticizing the withdrawal schedules for the tactical nuclear weapons (July 1, 1992) and the strategic nuclear warheads (December 31, 1994), as well as questioning the government's competence in handling national security affairs.

This coincided with the Rada's growing perception that Kravchuk had blundered badly at the December summits. In the first few months of independence, members of parliament had conducted what amounted to a seminar on nuclear weapons and foreign policy. In December 1991, the Rada had set up a commission to study the implications for Ukraine of the Strategic Arms Reduction Treaty (START). From meetings with military and scientific experts, the parliamentarians gradually understood that Kravchuk had simply handed the tactical nuclear weapons to Russia and received nothing in return.

Other motives may also have prompted Kravchuk's action. By this time, Kiev had started to perceive that international, especially American, interest in Ukraine was almost wholly confined to nuclear matters; once these weapons were returned, Ukraine feared that it would find itself isolated and alone in a dangerous part of the world. Second, Kiev began to realize that Moscow was the true beneficiary of Ukraine's denuclearization, both in terms of receiving the withdrawn weapons and their nuclear material and in terms of collecting U.S. dismantlement assistance ($400 million pledged in 1991, with promises of more to come). Ukraine might have thought that holding up the removal of the tactical nuclear weapons would guarantee it a share of the American aid.

Coincidentally, Kravchuk's key arms control advisers—National Security Adviser Anton Buteiko and, at the Foreign Ministry, Boris Tarasiuk and Constantine Hryshchenko—were also having second thoughts about the country's denuclearization. It had become clearer with time that the Russians had taken advantage of the Ukrainians' inexperience at the two December summits. In particular, Kiev had agreed to return the tactical nuclear weapons without any compensation for the highly enriched uranium (HEU) in each device. Now, however, Kiev demanded compensation for returning the tactical nuclear weapons to Russia. This disorganized approach to national security matters continued to plague Kiev throughout 1992 and 1993 and seriously harmed its credibility abroad, especially in the nuclear sphere.[13]

The background against which these complaints and reservations were aired was Moscow's increasingly heavy-handed approach to dealing with the newly independent states and with Ukraine in particular. Negotiations between Moscow and Kiev over the fate of the Black Sea Fleet (which by this time had clearly deteriorated to a coastal fleet) were becoming more contentious. Russia was also locked in a fierce debate with Ukraine (and the other republics) over how to divide the assets of the former USSR. This issue was particularly important to Ukraine, which wanted to sell these assets for hard currency and use the buildings to establish overseas embassies.[14]

A combination of pressure from Washington and concessions from Moscow persuaded Kravchuk to change his mind. In early April 1992,

Secretary of State James Baker told Ukraine that U.S. aid could be reduced and a planned Bush-Kravchuk meeting canceled if Kiev did not fulfill its commitment to return the tactical nuclear weapons to Russia. A week later, Kravchuk and Yeltsin finalized arrangements for Kiev's monitoring the removal and dismantlement of the tactical nuclear weapons, and withdrawal officially resumed.[15] Ukraine and Russia also signed agreements on servicing strategic nuclear missiles and redeploying warheads from Ukraine to Russia. These agreements stated that the export of warheads for servicing and repair would be carried out without hindrance and would not be subject to customs inspection. They did not mention any compensation for the fissile material in the warheads.

The Ukrainian leader arrived in Washington in early May believing that the July 1 removal date still held.[16] However, the last train carrying tactical nuclear weapons from Ukraine crossed the border into Russia at 1:30 in the morning on May 6. A few hours later, Marshall Evgeny Shaposhnikov, commander-in-chief of the CIS Joint Armed Forces, announced in Moscow that the last tactical nuclear weapons had been removed from Ukraine.[17] Russia had clearly timed the pullout and subsequent announcement to embarrass Kravchuk on his first official visit to the United States.

Ukraine did not disappoint. For the better part of May 6, confusion reigned in Kiev. Initially, both Kravchuk in Washington and his defense minister, Constantine Morozov, who had remained in Kiev, publicly discounted the Moscow report. After hearing the announcement, Morozov had tried to contact Kravchuk in Washington, reaching him only with the help of the State and Defense Departments. When the president and the defense minister finally spoke, Morozov could not confirm the accuracy of the news report. Kravchuk was furious with his advisers. The Foreign Ministry blamed the Defense Ministry for not informing it until late in the evening on May 6 that all the tactical nuclear weapons had left the country.[18] In an attempt to save face, Kravchuk announced before the National Press Club the following day that the accelerated withdrawal had been a *joint* decision by Ukraine and Russia.[19]

Putting aside the Keystone Kops aspects of this incident, the question remains as to how Russia could have removed the remaining tactical nuclear weapons from Ukraine so quickly after the Yeltsin-Kravchuk agreement in mid-April. If Russia had taken almost two months to remove just over half of the tactical nuclear weapons in Ukraine, how could it have removed the remainder in only three weeks?

The answer is that Russia had simply ignored Kravchuk's March 12 suspension order and had started the second round of withdrawals in late March as originally scheduled. Even as Yeltsin and Kravchuk negotiated the details on resuming withdrawals, the Russian military was spiriting the weapons out of the country. The Ukrainian military, which had only the most rudimentary ability to monitor the withdrawal, was kept in the dark until it went out in the field on May 6 to confirm Shaposhnikov's announcement.

Russia had succeeded in humiliating Ukraine but in the process had been too clever by half. Its gambit was both pointless and counterproductive. It was pointless because Ukraine had reconciled itself in December, and again in April, to the removal of the tactical nuclear weapons; Moscow had even acquiesced to having Ukrainian arms experts monitor the dismantlement of the weapons. Whether the tactical nuclear weapons were removed in May, in June, or by July 1 was immaterial; Russia was in complete control of the process. There was no chance that Kiev would block their removal. The move was counterproductive because it made the Ukrainian leadership much more wary of dealing with Russia. In addition, the episode made Washington more respectful of Ukrainian complaints of Moscow's arrogance and more sensitive to Kiev's national security anxieties. And it made the removal of the strategic nuclear warheads from Ukraine much more difficult.

THE LISBON PROTOCOL

The demise of the Soviet Union had thrown a legal monkey wrench into the strategic arms reduction talks between Moscow and Washington. Russia, not to mention Ukraine, Kazakhstan, and Belarus, had not been a signatory to START. For purposes of START, the question was, who under international law succeeded to the international rights and duties of the USSR—Russia alone, all of the former republics, or only those republics on which strategic nuclear weapons were based?

In late April 1992, the United States formally accepted that Russia, Ukraine, Kazakhstan, and Belarus succeeded the USSR for START purposes. Washington drafted a protocol to START recognizing this new situation. Article 5 of the protocol obligated Ukraine, Kazakhstan, and Belarus to join the NPT as nonnuclear weapon states "in the shortest possible time." Ukraine had not wanted the protocol to address the issue of its adherence to the NPT, preferring to take up the issue separately. But Washington insisted that this obligation be incorporated into the protocol's text. Fortunately for the United States, obtaining Kravchuk's agreement to these terms was eased because the document formally recognized Ukraine as one of the successors to the USSR. In addition to the status this conferred, it allowed Kiev to make a stronger claim for its fair share of the former Soviet Union's assets, especially its buildings and properties overseas.[20]

Even if the protocol now ensured that the four states were legal successors to the Soviet Union for START purposes, the United States still fell short of its goal of having all of the Soviet Union's nuclear arsenal concentrated in Russia. Although the 130 SS-19 intercontinental ballistic missiles (ICBMs) in Ukraine were expected to be eliminated under START, the treaty did not require the dismantlement of the 46 more modern SS-24 missiles or the 564 air-launched cruise missiles (ALCMs).[21] Pursuant to the overriding U.S. objective of having Russia as sole nuclear heir, the United States negotiated, with Ukraine, Kazakhstan, and Belarus, "side letters" that required these countries to return *all* the nuclear weapons on their territories to Russia. During Kravchuk's visit in May, the Ukrainian leader exchanged with President Bush two letters that finalized the language of the protocol and side letter. To minimize possible domestic recriminations, Kravchuk also insisted that the protocol be subject to the Rada's ratification.[22]

The four former Soviet republics and the United States were scheduled to meet in Lisbon on May 23 to officially sign what became known as the Lisbon Protocol; all three side letters had already been initialed. Washington had worked hard to choreograph the event and thought it had firm commitments from all the actors. But in the days leading up to Lisbon, Ukraine had second thoughts, and Foreign Minister Anatoly Zlenko reopened a debate with Baker over the language of both the protocol and the side letter.

One area of disagreement concerned the timetable for denuclearization, specifically when Ukraine would return all the nuclear weapons to Russia and join the NPT as a nonnuclear weapon state. Washington tried to include language from the December 1991 Minsk summit declaration that had stipulated a December 31, 1994, deadline for the removal of strategic nuclear weapons from Ukraine. Kiev refused. Kravchuk wanted as indefinite a commitment as possible. He did not trust Moscow and saw retention of the strategic nuclear weapons as a hedge against future Russian pressure and interference. Ukrainian officials justified their refusal to the Americans by citing their experience with Russia over the tactical nuclear weapons.[23]

At the same time, Baker had to contend with Moscow, which wanted iron-clad assurances on Ukraine's denuclearization. The protocol did not set a specific date for START ratification, a potential loophole that bothered Moscow. As the deadline for signing the protocol neared, an exasperated Secretary of State Baker finally informed Zlenko that Ukraine had made a commitment and that the United States was going ahead on that basis. He told Zlenko he was keeping the protocol's original language on NPT membership: Ukraine, Kazakhstan, and Belarus would join "in the shortest possible time." Regarding the protocol's submission to the Rada, Baker pointedly reminded his Ukrainian counterpart that he did not want any delay. Confronted with an annoyed and forceful U.S. secretary, Zlenko caved in, accepted the suggested language, and signed the protocol.

The haggling over the final wording of the Lisbon Protocol and side letter should not obscure their significance. Despite rising enmity between Kiev and Moscow, Ukraine had formally committed itself to becoming a nonnuclear weapon state. The United States had worked long and hard to reach this point. It had cajoled and coerced Ukraine to agree to remove all the nuclear warheads on its soil and accede to the NPT. All that remained was for the Rada to bless the handiwork. The United States thought that Kravchuk could win Rada approval for the Lisbon documents; in fact, Kravchuk had assured the Americans of the Rada's cooperation. The Rada had other ideas.

AFTER LISBON

The first sign that the Rada might be unwilling to play its designated role was when Kravchuk submitted a military doctrine for the Rada's consideration in late summer. In a surprising fit of independence, the Rada refused to pass it, instead remanding the document to committee for further study. Given Russia's behavior, Rada members questioned the wisdom of endorsing the statement "Ukraine does not consider any state its adversary." The Rada also considered revising the country's previous pledge not to accept, produce, or acquire nuclear weapons. The parliament's handling of the country's military doctrine was a watershed of sorts. The Rada was now convinced that it had real power that could be exerted to counter that of the executive branch.

If Kravchuk had miscalculated, the United States was not without fault either. In June, Presidents Bush and Yeltsin had agreed on the outline of an arms reduction agreement to follow START. Although the START II draft did not mention Ukraine, Belarus, or Kazakhstan (it was solely between the United States and Russia), not consulting with Kiev in advance particularly annoyed Ukrainian legislators. More important, Washington had relaxed the pressure on all the newly independent states after June 1992. The culprit was U.S. domestic politics. In July, Baker and his top aides left the State Department for the White House to help direct President Bush's reelection campaign. This disrupted continuity, and foreign policy suffered further from the reluctance of the White House to highlight international affairs, with the president's Democratic challenger focusing attention on domestic problems.[24]

SECURITY ASSURANCES AND FINANCIAL COMPENSATION

By summer 1992, the basic outlines of Ukraine's concerns were increasingly visible. Ukrainian officials remained committed to becoming a nonnuclear state, but they emphasized that certain conditions needed to be satisfied before Kiev would ratify START, the Lisbon Protocol and side letter, and the NPT. These conditions centered on national security and financial assistance.

National Security Considerations.   Virtually from the moment of independence, the gravest external threat to Ukraine's security derived from Russia's inability to reconcile itself to the idea of a sovereign Ukraine. According to one historian, the "defining characteristic" of Russia's relations with Ukraine through history has been "the Russian assumption that Ukraine is geographically and culturally an indivisible part of Russia."[25] With the exceptions of Yelena Bonner and Yuri Afanasev, no Russian democrat ever publicly conceded that Ukraine was an independent country.[26]

A major dispute arose over Crimea, a Black Sea peninsula that Khrushchev had transferred from Russia to Ukraine in 1954. Russian nationalists had never reconciled themselves to this loss.[27] Transforming this disagreement into a possible military crisis was the fact that the Crimean city of Sevastopol was home port to the 350-vessel Black Sea Fleet, to which both Kiev and Moscow laid claim. For Russia, the fleet was an emblem of vanished superpower status. For Ukraine, it was related to the disputed status of Crimea and thus epitomized the country's independence and sovereignty. The importance of these competing symbols far outweighed the fleet's military value, since neither party was able financially to maintain and operate it.

On July 9, 1993, the Russian parliament unanimously resolved that Sevastopol legally belonged to Russia. Yeltsin immediately denounced the resolution.[28] The month before, Yeltsin and Kravchuk had tried to put the disposition of the Black Sea Fleet behind them by deferring a final division of the fleet until the end of 1995; it would operate under joint Russian-Ukrainian command in the interim.[29] The parliament's action signaled to both Yeltsin and Ukraine that Russia's irredentist claims could not be dismissed so easily.

Kiev's insecurities over Crimea and the Black Sea Fleet increased when viewed against the larger pattern of Russian behavior in the "near abroad" (*blizhnee zarubezh'e*). The Russian military's interferences with the lawful governments of Moldova, Georgia, and Tajikistan were only a few of the ways Moscow was flexing its muscles in areas formerly part of the Soviet Union.[30] In February 1993, Yeltsin had first publicly raised the possibility of Russia's playing a larger role in settling regional disputes, by using military force if necessary, in places where Moscow had a "special responsibility."[31] Seven months later, Foreign Minister Andrei Kozyrev addressed the UN General Assembly. Kozyrev requested not only international approval for Russian intervention in the former Soviet republics but also international financial assistance to support such action. Offering cold comfort to Kiev, he advised that Ukraine should not join the "Partnership for Peace" program, a plan of the North Atlantic Treaty Organization (NATO) to gradually expand its membership eastward. He noted: "We would not like NATO to protect Ukraine from Russia. We ourselves can defend Ukraine from anyone."[32]

For Ukraine, Russia's regional military interventions and harsh rhetoric raised the specter that it might be reabsorbed in a replay of 1920–22. Ukraine's overwhelming energy dependence on Russia made it particularly vulnerable. Russia raised oil and gas prices 170 times during 1992 and 1993 and threatened to cut off fuel supplies over half a dozen times. Contributing to Ukraine's poor credibility with the international community were Russian disinformation efforts designed to portray Kiev as foolish, untrustworthy, or malevolent.[33]

That Ukraine did not belong to any security alliance magnified its sense of isolation. Kiev decided not to join the CIS security arrangement formed in May 1992 at Tashkent. Russian security guarantees at the January 1993 meeting between Yeltsin and Kravchuk were unsatisfactory because they remained in force only as long as Ukraine was a member of CIS.[34] President Kravchuk's February 1993 proposal for a security system that extended from the Baltics to the Black Sea and that excluded Russia generated a tepid response.[35] With the dissolution of the CIS Joint Military High Command in June 1993, all nuclear weapons officially came under the command of Russia's Strategic Rocket Forces. A few days later, Yeltsin announced Moscow's willingness to extend security guarantees to Kiev before ratification of START and the NPT, with the guarantees taking effect after ratification of both treaties.[36] This too hardly assuaged Ukraine's security concerns.

Finally, Ukraine was not immediately eligible to join the U.S. Partnership for Peace program. (Only Poland, Hungary, and the Czech and Slovak republics were initially invited to join.) Moreover, the Clinton administration's foreign policy setbacks in Somalia and Haiti, and especially its vacillation in Bosnia in the face of Serb aggression, did nothing to reassure Kiev that Washington would forcefully defend Ukrainian security interests.

In this inhospitable environment, Ukraine's primary security challenge was preserving its independence from Russian aggrandizement. Many Ukrainian officials saw nuclear weapons as the means to fortify the country's fragile independence, reduce Russian economic and political interference in its domestic affairs, gain international respect, and deter any possible Russian military aggression. In short, a nuclear prescription could cure Moscow's "imperial disease." Ukraine would part with its nuclear inheritance only if it could receive at least the same measure of security through other means.

Compensation.   The gravest internal threat to Ukraine's security derived from its inability to create an economically viable state. Although financial compensation could not, by itself, reverse wholesale economic mismanagement, Kiev saw the aid as a quick and easy fix—to bolster the government's sagging popularity, to quiet Rada opposition, and to create jobs. But compensation turned out to be neither quick nor easy.

The compensation issue actually involved two discrete categories that were usually lumped together: the cost Kiev would bear in dismantling the strategic nuclear weapons and transporting the warheads back to Russia and the market value it would forgo from the fissile material (U-235 and plutonium) they contained. Ukraine was slow to understand the economics of each; over time the compensation issue was manipulated by Rada lawmakers as it became a bellwether of relations with Moscow and Washington.

Ukraine was also slow to realize the potential windfall it could reap from the nuclear weapons on its territory. Caught up in the euphoria and romance of independence in late 1991, burdened by its own inexperience, enjoined by the United States and others to fulfill its pledges to become a nonnuclear state, Kiev did not insist in the Alma Ata Agreement on Joint Measures on Nuclear Arms on receiving any compensation from Russia for returning the tactical nuclear weapons. As Kiev later realized its error, its demand for compensation for the HEU in the tactical nuclear weapons became a major source of friction with Moscow.

Whatever compensation figure was eventually decided on, it was understood by all participants that the bulk of the funds would come from the United States, either directly or indirectly. In late 1991, the U.S. Congress passed the Soviet Nuclear Threat Reduction Act, also known as the Nunn-Lugar Act after its two Senate champions. This legislation authorized the Defense Department to transfer $400 million from other programs to assist the safe dismantlement and storage of nuclear weapons and materials in the former Soviet Union (i.e., Russia); Congress allocated additional funds in 1992 and 1993.[37] Depending on Ukraine's willingness to return the nuclear weapons to Russia, it would receive some of these U.S. funds.

Indirectly, Ukraine would also receive U.S. money that was channeled through Russia. In February 1993, Russia agreed to blend down five hundred metric tons of HEU from dismantled nuclear warheads and sell the resulting low-enriched uranium (LEU) to the United States for use in commercial nuclear power reactors.[38] Under the contract, which runs for twenty years, Washington is expected to pay Moscow an estimated $11 billion.[39]

The Defense Department originally came up with the idea of tying the purchase of Russian HEU to the condition that Moscow first work out bilateral compensation agreements with all three republics for the HEU in the nuclear warheads that would be returned. Not a penny would go to Russia before these deals were finalized.[40] This would provide an incentive for Moscow to negotiate quickly and in good faith. This linkage had actually been reinforced in November 1992 by the Russian Supreme Soviet's conditional ratification of START I, which called for the prior implementation of denuclearization agreements with Ukraine, Belarus, and Kazakhstan.

Complicating these negotiations was uncertainty over the precise value of the HEU and plutonium in the warheads. Washington had consistently told Kiev that plutonium had a negative value; there was no lawful international market for the material, and it was expensive to handle and store safely. The HEU, on the other hand, could be blended down and used in civilian nuclear power reactors.[41] How much HEU the nuclear warheads might contain was unclear to Ukraine, and Moscow was unwilling to divulge such information for fear of revealing weapon design secrets.

A key in accelerating Ukraine's nuclear learning was the appointment of Leonid Kuchma as prime minister in October 1992. Kuchma had trained as a mechanical engineer and had spent most of his working life at the world's largest rocket and missile production plant at Dnepropetrovsk. His technical and defense expertise gave him credibility with Kravchuk and other cabinet officials. The new prime minister viewed nuclear weapons not as military assets but as economic assets that were valuable bargaining chips with the United States, Russia, and the West. Kuchma contended that the $175 million offered by the United States for returning the nuclear warheads was a paltry sum. After Kuchma entered the cabinet, Kiev became a much tougher and more astute negotiator.

Over time, compensation demands escalated, with little or no regard for economic costs and benefits. For many Ukrainian officials, these claims became a way to raise high the Ukrainian trident to signal one's patriotism.[42] For others, compensation claims became a pretext for opposing the return of the nuclear warheads at any price.

At no point did anyone in the Ukrainian government undertake a systematic, rigorous analysis of the dismantlement costs, transportation expenses, and market value of the HEU in the nuclear warheads. At best, there were only rudimentary back-of-the-envelope calculations, which helped to explain why official Ukrainian compensation figures changed so frequently. For the latter part of 1993, Foreign Minister Zlenko settled on $2.8 billion, which apparently included the costs of building a nuclear warhead dismantlement facility in Ukraine. Even the meaning of "dismantlement" changed over time as the word came to be associated in Ukrainian eyes with environmental cleanup and new jobs for displaced personnel.

Command and Control.   To the extent that Ukraine could assert authority over the nuclear weapons stationed on its territory, it strengthened its bargaining leverage in negotiations over security assurances and financial compensation. Yet effective command and control meant that Kiev could maintain and launch these weapons if necessary.[43]

The December 1991 Minsk summit attempted to head off any future disputes over command and control of the nuclear arsenal. Russia, Ukraine, Kazakhstan, and Belarus established a telephone link to prevent any of these parties from launching nuclear weapons without the consent of the other three. Kravchuk told the news agency TASS after the summit that a device would be added to his office that would "be able, when necessary, to block the nuclear button." He added, "This means that it will be impossible to launch a missile from any point in the former Union without a joint decision by us."[44] In reality, Kravchuk had no such power. This consultative arrangement, ostensibly under CIS auspices, was a fig leaf designed to make preservation of Russian control over the nuclear stockpile politically palatable. Moscow alone retained operational control: the ability to launch these missiles anytime it wanted.

The control issue resurfaced in March 1992 when Kiev's aggravation over the removal of the tactical nuclear weapons to Russia spurred Kravchuk to "suspend" Moscow's withdrawal. On April 5, Kravchuk issued a decree that placed all military forces in Ukraine under the Ukrainian Ministry of Defense.[45] This permitted Kiev to "administer" the strategic nuclear forces in Ukraine, which meant that it was responsible for staff appointments and promotions, financing, social questions, and administration of the national oath.

In June 1992, Ukraine institutionalized this administrative control by creating within the Defense Ministry the Center for the Administrative Command and Control of the Troops of the Strategic Nuclear Forces.[46] In November 1992, Ukraine claimed legal ownership of the nuclear warheads and their delivery vehicles but denied that this transformed it into a nuclear weapon state.[47] In June 1993, Prime Minister Kuchma and Rada member Dmytro Pavlychko recommended that Kiev assume operational control of some nuclear weapons.[48] The next month, the Rada passed the "Fundamental Principles of Ukraine's Foreign Policy," which claimed for Ukraine temporary ownership of all nuclear weapons on its territory. Kravchuk supported it: "My feeling is that it should be set down that Ukraine must be the owner of nuclear weapons on its territory pending their destruction."[49]

The fear among those countries that wanted to prevent an independent Ukrainian nuclear force was that administrative control would lead over time to operational control—the ability to launch these weapons against an adversary on command. Russian experts estimated that Ukraine could break the launch control security systems within nine months.[50] U.S. intelligence agencies thought that Ukraine had the expertise and technical competence to assert operational control over nuclear weapons within twelve to eighteen months.[51]

In addition, Moscow used Kiev's claims of controlling the nuclear weapons to excite international pressure for Ukraine's denuclearization. It portrayed Ukraine as a careless nuclear custodian whose irresponsibility might result in the sale of some of these weapons to third parties (such as the Palestine Liberation Organization) or whose inexperience would cause a nuclear disaster.[52] Paradoxically, the more attention that was paid to Russian fears, the more leverage Ukraine gained for stronger security assurances and a larger financial compensation package.

THE CLINTON ADMINISTRATION CHANGES TACTICS

The Clinton administration initially continued the Bush administration's approach toward Ukraine: diplomatic pressure and isolation until Kiev fulfilled its previous disarmament pledges. This policy also convinced Kiev that Washington would turn its back on Ukraine as soon as Ukraine gave up the nuclear weapons. Foreign Minister Zlenko received a stern message during his March 1993 visit to Washington: Prime Minister Kuchma would "not necessarily" be able to meet with Clinton during his anticipated May visit.[53] The price of a long-term relationship with the United States, Clinton administration officials told Kiev, was signing START I and the NPT. The Russians also continued their pressure on Ukraine at this time by publicly claiming that Kiev was trying to gain operational control over the weapons on its territory.[54] For a Ukraine buffeted at home by a dismal economy and battered abroad by Russia, the Clinton administration's policy reinforced its already acute anxiety. Kiev hardened its resolve.

Concerned by the direction in which developments in Ukraine were headed, the Clinton administration decided in mid-April to rethink its policy. The National Security Council (NSC) chaired an interagency policy review, which concluded that the Clinton administration should actively and closely work with Ukraine to show that Kiev's interests in the security area lay in denuclearization and greater integration with the United States, Western Europe, and NATO (a policy the Pentagon had urged eighteen months earlier). In addition, the NSC working group recommended the "early deactivation" of the SS-19s, SS-24s, and ALCMs in Ukraine and advised Washington's greater engagement with Kiev on a host of political, economic, and military issues.[55] In early May, Strobe Talbott, ambassador to the CIS, visited Kiev to brief Ukrainian officials on the new policy and seek a commitment on deactivation.[56]

To implement this policy shift, the State Department entered into discussions with Ukraine concerning "three pillars": dismantlement assistance, economic aid, and security assurances. The Defense Department complemented this approach by strengthening military-to-military ties, suggesting confidence-building measures between Moscow and Kiev, drafting numerous agreements that expressed U.S. support for Ukraine's independence, and improving the quality of Ukraine's conventional forces to downgrade the importance of nuclear weapons and partially remedy the military imbalance with Russia.[57]

DISMANTLING THE SS-19S

Secretary of Defense Les Aspin visited Kiev in June 1993 to lend further support to this new policy. Aspin proposed that the nuclear missiles in Ukraine be deactivated and the warheads stored in Ukraine under international supervision. Eventually, the warheads would be withdrawn to Russia, and Ukraine would be compensated for the value of the uranium. Unfortunately, Aspin had not cleared the idea with his Russian counterparts, who opposed Washington's new "soft" line with Ukraine and thought this idea an American ploy to gain access to weapon design secrets.[58]

Ukrainian officials welcomed the Aspin plan, which focused greater attention on the fate of the SS-19s. Earlier, the United States and Russia had both urged Ukraine to deactivate the 130 SS-19s and the 46 SS-24s, just as Washington and Moscow were doing with some of their strategic systems. Aspin this time found Kiev receptive, at least as far as the SS-19s were concerned. The SS-19, code-named "Stiletto," could launch six warheads, each with an explosive yield of five hundred kilotons, a distance of ten thousand kilometers to targets in the United States. These missiles used a highly toxic liquid heptyl fuel, which presented certain maintenance hazards.[59] By mid-1993, they were either approaching or had already exceeded the end of their service life. In June, Kravchuk had stated that 36 SS-19s needed to be dismantled within the next few months because their fuel posed a serious environmental danger. Ukrainian officials, especially the minister of the environment, Yuri Kostenko, were very receptive to these arguments. On July 15, Ukraine began to deactivate these missiles, even before Defense Ministers Morozov and Aspin signed a memorandum of understanding under which Washington pledged $175 million to Ukraine for dismantlement assistance.[60] The entire SS-19 dismantlement effort was set to be completed by the end of 1995.

Curiously, Kiev made the decision to deactivate these missiles whether START was ratified or not. The issue was not submitted to the Rada for approval, and even ardent pronuclear nationalists did not raise a fuss.

THE MASSANDRA SUMMIT

All of the outstanding issues that had occupied Kiev and Moscow for the previous two years—security, compensation, nuclear weapons, command and control, and status—came to a head in early September at a hunting lodge built by Joseph Stalin in Massandra, a small town outside the Crimean resort of Yalta. Delegations from Ukraine and Russia met there all day on Friday, September 3, 1993. The negotiations were noisy, tense, and at times acrimonious. Further complicating matters was the fact that the parties had a lot of ground to cover in a very short period of time. This undoubtedly contributed to much of the subsequent confusion, controversy, and mutual recriminations.

The initial press accounts stated that Ukraine had decided to surrender two symbols of the country's sovereignty: its claim to the Black Sea Fleet and the remaining nuclear weapons on its territory. In exchange, Russia would write off Kiev's $2.5-billion oil and gas debt and provide fuel rods for Ukraine's nuclear power plants. If a deal along these lines was struck—and it appears that one was, at least in principle—it fell apart soon after the summit amid accusations by both sides of bad faith and double-dealing.[61]

What is clear was that the Russians surprised the Ukrainians at Massandra by their tough negotiating. Yeltsin was under pressure at home (his running feud with suspended Vice President Alexander Rutskoi, legislative leader Ruslan Khasbulatov, and the Russian parliament would lead him to disband the legislature the following month), and he wanted to use Massandra to bolster his domestic standing. Russian gloating after the summit made it politically more awkward for Kravchuk to sell the deal at home, where he was already besieged by ongoing domestic economic and political crises.

A major item on the agenda was the fate of the Black Sea Fleet. The Russians recommended that Ukraine immediately hand over its share of the fleet in return for debt forgiveness. The next day, Yeltsin recounted this "suggestion" for Moscow television: "Why don't you give up your part of the Black Sea Fleet, so there will be a Russian Black Sea Fleet, and we will cancel the debts."[62] According to Ukrainian officials, Yeltsin and Defense Minister Pavel Grachev had presented an ultimatum. They told Ukraine that it had to accept the deal or else Russia would cut off all oil and gas supplies—a highly credible threat, since Moscow had twice suspended such supplies the previous month. Moreover, unless Kiev acquiesced, Moscow would forcibly seize the fleet. Grachev taunted that Ukraine could then declare war on Russia if it wanted.[63]

As confusing as the Black Sea Fleet issue was, the competing interpretations of the nuclear issue were even more baffling.[64] Press reports of a deal that would rid Ukraine of all its nuclear weapons within two years grabbed international attention. Again, according to Yeltsin's interpretation of events, "There was also, I would say, a breakthrough regarding nuclear arms . . . we have agreed on compensation in the form of unenriched uranium [*sic*] in the quantity that they transfer to us as nuclear warheads."[65]

The written agreement to remove all strategic nuclear warheads from Ukraine was leaked to the press the following week. In its entirety, it read: "The prime minister of Ukraine and the chairman of the Council of Ministers of the Russian Federation agree that after ratification of the START I Treaty by the Ukrainian Supreme Council, the Ukrainian Government will provide for, no later than twenty-four months from the date of ratification, the withdrawal of all nuclear warheads of the strategic nuclear forces deployed in Ukraine to the Russian Federation for dismantling and destruction."[66] The two prime ministers, Leonid Kuchma and Viktor Chernomyrdin, initialed the document. However, at some point, the text was altered. The word "all" was struck out, and the phrase "subject to the treaty" was added after "strategic nuclear forces deployed in Ukraine." These emendations limited Ukraine's arms control obligations to the provisions of START I, which did not require dismantlement of the SS-19s (which Kiev was dismantling in any case) and, more important, did not require dismantlement of the more modern SS-24s, which Ukraine wanted to retain.

President Kravchuk's national security adviser, Anton Buteiko, made these revisions. The Russians had drafted this document, as they had all the documents at the summit. After both prime ministers had signed the document, Buteiko read it and immediately realized its implications. According to one source, he then made his alterations in the presence of the Russians.[67] Because of their inexperience, however, the Ukrainians never had these changes formally initialed by both parties. The Russians subsequently insisted on adhering to the original, unamended text. On Saturday, back in Moscow, an adamant Yeltsin declared: "All documents concerning this problem were signed yesterday. We consider the affair closed. For us, there is nothing left to clarify."[68] Yet on Monday, September 6, Yeltsin disavowed this agreement because Kravchuk had "reneged" on his part of the deal by saying back in Kiev that he would submit the agreement to the Rada for approval.[69]

The two sides at Massandra had also reached an agreement, of sorts, on compensation for the tactical nuclear weapons that had already exited Ukraine the previous year. Prime Ministers Chernomyrdin and Kuchma verbally agreed that Ukraine should receive compensation for the fissile material in the tactical nuclear weapons, with the exact amount to be determined later by a bilateral commission. This deal was never reduced to writing, in yet another Ukrainian snafu. In any event, this agreement was withdrawn by the Russians at the last minute when Yeltsin nixed the idea.[70] There was no need to give the Ukrainians one kopeck for these weapons, Yeltsin argued. "We have already destroyed them and we did not have such a compensation agreement in the past."[71]

Despite severe criticism in Ukraine of Kravchuk's performance at Massandra (some Rada members called him a traitor and demanded his impeachment), the proposed deal had much to commend it. As Kravchuk himself contended, Ukraine had to be realistic. Kiev's dire economic circumstances meant that it could not afford to operate the Black Sea Fleet. The majority of the fleet's officers were waiting to hoist the Russian Navy's flag of St. Andrew, over three-quarters of Crimea's population were ethnically Russian, and Ukraine could not hope to win a conflict with Russia over the fleet. In fact, a dispute with Moscow could result in losing both the fleet and the peninsula. What the Ukrainian leader could not admit, though, was that his poor bargaining position was a direct result of the misguided economic and political policies he had adopted. According to one knowledgeable observer, the Massandra summit "brought home very forcefully the perils of not putting one's own house in order, postponing economic reform, and simply muddling through," and "exposed Ukraine's weaknesses, isolation, and lack of options."[72]

The Massandra summit may have been a fiasco, but it was not a total failure. It brought together a number of ideas that had been floated in bilateral negotiations during the previous months. For the first time, senior Russian officials had agreed, in principle, to compensate Ukraine for the tactical nuclear weapons that had been removed the previous year. The summit moved the parties closer to the agreement that they would reach four months later, this time with help from the United States.

THE CHRISTOPHER VISIT AND "PARTIAL" START RATIFICATION

U.S. Secretary of State Warren Christopher traveled to Kiev in late October 1993 to reinvigorate the denuclearization process. His visit found Ukraine's turbulent political and economic conditions worse than usual. The coup attempt against Yeltsin by Russian antireformers in early October had made the already insecure Ukrainians even more nervous; Rada members warned of the "red-brown" threat to the country (from a communist-fascist coalition in Moscow). Economic conditions in Ukraine were appalling, with the inflation rate running at 90 percent per month.[73] Russia had stopped supplying Ukraine with nuclear fuel; it was also not taking back spent fuel, which was piling up to dangerous levels.[74]

Two trends that had become more pronounced in Ukrainian thinking during the preceding eighteen months impaired the chances for a successful visit by Christopher. First, Kiev was increasingly doubtful whether Russia would ever reconcile itself to Ukraine's independence, regardless of who held the reins of power in Moscow. Second, there was the growing perception that the West, and especially the United States despite the Clinton administration's policy shift, was interested in Ukraine only so long as it retained nuclear weapons. For many Ukrainian officials who had initially wanted to rid the country of nuclear arms, or perhaps saw them as a diplomatic card to trade for the right price, the passage of time had hardened their view that Kiev needed to keep nuclear weapons for its national security.

In Kiev, Christopher discussed U.S. security assurances and compensation for dismantlement.[75] But his larger message was that Washington wanted to broaden the dialogue with Ukraine beyond the nuclear sphere to include economic issues, and he emphasized that this would be the most reliable guarantor of peace.[76] Seemingly mollified, Kravchuk reversed his earlier position and promised to work for Ukraine's total nuclear disarmament.[77] In concrete terms, the two sides signed an umbrella agreement that transferred $175 million for dismantling the SS-19s.[78]

Ukraine was flattered by the high-level attention and welcomed the shift in the bilateral relationship away from purely nuclear matters. Although the United States dismissed Zlenko's request for $2.8 billion in dismantlement assistance, Christopher declared that the Clinton administration would seek another $155 million in economic assistance for Ukraine in fiscal year 1994.[79]

The trip almost accomplished more—and less. According to U.S. participants, Kiev was willing to deactivate the SS-24 ICBMs. In return, it demanded American security assurances, whose content the two sides had been debating for months. In the end, disagreement turned not on the nature of the assurances but on their timing. Ukraine insisted on tying U.S. security assurances to its deactivation pledge, a position that the American embassy in Kiev supported. But Talbott and Lynn Davis, under secretary of state for science and technology, thought that offering assurances at this time would expend a valuable bargaining chip that Washington wanted to retain to induce Kiev's ratification of START, the Lisbon Protocol, and the NPT. The State Department's view prevailed. After Ukrainian Foreign Ministry officials refused to budge, Talbott went over their heads. That evening during a state dinner, he presented Kravchuk with a document outlining an SS-24 deactivation schedule. Zlenko advised his president not to sign it.[80]

Whatever momentum the Christopher visit generated was slowed by events beyond Ukraine's borders. In early November, Russia released a new military doctrine that superseded Leonid Brezhnev's 1982 pledge never to use nuclear weapons first. Under the new formulation, Moscow promised not to use nuclear weapons against any nonnuclear state that was a member of the NPT and was not allied with a nuclear-armed country.[81] As Kiev was quick to point out, this change in Russia's no-first-use doctrine contravened the December 1991 Alma Ata Agreement on Joint Measures on Nuclear Arms. Although this doctrinal change may simply have been a more honest expression of military reality, many interpreted it as an attempt to intimidate Ukraine. Further, a few days later Moscow sounded the alarm that the nuclear weapons in Ukraine were unsafe. In the words of Foreign Minister Andrei Kozyrev, their deterioration "could lead to a tragedy much worse than Chernobyl." Kiev dismissed the charge as Russian "propaganda" intended to discredit it and to alarm the world to pressure Ukraine to denuclearize.[82]

On November 18, eleven months after START I had been submitted to the Rada for consideration, the Ukrainian parliament finally ratified the agreement. However, the Rada imposed seven conditions that needed to be satisfied before the treaty could be implemented.[83] Article 5 of the Lisbon Protocol, which called for Ukraine to join the NPT as soon as possible, was deliberately excluded from consideration, as was any mention of the NPT itself. Kravchuk's May 7, 1992, side letter to President Bush, the only document that obligated Ukraine to eliminate *all* nuclear weapons on its soil by a specific time period (and which was seen by Washington as an integral part of the Lisbon Protocol), was also not ratified. In a reprise of the Massandra summit, one condition called for compensation for the tactical nuclear weapons that had been removed in 1992. Particularly disturbing were the conditions that reaffirmed Ukraine's ownership of the nuclear warheads and its "administrative control" over the nuclear weapons deployed on its territory.

The Rada's action received a hostile reception in the United States, where commentators interpreted it as a repudiation of Kiev's pledge to become a nonnuclear state. The entire episode, from Kravchuk's repeated assurances to the Rada's irresolution, was seen as yet another example of Ukrainian perfidy and unreliability. Indeed, Clinton phoned Kravchuk a few days after the vote to express his displeasure.[84] Given that the separation of powers in Ukraine mirrored that in the United States—the executive branch proposes, but the legislative branch disposes—such criticism seemed a bit sanctimonious, especially coming from a country whose Congress had failed to ratify the SALT II treaty with the Soviet Union in 1979.[85]

Further, the Rada's resolution should not have come as a total surprise. The conditions merely reflected the concerns and anxieties that Rada members (and Ukrainian diplomats) had expressed before about their fragile independence. Kravchuk explained the result by emphasizing the need for security guarantees: "The world's other nuclear powers did not work together with us during the twelve months which preceded the START I agreement. [We] fear the territorial claims that are being expressed in certain nationalist circles in Russia. [The Rada] vote reflects the opinion—which is widely held here—that nuclear weapons are a means of protection against threats to the integrity of Ukrainian territory. . . . You must understand the fears of the Ukrainian people."[86]

In retrospect, it is more accurate to see the Rada's action as the first grudging step toward the country's stated long-term goal of nuclear disarmament. An important precedent had been set for future initiatives to build on. For the first time, the Rada had specifically endorsed dismantling the nuclear weapons on Ukrainian soil. (The Alma Ata agreement eliminating the tactical nuclear weapons from Ukraine had never been put to a vote in the Rada.) Although parliamentarians had reconciled themselves to Kiev's dismantling the SS-19s, again, there had been no legislative sanction.

The November START resolution thus marked the first time the Rada had formally supported eliminating nuclear weapons that it had earlier declared were the property of Ukraine and over which Ukraine exerted administrative control. And although the Rada did not sign the Lisbon documents that would have ensured total denuclearization, its conditional ratification of START included a proportionate reduction in all strategic nuclear weapons, including the SS-24s, that were not covered in the START I limits.[87] In other words, the Rada went beyond the strict letter of the START agreement and endorsed the dismantlement of some of the most modern missiles in Ukraine. Moreover, Ukraine pledged to "gradually rid itself of the nuclear weapons deployed on its territory" as it moved "toward nonnuclear status." The resolution also left open the possibility of eliminating "additional delivery vehicles and warheads in accordance with procedures that may be determined by Ukraine." Given Ukraine's unabated anxieties, the Rada's action was surprising not for refusing to ratify all these arms control agreements but for going as far as it did.

THE JANUARY 1994 TRILATERAL ACCORD

The Rada's resolution had now set down explicit markers on the nuclear issue. During the next two months, Ukrainian, Russian, and American diplomats tried to fill the potholes and smooth the speed bumps on the road to Ukraine's denuclearization.

Annoyed by the Rada's vote, in December the United States decided to redouble its diplomatic efforts. In particular, Washington now played a much more active role in refereeing the ongoing nuclear negotiations between Ukraine and Russia and, more generally, on a range of divisive security issues, such as the Black Sea Fleet and energy supplies.[88] Kravchuk had responded positively to President Clinton's phone call in late November; he replied that he too was unhappy with the Rada's behavior, would resubmit START and the NPT to the parliament, and as an earnest of his goodwill, would begin to deactivate some of the SS-24s.[89] The United States also reviewed with Russia the possibility of retargeting both countries' nuclear arsenals; not coincidentally, this would mean that U.S. missiles were not aimed at Ukraine, a concern Kiev had recently expressed during Christopher's visit.[90] On a more personal level, Washington indicated that President Clinton would not visit Kiev during his scheduled January trip to the region unless there was more progress in the nuclear sphere. In the meantime, Kiev continued to deactivate the SS-19s and began deactivating twenty SS-24 missiles.[91] These concrete steps in turn encouraged both the Russians and the Americans to press ahead.

The influence on Ukraine's thinking of three other factors is more difficult to ascertain. The abysmal economy may have convinced Kravchuk and other Ukrainian officials that denuclearization would bring much-needed Western financial assistance and lessen the country's dependence on Russia. Certainly, Kravchuk, the former Communist Party ideologue, was reluctant to alter the existing mismanaged, inefficient economic system. Despite the hyperinflation that devoured personal savings, Kravchuk had retreated in the fall from the few market reforms that had been implemented, and he moved back toward a Communist-era command economy.[92] One Western observer recorded that Ukraine was staggering under the highest inflation rate of all the former Soviet republics, a currency that had collapsed against both the dollar and the ruble, and a soaring budget deficit, shrinking production, and depressing living standards.[93] The coldest early winter in recent memory, coupled with the rationing of heating fuel and electricity, literally brought home to all Ukrainians the drawbacks of Kiev's current path.

Fishing in these troubled waters was ultranationalist Russian leader Vladimir Zhirinovsky. Zhirinovsky's misnamed Liberal Democratic Party was the leading vote-getter in Russia's December 12, 1993, parliamentary elections, immediately catapulting its leader onto the world stage. Zhirinovsky's previous calls for forcibly defending Russian minorities in the near abroad and, more alarmingly, for reincorporating Ukraine into the Russian Federation now assumed darker significance. For the ever-insecure Ukrainians, the specter of Zhirinovsky as president of Russia convinced them of the urgent need to obtain international security assurances, which could be won only if they surrendered the nuclear weapons.

Third, the uncertain safety of the remaining nuclear warheads may have induced greater flexibility by Ukraine. Russian charges of Ukraine's technical incompetence had been dismissed by Ukraine, but Kiev still might have had real worries over maintaining the force and averting a nuclear accident. Indeed, one of the conditions laid down in the Rada's START resolution had called for continued maintenance of existing strategic systems in Ukraine, maintenance that could be accomplished only with Moscow's assistance.

In the weeks after the Rada vote, Washington became much more directly involved in working with Moscow and Kiev on a denuclearization agreement. During U.S. Vice President Al Gore's meeting in Moscow in mid-December with Russian Prime Minister Viktor Chernomyrdin, Gore suggested that a senior Russian official accompany Deputy Secretary of Defense William Perry, who was also in Moscow, on his trip to Kiev; Chernomyrdin agreed and sent Deputy Foreign Minister Georgi Mamedov. The Kiev meeting helped to get a trilateral process started. Russian and Ukrainian delegations were then invited to Washington on January 3, 1994, to hammer out the details of an agreement. Moscow and Kiev decided on the amount of the HEU in the strategic nuclear warheads and agreed that Ukraine would receive compensation in the form of nuclear fuel rods; the primary hurdle was the cost of dismantling the weapons and shipping the warheads back to Russia, but this too was settled. Concerning the tactical nuclear weapons, Washington suggested a compensation formula that satisfied both parties. By January 5, the three parties had agreed on a draft text of a trilateral agreement and annex, along with a set of six secret letters.[94]

Details of the deal first started to leak out on the European leg of President Clinton's scheduled trip to Russia in early January 1994. On Monday, January 10, Clinton announced in Brussels that the three countries would sign an agreement in Moscow on Friday, January 14, to eliminate the nuclear weapons in Ukraine. Clinton called the deal "a hopeful and historic breakthrough."[95] Yet Ukraine began having second thoughts; reports from Kiev on Tuesday noting official reservations about the agreement, combined with Kravchuk's silence on the agreement, suggested that the deal might not be signed later that week.

Clinton the statesman became Clinton the politician during a planned stopover in Ukraine to bolster Kravchuk and drum up political support for the trilateral agreement. The idea was to present to Ukraine a concrete proposal with real benefits. But the American president's efforts did not immediately translate into Ukrainian support. During their joint press conference before a clutch of Ukrainians on Wednesday evening at Borispol airport, Kravchuk never endorsed the deal and never said that Ukraine would eliminate all its nuclear weapons.[96] In a sign that ratification would not be easy, Kravchuk's office had not invited any Rada members to meet with Clinton.

By Friday, Kravchuk was on board. In Moscow, Clinton, Kravchuk, and Yeltsin signed the Trilateral Agreement and Annex as planned. At a press conference after the signing ceremony, Kravchuk called it a "historic step." Recognizing potential problems with the Rada, he presented the deal as fulfilling the parliament's wishes: "We have been able to implement the provisions of a resolution of the Supreme Soviet about the ratification of the START I Treaty. . . . We have succeeded in complying." He confidently proclaimed, "Parliament will ratify the treaty."

Kravchuk correctly asserted that the Trilateral Agreement addressed many of Ukraine's long-standing concerns over security guarantees, compensation for the material in the nuclear warheads, and financial assistance.[97] The opening language of the agreement tried to assuage Ukraine's insecurity. The three presidents pledged to "deal with one another as full and equal partners" and to ensure that relations among their countries would be "conducted on the basis of respect for the independence, sovereignty, and territorial integrity of each nation." More substantively, the United States and Russia declared their willingness to provide security assurances to Ukraine. Once START I entered into force and Ukraine became a nonnuclear weapon state party to the NPT, Washington and Moscow would reaffirm their respect for Ukraine's territorial integrity, their obligation not to use or threaten military force or economic coercion against Ukraine, their commitment to seek immediate UN Security Council action if Ukraine became subject to a nuclear threat, and their promise not to use nuclear weapons against Ukraine.[98] Britain was prepared to offer the same security assurances under the same conditions. At a January 14 Moscow press conference, Kravchuk conceded that these were "not legally binding guarantees" but merely "political commitments." That these assurances were in a document signed by both Russia and the United States, however, gave them a political symbolism that partially transcended their formal shortcomings.

Financial compensation for both the tactical and the strategic nuclear warheads had also been a sticking point, most recently at the Massandra summit. The phrasing of the Trilateral Agreement tried to solve this problem by blurring the distinction between tactical and strategic nuclear warheads. As compensation for the strategic nuclear warheads, the Annex stipulated that Russia would provide to Ukraine, within ten months, one hundred tons of low-enriched uranium fuel rods for nuclear power stations, which would help alleviate a severe energy shortage. Within this same time period, at least two hundred nuclear warheads from SS-19s and SS-24s would be transferred from Ukraine to Russia for dismantling. Ukrainian representatives would monitor warhead dismantlement. The United States would provide a $60-million "advance payment" to Russia to help cover the expense of transporting and dismantling the strategic warheads and of producing fuel assemblies.[99] All SS-24s would be deactivated within ten months and all warheads transferred from Ukraine to Russia "in the shortest possible time."

Accompanying the Trilateral Agreement and Annex were six secret letters, two each by Kravchuk, Yeltsin, and Clinton. Kravchuk's letters to Yeltsin and Clinton contained Ukraine's promise to ensure the return of all the nuclear warheads on its territory to Russia within three years; the letters also contained a schedule for their removal. Yeltsin's letters to Kravchuk and Clinton discussed the issue of compensation. For the tactical nuclear weapons it had removed in early 1992, Russia promised to compensate Ukraine in the form of debt forgiveness of oil and gas supplies previously shipped from Russia.[100] This formulation was designed to satisfy the concerns of the two countries' respective domestic constituencies, should the compensation agreement become public. Kiev could assert that it had received "payment" for the tactical nuclear weapons, which it had previously claimed as its "material wealth." Moscow could placate nationalist critics by arguing that it was simply writing off the debt for unpaid energy supplies.

Clinton's letters to Kravchuk and Yeltsin simply acknowledged his receipt of their letters. His two letters did not contain any additional U.S. commitments.[101]

THE RADA RATIFIES START

A confidential cable dated January 14, 1994, from Secretary of State Christopher to the U.S. embassies in Moscow and Kiev stated that the Trilateral Agreement provided the basis for a major transformation of Ukrainian-American relations while simultaneously removing a "major irritant" in Russian-Ukrainian relations.[102] But before the accord could achieve either of these goals, it had to be ratified.

The United States and Russia had originally intended the Trilateral Agreement to be an executive agreement and had strong-armed Kravchuk to avoid submitting the document to the Rada. Kravchuk initially agreed.[103] At his January 14 press conference, he declared that ratification was unnecessary. "The first document is a political statement, and the second one is an appendix to this document. These are documents that do not require ratification or approval." But when faced with domestic criticism like that from Rukh opposition leader Vyacheslav Chornovil, who accused Kravchuk of "shameful capitulation" and national "betrayal,"[104] Kravchuk backed down, just as he had done after the Massandra summit.[105] Yet the Ukrainian president proved himself more adroit this time around. On February 3, 1994, the Rada voted overwhelmingly in favor of removing the conditions it had attached on November 18 to ratification of START and the Lisbon Protocol.[106]

The Rada vote came after heavy lobbying by Kravchuk, Zlenko, and Defense Minister Vitaly Radetsky; they argued that the Trilateral Agreement fulfilled the conditions the Rada had previously laid down. They also warned that the nuclear weapons in Ukraine were becoming increasingly unsafe. Colonel General Evgeni Maslin, chief of nuclear systems in the Ukrainian Defense Ministry, had stated the previous month: "The condition of nuclear safety in Ukraine continues to worsen. A moment may come when [Russia] will just simply refuse to accept such warheads for disassembly."[107] This represented a shift by Ukrainian officials, who had previously dismissed similar Russian assertions as misleading and inflammatory.

A changed political context also influenced the vote. The election as president of Crimea of Yuri Meshkov, who favored Crimean independence and close ties with Russia,[108] increased Kiev's insecurity and probably assisted passage of the resolution. The Trilateral Agreement included security assurances and Moscow's official recognition of Ukraine's territorial integrity; rejection of the resolution, Kravchuk cautioned, would lead to "international isolation," with Ukraine more vulnerable to separatist tendencies and Russian interference.

The Rada demonstrated greater maturity than before by placing the country's national interests ahead of scoring political points. It rejected the arbitrary value some officials assigned to the fissile material in the nuclear warheads.[109] The prospect of receiving some immediate assistance to alleviate the country's domestic hardships was far more attractive. On January 28, the Ukrainian State Committee on Nuclear Energy warned that all reactors could cease operating in 1995 without additional fuel supplies.[110] The Trilateral Agreement promised one hundred tons of nuclear fuel rods within ten months, an amount that would partially remedy the energy shortage that was hobbling an already moribund economy.

Washington astutely sweetened the pot at this time to influence the vote. In late January 1994, Economics Minister Roman Shpek visited Washington, where the Clinton administration promised to double U.S. financial assistance to $310 million if the Rada passed the Trilateral Agreement. President Clinton placed this promise in writing in a letter to Kravchuk, who used it to sway Rada lawmakers.

Technically, the Rada did not endorse the Trilateral Agreement. Rather, deputies were asked by Kravchuk to approve a resolution drafted by the president's office.[111] Clouding an already complicated situation was the fact that the Rada did not pass judgment on the resolution that Kravchuk had submitted but instead drafted and passed its own.[112] The Rada voted separately on the NPT and somewhat inconsistently fell thirty-three votes short of joining the treaty. Some Rada members were confused about exactly what they were endorsing. One deputy admitted, "I have no idea what we voted for."[113]

Some ambiguities remained as to whether the Rada voted for complete or partial denuclearization. Although its February resolution embraced START, the Rada's November resolution had stated that START obligated Ukraine to eliminate only 36 percent of the nuclear delivery vehicles and 42 percent of the nuclear warheads on its soil. Moreover, the February resolution did not mention Kravchuk's May 7, 1992, side letter, which committed Ukraine to rid itself of *all* nuclear weapons within START's seven-year period, even those not covered by the terms of START. Interestingly, Ukraine's refusal to join the NPT meant that it would not receive the American, Russian, and British security assurances contained in the Trilateral Agreement, including promises not to use nuclear weapons against Ukraine.

In early March, Kravchuk traveled to Washington. The Clinton administration used this meeting to underscore a broader partnership with Ukraine and to double again U.S. aid.[114] Regardless of whatever legal imperfections remained in Ukraine's arms control obligations,

Kiev began shipping the warheads back to Moscow immediately afterward. In May, Ukrainian Defense Minister Radetsky declared that nuclear warheads were being removed from the country at a rate of approximately 60 per month.[115] By early November 1994, Defense Department officials confirmed that 360 warheads had already been returned to Russia.[116] Under the terms of the Trilateral Agreement, all the warheads would be returned to Russia by the beginning of 1997.

UKRAINE JOINS THE NPT

In July 1994, Leonid Kuchma defeated Kravchuk in a runoff to become president of Ukraine. Kuchma's political platform was dedicated to market-based economic reform and the adoption of more pragmatic (i.e., closer) relations between Kiev and Moscow. Kuchma had been indifferent to NPT ratification during his campaign. But the month before the election, he had privately reassured the White House that he supported NPT membership, partly because it would accelerate the country's economic and political integration into the West.[117]

As before, the hurdle was winning the Rada's approval. Ukraine's apprehension derived from its long-standing fear that once it completely renounced all nuclear ambitions, the United States and the West would ignore it. Specifically, leading Rada members held the NPT hostage to two concerns. First, despite U.S. pledges to Ukraine totaling $700 million in Nunn-Lugar funding and economic assistance for 1994, Ukraine had received barely 10 percent of that amount. Second, the legislature insisted on stronger security assurances from the United States, Russia, and Britain.

The Clinton administration redoubled its efforts to meet both concerns and, more generally, to convince the Rada that the United States and the West were committed to a comprehensive and ongoing relationship with Ukraine. Vice President Gore, Assistant Secretary of Defense Ashton Carter, and other U.S. officials visited Kiev during the summer and early fall to assure Rada members that additional funding was in the pipeline and that a schedule of planned denuclearization programs for Ukraine would be expedited. In addition, in mid-November, fourteen European ambassadors delivered a demarche to Kuchma with a joint pledge of $234 million in assistance for Ukraine; Kuchma shared this news with the Rada.[118] The Clinton administration also tried to satisfy Ukrainian concerns on security assurances. By the first week of November, the United States, Russia, and Britain had finalized a new text on security assurances, one that was acceptable to Ukraine.

Still, this might not have been enough without the political leadership of President Kuchma. Kuchma clearly believed that NPT membership was in Ukraine's interests; he also knew that unless this issue was resolved, it would overshadow his upcoming address to the UN General Assembly, would dog his summit meeting with President Clinton at the White House on November 22, and would jeopardize a host of Ukrainian-American cooperation agreements that had already been drafted.

On November 16, 1994, the Rada voted overwhelmingly in favor of joining the NPT.[119] Kuchma thus succeeded where Kravchuk had earlier failed. Before the vote, Kuchma delivered an impassioned speech to the Rada, reminding the legislators that Ukraine could not test nuclear weapons, that keeping the weapons on Ukrainian territory would cost $10–30 billion, that in any case Moscow retained operational control, and that developing a nuclear arsenal from scratch would cost up to $200 billion over ten years.[120]

Ukraine deposited its instrument of NPT ratification at the December 5 summit meeting of the Conference on Security and Cooperation in Europe (CSCE) in Budapest, Hungary. President Clinton praised Kiev's decision as "a bold move away from the nuclear precipice." Ukraine received in turn a memorandum on security assurances signed by the United States, Russia, and Britain, to which it added its signature. The revised security assurances largely reiterated the general statements in the January 1994 Trilateral Accord but were now "customized" for Ukraine. They again included respect for Ukraine's sovereignty, independence, and existing borders, and a promise to refrain from the threat or use of force or "economic coercion" against Ukraine. A new wrinkle was a clause requiring consultations among the four parties in the event that "a situation" arose from the commitments in the document. Overall, the assurances amounted to little more than a change in form from the earlier agreement.[121]

Ukrainian accession to the NPT removed the last barrier to formal implementation of START I, which entered into force that same day. START I reduced the strategic nuclear arsenals of the United States and Russia to 7,000–8,000 warheads each and, more important, now permitted the U.S. Senate and the Russian Duma to proceed with ratification of START II, which would reduce Russian and American nuclear arsenals even further, to 3,000–3,500 warheads each.[122]

Potentially, the benefit of Kiev's ratification extended well beyond Ukraine or even the United States and Russia. On the eve of the 1995 NPT review and extension conference, the deep arms cuts in START I and II went some way toward meeting U.S. and Russian disarmament

obligations under Article 6 of the treaty. At a time when many nonnuclear members were criticizing the behavior of the nuclear weapon
states, Ukraine's action strengthened the U.S. position, which called
for the indefinite and unconditional extension of the NPT, and improved the chances for a successful outcome at the review and extension conference.

CONCLUSION: MISTAKES, SUCCESSES, AND LESSONS

All the key players in the denuclearization drama—Russia, the United
States, and most important, Ukraine—made policy errors and mis-
judgments. But at important junctures, they also responded to complex and difficult circumstances by making prudent decisions and implementing thoughtful policies.

An Assessment of Russian Policy.   Moscow deserves very high
marks for quickly crafting a CIS structure in December 1991 that
ensured a modicum of cohesion among the newly independent
republics of the former Soviet Union. The CIS Joint Military High
Command ensured single, centralized command and control over the
far-flung nuclear stockpile; although it may have been a fig leaf mask-
ing Russian authority, it nonetheless made such an arrangement politically palatable to Ukraine. The Alma Ata and Minsk summits won
formal commitments from Ukraine to remove the tactical and strategic
nuclear warheads and thus to become a nonnuclear weapon state by a
specific target date. This paved the way for the swift and safe removal
of tactical nuclear weapons from Ukraine by spring 1992. At the time
of the collapse of the Soviet empire in December 1991, none of these
achievements appeared inevitable or even obvious. And in late 1993,
Moscow reversed its previous stance and agreed to compensate Kiev
for the tactical nuclear weapons it had removed the year before, thereby paving the way for the January 1994 Trilateral Agreement. Russia's
fulfillment of its commitments under that agreement, along with its
willingness to endorse later another set of security assurances, eased
the Rada's vote for NPT membership in November 1994.

Moscow also deserves praise for what it did not do, namely, cut off
oil and gas supplies to Ukraine. Such a step could have been justified
on economic grounds alone; during 1993, subsidies to Ukraine
amounted to over $5 billion, according to U.S. government esti-
mates.[123] Kiev's energy dependence gave Russia enormous leverage,
which Moscow largely chose not to exploit in connection with the nuclear issue.[124]

On the other hand, Russia's acrimonious and at times antagonistic relations with Ukraine hindered the denuclearization effort. The main culprit was Russia's inability to accept the legitimacy of a sovereign Ukraine. Inflammatory statements from Russian politicians such as Rutskoi, Khasbulatov, and Zhirinovsky—on defending the rights of ethnic Russians in eastern Ukraine, on returning Crimea to the fold, and on asserting sole control of the Black Sea Fleet—exacerbated Kiev's anxieties over preserving its territorial integrity and aggravated already frayed nerves. Even after the January 1994 Trilateral Agreement, Kozyrev stated, "We should not withdraw from those regions which have been in the sphere of Russian interest for centuries."[125] Kiev viewed Moscow's aggressive use of military forces to back local insurgencies in the near abroad as a sinister precedent for meddling in Ukraine.

Further, Russia overplayed its hand with Ukraine. Timing the withdrawal of the last tactical nuclear weapons to embarrass Kravchuk during his first official visit to the United States in May 1992, issuing a stream of disinformation about Ukraine's shortcomings as a nuclear custodian, and suspending energy supplies during Kravchuk's second visit to Washington in March 1994 were all unnecessary. By increasing Kiev's suspicions, these provocations also ran counter to Moscow's larger goal of gathering in all the nuclear weapons stationed in Ukraine. The myriad gratuitous insults and personal slights that Russian negotiators directed to their Ukrainian counterparts also retarded a quicker resolution of the nuclear issue.

A more conciliatory approach by Moscow (which admittedly would have been difficult, if not impossible, for Yeltsin or any other leader given the political situation in Russia) would have reassured Ukraine and expedited the denuclearization process. Even if Moscow secretly harbored irredentist ambitions toward Ukraine, as many Ukrainians feared, a more patient strategy would have better achieved Russian objectives.

Finally, Russia (and the United States) faced another challenge in dealing with Ukraine: an uneven bargaining position. It was far more important to Russia that the warheads be removed from Ukraine than it was to Ukraine that they be sent back to Russia. Kiev needed to be convinced that its national security would be enhanced, or at least not diminished, if it transferred the nuclear weapons. Yet even if Ukraine could be assured that denuclearization was in its best interests, it had every incentive to delay the removal of nuclear weapons to extract additional benefits from Moscow and Washington. In other words, by practicing the "politics of procrastination," Kiev hoped to win more concessions tomorrow than it could today. Ukraine's nuclear games-manship was thus an unavoidable element that complicated Russian (and American) negotiations, dragged out the denuclearization process, and raised its cost.

Further, Moscow's diplomatic options were limited. Russian coercion would increase Ukraine's insecurity and produce the result Russia least wanted: retention of the nuclear warheads. (In fact, such pressure hardened the Rada's resolve first to delay a vote on START and then, in November 1993, to keep some nuclear weapons in the country.) Short of declaring war and forcibly seizing the nuclear warheads, which despite uneven relations was never a serious option, Russia had little flexibility. It could walk away from the table only at the cost of leaving Ukraine to become the world's third-largest nuclear power.

An Assessment of U.S. Policy.   Hindsight suggests that the United States should have initially pursued a different approach toward Ukraine. The Bush administration was willing to enter into a broader and closer relationship only after Ukraine first fulfilled its arms control commitments.[126] Kiev's performance in the nuclear sphere was thus seen as the litmus test of its good faith on all issues.

This American focus on nuclear weapons met with partial success in May 1992, when Secretary Baker persuaded Kiev to sign the Lisbon Protocol and the associated side letter that officially committed Ukraine to permanent nonnuclear status. Again, this achievement was neither inevitable nor obvious at the time.

But making the nuclear issue the centerpiece of Ukrainian-American relations ultimately did not succeed on its own terms. There were limits to what Washington could achieve through pressure alone. The Rada refused to vote on these agreements until November 1993. Washington's impatience with Kiev was understandable—Ukraine jeopardized all of Washington's labors in negotiating with Moscow the landmark arms control agreements that had been under discussion for many years. Yet at heart, the Bush administration's exclusive focus on nuclear arms was fundamentally nonstrategic. Washington was slow to realize that Ukraine's independence was the single greatest impediment to the Russian Federation's reconstitution of the Soviet empire, which could have once again menaced Europe and threatened American interests worldwide.

Kiev became more reluctant to part with its nuclear inheritance as Ukrainian officials became more knowledgeable, relations with Moscow deteriorated, suspicions grew that Washington had little interest in a nonnuclear Ukraine, the Rada became a true parliamentary body with its own prerogatives, Russia and its proxies meddled in the near abroad, and Ukraine witnessed NATO and especially U.S. indecisiveness over the bloodletting in Bosnia. Only after the Clinton administration wisely rejected the previous U.S. policy in the spring of 1993 and expanded its relationship with Ukraine was denuclearization progress possible. A Ukraine more certain of its ties to the United States was more willing to return the nuclear warheads to Russia. Pledges began to turn into deeds.

Visits by Talbott and Aspin to Kiev in spring 1993 provided the first concrete indications of the Clinton administration's broader engagement. Christopher's trip in October 1993 advanced the ball down the field. The U.S. refusal to trade security assurances at this time in return for Kiev's deactivating the SS-24s preserved a meaningful incentive that Washington later used to gain Ukraine's endorsement of a much broader denuclearization commitment. In general, the administration's determined and skillful diplomatic efforts to build on the Massandra summit and the Rada's partial ratification of START I deserve high marks. At all points, the Clinton team presented Ukraine with a vision of a nonnuclear country tied economically, politically, and militarily to the West.

These labors yielded tangible benefit in January 1994 with the Trilateral Agreement, which stipulated that all nuclear warheads would be transported to Russia within three years. After initially underestimating the Rada's importance, the Clinton administration crafted the agreement to address many of the precise reservations the Ukrainian parliament had expressed the previous November. In February, the Rada apparently agreed to endorse this new disarmament commitment. Trains taking the remaining nuclear warheads back to Russia began departing the following month. The Clinton administration again pressed forward after Kuchma's election in July, working through the fall to meet the Rada's concerns about receiving denuclearization funds and enhanced security assurances. To influence the pending Rada vote on the NPT, the Clinton administration made it known that it would increase U.S. economic assistance to Ukraine by another $200 million.[127] With Kuchma's help, the Rada voted in November to join the NPT, thereby opening the way for the entry into force of the START I agreement. Against great odds, the Clinton administration achieved a momentous nonproliferation success, one that is still largely underappreciated.

An Assessment of Ukrainian Policy.   "The fox knows many things," a classic Greek epigram observes, "but the hedgehog knows one great thing." Just as the hedgehog knows to beware the hungry fox, Ukraine knew that the nuclear weapons had some value, even if their precise benefit was difficult to quantify or even at times to articulate.

For some Ukrainians, the mere existence of nuclear weapons stationed on their territory alleviated the country's insecurity and deterred external threats. Falling between two security systems, Ukraine could anchor itself to neither one. It could not immediately join NATO; although the Partnership for Peace plan offered membership at some unspecified date, it did little to quiet Kiev's anxieties in the interim. Alternatively, the Tashkent Collective Security Treaty would have subordinated Ukraine to Russia's defense requirements, an option that was unacceptable to Kiev. Since Ukrainian independence in December 1991, Russia's psychological refusal to accept its loss of empire and acknowledge that its "little Russian" brothers now ruled a sovereign and independent state resulted in ongoing intrusions and interference in Ukrainian affairs. Retaining nuclear weapons would prevent a long history of Russian aggrandizement from repeating itself. Nuclear weapons appeared to offer Kiev the wherewithal to preserve the country's tenuous grasp on independence.

It was also thought that nuclear weapons enhanced the country's international prestige. News reports frequently noted that Ukraine was the world's third-largest nuclear power—but omitted that Ukraine did not have the capability to actually launch any nuclear weapons. During 1992 and 1993, Ukrainian officials and parliamentarians were feted in foreign capitals, and delegations from all over the world beat a path to Kiev's doorstep. This was intoxicating for a country that had been previously best known for a nuclear power plant disaster and a great famine. Kiev strongly suspected that all this care and attention related to its nuclear intentions; once the weapons left, so would this international flattery.

Given these perceptions, why did Ukraine slowly but steadily agree to return the nuclear weapons to Russia?

Technological constraints influenced Kiev's thinking. The inescapable technological fact was that Ukraine never had operational command and control over the nuclear weapons. Seizing the weapons would have provoked a war with Russia. Even if an open conflict could somehow have been avoided, other technical obstacles loomed. The liquid fuel for the SS-19 ICBMs made these weapons systems difficult to service and dangerous to keep. The SS-24s were also troublesome for Ukraine to maintain. Moreover, they were not really useful for deterring Russia; Kiev would have needed to retarget them to hit high-value sites such as Moscow or Saint Petersburg, and this would have been a technically daunting task. Defense Minister Morozov repeatedly told Kravchuk that the nuclear weapons had no deterrent value. All these reasons made it easier for Kiev to relinquish them to Russia.

The significance of Ukraine's fractious parliament, political inexperience, and attendant incompetence should also not be underestimated for understanding how the nuclear issue played out.[128] Ukraine was more a province of the Soviet Union than a republic; for decades there had been a brain drain of the country's best and brightest to Moscow, where honors were bestowed and careers were made. As one Western diplomat in Kiev phrased it in 1993, "The Ukrainians have been living on the dark side of the moon for seventy years." Ukraine was further hampered by a Soviet-era constitution that only vaguely delineated the powers of the president, the prime minister, and the Rada, further confusing an already chaotic political environment. The combination of erratic leadership, personal rivalries, and unclear policy produced a series of uncoordinated, halting steps toward a declared but distant goal of nuclear disarmament.

This inexperience repeatedly manifested itself: at the December 1991 Alma Ata summit, when Ukraine unilaterally conceded the removal of the tactical nuclear weapons on its territory by July 1, 1992; at its discovery in May 1992 that Moscow had spirited all the tactical nuclear weapons out of the country without its knowledge; at its last-minute hesitation to sign the Lisbon Protocol; at its default on the Minsk summit commitment to remove all strategic nuclear warheads from Ukraine by the end of 1994; at the missteps during and after the Massandra summit; and at the Rada's failure to ratify the NPT (which after January 1994 meant that Ukraine would not receive the Russian, American, and British security assurances promised in the Trilateral Agreement). In general, Ukraine's backsliding on arms control promises antagonized the Bush and Clinton administrations and eroded European support during the crucial time when Kiev was struggling to consolidate its independence.[129]

The prime engine for Ukraine's denuclearization was President Leonid Kravchuk. His precise motivations remain unclear. The most straightforward interpretation is that Kravchuk believed that eliminating nuclear weapons would best serve his, and his country's, interests. A consummate politician who consistently sought compromise over confrontation, Kravchuk told the United States and other Western countries what they wanted to hear: Ukraine would return the nuclear warheads to Russia. This was not necessarily because he was devoted to a nonnuclear Ukraine. Kravchuk's bottom line was to remain in office; he saw the nuclear issue as just one way to increase his power and prestige. With a recalcitrant Rada, Kravchuk could portray himself as the indispensable man who could break governmental gridlock.

After July 1994 (when Kravchuk proved quite dispensable), Leonid Kuchma moved smartly to eliminate any residual Western fears that Ukraine harbored nuclear ambitions and to reassure the international community that Kiev could be a responsible actor by not further delaying its membership in the NPT, a delay that impeded the entry into force of START I. In September, the IAEA General Conference approved a draft comprehensive safeguards agreement with Ukraine, an agreement that Kuchma was willing to implement even if the Rada did not approve Ukraine's accession to the NPT.[130] But due in no small measure to his influence, the Rada decided to join the NPT on November 16, and Ukraine officially became a member on December 5.

An argument can be made that Kiev actually played the nuclear card quite skillfully, if at times this was more by accident than by design. Ukraine convinced the international community, successfully in the end, that it should be compensated for returning the tactical nuclear weapons and strategic nuclear warheads to Russia. The case for compensation was not immediately obvious, even to Kiev, which had originally agreed to return the tactical nuclear weapons to Russia without any reimbursement. Ukraine had no operational control over any of these weapons. Ukraine had not enriched the uranium contained in the nuclear warheads. (Neither had Ukraine produced the plutonium, which had no commercial legal market value.) Ukraine had not manufactured the tactical nuclear weapons, the air-launched cruise missiles, or the SS-19 ICBMs. At most, Ukraine had a strong case for either keeping (without their nuclear payloads) the SS-24s, which had been manufactured in its factories, or selling them as scrap metal.

Nonetheless, given what was at stake—a potential new nuclear state in the heart of Europe and the end of START I and II—Ukraine successfully exploited the fears of others, especially the United States and Russia. Although retention of the nuclear weapons on its soil was of uncertain advantage to Ukraine, their removal was of considerable value to Washington and Moscow. Returning the weapons would remove a sticking point in Ukraine's relations with Russia. More important, it would facilitate greater Ukrainian integration with U.S. and Western financial, political, and military institutions that could far better bolster the country's fortunes.

For weapons that Ukraine did not control and had not built, it received (twice) American, Russian, and British security assurances, one hundred tons of nuclear fuel, forgiveness of its multibillion-dollar oil and gas debt to Russia, and a commitment of $900 million in U.S. financial assistance. Rather than entrusting its future to dubious notions of existential deterrence and a spurious nuclear status, Ukraine eventually concluded that the real value of these weapons could be realized only by giving them up.

Belarus: Pushing on an Open Door

In 1904, the father of geostrategy, Sir Halford Mackinder, wrote in the Royal Geographical Society's *Journal* that whichever power occupied the region linking the great landmasses of Europe and Asia would also rule the world. To describe the strategic importance of this region, he coined the phrase "the geographic pivot of history."[131]

In the center of this region lies Belarus (formerly Byelorussia). Surrounded by Russia, Ukraine, Poland, Latvia, and Lithuania, and lacking any natural boundaries, its territory lies along a traditional invasion route for foreign armies. Its vulnerability was exploited by outside aggressors repeatedly through the years, from the Mongols in the thirteenth century to the Germans during World War II, when the country lost a quarter of its inhabitants and 90 percent of its infrastructure. Given this doleful history, the region might more aptly be called "the geographic divot of history."

From the late eighteenth century to the early 1990s, Moscow ruled most of what is now Belarus. That a distinctive Belarusian people still exist is remarkable. Their survival is a testament to an ability to accommodate themselves to the prevailing power at the time. Despite the country's independence, this remains no less true today. According to one expert, "Of all the western republics of the former USSR, Belarus has traditionally been viewed as the most Russified and pliant in its relations with Russia."[132]

THE NONNUCLEAR POLICY

On July 27, 1990, the newly elected Byelorussian parliament (Supreme Soviet) passed the "Declaration on State Sovereignty," which proclaimed that the country should become neutral and nuclear-free.[133] The following year, the country's foreign minister, Petr Kravchenko, repeated these principles before the UN General Assembly.[134]

The most infamous reason for the country's strict nonnuclear policy was of course the Chernobyl disaster, which inflicted greater harm on

Belarus than on any other country. Whereas the accident contaminated less than 1 percent of Russian territory and 4 percent of Ukrainian territory, radioactive fallout poisoned roughly 20 percent of Belarus. Prime Minister Vyachaslav Kebich likened the accident to a nuclear explosion. Six years after the disaster, two million people, or one out of every five citizens, were reportedly living in contaminated zones, including eight hundred thousand children.[135] By the early 1990s, cows in these areas were still unable to produce uncontaminated milk.[136] The disaster produced in the populace a widespread, visceral hatred of all things nuclear.

That Belarus boasted one of the world's heaviest concentrations of soldiers and equipment also prompted the country to rid itself of the Soviet military presence, which included tactical and strategic nuclear weapons stationed on its territory. Another motivation was even more compelling, if less well-known. In the event of another European war, Soviet military doctrine and war plans envisioned that tactical nuclear weapons would be used on Belarusian territory to halt a NATO advance.[137]

Most important, removal of all nuclear weapons was entirely consistent with Belarus's foreign policy objectives of neutrality and nonalignment. Indeed, nuclear disarmament assisted the country's quest for independence. As long as the nuclear weapons remained on Belarusian soil, so would the thirty-five thousand members of the Strategic Rocket Forces (SRF), overwhelmingly Russian in ethnic composition. If the missiles went back to Russia, so would the soldiers.

THE DECEMBER 1991 AGREEMENTS

In the unpredictable period after the August 1991 coup attempt and before the formation of the CIS, Belarusian military and political leaders reassured Moscow that Minsk harbored no nuclear ambitions. In September, the commander of the Belarusian Military District emphasized "the indisputable fact that the defensive nuclear potential, including [those systems] deployed on the territories of the sovereign republics, must remain in the same hands and have the same command point."[138] Prime Minister Kebich declared that the nuclear weapons would "be moved to Russia." He added: "It is not desirable to distribute the nuclear weapons among the armies of the republics. It is better to put them under the central control of Russia. We are planning to make Belarus a nuclear-free state."[139]

As in Ukraine and Kazakhstan, the diplomatic maneuvers of December 1991 set the nuclear agenda in Belarus. The CIS founding document codified unified command and control over the nuclear arsenal, and the December 21 Agreement on Joint Measures on Nuclear Arms reached at Alma Ata further obligated the parties to a number of arms control measures. Belarus agreed to join the NPT as a nonnuclear weapon state, conclude a safeguards agreement with the IAEA, help remove tactical nuclear weapons from the country by July 1, 1992, and submit START I to its parliament for ratification.

To underscore further its nonnuclear stance, Stanislav Shushkevich, chairman of the Belarusian Supreme Soviet, declared in late December 1991: "We must eliminate any open questions in the world, and we do not want the world to be afraid of us. I am saying this directly—we are handing over the nuclear button to the President of Russia, Boris Nikolayevich Yeltsin."[140]

At the Minsk summit the following week, Belarus signed the Agreement on Strategic Forces, which outlined the joint command of strategic weapons and reaffirmed the nonnuclear commitment of Minsk and the other signatories. In this agreement, Ukraine pledged to remove all strategic nuclear weapons from its territory by the end of 1994. Interestingly, there was no similar obligation for Belarus, perhaps because no similar anxiety existed in Moscow about Minsk's intentions.

REMOVAL OF THE TACTICAL NUCLEAR WEAPONS

As it had done in Ukraine and Kazakhstan, Russia removed the tactical nuclear weapons from Belarus as quickly as possible, without coordinating or even consulting with the local authorities. In the four months following the Alma Ata and Minsk summits, Moscow withdrew all of the approximately fifteen hundred tactical nuclear weapons stationed in Belarus.[141]

In mid-February 1992, as this withdrawal was taking place, Belarusian officials announced their annoyance at Russia's behavior. According to the Moscow wire service *Postfactum,* one deputy complained that tactical nuclear arms were being removed from Belarus without any formal agreement or even the government's knowledge. Although Belarus would adhere to its nonnuclear objective, he stated, it would not speed up the removal of nuclear arms from its territory, since its opinion had not been taken into consideration.[142] How Minsk could have expedited withdrawal when it exercised no control over the tactical nuclear weapons, and had no information on how this process worked, was unclear. Minsk's public irritation was less than an empty threat and demonstrated how little ability Belarus actually had to influence this issue.

Still, the following month, Belarus Defense Minister-designate Petr Chaus applauded Ukrainian President Kravchuk's decision to suspend withdrawal of tactical nuclear weapons from Ukraine. He endorsed Kravchuk's protest that destruction of the weapons must be supervised, and he stated that Belarus had similar concerns.[143] However, Belarus never suspended the withdrawal process or insisted on monitoring dismantlement of the weapons. To ensure that Belarus did not rock the boat, Shushkevich emphasized that same day that Ukraine's decision was "an exclusively internal affair of state." He noted: "I can only say this decision had no influence on the Belarusian stand. We firmly keep to our opinion that Belarus should become a nonnuclear state. That is why all disarmament arrangements in the republic are following the adopted scheme."[144]

As if further reassurance was necessary, a few days later Shushkevich said that Belarus would ensure removal of all tactical nuclear weapons ahead of the scheduled July 1 date.[145] In fact, the Russians removed all tactical nuclear warheads without incident from Belarus by the end of April, two months ahead of schedule.[146] The associated missile launchers were dismantled over the following few weeks. Statements at the time indicated that Belarusian officials did not know whether tactical nuclear weapons were still based in their country or not.[147]

THE FATE OF THE SS-25s

Belarus was also home for eighty-one single-warhead, road-mobile SS-25 ballistic missiles. Code-named "Sickle" by NATO, each had a yield of 750 kilotons and a range of 10,500 kilometers. They were held at a dozen military operating bases and guarded by personnel of the elite SRF.

The Lisbon Protocol in May 1992 did not require Belarus to wait until START I ratification before removing the SS-25s. And, in fact, Minsk did not wait. Immediately after the Lisbon meeting, Belarus began preparations for withdrawing the SS-25s. Foreign Minister Kravchenko erroneously stated at the end of June that withdrawal of the SS-25s had begun. At this time, Minsk was only discussing the logistical details for removal.[148]

When the Supreme Soviet's newly formed Security Council met in early July, its members considered a draft treaty that Moscow had drawn up on the strategic forces "temporarily deployed" in Belarus.

In a secret signing ceremony in Moscow on July 20, 1992, Belarus formally assigned jurisdiction over the SS-25s to Russia. The classified agreement reaffirmed Minsk's legal right to veto a decision to use the nuclear weapons and stipulated that the strategic nuclear weapons would be withdrawn from Belarus within the seven-year time period set by the START I agreement.[149]

Moscow forced Belarus to accept this agreement, over Shushkevich's objections and despite the fact that it violated the December 1991 Alma Ata and Minsk agreements setting out joint CIS command over nuclear forces. The agreement appeared unnecessary given Moscow's absolute control over the nuclear forces inside Belarus. Although it may have been an attempt to soothe Belarusian sensitivities after Russia's heavy-handed approach to removing the tactical nuclear weapons, it more probably reflected a desire by the Russian military to formalize withdrawal procedures and logistical details.

In September 1992, Shushkevich instructed experts to devise a schedule to rid Belarus of the SS-25s "as soon as possible." These experts outlined four different scenarios, based on two-, three-, four-, and five-year withdrawal periods. According to news reports, problems surrounding the physical transportation of the missiles and uncertain funding prospects for withdrawal complicated planning. But the worst problems were intensely human: how to find new jobs for those soldiers who would remain in Belarus after the last SS-25 had exited the country and how to find billets back in Russia for those officers who would leave with the missiles.[150]

In late October, Minsk and Moscow engaged in "consultations on coordinating mechanisms" for removing the SS-25s.[151] Euphemism aside, the Russians had in fact scripted a withdrawal schedule, but they let Shushkevich announce the deal on October 26. The strategic nuclear weapons in Belarus would be removed over a period of two to three years. This schedule did not impose a rigid timetable but rather constituted a "statement of intent" to return the missiles within three years. Nonetheless, by December 30, 1994, Moscow intended that the last SRF units would be back in Russia and Belarus would be nonnuclear.[152]

Over the next few months, however, logistical and financial problems repeatedly deferred the start of the three-year withdrawal period. It was not until July 1993 that the first SS-25s left Belarus. Two months later, on September 24, 1993, Belarus and Russia secretly formalized a classified withdrawal schedule, which stipulated that all the SS-25s would now be removed by the end of 1996.[153] In November, the two parties also agreed that all SRF troops would exit Belarus accord-

ing to the same timetable. By the end of 1993, twenty-seven missiles had reportedly been returned to Russia, where they were integrated into an SS-17 SRF base midway between Moscow and Saint
Petersburg.[154]

START I, THE LISBON PROTOCOL, AND THE NPT

Although Belarus, in its July 1990 Declaration on State Sovereignty,
had committed itself in principle to becoming a nonnuclear state, it remained for it to codify this commitment by ratifying START I, the Lisbon Protocol, and the NPT.

In February 1993, the three agreements were debated in closed session first by the Belarusian parliamentary leadership and then by the
entire Supreme Soviet. The decision was taken quickly and with a
minimum of debate, with the vote 218–1 in favor of acceding to all
three agreements. According to the chairman of the Supreme Soviet's
commission on national security, Mechislav Grib, most of the secret,
four-hour discussion concerned the prohibitive costs of maintaining
the nuclear weapons and the subsequent risk of grave environmental
damage. Few argued in favor of retaining the missiles.[155]

In fact, most of the parliamentary debate had nothing to do with
the merits of becoming nonnuclear; rather, it confirmed the universal-
ity of the maxim "All politics is local." In addition to ratifying the
three arms control agreements, the deputies considered two bilateral
treaties with Russia on coordinating joint military activities inside Belarus and the July 20, 1992, agreement on the strategic forces still stationed in the country. The Supreme Soviet ratified the latter agreement, but only after deleting a provision that would have required all
Belarusian citizens drafted into units of the strategic forces based in
the country to take an oath of loyalty to the CIS Unified Armed
Forces. (Belarus had just administered its own loyalty oath to all military personnel five weeks earlier, and this oath overrode the pro-
Moscow leanings of the overwhelming majority of deputies.)

The nature of the debate indicated that the denuclearization decision enjoyed support across the political spectrum, albeit for different
reasons. For ardent nationalists like Zyanon Paznyak and for political
moderates like Shushkevich, the nuclear weapons and the thirty-five
thousand SRF troops were alien intrusions; the country could not
truly be independent and sovereign as long as they remained on Belarusian soil. Shushkevich also realized that denuclearization would
lead to greater foreign economic assistance, which would increase his
political stature and bolster his domestic standing. Conservative

deputies and the old Communist Party *nomenklatura*, who had been elected in the preindependence days of 1990 and constituted over 80 percent of the legislature, were predisposed to Russian sensitivities, especially regarding the return of nuclear weapons. For them, the solution was straightforward: if Moscow wanted the nuclear weapons back, then back they would go.[156]

The legacy of Chernobyl had sensitized the deputies to the possibility of environmental contamination from another nuclear accident, as implied in Grib's recounting of the secret parliamentary debate. Defense Minister Pavel Kozlovsky later alluded to this concern by asking rhetorically, "What is the use of bargaining [over nuclear weapons] if the state is unable even physically to sustain the nuclear arsenal?"[157] Further, public opinion sided with returning the nuclear weapons. Polls consistently revealed that an overwhelming majority of the Belarusian people wanted the country to be free of all nuclear weapons.[158]

Other motivations also influenced the vote. The presence of nuclear weapons in Belarus made the country less, not more, secure. In the event of a conflict between Russia and NATO, a nuclear-armed Belarus would certainly attract a devastating nuclear strike. As expressed by Shushkevich, "It is plain madness to have a powder keg on the highway from Russia to the countries of the West."[159] In addition, Minsk hoped that a formal renunciation of its nuclear ambitions would encourage other countries, especially Ukraine, to follow a similar path.

Although virtue may be its own reward, Washington had already put together an incentive package to encourage the Supreme Soviet to ratify the START I agreement and join the NPT. In October 1992, the two countries had signed an "umbrella" agreement, which provided a legal framework for U.S. assistance, and two implementing agreements—the first allocating $5 million to train and equip Belarusian personnel to deal with a possible emergency during the removal of the SS-25s and the second earmarking $1 million to establish an export control system.[160] Adding the cost of other technical assistance programs, by January 1993 Washington had committed over $7.5 million to denuclearization efforts and defense conversion in Belarus. Although these funds were devoted to activities judged to be in U.S. national interests, they conveniently whetted Minsk's appetite for additional aid on ratification of START, the Lisbon documents, and the NPT.

The United States made certain to follow through on its earlier promises of assistance to Belarus, not only to preserve its credibility with Minsk but also, and more important, to send a message to

Ukraine and Kazakhstan that Washington honored its commitments and that denuclearization brought tangible benefits. Immediately following the February 1993 vote, President Clinton called Shushkevich to congratulate him and discuss expanding bilateral cooperation, and American officials began putting together an assistance package for Belarus.[161] In March, Secretary of State Christopher pledged an additional $65 million to facilitate Minsk's denuclearization efforts. Four months later at the White House, Chairman Shushkevich formally presented President Clinton with Belarus's instruments of accession to the NPT. During this same visit, U.S. Secretary of Defense Aspin and Belarusian Defense Minister Kozlovsky signed three agreements ensuring the safety, security, and dismantlement of former Soviet nuclear weapons in Belarus.[162] By October 1993, the two countries had signed more than twenty agreements for military cooperation and economic assistance. During the next four months, Secretary Christopher and President Clinton each visited Minsk, providing symbolic demonstrations of American appreciation for Belarus's nonnuclear stance.

CONCLUSION

Why did Belarus, unlike Ukraine or Kazakhstan, decide to denuclearize so rapidly and in such a noncontroversial manner—indeed without even a public, or much of a private, debate?

For one Western ambassador in Minsk, the reason was simple: "Because the Russians told them to."[163] No doubt this is a large part of the answer. Russia exerted extraordinary influence over its much smaller and submissive neighbor. Indeed, the road to Belarusian independence was very different from that followed by its Baltic and East European neighbors—and even from that taken by Russia itself. The Belarusian path was more accommodating and less adversarial, and this relatively smooth process influenced the government's policies toward Russia after the Soviet Union's demise.[164]

This compliant line is not hard to understand. If the hallmarks of independence and sovereignty are economic and national security, Minsk was incapable of achieving either without the active cooperation, indeed participation, of Moscow. Russia absorbed nearly 70 percent of Belarusian exports and supplied 90 percent of its energy. In 1992 Moscow planned to begin charging Belarus and the other CIS republics world market prices for natural gas and oil; by 1993, Belarus's debt to Russia had mounted to 112 billion rubles.[165] Prime Minister Kebich did not exaggerate when he stated that Belarus could not part company with Russia without risking its very survival.

In addition, the Belarusian military closely integrated its operations with its Russian counterparts, which wielded inordinate influence in Belarus. Even after independence, large parts of the country were under the de facto administrative control of Russian military commanders. The majority of Belarusian officers were ethnically Russian, as were over 75 percent of the Ministry of Defense.[166] With its indefensible borders and budgetary woes, Belarus could not fend for itself. Acknowledging the obvious, Acting Defense Minister Chaus conceded that any military conflict between Belarus and Russia was impossible. Chairman Shushkevich said that regardless of who was in political power in Russia, Belarus would continue to seek good relations.[167]

To focus solely on Russia's influence, however, is to miss, and misunderstand, the role that Belarus played in its own story. Just because Minsk's behavior adhered to Russian objectives did not mean that it contradicted Belarusian ones. Nonnuclear status was in Minsk's own interests as well. On the question of removing the tactical and strategic nuclear weapons from Belarus, Russia was pushing on an open door.

Political factors contributed to and reinforced this submissive stance. The two key figures in the government, Prime Minister Kebich and Chairman of the Supreme Soviet Shushkevich, both leaned toward Moscow—Kebich because of his political inclinations as a long-time member of the Communist Party and Shushkevich because of his good personal relations with Yeltsin. Even if these pro-Moscow sentiments had not existed, Minsk could not have pursued a foreign policy independent from Moscow. In fact, its declared policy of neutrality and nonnuclear status dovetailed perfectly with Russia's desire to remove the nuclear weapons from the country.

Of course, none of this prevented Minsk from using the missiles as a lever to extract economic benefits from Washington and Moscow. Yet unlike Kazakhstan and especially Ukraine, Belarus did not even pretend to play the nuclear card. After an initial halfhearted attempt by Shushkevich in December 1991 to tie denuclearization to U.S. diplomatic recognition, Minsk ignored opportunities to engage in nuclear diplomacy. Beginning with Foreign Minister Kravchenko's January 1992 declaration that Belarus wanted to be the first CIS member free of all nuclear weapons, Belarusian officials, especially Shushkevich, repeatedly indicated their desire to remove the SS-25s as quickly as possible. Further, Shushkevich did not endorse Kravchuk's January 1993 proposal in Davos, Switzerland, for an international nuclear disarmament fund to pay for denuclearization; he merely said that the idea required further study.[168] Finally, Minsk did not raise the idea of compensation for the HEU in the strategic nuclear warheads until *after* it had ratified START and the NPT in February 1993. All these actions undercut any negotiating leverage Belarus might have had.

According to Vyachaslav Paznyak, director of Minsk's Center for Strategic Initiatives, the decisions to quickly rid the country of tactical and strategic nuclear weapons also testified to the government's inexperience in the conduct of foreign policy.[169] In contrast to both Ukrainian and Kazakh officials, no Belarusian official ever threatened to keep the nuclear weapons as a way to gain leverage over Moscow or even publicly requested that Minsk receive compensation for the HEU contained in the tactical nuclear weapons.

Finally, if denuclearization was going to take place anyway because Russian and Belarusian interests overlapped, how can the U.S. contribution to this process be evaluated? To call Washington's role wholly superfluous would be uncharitable and inaccurate. By providing technical advice and, more important, economic assistance at key moments, the United States greased the tracks for a train that was already in motion.

Kazakhstan: Deliberate Denuclearization

Located in central Asia between Russia and China, and covering an area roughly four times the size of Texas, Kazakhstan was destined to play an important role in the CIS. Its population of seventeen million comprised over one hundred nationalities, with the two main ones being ethnic Kazakhs and Russians. It also hosted 104 SS-18 ICBMs, each code-named "Satan," and carrying ten 550-kiloton nuclear warheads. These missiles, along with 40 nuclear-capable "Bear H" long-range bombers, ensured that Kazakhstan would be a key actor in efforts to return what had been the Soviet Union's nuclear weapons to Russia.

Nursultan Nazarbayev, an ethnic Kazakh and former steelworker whom Gorbachev had installed as Kazakh Communist Party chief, ruled Kazakhstan. Nazarbayev clearly intended to steer a delicate course between mollifying Russia (and Kazakhstan's large ethnic Russian population) and charting his country's economic growth, with considerable Western assistance. For Nazarbayev, nuclear weapons were a tool he could use to shape his country's relationship with Russia and the West, especially the United States.

EARLY STATEMENTS ON NUCLEAR WEAPONS

In their efforts to return all the Soviet Union's nuclear weapons to Russia, Washington and Moscow initially viewed Kazakhstan as more troublesome than Ukraine. Almost immediately after the failed putsch in August 1991, Nazarbayev's public statements on the future disposition of the nuclear missiles on Kazakh territory revealed an ambivalent commitment to returning these weapons to Russia. Two themes predominated. First, Nazarbayev and other Kazakh officials emphasized the importance of keeping centralized (i.e., CIS) control over the nuclear arsenal. Second, Nazarbayev insisted that Kazakhstan have a say on nuclear decision making. This latter theme was heard in calls for a Kazakh veto over any use of nuclear weapons and, more realistically, in arguments that the nuclear weapons should remain in Kazakhstan for the foreseeable future. One of Nazarbayev's first statements on nuclear weapons neatly captured both these points: "Our nation has nuclear weapons. It has been advocated that the nuclear weapons should be put under the unified control of the center of the Soviet Union. However, the cost of their relocation is high."[170]

During his first major international trip, to London in October 1991, Nazarbayev repeated his position that control of nuclear weapons could be exercised only by the center. He declared, "I do not recognize republics' individual control of nuclear weapons."[171] Other Kazakh officials at this time spoke of eliminating the country's nuclear weapons within the START framework, implementing a dual-key launch system with Kazakhstan possessing one of the keys, and requiring that Almaty (the name was changed in 1992 from Alma Ata) be informed before the central authority decided to use the nuclear weapons stationed on Kazakh territory.

For anyone familiar with Kazakhstan's history, Nazarbayev's public hesitancy over nuclear weapons was hard to fathom. Although Kazakhstan had not suffered a nuclear accident on the scale of Chernobyl, the Semipalatinsk nuclear testing site in the northeastern section of the country had inflicted more harm over a far longer period of time. Since 1949, an estimated five hundred nuclear explosions—what Nazarbayev called "death-bearing tests"—were conducted at Semipalatinsk, with almost two hundred of them above ground. These included hydrogen bomb tests. According to Kazakh estimates, hundreds of thousands of people still suffered from exposure to radioactivity, a situation that moved Nazarbayev to lament, "The Kazakh people have gone through hundreds of tragedies similar to that in Hiroshima."[172] Kazakhstan's October 1990 independence declaration included a provision prohibiting nuclear tests, demonstrating the depth of antinuclear sentiment, especially since the Soviet Ministries of Defense and Atomic Power and Industry supported continued weapons testing at the time.[173] Immediately after the August 1991 coup attempt, Nazarbayev had issued a decree closing the nuclear test site.

News reports that Nazarbayev favored nuclear weapons for the Islamic world (an aspect of the so-called loose nukes problem) combined with his earlier ambiguous stance to force the leader in late November to publicly reaffirm his support for central control over nuclear weapons. In reasserting how difficult it would be to transfer these weapons to third parties, he argued for keeping the weapons in Kazakhstan. "Each launching system encompasses an underground complex. To move it to another place is just impossible. In the most modest estimate, such a project might cost from twenty-five to thirty billion rubles."[174]

Stories depicting Almaty as an irresponsible nuclear custodian surfaced periodically in the media during the next few months.[175] The basis of these reports is obscure. Although it is possible that Almaty might have intimated about a transfer of nuclear weapons to Iran and other countries in the Middle East to increase Moscow's anxiety and thus gain leverage in the bilateral relationship, Nazarbayev must have realized that even hinting at such a transfer would have harmed rather than helped his cause. More likely, these allegations may have been part of a Russian attempt to embarrass and discredit Nazarbayev for his independent nuclear stance or may have constituted an Israeli disinformation campaign intended to draw the West's attention to Iran's nuclear ambitions.

Nazarbayev's strategy was thrown off-balance momentarily by the formation of the CIS on December 8; Kazakhstan had not been invited to attend the Minsk meeting of the three Slavic states and was unaware that the meeting was even taking place.[176] Nazarbayev reacted quickly to preserve his diplomatic flexibility and began actively using the nuclear card to shape his relations with Yeltsin, Russia, and the CIS, with the goal of creating a special role for his country. Within days, he organized a meeting with the four other central Asian states (Kyrgyzstan, Tajikistan, Turkmenistan, and Uzbekistan); at the meeting, they declared their wish to join the CIS.

This wish was granted a week later. The CIS admitted the central Asian states, along with Armenia, Azerbaijan, and Moldova, at its December 21 summit in Almaty. At this meeting, the full membership declared, "Single control over nuclear weapons will be preserved." In a separate Agreement on Joint Measures on Nuclear Arms, Kazakhstan, Ukraine, and Belarus promised to transfer to Russia by July 1, 1992, the tactical nuclear weapons based on their territories. Although Nazarbayev might have refused to repatriate the tactical nuclear weapons to gain another source of influence, circumstances compelled him to yield on this issue: the weapons were under strict Russian control, they were few in number, and their continued presence in Kazakhstan without expert maintenance posed unacceptable environmental risks for a country already heavily contaminated after decades of nuclear tests. Kazakhstan would retain sufficient influence with the strategic nuclear weapons that would remain on its territory for many more years.[177]

However, Kazakhstan refused to agree with Ukraine and Belarus that the head of the Russian Federation should have the authority, even after consultations, to decide how nuclear weapons on CIS territories were used. More important, Almaty refused to pledge that it would join the NPT as a nonnuclear weapon state, as Kiev and Minsk had agreed to do. Well-pleased with himself, Nazarbayev telephoned U.S. Secretary of State Baker after the Almaty summit to brag about how the meeting had gone.

Kazakhstan was also trying at this time to establish a relationship with the United States, which recognized Russia as the sole inheritor of the Soviet nuclear arsenal. Nazarbayev coveted a special relationship with the United States, wanted to ensure that Washington understood his country's geographic vulnerability between Russia and China, and sought both speedy U.S. diplomatic recognition and American support for UN membership.

Baker took a dim view of Kazakhstan's policy of nuclear ambiguity and played on Nazarbayev's objectives to move the country closer to denuclearization. First, Washington offered Almaty the prospect of early diplomatic recognition, although, once granted, this carrot could not have been used again.[178] A more durable source of leverage lay in using the nuclear issue as both a precondition to and a test of good relations between the United States and Kazakhstan.

Nazarbayev was willing to pay Washington's price, but only up to a point. Twice in December 1991, he privately told Baker that Kazakhstan would sign START and the NPT, once only minutes before a joint appearance in Almaty before the international press corps. On this occasion, Nazarbayev retreated from his private assurance and hedged on when and even whether Kazakhstan would join the NPT. In general, Nazarbayev was deliberately more ambiguous on the nuclear issue in public than he was in private with the Americans. Until it became clear that Nazarbayev's studied equivocation was aimed at influencing Moscow rather than deceiving Washington, such behavior frustrated the Bush administration.[179] At the Minsk summit at the end of the month, Kazakhstan continued to play this game, refusing to commit to removing all the strategic nuclear weapons in Kazakhstan by the end of 1994, as Ukraine had formally promised.

KAZAKHSTAN'S "NUCLEAR DEBATE"

What may not have been known to U.S. officials at this time was the nature of a behind-the-scenes nuclear debate then under way in Almaty. Government officials and military officers argued over the perceived political advantages and disadvantages that nuclear weapons conferred; the possible military use of nuclear arms was not raised. Although only the contours of this debate are known, it clearly influenced Kazakhstan's nuclear stance at the two December 1991 summits and afterward.

As a result of this private nuclear debate, Kazakhstan decided to pursue a middle path between abandonment and retention. This "deliberate denuclearization" approach consisted of three strands. First, Almaty would not try to assert direct control over the nuclear weapons, for several reasons. Kazakhstan did not have the resources or technical knowledge to maintain the weapons. It also recognized that the creation of a new nuclear state would alienate the international community, especially the United States, at a time when Kazakhstan desperately needed foreign assistance and investment. Most important, such a move would have drawn an immediate and harsh response from Russia to prevent nuclear weapons from falling into Almaty's hands.

Second, Kazakhstan would insist that the weapons remain under some form of "joint control." Although in reality this was a polite fiction, it would allow Almaty to assert not only its sovereignty but also its desire to be consulted over the future disposition of the missiles. As part of this strategy, during the next two years Kazakhstan rebuffed strong Russian pressure to officially relinquish command and control and insisted that the strategic nuclear weapons remain under the joint command of the CIS.

Third, Almaty would try to keep these weapons on Kazakh soil for as long as possible. The mere presence of these missiles, even if not under local control, created a modicum of anxiety over the country's nuclear intentions and conferred a corresponding amount of leverage. Of course, objective technical, financial, and logistical obstacles reinforced this policy; Moscow's limited financial and logistical resources hampered the speed with which deactivation, dismantlement, and destruction could occur. But Kazakhstan had subjective reasons for pursuing this policy. Retention of the missiles amplified Kazakhstan's voice within the CIS and introduced a measure of cautious respect in Moscow's, and Beijing's, bilateral relations with Almaty. It also allowed Kazakhstan's requests for U.S. and UN security assurances to play to a more receptive audience than would otherwise have been the case.[180]

This three-part denuclearization policy confirmed the wisdom of the stance Nazarbayev had tentatively sketched out in his public statements during the previous months. Its challenge lay in charting a steady course between capitulation and confrontation. Nazarbayev's position incorporated some of the features of both Ukraine's and Belarus's nuclear policies, but it better advanced the country's national security interests by not overly antagonizing Russia or alarming the United States. If Ukraine's policy appeared designed to eventually retain nuclear weapons, Kazakhstan's policy was intended to eliminate them as slowly as possible.

REMOVAL OF THE TACTICAL NUCLEAR WEAPONS

Russia did not give Kazakhstan the chance to keep the tactical nuclear weapons for very long. In December 1991 at the Alma Ata summit, Kazakhstan had agreed to ensure the transfer of these weapons within six months. In fact, Moscow removed all of them in less than a month, by the end of January 1992.

Three factors accounted for this expedited withdrawal. First, there were few tactical nuclear weapons located in Kazakhstan—open sources are silent on the exact number, but it was probably no more than a couple of hundred. Second, Moscow was no doubt agitated by Nazarbayev's independent stance and wanted to minimize the opportunities he might have to seize these weapons. Third, rumors had already been circulating concerning a "nuclear connection" between Kazakhstan and Iran; such a scenario terrified those Russian officers responsible for nuclear command and control. Interestingly, a raft of Russian media reports alleging that Almaty had sold nuclear weapons to Iran appeared in January at precisely the time these weapons were being withdrawn. Kazakhstan's deputy prime minister categorically denied one story that his country had sold three nuclear warheads to Iran: "I can give official assurances that the Kazakhstan government has signed no agreements of this kind and has no intention to."[181]

Yet these reports so alarmed Moscow that it checked its records and recounted the number of weapons it had removed from Kazakhstan. According to the Russian general entrusted with the security of the nuclear warheads, "We counted up and checked how many tactical weapons were introduced into Kazakhstan and how many were withdrawn; all the numbers tallied."[182] U.S. intelligence analysts responsible for tracking nuclear weapons in the former Soviet Union confirmed his accounting.[183] Indeed, Washington felt confident enough about the safety and security of the nuclear weapons in Kazakhstan that neither President Bush nor Secretary Baker brought up this subject with Nazarbayev during his visit to Washington in May 1992.[184]

An indirect source of evidence also supports the view that there was no leakage of Kazakh tactical nuclear weapons to third parties. According to some reports, Nazarbayev did not know that Russia had actually removed the tactical nuclear weapons from his country and was furious when informed after the fact by his aides.[185] Paradoxically, the Kazakh president's anger at his ignorance is persuasive evidence that Almaty did not sell nuclear weapons overseas. It indicates that Russia, not Kazakhstan, controlled these weapons, thereby greatly minimizing the chances that any of them found their way to Iran or other countries.

THE ROAD TO LISBON

In the first months of 1992, Almaty continued its cat-and-mouse game with Moscow and Washington over the future of the strategic nuclear weapons on its territory. In January and February, Nazarbayev personally declared that Kazakhstan would join the NPT as a nonnuclear weapon state.[186] Yet the very next month, Almaty started making noises that it should be allowed to join the NPT as a nuclear power. Nazarbayev explained his logic: "[Kazakhstan] is entitled to belong to the nuclear club because tests on its territory were being carried out eighteen months before the signing of the nuclear Nonproliferation Treaty."[187]

At an international conference in Parnu, Estonia, the following month, one of Nazarbayev's key foreign policy advisers elaborated on his president's reasoning; he claimed that Kazakhstan fulfilled the NPT's definition of a nuclear weapon state "as a former governmental formation within the Soviet federation, as one of the legal successors to the USSR, and as a producer of nuclear arms—not to mention as a nuclear testing ground."[188] And in an April 27 interview with the *Christian Science Monitor*, Nazarbayev stated that he had asked the United States to regard Kazakhstan as a "temporary nuclear state" that had embarked on the road to disarmament.[189] This rather imaginative interpretation of the NPT not only increased the anxieties of Russia and the United States but also led them to question Kazakhstan's understanding of nuclear matters.

During this same period, Almaty started placing conditions on the elimination of the SS-18s. In February 1992, Nazarbayev announced that eliminating the missiles would take at least fifteen years.[190] Less than a week later, he insisted that Kazakhstan would eliminate its nuclear potential only when the United States, Russia, and China did the same.[191] In March, the Kazakh president raised the question of cost: even if Kazakhstan decided to return the strategic nuclear weapons to Russia, this action would "cost billions of rubles," which Kazakhstan did not have.[192] Whether due to fear of Moscow's moves to establish its own army, anxiety over being a nonnuclear state wedged between nuclear-armed Russia and China, a desire to be included in the START negotiations, or a policy decision about how best to win financial concessions and security guarantees from Washington and Moscow, these and other statements strongly suggested that by the beginning of May 1992, Kazakhstan intended to retain strategic nuclear weapons on its territory for some time.[193]

Yet less than three weeks later, Nazarbayev stood by President Bush's side in the White House and pledged, for the first time, to ratify the START agreement, join the NPT "in the shortest possible time," and eliminate all nuclear weapons on Kazakh territory within seven years.[194] In Lisbon four days later, Kazakhstan formalized these pledges.

What caused this remarkable turnabout? A number of events dealing with both status and security had coalesced by the middle of May to change Nazarbayev's mind. The previous month, Washington had agreed to recognize Kazakhstan, Ukraine, and Belarus, in addition to Russia, as legal successors to the Soviet Union under START, a move these countries had long sought.[195] In addition, the week before the Washington summit, Nazarbayev had signed a Collective Security Treaty at Tashkent with Russia and other CIS countries. Under the Tashkent agreement, aggression against any CIS member would be treated as aggression against all members. From Almaty's perspective, this meant a Russian security guarantee against China. In public and in private conversations with U.S. officials, Nazarbayev cited Tashkent as an important spur to his signing of the Lisbon documents. At this time, Kazakhstan and Russia had also drafted a bilateral cooperation and friendship treaty, which Nazarbayev formally initialed after his Washington trip. These assurances, combined with a letter in mid-May from the Chinese Foreign Ministry stating that Beijing relinquished all claims to Kazakh territory, markedly increased Kazakhstan's national security.[196]

These developments occurred against the background of an ongoing dialogue between Baker and Nazarbayev on the advantages and disadvantages of denuclearization. Baker had been hard at work on this issue since the previous December, repeatedly calling and writing the Kazakh leader. According to a senior Kazakh Foreign Ministry official, Baker deserved much of the credit for changing Kazakhstan's perspective on returning the strategic nuclear weapons. The U.S. secretary of state consistently emphasized that Kazakhstan's relationship with the United States would improve if the weapons went back to Russia: Almaty would receive economic aid, military assistance, and political support.[197] To underscore this point, in May 1992 Baker sent Nazarbayev a letter reiterating the security assurances that the United States would extend to Kazakhstan if it joined the NPT as a nonnuclear weapon state. Indeed, following Nazarbayev's pledges at the White House, the Kazakh leader and Bush signed a host of economic and trade agreements.

In Lisbon the next week, Kazakhstan, along with Ukraine, Belarus, and Russia, signed a protocol that formally established these countries as the "successor states" of the former Soviet Union and obligated Almaty, Kiev, and Minsk to join the NPT.[198] In addition to this protocol, Nazarbayev had already guaranteed, in a "side letter" to President Bush, that all nuclear weapons would be removed from Kazakh territory within seven years. This letter, as well as the issue of why it differs from its Ukrainian and Belarusian counterparts, contains its own drama.

Under the START agreement, only half of the 104 SS-18s deployed in Kazakhstan had to be eliminated within the prescribed seven-year implementation period.[199] But both Moscow and Washington wanted to ensure that *all* the missiles were returned to Russia during this period. En route to the United States after the Tashkent summit, Nazarbayev stopped in Moscow to meet with Yeltsin on Sunday, May 17. From his press statement after this meeting, it was clear that Nazarbayev had fooled Yeltsin into allowing Almaty to keep half of its SS-18s beyond the seven-year START framework. He noted, "We agreed that after the fulfillment of the START treaty the question of *further cuts in nuclear arms stationed in Kazakhstan's territory* will be decided by Russia and Kazakhstan."[200] After he arrived in Washington and disclosed the formula he and Yeltsin had agreed on, the State Department questioned Moscow, which made excuses for the mishap.

Nazarbayev's cleverness alerted Washington to the possibility that he might attempt a similar ploy in Lisbon. Over a working breakfast at Blair House during Nazarbayev's Washington visit, Baker warned Nazarbayev not to attempt the same formula he had used with Yeltsin and stressed that good relations with the United States depended on Kazakhstan's living up to its international commitments.[201] The pressure worked. The Lisbon side letter was brief and unambiguous; Kazakhstan agreed to remove all the SS-18 missiles during the seven-year START period.

Six weeks after Lisbon, in early July 1992, Kazakhstan ratified the START agreement. In the very brief debate that preceded the vote, a few nationalist parliamentarians portrayed START as a betrayal of the country's national interests. These legislators carried little influence, however. Quick START ratification was a dividend from the Washington and Lisbon summits, since Kazakhstan wanted to impress the United States with a demonstration of its good faith.[202]

THE NONPROLIFERATION TREATY

During his May 1992 visit to Washington, Nazarbayev assured Bush that Kazakhstan did not have any substantive questions concerning NPT ratification. All that remained were routine procedural matters, such as preparing the appropriate documents for the parliament, matters that would require only a few months to complete.[203] Yet it took another year and a half and the intervention of Vice President Gore before Kazakhstan finally ratified the NPT.

This delay could be attributed to several factors: the rhythm of American domestic politics, internal disorder in Russia, more pressing international crises, Moscow's heavy-handed negotiating methods,[204] and most important, no sense of urgency on Almaty's part to join the NPT. Soon after Kazakhstan ratified START, Secretary Baker and his top aides left the State Department to work on President Bush's reelection campaign. Facing charges that Bush spent too much time on foreign policy and not enough on domestic policy, the Bush State Department toned down its active, internationalist role. Clinton's election victory in November meant further delay, since the new president had to assemble a new national security team, which then had to be confirmed and fully briefed. This took time, which the Clinton administration found it did not have. Weeks after the inauguration, North Korea refused IAEA inspections and gave notice that it intended to withdraw from the NPT. Foreign policy setbacks in Bosnia, Somalia, and Haiti stole the administration's attention as it confronted bitter sniping from critics over the stewardship of American foreign policy.

In Russia, Yeltsin continued to battle conservatives and unreconstructed Communists as he tried to institute an economic reform package. This political dispute turned bloody after disaffected legislators seized the Russian parliament building in early October 1993; Yeltsin had to use the army to dislodge them. When Washington and Moscow focused on the other CIS members, their attention primarily centered not on Kazakhstan but on Ukraine, which for most of the year refused to even vote on the START agreement, the Lisbon documents, and the NPT.

Compared with these events, Kazakhstan's NPT status was very much a second-order problem. Almaty understandably interpreted this neglect as a slight. As one senior Foreign Ministry official bemoaned: "When the Clinton administration talks about nuclear weapons in the former Soviet Union, it goes first to Russia, then to Ukraine, and then to other countries. In his [September 1993] UN speech, Clinton mentioned Russia, Ukraine, and others, but not Kazakhstan."[205]

Still, nothing prevented Kazakhstan from simply ratifying the NPT anytime it wanted. But given the fresh American administration and the time lapse since START ratification, Almaty realized that it could take advantage of the Clinton administration's lack of a proven record on nuclear issues and parlay NPT membership into further concessions. Despite all the diplomatic exchanges, bilateral agreements, and pledges to the Bush administration, Kazakhstan's attitude was now: "What have you done for me lately?"

Consequently, when U.S. Secretary of State Christopher visited Kazakhstan in October 1993, he was surprised by Nazarbayev's refusal to sign an agreement that would release U.S. funds to Kazakhstan for nuclear dismantlement. The Kazakh leader insisted on signing it with Clinton, and he reportedly unrolled a map and pointed out to Christopher all the dangers on Kazakhstan's borders.[206] Kazakh insecurity was not a new issue; Baker had repeatedly explained the U.S. security assurances Almaty could expect if it ratified the NPT. Moreover, Nazarbayev had just returned from a visit to China, where he and President Jiang Zemin had issued a joint declaration that included China's promise never to use nuclear weapons first against Kazakhstan, a nonaggression pledge, and an expression of mutual respect for each other's sovereignty and territorial integrity.[207] Nevertheless, Nazarbayev felt that he had little to lose by probing Christopher to see if he could win any additional security commitments from Washington.

In the weeks after the Christopher trip, negotiations between the United States and Kazakhstan continued. The Clinton administration told Kazakhstan that Nazarbayev would receive his meeting with the president only if it signed an "umbrella agreement" to provide U.S. dismantlement funds to Almaty and, more important, if it joined the NPT. In mid-December, Vice President Gore met with Nazarbayev in Almaty and closed the deal. Gore reiterated the importance the United

States attached to NPT membership. Nazarbayev immediately telephoned the parliament, which two hours later voted 238–1 in favor of
joining the NPT.[208]

The lopsided vote proved that Nazarbayev could have had Kazakhstan ratify the NPT anytime he wanted. Clearly, he hoped to use this
remaining piece of leverage to its maximum benefit. And he succeeded. In return for NPT ratification, Gore agreed that Nazarbayev
could meet in Washington with Clinton. Kazakhstan would also receive an estimated $84 million in dismantlement and other nuclear-re-
lated assistance, and the United States pledged to invest close to $200
million in economic assistance in Kazakhstan and other central Asian
countries during the next three years.[209] At a February 1994 meeting at
the White House, Clinton told Nazarbayev that the United States
would triple its foreign aid to Kazakhstan.[210]

CONCLUSION

By the end of 1993, the entire SS-18 force in Kazakhstan was deactivated, and 120 warheads from 10 missiles had been shipped back to
Russia.[211] Moscow had probably rotated these warheads out of the
country under the guise of "servicing the missiles" and then simply
not rotated them back in. Kazakhstan had not protested, even though
the START agreement had not yet entered into force. By February
1994, all 40 long-range bombers had flown back to Russia.[212] According to Russian news reports, during the March 28 summit Yeltsin and
Nazarbayev agreed that all nuclear warheads would be removed from
Kazakhstan within fourteen months and the missiles and their silos
destroyed within three years.[213]

Why did Kazakhstan choose this pragmatic path to denuclearization? According to U.S. Ambassador William Courtney, Kazakhstan's
strategic position played an important role. Kazakhstan's location and
ethnic composition demanded that it not aggravate Russia, which offered the only possible counter to any future threats from its other nuclear-armed neighbor, China.[214] For example, unlike Ukraine, Kazakhstan never insisted on compensation for the fissile material contained
in the tactical nuclear warheads returned to Russia. Almaty had not
requested reimbursement when Moscow removed the weapons in
January 1992, and the Kazakh Foreign Ministry thought that raising
this issue later would needlessly inflame tensions with Russia.[215] In
addition, Almaty's policy of deliberate denuclearization was aimed at
eliciting tangible benefits from Washington, with which it hoped to establish good relations. Blocking or retarding the return of nuclear

weapons to Russia would have poisoned ties between Kazakhstan and the United States. Also, local considerations strongly influenced this policy. The tragic legacy of the Semipalatinsk nuclear testing site ensured that Almaty had little desire to retain nuclear arms.

To these factors must be added the personality of Nursultan Nazarbayev. Kazakhstan possessed an astute leader who understood sooner and more clearly than others the limits within which he could maneuver to best promote his country's interests. According to a presidential adviser, the Kazakh leader had decided from the very beginning that the nuclear weapons had to be returned to Russia.[216] But he adroitly negotiated the pace, terms, and price of their return to extract maximum advantage. He was able to parlay a weak hand—a poor economy, fewer nuclear weapons than in Ukraine, borders with two nuclear-armed states, enormous human suffering and environmental harm from past nuclear tests, and suspicion over ties to other Moslem states—into a winning hand, gaining kudos for his statesmanship and international status for his country.

Chronology

AUGUST 1991 The Moscow coup fails.

NOVEMBER The U.S. Congress passes the Soviet Nuclear Threat Reduction Act, which pledges $400 million to assist the safe dismantlement and storage of nuclear weapons and materials in the former Soviet Union.

DECEMBER 1 In a national referendum, Ukraine votes overwhelmingly in favor of independence.

DECEMBER 8 Boris Yeltsin, Leonid Kravchuk, and Stanislav Shushkevich announce the formation of the Commonwealth of Independent States (CIS) to replace the Soviet Union.

DECEMBER 21 The Agreement on Joint Measures on Nuclear Arms is signed at the CIS summit in Alma Ata; Ukraine, Kazakhstan, and Belarus pledge to return all tactical nuclear weapons to Russia by July 1, 1992, and to accept comprehensive IAEA safeguards; Ukraine and Belarus pledge to join the NPT as nonnuclear weapon states.

DECEMBER 30 Ukraine pledges at the CIS summit in Minsk to return all strategic nuclear weapons to Russia by December 31, 1994; Ukraine agrees that nuclear weapons on its soil are under the joint command of the Combined Strategic Forces Command.

JANUARY 1992 Russia begins removing tactical nuclear weapons from Ukraine and Belarus and withdraws all such weapons from Kazakhstan.

MARCH Kravchuk announces that he is suspending further withdrawals of tactical nuclear weapons.

APRIL Kravchuk decrees that all military forces in Ukraine, including those responsible for guarding nuclear weapons, are under the control of the Ministry of Defense.

The United States formally accepts that Ukraine, Kazakhstan, and Belarus, along with Russia, are successors to the Soviet Union for purposes of the Strategic Arms Reduction Treaty (START).

Russia removes the last tactical nuclear weapons from Belarus.

MAY 6–7 Moscow surprises Kiev by announcing that all tactical nuclear weapons have been removed from Ukraine; Ukrainian officials scramble to confirm the news; Kravchuk announces, before the U.S. National Press Club, that the accelerated withdrawal was a joint decision by Ukraine and Russia.

The United States negotiates "side letters" with Ukraine, Kazakhstan, and Belarus—letters that require the return to Russia of all nuclear warheads on their territories, not just those covered by START, within the seven-year START time frame.

Kazakhstan signs the Tashkent Collective Security Treaty, which grants Almaty a Russian security guarantee against China.

MAY 23 The United States, Russia, Ukraine, Kazakhstan, and Belarus meet in Lisbon to sign the Lisbon Protocol, which formally makes Ukraine, Kazakhstan, and Belarus parties to START and obligates them to join the NPT as nonnuclear weapon states "in the shortest possible time"; the side letters are also formally signed.

JULY Kazakhstan ratifies START I.

Belarus assigns jurisdiction over the SS-25s to Russia.

OCTOBER Shushkevich announces that all strategic nuclear warheads in Belarus will be returned to Russia by the end of 1994.

NOVEMBER Russia ratifies START, conditioned on prior implementation of denuclearization agreements with Ukraine, Kazakhstan, and Belarus.

FEBRUARY 4, 1993 Belarus ratifies START I, the Lisbon documents, and the NPT.

MARCH The United States pledges an additional $65 million to Belarus to assist denuclearization efforts.

APRIL–MAY The administration of U.S. President Bill Clinton reverses its initial pressure tactics toward Ukraine and instead opts for a broader engagement that encompasses economic, military, and political ties.

JUNE With the dissolution of the CIS Joint Military High Command, all nuclear forces now come under the command of Russia's Strategic Rocket Forces (SRF).

JULY The Rada claims temporary ownership of all nuclear weapons on its territory and is supported by Kravchuk.

Ukraine begins to deactivate the SS-19 missiles.

SEPTEMBER The Massandra summit between Russia and Ukraine ends with mutual recriminations.

Belarus and Russia formally agree that all strategic nuclear warheads will be returned to Russia by the end of 1996.

U.S. Secretary of State Warren Christopher visits Ukraine; the United States refuses to provide security assurances in return for SS-19 and SS-24 deactivation and holds out for ratification of START, the Lisbon documents, and the NPT.

NOVEMBER 18 The Rada ratifies START I with seven conditions; Clinton calls Kravchuk to express his disappointment; Kravchuk orders SS-24s to be deactivated.

DECEMBER Vladimir Zhirinovsky's Liberal Democratic Party is the leading vote-getter in Russian parliamentary elections; Ukraine's economy sinks lower; concerns increase over the safety of nuclear warheads in Ukraine.

U.S. Vice President Al Gore meets with Nursultan Nazarbayev in Almaty; Kazakhstan ratifies the NPT; by the end of December, the entire SS-18 force in Kazakhstan is deactivated.

JANUARY 1994 Clinton, Yeltsin, and Kravchuk sign the Trilateral Agreement and Annex, along with six secret letters; the United States, Russia, and Britain condition security assurances to Ukraine on ratification of START and the NPT; Ukraine pledges to return all strategic nuclear warheads to Russia within three years in exchange for nuclear fuel and debt forgiveness.

Ukrainian Economics Minister Roman Shpek visits Washington; the Clinton administration promises to double U.S. financial assistance if the Rada passes the Trilateral Agreement.

FEBRUARY The Rada votes to remove the conditions it had imposed on START and the Lisbon documents in November 1993; it does not ratify the NPT.

At a White House meeting, Clinton promises Nazarbayev that the United States will triple U.S. assistance to Kazakhstan.

MARCH SS-19 and SS-24 nuclear warheads begin to leave Ukraine for Russia at the rate of sixty per month.

NOVEMBER The Rada approves Ukraine's joining the NPT; by this time, 360 strategic nuclear warheads have been removed from Ukraine and returned to Russia; at a White House ceremony, Clinton promises Kuchma an additional $200 million in U.S. economic aid.

DECEMBER 5 Ukraine formally joins the NPT, and the United States, Russia, and Britain provide "additional" security assurances; START I officially enters into force.

Notes

Ukraine

[1] See Robert Conquest, *The Harvest of Sorrow: Soviet Collectivization and the Terror-Famine* (Oxford: Oxford University Press, 1986), pp. 299–307.

[2] Ukrainian nationalists claim that Ukrainian and Russian history is not a continuum from Kievan Rus to the late twentieth century; rather, Ukrainian history was suspended from Kievan Rus until 1991, except for the short-lived period after World War I. For an excellent one-volume history of Ukraine, see Orest Subtelny, *Ukraine: A History* (Toronto: University of Toronto Press, 1988); see also John A. Armstrong, *Ukrainian Nationalism*, 3d ed. (Englewood, Colo.: Ukrainian Academic Press, 1990).

[3] See David Marples, "One Million Ukrainians Affected by Chernobyl," *Radio Liberty Report on the USSR* 2, no. 13 (March 30, 1990): 19–21. For additional information on the Chernobyl disaster, see *The International Chernobyl Project: Technical Report* (Vienna: IAEA, 1991); Grigorii Medvedev, *The Truth about Chernobyl* (New York: Basic Books, 1991); Zhores A. Medvedev, *The Legacy of Chernobyl* (New York: Norton, 1990); Iurii Shcherbak, *Chernobyl: A Documentary Story* (New York: St. Martin's, 1989); Richard F. Mould, *Chernobyl—The Real Story* (New York: Pergamon, 1988).

[4] Complicating any new policy formulation was the fact that U.S. influence with Ukraine had suffered a severe setback earlier in the month. On August 1, 1991, President George Bush delivered a speech in Kiev that poisoned Ukrainian-American relations and handicapped subsequent U.S. efforts to rid Ukraine of nuclear arms. To a people who had endured tragedies of biblical proportions for over seventy years, Bush lectured: "Freedom is not the same as independence. Americans will not support those who seek independence in order to replace a far-off tyranny with a local despotism. They will not aid those who promote a suicidal nationalism based on ethnic hatred." Dubbed the "chicken Kiev" speech by *New York Times* columnist William Safire, this injunction was interpreted by Ukrainians as an official American rejection of their aspirations for freedom.

Bush was acutely sensitive to Soviet feelings about his visit to Kiev; Moscow had in fact asked him not to go. Further, according to one account, "During a discussion of the Kiev stop, Bush told Baker, Scowcroft, and Sununu, `Whatever we do, I don't want to make trouble for Gorbachev, so let's handle it with that in mind.'" Michael R. Beschloss and Strobe Talbott, *At the Highest Levels: The Inside Story of the End of the Cold War* (Boston: Little, Brown, 1993), pp. 408ff. The Beschloss and Talbott treatment of the Kiev visit is extremely forgiving to the president and his advisers. For a much more critical assessment, which suggests that Bush inserted the specific phrase "suicidal nationalism" into his speech at Gorbachev's personal request, see Susan D. Fink, "From 'Chicken Kiev' to Ukrainian Recognition: Domestic Politics in U.S. Foreign Policy" (master's thesis, Naval Postgraduate School, Monterey, California, June 1993). The text of the president's speech can be found in *Public Papers of the Presidents of the United States: George Bush*, book 2 (Washington, D.C.: USGPO, 1992), pp. 1005–8.

[5] There was a brief, almost theoretical, debate within the Bush administration about whether Washington could or should prevent Ukraine from acquiring nuclear weapons. Some Pentagon officials thought that a nuclear Ukraine might

counter future Russian expansionism but would have a neuralgic influence on Poland and Germany. State Department officials also warned that Ukraine's assertion of operational control over the nuclear weapons on its territory would entail an unstable transition period, during which time Ukraine would be vulnerable to a preemptive Russian military strike. Further, an encircled and insecure Russia would feel threatened and might lash out in other ways contrary to U.S. interests. Dennis Ross, personal interview, Washington, D.C., February 8, 1994; Steven Hadley, personal interview, Washington, D.C., May 2, 1994; Paul Wolfowitz, personal interview, Washington, D.C., June 29, 1994.

[6]This go-slow approach was also favored because of Washington's uncertainty over Ukraine's intentions. In late October, Washington did not know whether Ukraine would vote for independence in the December 1 referendum. The American Embassy in Moscow had cabled that the high percentage of ethnic Russians in eastern Ukraine, coupled with the fact that Ukraine had voted in favor of the Union Treaty in March 1991, made the outcome in December unclear. At a NATO summit in mid-November, the United States opposed those allies who wanted to extend diplomatic recognition to Ukraine. (Canada was Kiev's strongest advocate at this meeting; Ottawa was especially sensitive to Ukrainian independence because of the large Ukrainian diaspora living in Canada.) As the December 1 vote approached, the way Ukraine would vote became clearer. In mid-November, the U.S. consulate in Kiev concluded that 70–75 percent of the country would vote for independence; at the time this was a still-radical (and unwelcome) view within much of the U.S. foreign policy establishment. Current and former senior U.S. government officials, personal interviews, Washington, D.C., January, February, and May 1994. After the creation of the CIS, the Bush administration quickly shifted gears to emphasize single, central control over the nuclear weapons arsenal. See James A. Baker III, "America and the Collapse of the Soviet Empire: What Has to Be Done," address at Princeton University, December 12, 1991, reprinted in U.S. Department of State, *Dispatch* 2, no. 50 (December 16, 1991): 887–93.

[7]Senior U.S. government official, personal interview, Washington, D.C., January 1994. For an excellent treatment of U.S. and NATO nuclear diplomacy during December 1991, see Steven Miller, "Western Diplomacy and the Soviet Nuclear Legacy," *Survival* 34, no. 3 (Autumn 1992): 3–27.

[8]To be sure, Ukraine was recognized as an independent state by the Central Powers in 1918 and by the United Nations in 1945. The first period of independence was short-lived, and recognition in 1945 was a sham designed to mollify Joseph Stalin.

[9]Kravchuk actually tried to prevent Moscow from restarting the removal of tactical nuclear weapons; this was somewhat easier than trying to stop a withdrawal process that was already under way. For the Kravchuk suspension announcement, see *TASS*, March 12, 1992, reported in Foreign Broadcast Information Service, *Daily Report, Central Eurasia* (hereafter cited as FBIS-SOV), 92-050 (March 13, 1992), p. 5; for Russia's reaction, see FBIS-SOV-92-051 (March 16, 1992), pp. 3–6; FBIS-SOV-92-052 (March 17, 1992), pp. 1–3.

[10]Article 8 of the Agreement on Joint Measures on Nuclear Arms stipulated, "The present Agreement requires ratification." Anton Buteiko defended Kravchuk's suspension decision on this basis, saying that prior Ukrainian cooperation had been a goodwill gesture. *Krasnaya Zvezda*, March 17, 1992, reported in FBIS-SOV-92-053 (March 18, 1992), p. 3.

[11]*Krasnaya Zvezda*, March 17, 1992, reported in FBIS-SOV-92-053 (March 18, 1992), p. 3.

[12]Margaret Shapiro, "Ex-Soviet Leaders Fail to Settle Disputes," *Washington Post*, March 21, 1992; see also Fred Hiatt, "Commonwealth Faces Unstable Future," *Washington Post*, March 22, 1992.

[13]One example was Kravchuk's March 12 declaration; less than a week later, Ukrainian Foreign Minister Anatoly Zlenko wrote NATO Secretary General Manfred Wörner, stating that Kiev would adhere to the July 1 withdrawal date. Kravchuk's press secretary immediately refuted this report, as did Kravchuk himself at the Kiev CIS summit. See FBIS-SOV-92-055 (March 20, 1992), p. 1. One reason for the lack of coordination was that Kravchuk had established a defense advisory committee, which did not include Zlenko or any other Foreign Ministry officials. It was this committee that had advised Kravchuk to suspend the removal of the tactical nuclear weapons. Even if the Foreign Ministry had been more closely consulted, it is unclear what effect the ministry would have had on policy-making. For example, the senior arms control expert at the Foreign Ministry relied on U.S. officials at the American Embassy in Kiev to educate him on the CFE treaty, the Helsinki Final Act, the differences between liquid- and solid-fueled missiles, and other arms control and security matters.

[14]On Russian-Ukrainian tensions at this time, see *Izvestiya*, February 7, 1992, reported in FBIS-USR-92-015 (February 18, 1992), pp. 18–21. A bizarre incident also contributed to bad blood between Moscow and Kiev in early 1992. On February 6, six Su-24 strategic bombers left the Ciscarpathian Military District in western Ukraine on a routine training mission to Belarus. They were scheduled to return two weeks later but never did, despite repeated Ukrainian protests. See *TASS*, February 17, 1992, reported in FBIS-SOV-92-032 (February 18, 1992), p. 57; *Komsomolskaya*, February 20, 1992, reported in FBIS-SOV-92-034 (February 20, 1992), p. 77; see also FBIS-SOV-92-064 (April 2, 1992), p. 67; FBIS-SOV-92-158 (August 14, 1992), p. 31.

[15]*ITAR-TASS*, April 16, 1992, reported in FBIS-SOV-92-075 (April 17, 1992), p. 2. Under the terms of the agreement, Ukrainian officers could monitor portal-to-border removal and then dismantlement at the dismantlement site. This was thus not a closed-loop portal-to-portal system, so there was no guarantee that any tactical nuclear weapon that was dismantled in Russia had actually come from Ukraine. Senior U.S. government official, personal interview, Washington, D.C., January 1994.

[16]Kravchuk was scheduled to visit Iran in late April before coming to Washington. The United States was very concerned about a possible Ukraine-Iran nuclear connection. Before Kravchuk's visit to Tehran, the U.S. government informed him that his visit to Washington would be canceled if the United States learned of any nuclear deal. U.S. government official, personal interview, Washington, D.C., January 1994. See also FBIS-SOV-92-081 (April 27, 1992), pp. 49–50.

[17]See *Izvestiya*, May 7, 1992, reported in FBIS-SOV-92-089 (May 7, 1992), p. 2.

[18]Boris Tarasiuk, personal interview, Kiev, Ukraine, October 29, 1993. See also FBIS-SOV-92-089 (May 7, 1992), p. 2; FBIS-SOV-92-088 (May 6, 1992), p. 2; FBIS-SOV-92-090 (May 8, 1992), pp. 2–3, 44–45. Russia claimed that Ukrainian military officers had monitored the pullout but that they had neglected to inform the Foreign Ministry or the president's office.

[19]For Kravchuk's appearance before the National Press Club, see Don Oberdorfer, "Ukraine Shifts Nuclear Arms to Russia," *Washington Post,* May 8, 1992. It appears that the United States was also overtaken by events; in the joint statement of Presidents Bush and Kravchuk, issued by the White House on May 6, Kiev affirmed "its resolution to complete the removal of all tactical nuclear arms from its territory prior to 1 July 1992."

[20]On April 11, 1992, Ukraine, Kazakhstan, and Belarus had issued a joint statement that they and Russia were the legal heirs of the assets of the Soviet Union. This statement accelerated Washington's policy reversal later that month. In addition, Ukrainian Defense Minister Morozov visited Washington at this time; he was the first senior Ukrainian official to visit Washington, and his visit may also have influenced the change in U.S. policy.

[21]Strictly speaking, the START I agreement did not require the elimination of the SS-19s. The agreement allowed each party great flexibility in deciding which weapon systems to cut, with the presumption that the oldest systems, such as the SS-19s, would be eliminated first. The exception to this general rule was that twenty-two SS-18s had to be eliminated each year during START's seven-year implementation period. See *START: Treaty between the United States of America and the Union of Soviet Socialist Republics on the Reduction and Limitation of Strategic Offensive Arms* (Washington, D.C.: U.S. ACDA, 1991).

[22]Senior U.S. government official, personal interview, Washington, D.C., January 1994. This condition was stipulated in Article 6 of the protocol.

[23]Ross, personal interview, Washington, D.C., February 8, 1994. For an excellent examination of Russian-Ukrainian economic, political, and security relations from 1990 to 1993 and of how competing interpretations of history complicated this relationship, see John Morrison, "Pereyaslav and After: The Russian-Ukrainian Relationship," *International Affairs* 69, no. 4 (October 1993): 677–703.

[24]Ross, personal interview, Washington, D.C., February 8, 1994. To be sure, Acting Secretary of State Lawrence Eagleburger visited Kiev during this period to discuss the nuclear issue, but by this time the Ukrainians may have decided to await the outcome of the U.S. presidential election. A lesser factor in Washington's decision not to pressure Kiev was the Bush campaign's fear of alienating Ukrainian-American voters, who already mistrusted the administration after the president's speech in Kiev the previous year.

[25]Roman Solchanyk, "Kravchuk Defines Ukrainian-CIS Relations," *Radio Free Europe/Radio Liberty Research Report* (hereafter cited as *RFE/RL Research Report*) 1, no. 11 (March 13, 1992): 8. For traditional Soviet attitudes toward Ukraine, see Roman Szporluk, "The Ukraine and Russia," in Robert Conquest, ed., *The Last Empire: Nationality and the Soviet Future* (Stanford, Calif.: Hoover Institution Press, 1986), pp. 151–82; idem, "The Imperial Legacy and the Soviet Nationalities Problem," in Lubomyr Hajda and Mark Beissinger, eds., *The Nationalities Factor in Soviet Politics and Society* (Boulder, Colo.: Westview, 1990), pp. 1–23.

[26]I am indebted to Markian Bilynsky for bringing this point to my attention. Russian officials periodically revealed their dreams of reincorporating Ukraine into the Russian fold. When Russian Foreign Minister Andrei Kozyrev was asked in June 1993 what he thought of the idea of reunification of Ukraine and Russia, he said, "I am for it." Quoted in Roman Solchanyk, "The Ukrainian-Russian Summit: Problems and Prospects," *RFE/RL Research Report* 2, no. 27 (July 2, 1993): 28. The

Russian ambassador to the United States at the time, Vladimir Lukin, urged Ukraine to recognize Russia's "special interests and influence" and "Russia's zone of natural gravity" in Ukraine, a nod not only to the past but also to the large ethnic Russian population in Ukraine. Lukin favored a "confederative type" of arrangement between the two countries. *Segodnya* (Moscow), September 3, 1993, reported in FBIS-SOV-93-172 (September 8, 1993), pp. 16–19. Russian Defense Minister Pavel Grachev went further, calling for a "military union" between Ukraine and Russia. *ITAR-TASS,* September 4, 1993, reported in FBIS-SOV-93-171 (September 7, 1993), p. 10.

[27]In April 1992, Russian Vice President Alexander Rutskoi stated that Crimea belonged to Russia: "If in 1954, perhaps under the influence of a hang-over or maybe of sunstroke, the appropriate documents were signed according to which the Crimea was transferred to the jurisdiction of Ukraine, I am sorry, such a document does not cancel out the history of the Crimea." Alexander Rutskoi in *Pravda Ukrainy,* April 7, 1992, quoted in Roman Solchanyk, "Ukraine and Russia: The Politics of Independence," *RFE/RL Research Report 1,* no. 19 (May 8, 1992): 15. Anatoly Sobchak, mayor of Saint Petersburg, and Ruslan Khasbulatov, chairman of the Russian parliament, made similar statements.

[28]See James Rupert, "Russian Deputies Claim Ukraine's Naval Base," *Washington Post,* July 10, 1993; Serge Schmemann, "Russian Parliament Votes a Claim to Ukrainian Port of Sevastopol," *New York Times,* July 10, 1993; *ITAR-TASS,* July 9, 1993, reported in FBIS-SOV-93-131 (July 12, 1993), p. 32. For the immediate reaction to the resolution in Ukraine, see FBIS-SOV-93-131 (July 12, 1993), pp. 35–38; FBIS-SOV-93-133 (July 14, 1993), pp. 44–45. On Yeltsin's denunciation, see *New York Times,* July 11, 1993.

Sevastopol resonates throughout Russian and Soviet history from the days of Catherine the Great to its heroic stance against the Germans during World War II. See Jane Perlez, "All at Sea off Crimea: Whose Navy Is It, Anyway?" *New York Times,* July 22, 1993; Suzanne Crow, "Russian Parliament Asserts Control over Sevastopol," *RFE/RL Research Report 2,* no. 31 (July 30, 1993): 37–41; Celestine Bohlen, "For Russia and Ukraine, Crimea Is a Sore Nerve," *New York Times,* March 23, 1994; more generally, Alan Fisher, *The Crimean Tatars* (Stanford: Hoover Institution Press, 1978).

[29]The agreement was signed in Moscow on June 17, 1993. See FBIS-SOV-93-116 (June 18, 1993), pp. 40–42; see also Douglas L. Clarke, "The Saga of the Black Sea Fleet," *RFE/RL Research Report 1,* no. 4 (January 24, 1992): 45–49; Solchanyk, "The Ukrainian-Russian Summit," pp. 29–30; John W. R. Lepingwell, "The Black Sea Fleet Agreement: Progress or Empty Promises?" *RFE/RL Research Report 2,* no. 28 (July 9, 1993): 48–55.

[30]See John Lough, "The Place of the 'Near Abroad' in Russian Foreign Policy," *RFE/RL Research Report 2,* no. 11 (March 12, 1993): 21–29. See generally Teresa Pelton Johnson and Steven E. Miller, eds., *Russian Security after the Cold War,* CSIA Studies in International Security No. 3 (Washington, D.C.: Brassey's, 1994).

[31]Yeltsin was quoted as saying: "I think the moment has come when responsible international organizations, including the United Nations, should grant Russia special powers as a guarantor of peace and stability in the region of the former Soviet Union. Russia has a heartfelt interest in stopping all armed conflicts on the territory of the former Soviet Union." Serge Schmemann, "Yeltsin Suggests Russian Regional Role," *New York Times,* March 1, 1993.

[32]*RIA* (Moscow), November 20, 1993, reported in FBIS-SOV-93-231-A (December 3, 1993), p. 1; Daniel Williams, "Russia Asserts Role in Ex-Soviet Republics,"

Washington Post, September 29, 1993; Paul Lewis, "At U.N., Russian Stresses Peril of Ethnic Conflict," *New York Times,* September 29, 1993. Kozyrev's speech was a forceful rejoinder to U.S. offers to mediate disputes between Ukraine and Russia and play a larger role in the newly independent states of the former Soviet Union. On the Partnership for Peace proposal, see *RFE/RL Research Report* 3, no. 12 (March 25, 1994): 1–43.

[33]Western diplomats, personal interviews, Kiev, October 25, 27, 1993.

[34]See John W. R. Lepingwell, "Negotiations over Nuclear Weapons: The Past as Prologue?" *RFE/RL Research Report* 3, no. 4 (January 28, 1994): 1–11.

[35]The Central and East European countries rebuffed Kravchuk's proposal because they did not want to antagonize Russia. See Roman Solchanyk, "Ukraine's Search for Security," *RFE/RL Research Report* 2, no. 21 (May 21, 1993): 1–6.

[36]See Celestine Bohlen, "Yeltsin Promises Ukraine Security Guarantees," *New York Times,* June 18, 1993. This offer came just before the Rada was about to consider ratifying START I, the Lisbon documents, and the NPT.

[37]The Soviet Nuclear Threat Reduction Act of 1991 can be found in Title II of the "Conventional Forces in Europe Treaty Implementation Act of 1991," Public Law 102-228, December 12, 1991. By the end of 1993, *none* of the $177 million proposed for Ukraine had actually been obligated; only one-quarter of the proposed funds for Russia had been obligated. See "U.S. Security Assistance to the Former Soviet Union," *Arms Control Today* (January-February 1994), pp. 32–33; see also Theodor Galdi, "The Nunn-Lugar Cooperative Threat Reduction Program for Soviet Weapons Dismantlement: Background and Implementation," *Congressional Research Service Report* (December 29, 1993); John Fialka, "Helping Ourselves: U.S. Aid to Russia Is Quite a Windfall—for U.S. Consultants," *Wall Street Journal,* February 24, 1994. The reasons why so little funding had actually reached these states include bureaucratic obstacles encountered by the United States, both at the Pentagon, which had to transfer money from existing Defense Department programs, and at the ministries in Moscow, Kiev, Minsk, and Almaty.

[38]U.S. Arms Control and Disarmament Agency, "Agreement between the Government of the United States of America and the Government of the Russian Federation Concerning the Disposition of Highly Enriched Uranium Extracted from Nuclear Weapons," February 18, 1993.

Uranium with less than 20 percent U-235 is considered low-enriched uranium; if it contains 20 percent or more U-235, it is considered highly enriched uranium. For nuclear explosives, weapons designers prefer to use uranium with a concentration of greater than 90 percent U-235.

The United States has established a quasi-independent company, the U.S. Enrichment Corporation (USEC), which will be responsible for purchasing the Russian uranium and marketing it to U.S. and international utilities. For U.S. taxpayers there is some risk that the Department of the Treasury may have to assume any losses suffered by the USEC. See U.S. Congress, Office of Technology Assessment, *Dismantling the Bomb and Managing the Nuclear Materials,* OTA-O-572 (Washington, D.C.: USGPO, 1993), pp. 137–45.

[39]A number of rationales were used to justify this purchase. The most persuasive was that the money from the HEU sale could be used by Russia to bolster its economy, underwrite dismantlement activities, and improve nuclear safety and security at nuclear power stations and dismantlement and storage facilities. Yet the

agreement contains no provisions tying U.S. funds to Russia's upgrading its reactor operations or improving the safety and security of nuclear dismantlement and storage sites. Indeed, there are no conditions on how Russia uses the money at all.

The deal was also justified on nonproliferation grounds. The following statement from the Office of Technology Assessment is representative: "A major incentive for U.S. purchase of Russian weapons HEU is to limit the security and proliferation threat represented by this material as long as it remains in Russia." Office of Technology Assessment, *Dismantling the Bomb*, p. 140; see also The White House, Office of the Press Secretary, "U.S.-Russian Agreement on Highly Enriched Uranium," Washington, D.C., August 31, 1992. Yet Washington has attached no strings that would prevent Russia from using this money to produce additional HEU to replace that sold to the United States, thereby vitiating whatever nonproliferation benefit may be achieved from removing the material from Russia. In fact, some Russian officials have stated that Russia will continue to produce HEU.

Unless Washington commits itself to purchasing *all* of Russia's HEU, the non-proliferation benefit from a *partial* purchase is unclear if hundreds of tons of HEU remain in Russia. This is a distinct possibility. See Office of Technology Assessment, *Dismantling the Bomb*, p. 141. As of 1995, American officials did not have an accurate accounting of Russia's HEU inventory, which has been estimated at one thousand tons. And even if the United States somehow purchased all of Russia's HEU (which is not current U.S. policy) and obtained Moscow's pledge not to produce any more (and could verify this), approximately one hundred metric tons of weapons-grade plutonium would still be left in Russia. In sum, a partial approach to the fissile material situation in Russia may be justifiable on other grounds but not in terms of significantly advancing the cause of nuclear nonproliferation.

It is also unclear whether this deal will be "budget-neutral for the U.S. government on a year-to-year basis," as both the Bush and the Clinton administrations claimed. See ibid., pp. 142–43; Dick Kovan, "Russia's HEU Sell-off: What Cost to the West's Nuclear Industry?" *Nuclear Engineering International* (January 1994), pp. 50–53; see also Heather Wilson, "Missed Opportunities: Washington Politics and Nuclear Proliferation," *National Interest*, no. 34 (Winter 1993–94), pp. 26–36; Peter Passell, "A Deal with Russia on Uranium Draws Protest from U.S. Industry," *New York Times*, June 8, 1994.

40The two Pentagon officials credited with this idea are Scooter Libby and Eric Adelman. Defense Department official, personal interview, January 28, 1994.

41On the disposition of plutonium, see Office of Technology Assessment, *Dismantling the Bomb*, pp. 67–108; see also Zachary S. Davis, "Nuclear Weapons: Dismantlement and Disposal in the States of the Former Soviet Union," *CRS Issue Brief* (June 7, 1993). Moscow has asserted that weapons-grade plutonium has economic value. See Thomas W. Lippman, "Russia Thinks Plutonium from Arms Has Commercial Value, Congress Told," *Washington Post*, March 10, 1993.

The U.S. government independently calculated the "true" value of the HEU in the nuclear warheads in Ukraine. The costs of dismantling the devices and blending down the HEU to obtain low-enriched uranium equaled 50–60 percent of the market value of the low-enriched uranium. U.S. State Department official, personal interview, Washington, D.C., May 27, 1994. See also John W. R. Lepingwell, "How Much Is a Warhead Worth?" *RFE/RL Research Report* 2, no. 8 (February 19, 1993): 62–64. Lepingwell concludes that Ukraine overestimated the amount of compensation it was due. See also, in the same issue, John W. R. Lepingwell, "Beyond START: Ukrainian-Russian Negotiations," pp. 46–58.

[42]Nationalist Vyacheslav Chornovil, leader of the Rukh opposition party in the Rada, declared in February 1993 that Ukraine's dismantlement costs could run to $2 billion. Two months later, Yuri Kostenko, citing the environmental problems in disposing of liquid fuel from the SS-19s, put a price tag of $3 billion on complete disarmament. See *Interfax*, February 1, 1993, reported in Joint Publications Research Service, *Proliferation Issues* (hereafter referred to as JPRS-TND), 93-005 (February 12, 1993), p. 28; *ITAR-TASS*, April 23, 1993, reported in JPRS-TND-93-012 (May 4, 1993), pp. 37–38. Dmytro Pavlychko, chairman of the Rada's Foreign Affairs Committee, claimed in October 1993 that the amount of HEU and plutonium in the tactical nuclear weapons alone was worth $3 billion. Dmytro Pavlychko, personal interview, Kiev, Ukraine, October 27, 1993. His colleague and chairman of the Supreme Council, Ivan Pliushch, trumped him by telling Secretary of State Warren Christopher later that month that Ukraine required $5 billion for returning the strategic nuclear warheads to Russia. JPRS-TND-93-036 (November 17, 1993), p. 28.

[43]A thorough examination of this complex and arcane subject is beyond the scope of this chapter. Interested readers are directed to an excellent study by Bruce Blair, *The Logic of Accidental Nuclear War* (Washington, D.C.: Brookings, 1993). On this topic, see also John W. R. Lepingwell, "Ukraine, Russia, and the Control of Nuclear Weapons," *RFE/RL Research Report* 2, no. 8 (February 19, 1993): 4–20; Martin J. Dewing, "Ukraine: Independent Nuclear Weapons Capability Rising" (master's thesis, Naval Postgraduate School, Monterey, California, June 1993); William H. Kincaide, "Nuclear Weapons in Ukraine: Hollow Threat, Wasting Asset," *Arms Control Today* (July-August 1993), pp. 13–18.

[44]According to a U.S. State Department official who met with Kravchuk in 1992, the Ukrainian leader clearly did not understand how the telephone link worked. Personal interview, Washington, D.C., June 5, 1994. Kravchuk appeared to be a slow learner. In August 1993, he asserted Ukrainian control of the missiles that were under CIS unified command: "Our authority only concerns the fact that we will not allow them to be launched from the Ukrainian territory." *Interfax*, August 25, 1993, reported in JPRS-TND-93-009-L (November 9, 1993), p. 26.

[45]For the text of this decree, see *Holos Ukrainy*, April 8, 1992.

[46]See FBIS-SOV-92-113 (June 11, 1992), p. 2. The title of this center varies slightly in different news reports.

[47]Lepingwell, "Ukraine, Russia, and the Control of Nuclear Weapons," pp. 14–15; see also JPRS-TND-92-008-L (October 9, 1992), p. 11; John W. R. Lepingwell, "The Bishkek Summit and Nuclear Weapons Control," *RFE/RL Research Report* 1, no. 42 (October 23, 1992): 42–43. Sherman W. Garnett, former deputy assistant secretary of defense, speculated that Kiev might have thought that it needed to assert ownership over the nuclear weapons in order to support its claim for compensation. Presentation at the Carnegie Endowment for International Peace, Washington, D.C., November 17, 1994.

Some April 1993 news reports had Ukraine attempting to administer loyalty oaths to personnel of the 43rd Missile Army, which was part of the Strategic Rocket Forces in Ukraine. FBIS-SOV-93-068 (April 12, 1993), pp. 47–48.

[48]Chrystia Freeland and R. Jeffrey Smith, "Ukrainian Premier Urges Keeping Nuclear Arms," *Washington Post*, June 4, 1993.

[49]Receiving less publicity was the fact that the same legislation also ruled out the use of nuclear weapons or their influence in the country's foreign policy. See ibid.; Jane Perlez, "Ukraine May Ask Special Status in Atom Pact," *New York Times*, July 26, 1993; *Agence France Presse* (Paris), July 2, 1993, reported in FBIS-SOV-93-127 (July 6, 1993), p. 51; *Washington Post* and *New York Times*, July 8, 1993; see also *Interfax*, July 6, 1993, FBIS-SOV-93-128-A (July 7, 1993), p. 8; *Izvestiya*, July 7, 1993, reported in FBIS-SOV-93-128 (July 7, 1993), p. 44; *Interfax*, July 7, 1993, reported in FBIS-SOV-93-130-A (July 9, 1993), p. 7; Michael Dobbs, "Ukraine Claims All Nuclear Weapons on Its Territory," *Washington Post*, July 3, 1993. For a more measured analysis of the legislation, see *Ukrinform*, August 10, 1993, reported in FBIS-SOV-93-153 (August 11, 1993), p. 39.

[50]Dewing, "Ukraine," p. xi. According to one news report, Ukraine produced the blocking devices for the ICBMs stationed in Ukraine and some of the hardware and software for targeting these missiles. Steve Coll and R. Jeffrey Smith, "Ukraine Could Seize Control over Nuclear Arms," *Washington Post*, June 3, 1993.

[51]Michael R. Gordon, "Russians Fault U.S. on Shifting Ukraine's Arms," *New York Times*, June 7, 1993.

[52]On Ukraine's "sale" of nuclear warheads to the PLO, see *Interfax*, February 26, 1993, reported in FBIS-SOV-93-038 (March 1, 1993), p. 51; FBIS-SOV-93-114 (June 16, 1993), p. 47. News accounts in October 1991 reported that Yeltsin had contemplated a "preventive nuclear strike" against Ukraine at a time when Ukraine was taking steps to create its own armed forces, a step that Moscow might have feared would lead Kiev to exercise control over the nuclear weapons on its territory. See Paul Quinn-Jones, "Yeltsin Weighed Nuclear Strike on Ukraine, Soviet Report Says," *Boston Globe*, October 25, 1991; John Lloyd and Chrystia Freeland, "Ukraine Accuses Yeltsin of Nuclear Attack Threat," *Financial Times*, October 25, 1991.

[53]Michael R. Gordon, "Clinton Pressing Ukraine on A-Arms," *New York Times*, April 8, 1993. In this same article Paul Goble, of the Carnegie Endowment for International Peace, was quoted as saying that if the Clinton administration wanted "to send a signal to the Ukrainians that they are isolated and nobody loves them and therefore they might want to think about how to defend themselves, this is a good way to do it." See also Don Oberdorfer, "Ukraine Is Loath to Yield Nuclear Arms," *Washington Post*, March 25, 1993; Steven Erlanger, "Ukraine and Arms Accords: Kiev Reluctant to Say 'I Do,'" *New York Times*, March 31, 1993.

[54]*Segodnya*, May 18, 1993, reported in FBIS-SOV-93-097 (May 21, 1993), p. 45.

[55]White House official, personal interview, Washington, D.C., July 13, 1994.

[56]See Chrystia Freeland, "U.S. Shifts Policy on Ukraine," *Washington Post*, May 11, 1993; *Washington Post*, May 31, 1993; Dunbar Lockwood, "United States Modifies Approach to Broaden Relations with Ukraine," *Arms Control Today* (June 1993), pp. 25, 34. U.S. State Department official, personal interview, Washington, D.C., May 27, 1994.

[57]Michael R. Gordon, "Ukrainian Official Backs U.S. Plan on Atom Arms," *New York Times*, June 8, 1993.

[58]See Michael R. Gordon, "Aspin Meets Russian in Bid to Take Ukraine's A-Arms," *New York Times*, June 6, 1993; R. Jeffrey Smith, "Russian Rebuffs U.S. Plan on A-Arms," *Washington Post*, June 7, 1993; Michael R. Gordon, "Russians Fault U.S. on Shifting Ukraine's Arms," *New York Times*, June 7, 1993; FBIS-SOV-93-107 (June 7, 1993), p. 64; FBIS-SOV-93-108 (June 8, 1993), pp. 49–50.

[59]For a discussion of the dangers of heptyl fuel, see *Nezavisimaya Gazeta*, March 25, 1992, reported in FBIS-SOV-92-059 (March 26, 1992), pp. 4–6. Before the Aspin visit, Kiev had been haggling for months with Moscow over maintaining the SS-19s. Nicholas Krawciw, telephone interview, Washington, D.C., June 15, 1994. Krawciw, a retired U.S. Army major general of Ukrainian descent, informally advised the Ukrainian government on military matters.

[60]Morozov described the deactivation of those missiles aimed at the United States as an "act of goodwill." *ITAR-TASS*, July 28, 1993, reported in FBIS-SOV-93-143 (July 28, 1993), p. 47; FBIS-SOV-93-145 (July 30, 1993), pp. 43–44; FBIS-SOV-93-148 (August 4, 1993), p. 41; R. Jeffrey Smith, "Ukraine Begins to Dismantle Nuclear Missiles Aimed at U.S.," *Washington Post*, July 28, 1993; Michael R. Gordon, "U.S. Says Ukraine Has Begun Dismantling Nuclear Missiles," *New York Times*, July 28, 1993. The memorandum of understanding was signed on July 27, 1993.

The $175 million figure was proposed by the Ukrainians to the United States in 1992. The State Department originally countered with a much lower amount, but this figure was increased to $175 million after the Pentagon objected. Wolfowitz, personal interview, Washington, D.C., June 29, 1994. See, generally, Don Oberdorfer, "Bush Offers $175 Million for Nonnuclear Ukraine," *Washington Post*, December 10, 1992. Ukraine could not receive the $175 million until it signed a Safe, Secure, Dismantlement (SSD) agreement, which it signed on October 26, 1993.

[61]For an analysis of the Massandra summit and its implications, see Bohdan Nahaylo, "The Massandra Summit and Ukraine," *RFE/RL Research Report* 2, no. 37 (September 17, 1993): 1–6. For press coverage of Massandra and its aftermath, see *Interfax*, September 3, 6, 8, 20, reported in JPRS-TND-93-009-L (November 9, 1993), pp. 26–27; Celestine Bohlen, "Ukraine Agrees to Allow Russians to Buy Fleet and Destroy Arsenal," *New York Times*, September 4, 1993; Fred Hiatt, "Ukraine and Russia Reach Accord," *Washington Post*, September 4, 1993; Fred Hiatt, "Russia, Ukraine Differ on Deal," *Washington Post*, September 5, 1993; Steven Erlanger, "Ukraine Questions the Price Tag of Independence," *New York Times*, September 8, 1993; Marta Kolomayets, "Ukraine to Surrender Fleet, Nukes to Russia," *Ukrainian Weekly*, September 12, 1993.

[62]Moscow Russian Television, September 4, 1993, reported in FBIS-SOV-93-171 (September 7, 1993), p. 7.

[63]Boris Bazilewski, director, Rada Committee for Foreign Affairs, personal interview, Kiev, October 27, 1993; Pavlychko, personal interview, Kiev, October 27, 1993. During a break in the proceedings, Yeltsin and Kravchuk appeared together at an impromptu press conference. Yeltsin announced that Ukraine would give Russia its share of the Black Sea Fleet in return for the settling of Ukraine's debts to Russia. Kravchuk stood silently by his side and did not contradict these remarks. Kravchuk's national security adviser, Anton Buteiko, immediately realized the harm to Ukraine's interests caused by Kravchuk's silence. By the time the Ukrainian delegation had reached Borispol airport outside Kiev only a few hours later, Buteiko had stiffened Kravchuk's spine. At the airport, Kravchuk denied that any deal exchanging the Black Sea Fleet for debt had been struck. According to the Ukrainian president, nothing fundamental had changed; the two sides had merely agreed to establish a joint commission to study the Russian proposal. Kravchuk stated, "No other decision was made." State Department official, personal interview, Washington, D.C., June 5, 1994.

[64]What is undisputed is that the parties signed three agreements on nuclear weapons: (1) on the scrapping of nuclear warheads; (2) on general principles for scrapping the nuclear warheads of the strategic missiles in Ukraine; and (3) on the exercising of supervisory control over the maintenance of the nuclear complexes of the strategic nuclear weapons stationed in Ukraine and Russia.

[65]Moscow Russian Television, September 4, 1993, reported in FBIS-SOV-93-171 (September 7, 1993), p. 7. Russia had agreed to compensate Ukraine with low-enriched uranium (typically 3–5 percent U-235) in fuel rods for its nuclear power stations.

[66]The heading of this agreement is "Protocol on Withdrawal to Russia of All Nuclear Warheads of the Strategic Nuclear Forces Deployed in Ukraine." The text can be found in *Nezavisimost* (Kiev), reported in FBIS-SOV-93-177 (September 15, 1993), p. 47, and *RFE/RL Research Report* 3, no. 4 (January 28, 1994): 6. Copies of all the original Massandra agreements were provided to the author by a Western diplomat in Kiev, October 1993.

Other Massandra agreements stated that schedules for nuclear weapons removal would be worked out subsequently in bilateral talks and that Ukraine would be compensated for the nuclear material within one year after the warheads were removed.

[67]Western diplomat, personal interview, Kiev, October 25, 1993. Ukrainian officials claim that Buteiko changed the text before Kuchma signed it, a story that has the benefit of making both Kuchma and Buteiko look better than they do in the alternative account. Russian Foreign Minister Andrei Kozyrev tore up his copy of the denuclearization document after he saw what Buteiko had done. James Goodby, personal interview, Washington, D.C., December 9, 1993.

[68]Moscow Russian Television, September 4, 1993, reported in FBIS-SOV-93-171 (September 7, 1993), p. 7.

[69]Goodby, personal interview, Washington, D.C., December 9, 1993. To confuse matters further, the Russian Foreign Ministry issued a statement on October 1, 1993, that claimed that all the agreements reached at Massandra on nuclear arms remained fully valid. *ITAR-TASS*, October 1, 1993, reported in JPRS-TND-93-034 (October 27, 1993), p. 31. The Ukrainians refused to honor the unamended version of the agreement. Almost three weeks later, the Ukrainian Foreign Ministry explained that the Russian delegation had presented a version at odds with what the two delegations had negotiated. Why Kuchma had signed such a document in the first place, why the amended version had not been retyped and resigned, and, indeed, why it took the Ukrainian Foreign Ministry three weeks to put out this story are unknown. *UNIAR* (Kiev), September 24, 1993, reported in FBIS-SOV-93-185 (September 27, 1993), p. 21. UNIAR was an independent Ukrainian news service that started at this time.

[70]Tarasiuk, personal interview, Kiev, October 29, 1993; Western diplomats, personal interviews, Kiev, October 25 and 27, 1993; Bazilewski, director, Rada Committee for Foreign Affairs, personal interview, Kiev, October 27, 1993; Pavlychko, personal interview, Kiev, October 27, 1993.

[71]Moscow Russian Television, September 4, 1993, reported in FBIS-SOV-93-171 (September 7, 1993), p. 7. Boris Tarasiuk stated after the summit that no warheads would go to Russia until compensation for the tactical nuclear weapons was resolved. *Interfax*, September 20, 1993, reported in JPRS-TND-93-009-L (November 9,

1993), p. 20. In response to Tarasiuk's comment, Russia reiterated its refusal to compensate Ukraine for these weapons. *Interfax,* September 21, 1993, reported in JPRS-TND-93-009-L (November 9, 1993), p. 20.

[72]Nahaylo, "The Massandra Summit and Ukraine," p. 6.

[73]See Simon Johnson and Oleg Ustenko, "Ukraine Slips into Hyperinflation," *RFE/RL Research Report* 2, no. 26 (June 25, 1993): 24–32.

[74]Ukraine's nuclear policy theoretically impeded it from obtaining nuclear fuel from members of the Nuclear Suppliers Group (NSG). The NSG required nonnuclear weapon state recipients of nuclear technology and fuel to enter into full-scope safeguards agreements with the IAEA (based on the model agreement INF-CIRC/153).

As a further complicating factor, Kiev earlier had claimed "administrative" control and ownership of the nuclear weapons based on its territory. In fall 1993, the American embassy in Kiev reportedly advised Ukraine to negotiate with the IAEA a safeguards agreement as close as possible to INFCIRC/153. West European countries, including Germany, criticized the arrangement. In any event, Ukraine balked at signing the agreement. Personal correspondence with David Fischer, June 17 and 28, 1994.

Russia's refusal to take back Ukraine's used nuclear fuel reversed a nonproliferation policy the Soviet Union had followed for decades for all countries that it had supplied with nuclear fuel.

[75]Washington and Kiev had been conducting a security dialogue for some time. In January 1993, Boris Tarasiuk had traveled to Washington, where President Bush handed him a draft declaration with specific security assurances. The U.S. draft contained essentially recycled security assurances that Washington had offered before. The trip was really intended to reassure Rada members, who insisted that Ukraine should receive these assurances in written form before they would vote for START I. Tarasiuk, personal interview, Kiev, Ukraine, October 29, 1993.

Causing some confusion in press reports of the security issue generally was that Ukrainian officials habitually used the words "assurances" and "guarantees" interchangeably when discussing external security pledges. The Russian and Ukrainian word *"obespechienye"* means both "to guarantee" and "to assure."

[76]Kiev Radio, October 25, 1993, reported in JPRS-TND-93-035 (November 10, 1993), p. 71. The week before the secretary's visit a U.S. delegation led by the senior director at the National Security Council for the newly independent states, Nicholas Burns, had visited Kiev to discuss a range of economic issues. Earlier in October, the Pentagon's Graham Allison had also led a U.S. delegation to Kiev that signed seventeen military-to-military agreements with Ukraine. U.S. State Department official, personal interview, Washington, D.C., May 27, 1994.

[77]Thomas W. Lippman, "U.S. Clears Way to Give Ukraine $175 Million to Destroy A-Arms," *Washington Post,* October 26, 1993; Elaine Sciolino, "Ukraine Missiles: Terms Are Tough," *New York Times,* October 26, 1993.

Christopher did not help his cause by missing an easy opportunity to score diplomatic points. A new secretary of state speaking for a new president, Christopher could have distanced the United States from President Bush's August 1991 "chicken Kiev" speech, which, over two years later, still rankled Ukrainian officials. Indeed, three weeks before his trip, the American Embassy in Kiev had cabled to the State Department the secretary's talking points, which included this message. The language was excised. State Department official, personal interview, Kiev, October 27, 1993.

[78]See FBIS-SOV-93-206 (October 27, 1993), p. 51; FBIS-SOV-93-205 (October 26, 1993), pp. 54–57. The prospect of Christopher's visit resulted in another tangible (albeit unintended) accomplishment. Ukraine returned the first two strategic nuclear warheads, whose "condition" was "deemed pre-accident" to Russia on October 23. (Other news reports state that three warheads were shipped to Russia.) The warheads had been held up at the border from October 5 to October 22 by customs officials who insisted on inspecting the shipment. The issue was finally resolved because Ukraine did not want an incident with Russia before Christopher's visit. *Izvestiya*, October 26, 1993, reported in JPRS-TND-93-035 (November 10, 1993), p. 42. This delay apparently violated the terms of the April 1992 Russian-Ukrainian agreement on removal of warheads.

[79]See interview with Boris Tarasiuk in *Holos Ukrainy*, November 2, 1993, reported in FBIS-SOV-93-212 (November 4, 1993), pp. 62–63. The United States also promised to retarget its nuclear missiles away from sites in Ukraine.

[80]State Department officials, personal interviews, Kiev and Washington, D.C., October 27, 1993, May 27, 1994; White House official, personal interview, Washington, D.C., July 13, 1994. One reason for Talbott's repeated exertions at this time was that key U.S. senators had informed the State Department of their reluctance to provide Nunn-Lugar funds to Ukraine as long as the SS-24 ICBMs were not deactivated.

Christopher did not help the U.S. cause by his unimpressive performance at the October 25 press conference. The author's notes, Kiev, October 25, 1993. In addition, the lack of personal chemistry between the U.S. secretary of state and Ukrainian leaders may have limited what could have been accomplished on this trip. On Christopher's personal antipathy toward Anatoly Zlenko: U.S. State Department officials, personal interviews, Washington, D.C., 1993 and 1994. On the American secretary of state's failure to impress Zlenko and Kravchuk: Bohdan Mysko, personal interview, Kiev, October 27, 1994. Mysko is a Ukrainian-American who became part of Kravchuk's inner circle; as "Adviser to the President of Ukraine on International Economic Affairs" (the title on his business card), Mysko accompanied the Ukrainian president on foreign trips and attended official meetings, including ones with Christopher.

[81]Russian Defense Minister Pavel Grachev underscored this difference: "The new military doctrine says nothing about countries that do have nuclear arms. Indeed, this is a new concept." *La Republica* (Rome), reported in JPRS-TND-93-036 (November 17, 1993), pp. 22ff. On the new military doctrine, see FBIS-SOV-93-212 (November 4, 1993), pp. 34–41; *Rossiyskiye Vesti*, November 18, 1993, reported in FBIS-SOV-93-222-S (November 19, 1993), p. 1–11; Dunbar Lockwood, "Russia Revises Nuclear Policy, Ends Soviet 'No-First-Use' Pledge," *Arms Control Today* (December 1993), p. 19; see also Serge Schmemann, "Russians Drop 'First-Use' Vow on Atom Arms," *International Herald Tribune*, November 4, 1993; Fred Hiatt, "Russia Shifts Doctrine on Military Use," *Washington Post*, November 4, 1993. An English-language summary of the new military doctrine was provided to the author by a member of the Russian Embassy in Washington.

[82]"Nuclear Arms in Ukraine Are Unsafe, Russia Says," *International Herald Tribune*, November 6–7, 1993; see also "Russia Warns Ukraine on Decay of Warheads," *New York Times*, November 6, 1993; "Russian Warns of Nuclear Risk in Ukraine," *Washington Post*, November 6, 1993.

[83]The exact vote was 254–9, with 30 abstentions. For the text of the Rada's START resolution, see *UNIAR*, November 18, 1993, reported in FBIS-SOV-93-222 (November 19, 1993), pp. 45–47; see also "Ukraine Ratifies the Missile Pact, but Delays Ending Nuclear Status," *New York Times*, November 19, 1993; Dunbar Lockwood, "Ukrainian Rada Ratifies START I, but Adds 13 Conditions for Approval," *Arms Control Today* (December 1993), p. 17. The Rada's resolution contained thirteen provisions, but the Rada explicitly stipulated that only seven provisions (according to *UNIAR*'s version) or six provisions (according to the November 19, 1993, press release of the Embassy of Ukraine in Washington, D.C.) needed to be satisfied before it would agree to complete denuclearization. The embassy's version did not include Article 8 of the resolution as a condition.

Some Rada members invoked an interesting rationale for not joining the NPT as a nonnuclear weapon state. To do so, Serhiy Holovaty and others argued, would undercut Ukraine's claim of ownership—and its right to receive financial compensation—for the nuclear warheads it returned to Russia. In other words, Kiev could not demand compensation from Moscow if it did not have a legal claim to the warheads, and it could not join the NPT if it did.

[84]See Ann Devroy, "Clinton Presses Ukraine on Disarming," *Washington Post*, November 30, 1993; Thomas L. Friedman, "Ukraine Retreats on Nuclear Arms," *New York Times*, November 30, 1993; "Ukraine Calls Arms 'Material Wealth,'" *Washington Post*, December 1, 1993.

One reason for U.S. irritation was that the Rada's action threatened implementation of both the START I and the START II agreements. When the Russian Supreme Soviet ratified START in November 1992, it had conditioned Russia's agreement on the stipulation that the three other former Soviet republics with nuclear weapons on their territories would first ratify START and join the NPT. See "Text of Russian Federation Supreme Soviet Resolution on the Ratification of the Treaty between the Union of Soviet Socialist Republics and the United States of America on the Reduction and Limitation of Strategic Offensive Arms," November 4, 1992; the text is reprinted in *Rossiyskaya Gazeta*, November 21, 1992, reported in FBIS-SOV-92-227 (November 24, 1992), p. 2; see also Fred Hiatt, "Russian Legislature Ratifies START Pact," *Washington Post*, November 5, 1992; "Russia Ratifies Nuclear Arms Pact with U.S.," *New York Times*, November 5, 1992. Unless START I was ratified, it was doubted that the deep cuts dictated by START II in the American and Russian nuclear arsenals would take place.

[85]See Strobe Talbott, *Endgame: The Inside Story of SALT II* (New York: Harper and Row, 1979). Those with still longer memories noted that the United States waited fifty years to ratify the 1925 "Geneva Protocol on the Prohibition of the Development, Production, and Stockpiling of Bacteriological (Biological) and Toxin Weapons and on Their Destruction."

[86]In response to being asked whether Ukraine wanted a defense agreement with the West or NATO membership, Kravchuk replied that it wanted neither, but he added that Ukraine did want "simple declarations by the major nuclear powers undertaking not to attack Ukraine and, at the same time, to guarantee its territorial integrity." He noted, "If we receive such undertaking from Russia, the United States, France, and Great Britain, the Ukrainian population will feel they are living in safety." *Le Figaro* (Paris), November 29, 1993, reported in JPRS-TND-93-001 (January 6, 1994), p. 29.

A number of different schools of thought had arisen by this time concerning the feasibility of a Ukrainian nuclear deterrent. Some influential Rada members believed that Ukraine could rapidly develop a credible nuclear deterrent. If the United States had used nuclear arms to deter the Soviet Union during the cold war, this thinking went, so could Ukraine. To some outside observers, this appeared to be an example of technology leading policy: since Kiev had inherited nuclear arms, it should now develop a rationale for keeping them.

Providing the intellectual scaffolding on which probomb Rada members hung their arguments was an article by University of Chicago Professor John J. Mearsheimer in the summer 1993 edition of *Foreign Affairs*. Entitled "The Case for a Ukrainian Nuclear Deterrent," Mearsheimer relied heavily on international relations theory to contend that a nuclear Ukraine would promote peace. The Kiev-based Pylip Orlyk Institute for Democracy translated Mearsheimer's article into Ukrainian, along with Steven Miller's companion piece in *Foreign Affairs* entitled "The Case against a Ukrainian Nuclear Deterrent," with the intention of raising the intellectual level of Ukraine's nuclear debate. According to the institute's director, Markian Bilynskyj, only copies of Mearsheimer's article were requested. On the influence of Mearsheimer's article, see *Krasnaya Zvezda*, August 20, 1993, reported in JPRS-TND-93-027 (September 3, 1993), pp. 50–52. The Mearsheimer and Miller articles can be found in *Foreign Affairs* 72, no. 3 (Summer 1993): 50–66, 67–80.

Questions over doctrine, strategy, command and control, and targeting largely went unasked and unanswered by Ukrainian officials and experts who favored Kiev's retaining the nuclear arsenal. But as American and Western visitors to Kiev increasingly raised these uncomfortable questions, some Ukrainians cobbled together the notion of "existential deterrence." In this formulation, nuclear arms had intrinsic utility. Their mere presence on Ukrainian soil worked as a kind of "existential deterrent" against Russian aggression. It was irrelevant whether Kiev had operational control and, if so, whether the missiles could hit targets in Russia. As Yuri Kostenko asserted, "No matter who currently controls the launch button for the nuclear weapons deployed on Ukrainian territory, these weapons do defend Ukrainian sovereignty." Letter to the Editor, *Foreign Affairs* 72, no. 4 (September-October 1993): 183.

Finally, a third school believed that nuclear weapons damaged Ukraine's national security because they interfered with Kiev's full and fast integration into European economic and security structures. Kravchuk and his senior Foreign Ministry officials were the strongest adherents to this view. For this analysis of the nuclear debate in Ukraine, I am indebted to Markian Bilynsky, "Nuclear Weapons and Ukrainian Security: A Personal Overview" (unpublished paper provided to the author, October 1993).

[87]The Rada stated that 36 percent of the delivery vehicles and 42 percent of the nuclear warheads in Ukraine should be dismantled. Apparently, Ukraine obtained these percentages by calculating the START II general percentage reductions that would be applicable to the former Soviet Union's entire nuclear stockpile and then applying them to Ukraine. But Ukraine was willing to go beyond these percentage reductions in completely eliminating the SS-19 force on its soil.

[88]December 1993 marked the first time the United States directly intervened in Ukrainian-Russian affairs. See Elaine Sciolino, "U.S. Offering to Mediate Russian-Ukrainian Disputes on Security," *New York Times*, December 4, 1993. The U.S. offer to mediate disputes originally came in spring 1993 as part of the Clinton administration's reappraisal of its policy toward the former Soviet Union. See R. Jeffrey Smith, "U.S. Fears Ukrainian-Russian Clash," *Washington Post*, June 6, 1993; R. Jef-

frey Smith and Barton Gellman, "U.S. Will Seek to Mediate Ex-Soviet States' Disputes," *Washington Post,* August 5, 1993.

[89]State Department official, personal interview, Washington, D.C., May 27, 1994.

[90]See Michael R. Gordon and Eric Schmitt, "U.S. Is Considering Aiming Its Missiles away from Russia," *New York Times,* December 6, 1993; "U.S., Russia Mull Reaiming Nuclear Arms," *Washington Post,* December 7, 1993. In January 1994, the United States and Russia agreed to retarget their nuclear missiles away from sites on each other's homeland by May 30, 1994. It is likely, however, that the original target sets remained on backup programs that both sides could use on short notice.

The United States and other NATO members also warned Kiev during the fall that its nuclear policy would determine the level of economic assistance and participation in NATO's Partnership for Peace. See John W. R. Lepingwell, "The Trilateral Agreement on Nuclear Weapons," *RFE/RL Research Report* 3, no. 4 (January 28, 1994): 12.

[91]One reading of Articles 6 and 12 of the Rada's November 18 resolution authorized President Kravchuk to go beyond the stipulated percentage reductions. Kravchuk authorized the dismantlement of the SS-24s after the Rada's resolution, as he had promised to President Clinton.

By the end of December, 41 (out of a total of 130) SS-19s had already been taken off alert. News accounts also reported that Kiev had decided to remove all warheads from 20 (out of a total of 46) SS-24s by the end of the year and keep them in storage depots in Ukraine and that the remaining SS-24s would be deactivated by the end of 1994. See *Agence France Presse,* December 20, 1993, reported in FBIS-SOV-93-243 (December 21, 1993), p. 48; *Segodnya* (Moscow), December 22, 1993, reported in JPRS-TND-93-003 (January 31, 1994), pp. 27–28; *Interfax,* December 20, 1993, reported in JPRS-TND-93-003-L (January 31, 1994), p. 28. For slightly different numbers, see R. Jeffrey Smith, *Washington Post,* December 10, 1993.

[92]See "Shifting Back to Communist Era, Ukraine Bars Hard Currency Sale," *New York Times,* November 4, 1993.

[93]Lee Hockstader, "Ukraine: A Breadbasket Becomes a Basket Case," *Washington Post,* November 8, 1993. See also "Shifting Back to Communist Era, Ukraine Bars Hard Currency Sale," *New York Times,* November 4, 1993; "Fuel-Short Ukraine Is Caught in Wintry Vise," *New York Times,* November 23, 1993; Margaret Shapiro, "Winter Lashes Fuel-Short Former Soviets," *Washington Post,* December 7, 1993. In January 1994, a National Intelligence Estimate reportedly concluded that Ukraine's economic problems could spur ethnic conflict and the country's partition. See Daniel Williams and R. Jeffrey Smith, "U.S. Intelligence Sees Economic Plight Leading to Breakup of Ukraine," *Washington Post,* January 25, 1994.

[94]State Department officials, personal interviews, Washington, D.C., May 27 and June 1, 1994.

[95]Quoted in R. W. Apple, Jr., "Ukraine Gives In on Surrendering Its Nuclear Arms," *New York Times,* January 11, 1994; see also Ann Devroy, "Pact Reached to Dismantle Ukraine's Nuclear Force," *Washington Post,* January 11, 1994. After Clinton's statement, the press conference became confrontational and reporters grew short-tempered over the inability or unwillingness of senior U.S. officials to clarify conflicting or confusing statements. This was due to the U.S. government's uncertainty over how much information to reveal at this time. Still, it is unclear why U.S. officials publicly stated that some aspects of the deal would remain secret. The explanation subsequently given—that Kravchuk and Yeltsin should each have been

allowed to decide how best to handle the secret parts of the agreement, which concerned compensation and the timetable for withdrawal—does not adequately answer this criticism.

[96]See Clinton and Kravchuk joint press briefing, FBIS-SOV-94-009 (January 13, 1994), pp. 59–61; Lee Hockstader, "Battle Brewing in Ukraine over Ratification of Pact," *Washington Post*, January 13, 1994; Ann Devroy and Daniel Williams, "Clinton Boosts A-Arms Pact in Ukraine," *Washington Post*, January 13, 1994; Douglas Jehl, "Ukrainian Agrees to Dismantle A-Arms," *New York Times*, January 13, 1994. See also Lee Hockstader, "In Ukraine, Arms Deal May Hinge on the Deftness of the Salesman," *Washington Post*, January 14, 1994.

Originally, Kravchuk was supposed to host a summit with Clinton, but because Ukraine delayed completion of the Trilateral Agreement for so long, all it could get was a brief rally on the airport tarmac. Alternative sites, including a planned ceremony at the ornate Marinsky Palace in Kiev or a meeting at a private hunting lodge, also had to be scrapped. But the Ukrainians held up Clinton's departure as long as possible to try to milk as much political capital from the visit as possible. Not surprisingly, the Russians had delayed Clinton's departure from Moscow earlier on Wednesday to ensure that the president would spend as little time as possible in Ukraine.

[97]For a useful discussion of the Trilateral Agreement and Annex, see Lepingwell, "The Trilateral Agreement on Nuclear Weapons," pp. 12–20. The text of the Trilateral Agreement and Annex can be found here on pp. 14–15 and also in FBIS-SOV-94-012 (January 19, 1994), pp. 49–50.

[98]Specifically, Washington and Moscow reaffirmed (1) their respect for Ukraine's territorial integrity and the recognition that border changes could be made only by peaceful and consensual means, (2) their obligation to refrain from the threat or use of force and the agreement that none of their weapons would ever be used except in self-defense or in accordance with the Charter of the United Nations, (3) their commitment to refrain from economic coercion, (4) their commitment to seek immediate UN Security Council action if Ukraine should become a victim of aggression or a threat of aggression in which nuclear weapons were used, and (5) their commitment not to use nuclear weapons against Ukraine except in case of an attack on themselves or their allies by Ukraine or an ally of Ukraine.

[99]The $60-million payment would be deducted from money due to Russia under the February 18, 1993, HEU contract. The United States and Russia had signed the implementing agreement in Moscow on January 14, 1994. This payment marked a change in U.S. policy. Previously, the United States would not sign an agreement with Russia until Russia had negotiated bilateral compensation agreements with Ukraine, Kazakhstan, and Belarus. By signing the Trilateral Agreement deal, the United States now promised to provide Russia with $60 million *before* Russia had closed on all three compensation agreements. According to a State Department official involved in these issues, the reason for this change was that before signing the implementing agreement, Russia had sent letters to Kazakhstan and Belarus, assuring them that they would receive a "no less favorable compensation deal" than the one Ukraine had received. On this basis, the United States decided to modify its previous policy. Personal interview, Washington, D.C., May 27, 1994.

Under the Trilateral Agreement, Russia's transfer of fuel rods to nuclear installations in Ukraine not covered by IAEA safeguards violated its obligations under

Article 3(2) of the NPT. Officials at the State Department and White House concede that this issue had not occurred to them at the time. Personal interviews, Washington, D.C., May 27 and July 13, 1994.

[100]Defense Department official, personal interview, January 28, 1994; see also Federal News Service, Kravchuk press conference, Moscow, January 14, 1994, p. 9. A compensation formula for Ukraine was devised by the State Department's James Timbie, who came up with a compromise $/separative work unit (SWU) figure based on a range of U.S. estimates on how much HEU was contained in the strategic nuclear warheads. It was agreed that the actual amount of compensation for the tactical nuclear weapons would be decided in subsequent Russian-Ukrainian talks, with U.S. mediation.

[101]State Department official, personal interview, Washington, D.C., May 27, 1994.

[102]Department of State, cable from the American Embassy in Moscow to the secretary of state and the White House, January 14, 1994.

[103]Defense Department official, personal interview, January 28, 1994. For general reaction to the Trilateral Agreement in Ukraine, see JPRS-TND-94-004 (February 11, 1994), pp. 22–32. For opposition by Rada members to the Trilateral Agreement, see *Interfax*, January 16, 18, 1994, reported in JPRS-TND-94-001-L (January 31, 1994), p. 29.

[104]*UNIAR*, January 14, 1994, reported in Daily Report, *Central Eurasia*, FBIS-SOV-94-010 (January 14, 1994), p. 71. Another parliamentarian, Serhiy Holovaty, was quoted as saying: "The U.S. has described Kravchuk as a brave man. I agree. You must have courage to betray your country's interests so brazenly." Robert Seely, "Ukraine Nuclear Accord Survives Its First Test," *Washington Post*, January 21, 1994.

[105]Gerald Stacy, State Department official, personal interview, Washington, D.C., January 31, 1994. Two Ukrainian defense experts stated that Kravchuk did not have to submit the agreement to the Rada. See Jane Perlez, "Kravchuk Can Act on His Own, Experts Say," *New York Times*, January 16, 1994. During Clinton's overseas trip, U.S. officials hinted to the media that Kravchuk did not have the legal authority to bind Ukraine to the agreement.

[106]See Robert Seely, "A-Arms Pact Is Approved in Ukraine," *Washington Post*, February 4, 1994; "Ukrainian Parliament Edges Closer to Atomic Disarmament," *New York Times*, February 4, 1994. For information on the nuclear debate in Ukraine, see Lepingwell, "Negotiations over Nuclear Weapons," pp. 1–11.

[107]Fred Hiatt, "Warheads in Ukraine Decaying, Russians Say," *Washington Post*, January 19, 1994; John W. R. Lepingwell, "Ukrainian Parliament Removes START-1 Conditions," *RFE/RL Research Report* 3, no. 8 (February 25, 1994): 37–42.

[108]See Robert Seely, "Russian Nationalist Favored in Crimea," *Washington Post*, January 31, 1994; *New York Times*, January 31, 1994. See also Lee Hockstader, "Separatist Storm Brewing in Crimea," *Washington Post*, May 14, 1994. For a chronology of events in Crimea, see *RFE/RL Research Report* 3, no. 19 (May 13, 1994): 27–33.

[109]In particular, Yuri Kostenko, minister for the environment and a Rada member, had contended that Russia owed Ukraine $10 billion for the plutonium in the warheads, an estimate that overlooked the expense of storing the material and the fact that there was no legal world market for plutonium. Kostenko's statement can be found in *Nezavisimaya Gazeta*, January 26, 1994, reported in JPRS-TND-94-004 (February 11, 1994), p. 32. For a more realistic assessment, see Lepingwell, "How Much Is a

Warhead Worth?" pp. 62–64; see also Ashton B. Carter and Owen Coté, "Disposition of Fissile Materials," in Graham Allison, Ashton B. Carter, Steven E. Miller, and Philip Zelikow, eds., *Cooperative Denuclearization: From Pledges to Deeds*, CSIA Studies in International Security No. 2 (Cambridge: Harvard University, 1993), pp. 117–35.

[110]Lepingwell, "Ukrainian Parliament Removes START-1 Conditions," p. 39.

[111]This resolution contained three provisions. The first two called for removing the conditions the Rada had imposed when it had partially ratified START in November. The third provision called for joining the NPT as a nonnuclear weapon state. The text of this resolution can be found in Lepingwell, "Ukrainian Parliament Removes START-1 Conditions," p. 41.

[112]One clause removed the Rada's prior objection to Article 5 of the Lisbon Protocol (which called for Ukraine's adherence to the NPT "in the shortest possible time"); the other clause removed the conditions the Rada had imposed on START ratification. The text of the Rada's resolution can be found in Lepingwell, "Ukrainian Parliament Removes START-1 Conditions," p. 41.

[113]Mary Mycio, "Ukraine Lawmakers OK Nuclear Arms Cuts," *Los Angeles Times*, February 4, 1994. The deputy cited was Ihor Derkach. According to one report, Rada member Sergei Holovaty added an amendment stipulating that no warheads would be returned to Russia until agreements on compensation and security guarantees were signed. The amended resolution was passed, but all reference to the amendment was omitted from the official text as published by the Ukrainian wire service UNIAR. Lepingwell, "Ukrainian Parliament Removes START-1 Conditions," p. 40.

[114]By this time, the promised figure was up to $700 million. See Steven Greenhouse, "U.S. Ready to Help Ukraine and Georgia, If They Help Themselves," *New York Times*, March 4, 1994; Steven Greenhouse, "Clinton Vows to Improve Relations with Ukraine," *New York Times*, March 5, 1994; Thomas W. Lippman, "Clinton Increases Aid, Support to Ukraine," *Washington Post*, March 5, 1994.

[115]For the Radetsky statement, see *Interfax*, May 16, 1994, reported in FBIS-SOV-94-095 (May 17, 1994), p. 35. By the end of March, two consignments of SS-19 and SS-24 warheads had left Ukraine for Russia. There was some initial confusion over the second shipment when Ukraine threatened to delay the transfer because it had not received the promised fuel rods from Russia; Russia blamed the United States for not providing the promised $60-million advance payment. The money was supposed to have come from the U.S. Enrichment Corporation (USEC) as an advance payment for the low-enriched uranium Russia was contracted to provide under the February 1993 HEU deal. The USEC and Moscow worked out their differences on the timing of repayment by the end of March 1994. The USEC advanced two tranches of $15 million in April and May; the remaining $30 million was scheduled to be transferred by the end of the summer. See R. Jeffrey Smith, "Ukraine Begins Moving Nuclear Warheads to Russia," *Washington Post*, March 6, 1994; *RFE/RL News Briefs* 3, no. 13 (March 21–25, 1994), pp. 12–13; *RFE/RL Daily Report*, no. 64 (April 5, 1994), p. 3; statement of Ashton B. Carter, assistant secretary of defense, Senate Committee on Armed Services, April 28, 1994, p. 17.

[116]Defense Department officials, personal interviews, Washington, D.C., November 4, 1994.

[117]White House official, personal interview, Washington, D.C., July 13, 1994. On Kuchma's politics, see Dominque Arel and Andrew Wilson, "Ukraine under

Kuchma: Back to 'Eurasia?' " *RFE/RL Research Report* 3, no. 32 (August 19, 1994): 1–12.

[118]*UNIAR*, November 15, 1994, reported in FBIS-SOV-94-221 (November 16, 1994), p. 31; State Department official, telephone interview, December 2, 1994. There is some double-counting here, since the $234 million figure includes $75 million of U.S. FY95 funds. Kuchma announced on November 15 that Russia had stopped delivering nuclear fuel to Ukraine and would resume shipments only after Ukraine ratified the NPT. See *Interfax*, November 15, 1994, reported in FBIS-SOV-94-221 (November 16, 1994), p. 31.

[119]The text of the Rada's resolution can be found in FBIS-SOV-94-222 (November 17, 1994), pp. 39–40. See also James Rupert, "Ukraine Joins Treaty Curbing Nuclear Arms," *Washington Post*, November 17, 1994; Steven Greenhouse, "Ukraine Votes to Become a Nuclear-Free Country," *New York Times*, November 17, 1994. The resolution contained a number of "reservations," which included the claim that Ukraine was "the owner of the nuclear weapons inherited by it from the former USSR" and the statement that the law would take effect once Ukraine received "security guarantees from the nuclear states" in an "international legal document."

[120]For the text of Kuchma's speech, see FBIS-SOV-94-222 (November 17, 1994), pp. 40–42.

[121]See "Memorandum on Security Assurances in Connection with Ukraine's Accession to the Treaty on the Nonproliferation of Nuclear Weapons," copy provided to the author by the Office of the Legal Adviser, U.S. State Department. Two other revisions from the Trilateral Accord are worth noting: (1) the document had a new "chapeau"; and (2) Ukraine actually affixed its signature to this document, an act that was important to Kiev. State Department lawyers had originally opined that Ukraine's signing of the new document would impose new obligations on the United States. They were told to go away and study the issue further. They later revised their opinion: the United States would not assume any new obligations under the document, which merely reaffirmed previous U.S. security assurances. France made a similar commitment on security assurances to Ukraine. See *ITAR-TASS*, November 17, 1994, reported in FBIS-SOV-94-223 (November 18, 1994), p. 36. China issued a statement on December 4 recognizing Ukraine's sovereignty, independence, and territorial integrity and welcoming its accession to the NPT. See *RFE/RL Daily Report*, no. 228 (December 5, 1994).

[122]START I stipulates that each party will reduce its nuclear forces to six thousand warheads. This warhead figure is calculated according to START I counting rules, which discount certain types of warheads. For example, non-ALCM bombers are counted as carrying one warhead, no matter how many warheads they actually may carry. The warhead figures in START II, on the other hand, correspond one-for-one with actual deployed warheads.

[123]State Department official, personal interview, Washington, D.C., May 27, 1994. Oil and natural gas subsidies accounted for the bulk of this amount.

[124]Sherman Garnett observed in a 1994 article: "Russian strategy to date appears to be based on an understanding of Ukraine's weakness and Russia's inability to assume greater burdens than it already carries. The Russian government has focused instead on preserving its interests and influence over Ukraine, attempting to retain its economic and political leverage while it addresses its own crisis." See "The Ukrainian Question and the Future of Russia," *Politchna Dumka*, no. 4 (1994).

[125]Quoted in Hiatt, "Warheads in Ukraine Decaying." In the May-June 1994 issue of *Foreign Affairs*, Kozyrev stated, "Russian foreign policy inevitably has to be of an independent and assertive nature." See Kozyrev, "The Lagging Partnership," *Foreign Affairs* 73, no. 3 (May-June 1994): 61.

[126]The reasons for this approach involved a mix of personal and bureaucratic interests. The Bush administration, and President Bush personally, did not want to undermine Gorbachev—the personification of Washington's hopes for a benign and cooperative Soviet Union. Early U.S. recognition of Ukraine would have weakened Gorbachev's hold on power. In addition, American diplomats were overwhelmingly Russophiles—they read, spoke, and studied Russian, not Ukrainian. During the cold war, they had served in Moscow, not Kiev or Lviv. Ukraine was an outlying province, infrequently visited and rarely considered. Consequently, many U.S. officials willingly believed the Russian interpretation of Ukrainian-Russian affairs, an interpretation that invariably portrayed Kiev as foolish, malevolent, and untrustworthy.

[127]See Steven Greenhouse, "Clinton Thanks Ukraine with $200 Million," *New York Times*, November 23, 1994.

[128]Traditionally, Ukraine suffered from a shortage of qualified officials. According to one commentator, the 1917 revolution placed "idealistic, patriotic but inexperienced intellectuals into positions of leadership [in Ukraine] and forced them to act before they were sure of what they wanted or how to get it." Subtelny, *Ukraine*, p. 377. A Western diplomat in Kiev in 1993 expressed this same sentiment more tactfully; in his words, Ukraine was "institutionally thin." See, generally, Alexander J. Motyl, *Dilemmas of Independence: Ukraine after Totalitarianism* (New York: Council on Foreign Relations, 1993); Taras Kuzio and Andrew Wilson, *Ukraine: Perestroika to Independence* (New York: St. Martin's Press, 1994).

[129]Arguably, the more severe blunder occurred in the economic sphere. Through his misguided economic policies, Kravchuk was more effective than any Russian fifth column in undermining Ukrainian sovereignty. Kiev seemed oblivious to how its failure to implement effective market reforms lowered living standards, increased unrest (especially in the eastern part of the country), generally eroded its independence, and narrowed its room for maneuver on the nuclear issue.

[130]Ukrainian Foreign Ministry official, personal interview, Stockholm, October 3, 1994. According to this official, the agreement did not require Rada approval. But before implementing it as an executive agreement, Kuchma was waiting to see if the Rada would vote the following month in favor of the NPT.

Belarus

[131]Sir Halford Mackinder, "The Geographic Pivot of History," *Geographic Journal* 23 (1904): 421–44. According to Mackinder's famous maxim: "Who rules East Europe commands the Heartland. / Who rules the Heartland commands the World-Island. / Who rules the World-Island commands the World."

[132]Ustina Markus, "Belarus a 'Weak Link' in Eastern Europe?" *RFE/RL Research Report* 2, no. 49 (December 10, 1993): 22.

[133]The country changed its name from the Byelorussian Soviet Socialist Republic to the Republic of Belarus on September 19, 1991.

[134]Statement of Belarus Foreign Minister Petr Kravchenko, 46th session of the UN General Assembly, September 27, 1991, reported in FBIS-SOV-91-189 (September 30, 1991), p. 70.

[135]FBIS-SOV-92-083 (April 29, 1992), p. 53. See also David R. Marples, "Ukraine, Belarus, and the Energy Dilemma," *RFE/RL Research Report* 2, no. 27 (July 2, 1993): 44. It is now mandatory for all Belarusian secondary school students to learn about Chernobyl and the hazards of radioactivity.

[136]For additional information on Chernobyl's impact on Belarus, see David Marples, "The Medical Consequences of Chernobyl," *Radio Liberty Report on the USSR* 2, no. 10 (March 9, 1990): 21–22; David Marples, "The Legacy of the Chernobyl Disaster in Belarus," *RFE/RL Research Report* 2, no. 5 (January 29, 1993): 46–50; *The International Chernobyl Project: Technical Report* (Vienna: IAEA, 1991); Grigorii Medvedev, *The Truth about Chernobyl* (New York: Basic Books, 1991); Zhores A. Medvedev, *The Legacy of Chernobyl* (New York: Norton, 1990); Iurii Shcherbak, *Chernobyl: A Documentary Story* (New York: St. Martin's, 1989); Richard F. Mould, *Chernobyl—The Real Story* (New York: Pergamon, 1988).

[137]Testimony of Colonel General Anatoly Kostenko, Belarusian military district commander, before the Supreme Soviet, November 15, 1991, cited in Vyacheslav Paznyak, "Nonproliferation from Belarus's Perspective" (paper presented at the CIS Nonproliferation Conference, April 6–9, 1992, Monterey, California), p. 5.

[138]*TASS*, September 23, 1991, reported in FBIS-SOV-91-185 (September 24, 1991), p. 76.

[139]Interview with Japanese newspaper *Asahi Shimbun*, October 8, 1991, reported in FBIS-SOV-91-198-A (October 11, 1991), p. 9.

[140]Quoted on December 22, 1991, reported in FBIS-SOV-91-247 (December 24, 1991), p. 57. Shushkevich was an unknown professor at Belarus State University before the Chernobyl accident. Trained as a nuclear physicist, he quickly grasped the deadly consequences of the radioactive fallout for the country and publicly criticized the government for not doing enough to safeguard the public's health. On the basis of his newfound notoriety, Shushkevich was elected a deputy of the Supreme Soviet in the 1990 national election and was voted to the largely ceremonial position of chairman in September 1991. For the next two and a half years, Shushkevich used what little authority he had to modernize the economy and carve out a nonaligned foreign policy.

[141]On the number of tactical nuclear weapons in Belarus, see Robert S. Norris, "The Soviet Nuclear Archipelago," *Bulletin of the Atomic Scientists* (January-February 1992), p. 25. Other sources give slightly different estimates. Reportedly, over half of these weapons were assigned to the air force.

[142]*Postfactum*, February 12, 1992, reported in FBIS-SOV-92-030 (February 13, 1992), p. 81. The first voices calling for Belarus to retain tactical nuclear weapons were heard in late February 1992. See *Nezavisimaya Gazeta*, February 22, 1992, reported in FBIS-SOV-92-037 (February 25, 1992), p. 64.

[143]*Interfax*, March 17, 1992, reported in FBIS-SOV-92-053 (March 18, 1992), p. 3; see also Douglas L. Clarke, "Uproar over Nuclear Weapons," *RFE/RL Research Report* 1, no. 13 (March 27, 1992): 51.

[144]*TASS*, March 17, 1992, reported in FBIS-SOV-92-054 (March 19, 1992), p. 2.

[145]Radio Rossii (Moscow), March 21, 1992, reported in FBIS-SOV-92-056 (March 23, 1992), p. 2.

[146]FBIS-SOV-92-082 (April 28, 1992), p. 2.

[147]See FBIS-SOV-92-079 (April 23, 1992), p. 2; *RFE/RL Research Report* 1, no. 20 (May 15, 1992): 26.

[148]State Department official, personal interview, Washington, D.C., February 9, 1994; Vyachaslav Paznyak, personal interview, Washington, D.C., July 7, 1994.

[149]See "Agreement between the Republic of Belarus and the Russian Federation on the Strategic Forces Temporarily Deployed in the Territory of the Republic of Belarus," copy in author's possession. Minsk has never released the text of this agreement, although Belarusian and Russian officials have referred to it publicly. See *Nezavisimaya Gazeta*, July 22, 1992, reported in FBIS-SOV-92-142 (July 23, 1992), p. 9; *Interfax*, July 24, 1992, reported in FBIS-SOV-92-144 (July 27, 1992), p. 2; FBIS-SOV-92-145 (July 28, 1992), p. 53; FBIS-SOV-92-152 (August 6, 1992), p. 60; FBIS-SOV-92-183 (September 21, 1992), pp. 47–48; *Interfax*, November 24, 1992, reported in FBIS-SOV-92-228 (November 25, 1992), p. 53; *Nezavisimaya Gazeta*, November 26, 1992, reported in FBIS-SOV-92-234 (December 4, 1992), p. 36; John W. R. Lepingwell, "The Bishkek Summit and Nuclear Weapons Control," *RFE/RL Research Report* 1, no. 42 (October 23, 1992): 42–43.

[150]See *Interfax*, September 24, 1992, reported in FBIS-SOV-92-187 (September 25, 1992), p. 36; see also Moscow *Interfax*, February 11, 1993, reported in FBIS-SOV-93-028 (February 12, 1993), p. 48; Minsk radio, March 9, 1993, reported in FBIS-SOV-93-044 (March 9, 1993), p. 41.

[151]*Vesti* (Moscow television), October 23, 1992, reported in FBIS-SOV-92-207 (October 26, 1992), p. 63. The two parties also agreed at this time on a method to limit the number of armed forces in accordance with the Conventional Forces in Europe (CFE) Treaty.

[152]*Interfax*, October 26, 1992, reported in FBIS-SOV-92-208 (October 27, 1992), p. 3. In November 1992, the Belarusian Supreme Soviet endorsed a military doctrine that followed this timetable. See *Reuters*, December 31, 1992. On the general subject of withdrawing the strategic nuclear weapons, see Paznyak, "Nonproliferation from Belarus's Perspective," pp. 12–14.

[153]"Agreement between the Government of the Republic of Belarus and the Government of the Russian Federation on the Procedure of Withdrawal of Russian Federation Military Units of the Strategic Forces Temporarily Stationed on the Territory of the Republic of Belarus to the Territory of the Russian Federation," September 24, 1993, copy in author's possession.

[154]*Agence France Presse* (Paris), December 22, 1993, reported in JPRS-TND-94-003 (January 31, 1994), p. 18; see also *RFE/RL Daily Report*, no. 54 (March 18, 1994), pp. 8–9. See also Dunbar Lockwood, "Strategic Nuclear Forces of the United States and the Commonwealth of Independent States," *Arms Control Association Fact Sheet*, January 10, 1994. Other Western sources cite slightly different numbers of missiles and the times when they were scheduled to be withdrawn from the country.

[155]Personal interview, Minsk, November 2, 1993; this account was corroborated by a knowledgeable Western ambassador, personal interview, Minsk, November 2, 1993; see also FBIS-SOV-93-023 (February 5, 1993), p. 50; *Belinform*, February 5, 1993, reported in FBIS-SOV-93-024 (February 8, 1993), p. 34; *Belinform*, February 11, 1993, reported in FBIS-SOV-93-027 (February 11, 1993), p. 40.

[156]A physical testament to the continued close relations between Minsk and Moscow was the outsize statue of Lenin in front of the Supreme Soviet Assembly

building, one of the few Communist Party icons that remained intact and upright in the former Soviet Union.

[157]*Moskovskiye Novosti,* August 17, 1993, reported in FBIS-SOV-93-159 (August 19, 1993), p. 60.

[158]See, for example, USIA Opinion Research memorandum, December 10, 1992 (based on sampling survey of October 10–24, 1992), p. 6.

[159]*Izvestiya,* September 11, 1993, reported in FBIS-SOV-93-175 (September 13, 1993), p. 56. Shushkevich's assessment that nuclear weapons would decrease Belarus's security by attracting a nuclear strike echoes the calculations of Swedish officials in the late 1950s on whether Sweden should acquire nuclear weapons. See Mitchell Reiss, *Without the Bomb: The Politics of Nuclear Nonproliferation* (New York: Columbia University Press, 1988), pp. 37–77.

[160]*Interfax,* October 2, 1992, reported in FBIS-SOV-92-192 (October 2, 1992), p. 27; see also *RFE/RL Research Report* 1, no. 44 (November 6, 1992): 57.

[161]See Press Release, Embassy of Belarus, "A Telephone Call from President Clinton to Belarus Chairman Shushkevich," February 9, 1993. A few days after the vote, Minsk announced that during this call the president had given Shushkevich "security guarantees." *Belinform* (Minsk), reported in FBIS-SOV-93-026 (February 10, 1993), p. 36. This was untrue. The previous year, Washington had told the Belarusian foreign minister that when Minsk ratified START and joined the NPT, the United States would extend the same type of "security assurances" that it extends to all nonnuclear weapon states that are members of the NPT. This was the same formula that Washington offered to both Ukraine and Kazakhstan. State Department official, personal interview, Washington, D.C., February 9, 1994.

[162]The three agreements provided (1) $25 million for environmental restoration of former Soviet SRF sites, (2) $20 million for defense conversion and military housing and retraining for decommissioned SRF officers, and (3) $14 million for export control assistance to prevent the spread of weapons of mass destruction. The Nunn-Lugar amendment to the FY92 Defense Authorization bill allocated these funds, which came from the FY92 and FY93 Defense Department budgets. See Office of the Assistant Secretary of Defense for Public Affairs, Fact Sheet, "Signing of Agreements between U.S. Department of Defense and Belarus Ministry of Defense," July 22, 1993. These funds were actually part of the $65-million assistance package that had been announced in March by Secretary of State Christopher. Left in suspension between the March announcement and the July agreements (and beyond) was $6 million because Washington and Minsk disagreed over how to spend this money.

[163]Personal interview, Minsk, November 2, 1993.

[164]For example, the Byelorussian KGB was left virtually intact after independence. The sole change occurred at the top: the director was replaced by the head of counterintelligence. Unlike in East Germany, in Belarus there was no popular clamor to see personal files or learn who had informed for the state.

[165]See Marples, "Ukraine, Belarus, and the Energy Dilemma," pp. 39–44.

[166]Kathleen Mihalisko, "The Belarusian National Dilemma: And Its Implications for U.S. Policy-Makers," *Demokratizatsiya: The Journal of Post-Soviet Democratization* 2, no. 1 (1994): 112.

[167]For the Chaus comment, see *TASS,* February 12, 1992, reported in FBIS-SOV-92-030 (February 13, 1992), p. 81; Shushkevich made his statement on Minsk radio, August 27, 1993, p. 27, reported in FBIS-SOV-93-167 (August 31, 1993), p. 48.

[168]Radio Minsk, February 1, 1993, reported in FBIS-SOV-93-021 (February 3, 1993), p. 1; see also *ITAR-TASS*, January 30, 1993, reported in FBIS-SOV-93-020 (February 2, 1993), p. 1.

[169]Personal interview, Minsk, November 1, 1993. Paznyak is now director at the International Institute for Policy Studies, also in Minsk.

Kazakhstan

[170]Interview with Japanese newspaper *Asahi Shimbun*, September 21, 1991, reported in FBIS-SOV-91-191-A (October 2, 1991), p. 8. See also the statement of General Sagadat Nurbagambetov, head of the Kazakhstan State Committee for Defense, in FBIS-SOV-91-208 (October 28, 1991), p. 88.

[171]*TASS*, October 28, 1991, reported in FBIS-SOV-91-210 (October 30, 1991), p. 87.

[172]For a devastating portrait of the legacy of Semipalatinsk, see Max Eastman, "Mutant Children of a Failed God," *Spectator* (London), April 3, 1993, pp. 11–12; see also FBIS-SOV-92-156 (August 12, 1992), pp. 54–55.

[173]See Bess Brown, "The Strength of Kazakhstan's Antinuclear Lobby," *RFE/RL Report on the USSR* 3, no. 4 (January 25, 1991): 23–24. Without access to Semipalatinsk, Russia has only one other nuclear testing site, at Novaya Zemlya, an island in the Barents Sea.

[174]*Interfax*, November 25, 1991, reported in FBIS-SOV-91-228 (November 26, 1991), p. 88.

[175]In November 1994, the Clinton administration announced that it had removed approximately 600 kilograms of highly enriched uranium from a nuclear fuel fabrication plant at Ust-Kamenogorsk in northeastern Kazakhstan and had shipped it to the Oak Ridge nuclear facility in Tennessee. The highly classified operation was codenamed "Project Sapphire." See Michael R. Gordon, "Big Cache of Nuclear Bomb Fuel Found in an Ex-Soviet Republic," *New York Times*, November 23, 1994; Michael R. Gordon, "Months of Delicate Talks in Kazakhstan Atom Deal," *New York Times*, November 24, 1994; R. Jeffrey Smith, "U.S. Takes Nuclear Fuel," *Washington Post*, November 23, 1994. Questions later arose over how much of the enriched uranium was actually bomb-grade and whether the price the United States paid (estimated to be around $30 million) was too high. See Steven Erlanger, "Kazakhstan Thanks U.S. on Uranium, but Says It Wasn't in Danger of Theft," *New York Times*, November 25, 1994; Jack Anderson and Michael Binstein, "Uranium: Buy It or Else?" *Washington Post*, December 4, 1994. In a telephone interview in mid-November 1994, the inspection team chief at the On-Site Inspection Agency, Commander Paul Shaffer, who participated in the removal effort in Kazakhstan, stated that the United States had paid fair market value for the HEU. Regardless of whether Washington paid too much for this material, the Clinton administration's trumpeting of this operation as a nonproliferation and foreign policy success embarrassed the Kazakh government by publicly claiming that the material had been kept in an insecure manner; it also drew unwanted international attention not only to the fact that other caches of this material were vulnerable to theft but also to the fact that the United States was willing to bargain for them.

[176]This statement requires some clarification. Nazarbayev actually received a telephone call from Yeltsin and Shushkevich the weekend of December 7–8, inviting him to Minsk to sign the CIS charter. Nazarbayev declined, stating that he did not want to sign the document because he had not helped draft it. That both Yeltsin and Shushkevich were clearly "tired and emotional" at the time of the phone call—they had already drunk a toast to each of the charter's fourteen provisions—did not help persuade the Kazakh leader to fly to Belarus.

[177]Inexperience and lack of expertise by Kazakh diplomats may also have contributed to the policy on tactical nuclear weapons. These and some of the reasons mentioned in the text were cited by Bolat Nurgaliev, head of the international security and arms control department at the Kazakh Foreign Ministry, in a personal interview, Almaty, October 20, 1993.

[178]Baker telephoned Nazarbayev on December 24 with the news that the United States wanted to officially recognize the independence of the republics sometime soon and that it hoped Kazakhstan would be one of the first. FBIS-SOV-91-248 (December 26, 1991), p. 72. The next day, Washington recognized the independence of all five Central Asian republics (along with seven other former Soviet republics) but moved to conduct diplomatic relations with only two—Kazakhstan and Kyrgyzstan. Kyrgyzstan was so honored because it had strongly condemned the August 1991 coup attempt and because Kyrgyz President Askar Akayev, unlike the other central Asian leaders, was committed to economic reform.

[179]James Baker, personal interview, Washington, D.C., May 4, 1994; Ross, U.S. Department of State, personal interview, Washington, D.C., February 8, 1994. Ross thinks that Nazarbayev would have been wiser to explain his strategy explicitly to Baker.

[180]Nurgaliev, personal interview, Almaty, October 20, 1993; Oumirserik Kasenov and Kairat Abuseitov, *The Future of Nuclear Weapons in the Kazakh Republic's National Security* (Mclean, Va.: Potomac Foundation, 1993), pp. 7–11; see also Oumirserik Kasenov, "The Role of Kazakhstan in Strengthening the Nonproliferation Regime" (paper prepared for the Monterey Institute of International Studies, November 1993).

[181]Quoted in *TASS*, January 14, 1992, reported in FBIS-SOV-92-010 (January 15, 1992), p. 70. Nazarbayev personally denied at this time that Kazakhstan was considering the sale of nuclear weapons abroad; see *Interfax*, January 10, 11, 1992, reported in FBIS-SOV-92-008 (January 13, 1992), p. 56. For other official Kazakh denials of nuclear-related sales abroad, see FBIS-SOV-92-012 (January 17, 1992), p. 69; *Interfax*, January 20, 1992, reported in FBIS-SOV-92-014 (January 22, 1992), p. 83; *Rossiyskaya Gazeta*, January 22, 1992, reported in FBIS-SOV-92-015 (January 23, 1992), p. 99; *Postfactum*, January 25, 1992, reported in FBIS-SOV-92-017 (January 27, 1992), p. 63; *Interfax*, January 25, 1992, reported in FBIS-SOV-92-017 (January 27, 1992), p. 63; *TASS*, January 28, 1992, reported in FBIS-SOV-92-019 (January 29, 1992), p. 68; *Ekspress* (Almaty), January 29, 1992, reported in FBIS-SOV-92-041 (March 2, 1992); *ITAR-TASS*, May 2, 1992, reported in FBIS-SOV-92-086 (May 4, 1992), p. 3; FBIS-SOV-92-167 (August 27, 1992), p. 62; *ITAR-TASS*, October 15, 1992, reported in FBIS-SOV-92-200 (October 15, 1992), p. 41.

[182]Quotation of Lt. Gen. Sergey Zelentsov, deputy chief of the Main Directorate within the CIS Joint Armed Forces High Command, in *Nezavisimaya Gazeta*, March 18, 1992, reported in FBIS-SOV-92-054 (March 19, 1992), pp. 4–5.

[183]Personal interviews, Washington, D.C., 1993 and 1994.

[184]The White House, Office of the Press Secretary, "Press Briefing by Assistant Secretary of State for European and Canadian Affairs, Ambassador Thomas Niles," May 19, 1992 (hereafter cited as Niles Press Briefing), p. 7.

[185]U.S. government official, personal interview, Washington, D.C., 1993; Oumirserik Kasenov, director of the Kazakhstan Institute of Strategic Studies and foreign policy adviser to President Nazarbayev, personal interview, Almaty, October 19, 1993. Nurgaliev stated that Nazarbayev knew generally of the withdrawal process but conceded that he may not have known when the last weapon was removed. Personal interview, Almaty, October 20, 1993.

[186]Reuters, January 18, 1992; TASS, February 24, 1992, reported in JPRS-TND-92-036 (February 24, 1992), p. 72.

[187]Agence France Presse, March 20, 1992, reported in FBIS-SOV-92-057 (March 24, 1992), p. 1. Under article 9(3) of the NPT, a nuclear weapon state "is one which has manufactured and exploded a nuclear weapon or other nuclear explosive device prior to January 1, 1967."

[188]See Oumirserik Kasenov, "Nuclear Arms in Kazakhstan: Real Problems and False Myths," in Carin Wedar, Michael Intriligator, and Peter Vares, eds., Implications of the Dissolution of the Soviet Union for Accidental/Inadvertent Use of Weapons of Mass Destruction (Paide, Estonia: A/S Multipress, 1992), p. 180.

[189]See Daniel Sneider, "Kazakhstan Seeks US Pact for Further Cuts," Christian Science Monitor, April 27, 1992.

[190]TASS, February 20, 1992, reported in FBIS-SOV-92-037 (February 25, 1992), p. 65.

[191]Izvestiya, February 25, 1992, reported in FBIS-SOV-92-036 (February 24, 1992), p. 72.

[192]Agence France Presse, March 20, 1992, reported in FBIS-SOV-92-057 (March 24, 1992), p. 1.

[193]See John W. R. Lepingwell, "Kazakhstan and Nuclear Weapons," RFE/RL Research Report 2, no. 8 (February 19, 1993): 59; Kyodo (Tokyo), May 2, 1992, reported in FBIS-SOV-92-086 (May 4, 1992), p. 48; NHK (Japanese television), May 1, 1992, reported in FBIS-SOV-92-086 (May 4, 1992), p. 47. If Almaty thought these statements would win U.S. funding for dismantlement, it miscalculated. In April 1992, the State Department certified that the Russian Federation, Ukraine, and Belarus qualified for U.S. assistance under the Soviet Nuclear Threat Reduction (Nunn-Lugar) Act of 1991; Kazakhstan did not. The official U.S. statement said: "In making the required certification . . . the oral and written representations made by the leadership of these states, as well as their practices and patterns of activity, and trends in such activity, provide the basis for the Deputy Secretary of State's conclusion that their commitments satisfy the requirements of the legislation" (emphasis added). "Statement by Margaret Tutwiler," U.S. Department of State, April 10, 1992.

[194]The White House, Office of the Press Secretary, "Declaration by President Bush and President Nazarbayev on Relations between the United States and Kazakhstan," May 19, 1992.

[195]The START agreement, signed on July 31, 1991, was originally between the United States and the Soviet Union. Washington's recognition of Ukraine, Belarus, and Kazakhstan as legal successors to the Soviet Union was important because it granted greater legitimacy to their claims to share equitably with Russia the former Soviet Union's overseas properties and other assets.

[196]Don Oberdorfer, "Kazakhstan Agrees to Give Up A-Arms," *Washington Post,* May 20, 1992; Kasenov and Abuseitov, *The Future of Nuclear Weapons in the Kazakh Republic's National Security,* p. 6; FBIS-SOV-92-096 (May 18, 1992), p. 2. Kazakhstan's anxiety concerning China was reinforced by Almaty's proximity to the Chinese border.

[197]Nurgaliev, personal interview, Almaty, October 20, 1993.

[198]For the text of the Lisbon Protocol and associated side letters, see *United Nations Institute for Disarmament Research Newsletter,* nos. 22 and 23 (June-September 1993), pp. 44–45. For coverage of the Lisbon summit, see Don Oberdorfer, "Ex-Soviet States to Give Up A-Arms," *Washington Post,* May 24, 1992; Barbara Crossette, "4 Ex-Soviet States and U.S. in Accord on 1991 Arms Pact," *New York Times,* May 25, 1992.

[199]Technically, this statement is untrue; START did not require that any of the SS-18s in Kazakhstan be eliminated. START I specified that 50 percent of the Soviet Union's 308 SS-18s had to be destroyed during its seven-year implementation period. Because the agreement had not contemplated the dissolution of the USSR, it was silent on which particular missiles would be destroyed. Theoretically, Russia could have abided by the treaty's terms if it destroyed 154 of the 204 SS-18s on its territory while leaving untouched the 104 SS-18s based in Kazakhstan. However, the U.S. Senate and the Russian parliament later conditioned their ratification of START I on formal adherence by Kazakhstan (and Ukraine and Belarus) to the Lisbon documents as well as START I. As a practical matter, then, START I could not enter into force until all strategic nuclear warheads outside of Russia, including those associated with the SS-18s based in Kazakhstan, were pledged to return to Russia.

START II later made this point moot. START II called for the elimination of all SS-18s and for their nontransfer to a third state, including signatories of START I; this clause was intended to prevent the transfer of the missiles to Kazakhstan. See Douglas L. Clarke, "The Impact of START-2 on the Russian Strategic Forces," *RFE/RL Research Report* 2, no. 8 (February 19, 1993): 65–70.

[200]*ITAR-TASS,* May 18, 1992, reported in FBIS-SOV-92-096 (May 18, 1992), p. 2 (emphasis added).

[201]James Baker, personal interview, Washington, D.C., May 4, 1994; Ross, personal interview, Washington, D.C., February 8, 1993. See also Niles Press Briefing, May 19, 1992; *ITAR-TASS,* May 19, 1992, reported in FBIS-SOV-92-097 (May 19, 1992), p. 42.

[202]Kasenov, personal interview, Almaty, October 19, 1993; Nurgaliev, personal interview, Almaty, October 20, 1993. For an example of parliamentary opposition to Kazakhstan's ratifying of START I, see *Interfax,* May 25, 1992, reported in FBIS-SOV-92-102 (May 27, 1992), p. 2.

[203]Niles Press Briefing, May 19, 1992, pp. 7–8.

[204]Kazakh negotiators repeatedly complained about the arrogant approach Russia adopted in the bilateral denuclearization negotiations. For example, in August 1992, Russia drafted a treaty formally assigning jurisdiction over the strategic nuclear weapons in Kazakhstan to Russia (just as Russia did with Belarus). According to Kasenov, Kazakhstan refused to accede to this arrangement. Personal interview, Almaty, October 19, 1993; see also *RFE/RL Research Report* 1, no. 35 (September 4, 1992): 41–42. Almaty reportedly relented in a March 28, 1994, sum-

mit meeting between Presidents Nazarbayev and Yeltsin, who agreed that Russia would have jurisdiction over all nuclear forces in Kazakhstan. See *RFE/RL News Briefs* 3, no. 19 (May 2–6, 1994): 9.

205Nurgaliev, personal interview, Almaty, October 20, 1993.

206Elaine Sciolino, "Kazakh Uses America to Enhance His Stature," *New York Times,* October 25, 1993; see also FBIS-SOV-93-204, October 25, 1993, p. 63. Secretary of State Christopher may have been the victim of bad timing. His trip immediately preceded the visit to Almaty of Iranian President Akbar Hashemi Rafsanjani; Nazarbayev may have been reluctant to signal a closer relationship with the United States at that precise moment for fear of irritating his Iranian visitor.

207*Kazakhstanskaya Pravda,* October 22, 1993, p. 1. See also FBIS-SOV-93-199 (October 18, 1993), p. 85; JPRS-TND-93-034 (October 27, 1993), p. 37.

208*Izvestiya,* December 15, 1993, reported in FBIS-SOV-93-239 (December 15, 1993), p. 91. On July 26, 1994, Kazakhstan signed a comprehensive safeguards agreement with the IAEA. See *RFE/RL Daily Report,* no. 141 (July 27, 1994); IAEA Press Release 94/30, July 27, 1994.

209See R. Jeffrey Smith, "Kazakhstan Ratifies Nuclear Control Pact, Will Get U.S. Aid," *Washington Post,* December 14, 1993; Richard L. Berke, "Prodded by Gore, Kazakhstan Signs Arms Accord," *New York Times,* December 14, 1993.

210Gwen Ifill, "U.S. Will Triple Its Foreign Aid to Kazakhstan," *New York Times,* February 15, 1994; Ann Devroy, "Clinton Pledges Increase in Aid to Kazakhstan, Citing Reforms," *Washington Post,* February 15, 1994.

211On deactivation, see U.S. government official, personal interview, Washington, D.C., 1993; on the return of the warheads to Russia, see Fred Hiatt, "U.S. Reward Sought for Ceding A-Arms," *Washington Post,* February 14, 1993.

212*RFE/RL Daily Report,* no. 37 (February 23, 1994), pp. 2–3.

213See *RFE/RL Daily Report,* no. 85 (May 4, 1994); *ITAR-TASS,* May 17, 1994, reported in FBIS-SOV-94-095 (May 17, 1994), p. 4. There is one possible exception. In late 1992, reports of a bizarre story started to surface in the local Kazakh press. An unexploded nuclear device had been left in a shaft five hundred meters under Tekelen Mountain at the Semipalatinsk testing complex. Moscow had intended to explode the device in 1989, but Nazarbayev had banned all nuclear tests at that time. The military decided not to detonate it but to leave it in the shaft. See JPRS-TND-92-034 (September 22, 1992), p. 26; FBIS-SOV-92-231 (December 1, 1992), pp. 1–2; FBIS-SOV-92-232 (December 2, 1992), p. 22; *Komsomolskaya Pravda* (Moscow), November 28, 1992, reported in JPRS-TND-92-047 (December 18, 1992), pp. 27–28; *ITAR-TASS,* November 4, 1993, reported in JPRS-TND-93-036 (November 17, 1993), p. 27; *Komsomolskaya Pravda,* November 9, 1993, reported in JPRS-TND-93-037 (December 8, 1993), p. 43; *Krasnaya Zvezda* (Moscow), January 14, 1994, reported in JPRS-TND-94-004 (February 11, 1994), p. 22. Disarming and removing the nuclear device will be expensive, time-consuming, and dangerous. By the start of 1995, the situation had still not been resolved.

214Personal interview, Almaty, October 19, 1993.

215Kazakhstan later insisted on receiving compensation for the fissile material contained in the strategic nuclear warheads that were stationed on its territory, but by this time Moscow had already signaled to Kiev that it was willing to discuss this issue.

216Kasenov, personal interview, Washington, D.C., March 17, 1994.

Chapter 5

South Asia: The Zero-Sum Subcontinent?

Twice during 1993 the director of the Central Intelligence Agency, James Woolsey, testified before the U.S. Congress that the arms race between India and Pakistan represented "the most probable prospect" for the future use of nuclear weapons. According to Woolsey, the U.S. intelligence community believed that both countries had the capability to construct nuclear weapons "on short notice."[1] The CIA's Russian counterpart, the Foreign Intelligence Service, offered a similarly chilling analysis in a 1993 estimate of the nuclear situation on the Indian subcontinent. Its report concluded, "In the event that the India-Pakistan conflict shifts to the crisis stage . . . the matter will not be limited to the employment of conventional weapons."[2] Scholars in South Asia and the United States have painted distressing pictures of the wholesale devastation that even a limited nuclear war in the region would leave behind.[3]

The history of strained relations between the two countries contributed to these alarming assessments. India and Pakistan have fought three wars against each other since 1947, and miscalculation or misunderstanding between the two almost led to the outbreak of hostilities in 1987 and 1990. Neither country is a party to the NPT, neither accepts international safeguards over all its nuclear facilities, and each is actively enhancing its ballistic missile capabilities. Even if intentional escalation can be avoided, the risk of inadvertent or accidental nuclear war is now a fixture on the South Asian landscape.

Although this history alone would be sufficient cause for concern, the deteriorating domestic and regional environments in which this competition occurs make it particularly worrisome. Communal passions erupted in early December 1992, when Hindu fanatics destroyed the Babri mosque and local authorities failed to intervene. This incident revealed long-simmering resentment among some Hindus against Moslems in India, sentiments that have achieved political respectability with the growing popularity of the Bharatiya Janata Party.

Human rights atrocities have continued in Kashmir, due to an ever-mounting cycle of violence by Moslem separatists and Indian security forces. Migrations across porous borders created new national security problems in the region and have contributed to growing incidents of criminal behavior and terrorism. The increasing strain placed on limited natural resources by rapid population growth has also aggravated both interstate and intrastate tensions on the subcontinent.[4]

Amid these tensions and troubles, however, India and Pakistan have exercised some prudence and restraint over their nuclear behavior. Although they have rejected formalized legal curbs, the two parties have accepted tacit, informal constraints. India has not tested a nuclear device since its self-proclaimed peaceful nuclear explosion in 1974. Pakistan has never detonated a nuclear device and reportedly froze its nuclear weapons program in 1990. Neither country is believed to have a ready stockpile of assembled nuclear weapons, and neither has deployed nuclear weapons or officially declared that it possesses nuclear arms. Nor is either thought to have exported sensitive nuclear technologies or materials to third parties.

Further, with the end of the cold war, India has had to rethink its foreign policy priorities. The Soviet Union, India's superpower benefactor and primary source of military equipment, is no more, the Non-Aligned Movement is moribund, and China's economy and armed forces have grown by leaps and bounds. In this new environment, Washington has assumed relatively greater influence as New Delhi has realized that it can no longer play its "Soviet card" and as Indian economic policy has actively sought to attract overseas investment capital. The United States has used this opportunity to press its non-proliferation concerns, and other key donor states, such as Japan and Germany, have called for New Delhi to reconsider its opposition to full-scope safeguards and the NPT.

At the same time, Pakistan's strategic value to the West has greatly diminished with the removal of Soviet troops from Afghanistan in February 1989 and the end of the Soviet-American competition. Washington's military and economic assistance to Islamabad stopped in 1990 because of the country's nuclear weapons program. With the end of Soviet support for India, it is unclear how long China will continue to back Pakistan, especially as Beijing's relations with New Delhi gradually warm.

Many South Asian and some American analysts now believe that India and Pakistan have reached a nuclear modus vivendi based on arsenals of unassembled nuclear weapons. This "nonweaponized" or "existential" deterrence may well contribute to stability on the Indian subcontinent by providing more time for the two sides to consider developments, communicate with each other, and increase military preparedness gradually, instead of placing deployed nuclear forces on hair-trigger alert and operating in the fog of war.[5] The Clinton administration apparently concurs. According to a senior State Department official interviewed in January 1994, "Nuclear deterrence is probably operative in South Asia."[6] It may well be that the crises between India and Pakistan in 1987 and 1990 did not erupt into full-scale violence because each party retained its nuclear weapons capabilities.

Nuclear Capabilities

INDIA

India's interest in nuclear energy dates back to World War II, when a young Indian student at Cambridge University, Homi Bhabha, envisioned this new source of inexpensive electrical power as the engine to pull his country out of poverty. Bhabha returned to India after the war and directed his country's ambitious nuclear efforts as the first chairman of the Indian Atomic Energy Commission.[7]

By the early 1970s, India had built one of the most sophisticated nuclear programs in the developing world while ensuring that many nuclear facilities were not subject to IAEA safeguards. At this time, India irradiated nuclear fuel in a Canadian-supplied research reactor and then reprocessed the spent fuel to extract weapons-grade plutonium. On May 18, 1974, New Delhi detonated a self-proclaimed peaceful nuclear explosion in the sparsely populated Rajasthan Desert in western India.[8]

During the next two decades, India aggressively expanded and diversified its nuclear activities, again largely outside of IAEA safeguards. Woolsey declined to speculate in open session on the size of India's nuclear arsenal, but according to a senior State Department official, in 1994 India had enough fissile material for twenty to twenty-five nuclear weapons. It "could assemble several within a few days." By the year 2000, he added, India may have enough fissile material for a stockpile of up to fifty-five nuclear weapons.[9] India has also conducted research on thermonuclear weapons and is trying to reduce the size and increase the reliability and yield of its nuclear devices.[10]

PAKISTAN

India's nuclear test energized a nascent Pakistani nuclear program.[11] Outnumbered and outgunned by its much larger and wealthier neighbor, Pakistan saw nuclear weapons as vital to ensuring its sovereignty and survival. During the 1970s, Islamabad attempted to purchase from France a reprocessing facility that would have enabled it to extract weapons-usable plutonium from spent nuclear fuel. Washington pressured Paris and Islamabad into canceling the deal, after which Pakistan clandestinely acquired the technology to enrich uranium. The Kahuta enrichment facility, located just east of Islamabad, reportedly began producing weapons-grade uranium in the mid-1980s.[12]

The Soviet invasion of Afghanistan in late December 1979 transformed the security situation in South Asia. Despite the influx of millions of Afghan refugees, recurrent Soviet violations of Pakistani air space, and the renewed threat of ethnic unrest in Baluchistan and other provinces, no country in the region benefited more from the Soviet aggression than Pakistan. In June 1981, the administration of President Ronald Reagan provided Pakistan with a six-year, $3.2-billion aid package, marking the beginning of a renewed appreciation of Pakistan's strategic importance. Containing and rolling back Soviet expansion in Southwest Asia now took precedence over concerns about Islamabad's pursuit of nuclear weapons. The United States would support Pakistan, which in turn would funnel military and logistical assistance to the Afghan resistance and so counter Soviet influence.[13] In 1986, Congress approved a second assistance package, totaling over $4 billion.

Yet even by its own standards, the United States conceded that this policy was ineffectual in preventing, or even retarding, the progress of Pakistan's nuclear program. Pakistan's zealous pursuit of nuclear weapons repeatedly brought it into conflict with U.S. nonproliferation policy and domestic legislation. Five times during the 1980s Washington, in order to continue its assistance to Pakistan, waived U.S. laws intended to restrict the dissemination of sophisticated nuclear technologies.[14]

THE PRESSLER AMENDMENT

In 1985, Senator Larry Pressler introduced legislation that required the president to certify annually to Congress that Pakistan "does not possess a nuclear explosive device and that the proposed United States assistance program will reduce significantly the risk that Pakistan will possess a nuclear explosive device."[15] According to a 1987 opinion by the State Department's Office of the Legal Adviser, a nuclear explosive device did not have to be fully assembled to meet the Pressler standard; possession of all the unassembled components for a nuclear explosive device would prevent certification.[16] If the president cannot make this certification, the Pressler amendment requires the ending of U.S. military and economic assistance to Pakistan. Unlike previous legislation in the nonproliferation area, the Pressler amendment singled out one country—Pakistan—and did not allow the president to waive its application in the interests of U.S. national security.

In 1986, 1987, and 1988, President Reagan certified that Pakistan met the Pressler amendment criteria; in 1989, President Bush did the same. In October 1990, however, the Bush administration could not provide this certification, and Washington suspended the remaining three years of economic and military assistance to Pakistan under the 1986 aid commitment.[17]

The consequences of the 1990 certification decision reverberate to this day as both Americans and Pakistanis trade recriminations and allege bad faith and deceptive practices. In the aftermath of President Bush's October 1990 decision, Pakistan thought itself badly wronged by the United States; it believed it had reached an understanding with Washington about its nuclear program. Many Pakistanis argue, and some U.S. officials agree, that Islamabad's actions in the nuclear sphere in 1990 were not very different from what they had been in previous years.

Evidence strongly suggests that Washington knew, at least as early as 1987, that Pakistan had acquired a nuclear weapons capability. Dr. Abdul Qadeer Khan, director of the Kahuta uranium enrichment facility, explicitly stated to an Indian journalist in January 1987 that Pakistan could build nuclear weapons, that it did not need to conduct a nuclear test, and that the CIA knew of these capabilities. The "father of the Islamic bomb" warned: "Nobody can undo Pakistan or take us for granted. We are here to stay and let it be clear that we shall use the bomb if our existence is threatened."[18] The former chief of the army staff in Pakistan, General Mirza Aslam Beg, publicly declared in both 1993 and 1994 that Pakistan had assembled a nuclear bomb in 1987.[19] On the American side, a senior U.S. official in a 1993 interview stated that Washington "knew" from its intelligence sources in 1987 that the Pakistanis had built nuclear cores.[20] A former U.S. intelligence analyst added, "There was never any meaningful freeze on the Pakistani program from 1987 forward."[21] Most authoritatively and credibly, Richard Kerr, a career CIA official who rose to the position of deputy director of intelligence, said in 1993, "There is no question that we had an intelligence basis for not certifying from 1987 on."[22] In other words, according to Kerr, since 1987 the United States had believed that Pakistan possessed either a nuclear explosive device or all the unassembled components to make one.

In May 1990, the U.S. government concluded that Pakistan had fully assembled nuclear weapons. The American ambassador to Pakistan, Robert Oakley, later stated, "We had ascertained *beyond a shadow of a doubt* that the promises that [Prime Minister Benazir] Bhutto had made and kept in 1989, and that [General Beg] had made and kept during 1989, had been broken and the nuclear program had been reactivated."[23] Paul Wolfowitz, the under secretary of defense in the Bush administration, was more explicit: "We knew that Pakistan assembled a nuclear weapon. That is why we cut off assistance under the Pressler amendment later that year."[24] Richard Haass, senior director for the Near East and South Asia at the National Security Council, explained that there was "not one piece of 'A-Ha!' intelligence" but that the accumulation of discrete data led him to believe in early May that Pakistan had probably assembled "one or even more nuclear weapons."[25]

The decision to weaponize was most probably taken by General Beg. With the Soviet forces out of Afghanistan, and with Pakistan's strategic significance receding, Islamabad's long-standing fear of American unreliability and its suspicions of a U.S. "tilt" toward India resurfaced. According to Oakley, this may have triggered Beg's decision to assemble the nuclear devices.[26]

Despite the war scare in the spring and the fact that Pakistan had actually constructed nuclear weapons, U.S. officials entered into highly confidential discussions during 1990 to determine how Pakistan could once more receive presidential certification. The United States specified the three requirements Pakistan would have to satisfy to meet the Pressler standard: (1) no more production of uranium enriched to above 20 percent U-235; (2) no conversion of highly enriched uranium (HEU) hexafluoride gas (UF6) into metal; and (3) no working of the metal into weapons cores.

The third condition was essential. Although Pakistan could keep the bomb-grade material it had already produced, this condition effectively meant that Pakistan would have to dismantle or destroy its existing nuclear cores. In other words, it would have to walk the program back, perhaps to a pre-1987 nuclear capability. Islamabad agreed to the first two conditions but balked at the third. The Pakistanis refused to "roll back" their program, especially given their suspicions of an Indian nuclear weapon arsenal and New Delhi's continued work in this area.[27]

At the beginning of October 1990, President Bush did not certify Pakistan, which ironically provided something akin to independent verification that Islamabad had acquired nuclear weapons. Later that same month President Ghulam Ishaq Khan personally promised President Bush that Pakistan would not assemble a nuclear device, would not conduct a nuclear test, and would not transfer sensitive nuclear technology, but the pledge fell on deaf ears.[28]

1990: HOW REAL A NUCLEAR CRISIS?

In the March 29, 1993, issue of the *New Yorker* magazine, the investigative journalist Seymour M. Hersh wrote an article entitled "On the Nuclear Edge." Relying on U.S. intelligence sources and on-the-record interviews with senior CIA officials Robert Gates and Richard Kerr, Hersh claimed that in spring 1990 India and Pakistan had squared off in the most dangerous nuclear confrontation since the Cuban Missile Crisis. The dispatch of Gates to the region in May as President Bush's special envoy eased tensions and allowed India and Pakistan to avert disaster.[29] Kerr sounded the loudest alarm: "There's no question in my mind that we were right on the edge. . . . This period was very tense. The intelligence community believed that without some intervention the two parties could miscalculate—and miscalculation could lead to a nuclear exchange. . . . It was the most dangerous nuclear situation we have ever faced since I've been in the U.S. government. It may be as close as we've come to a nuclear exchange. It was far more frightening than the Cuban Missile Crisis."[30] The Hersh article prompted a storm of controversy, which still rages in the United States, India, and Pakistan, with most observers disputing Hersh's facts and downplaying the risk of nuclear war in South Asia at that time.[31]

Some general facts are undisputed, however. In December 1989, Moslem separatists escalated their militancy against Indian rule in the state of Jammu and Kashmir, which had been incorporated into India after partition in 1947. Pakistan's Inter-Services Intelligence Agency (ISI) took advantage of the situation by redirecting fundamentalist Islamic groups that had proved effective in fighting the Soviet forces in Afghanistan and by providing other forms of support to the insurgents. To combat these efforts, India stepped up border patrols along the Line of Control separating the Indian- and Pakistani-held territories in Kashmir and deployed large numbers of policemen, paramilitary troops, and armed forces to Kashmir to suppress the uprising.

New Delhi also began military training exercises in the Rajasthan Desert. This action rekindled Pakistan's historical fears of a swift Indian incursion into Sind, a move that could cut the slender country in half. Further, it summoned still-fresh memories of the 1986–87 "Brass

Tacks" exercise, when major Indian military maneuvers in the Rajasthan Desert had prompted Pakistan to send its armed forces into Punjab, almost triggering a fourth round of hostilities.[32] This time Islamabad responded by moving two armored tank units to positions near the border.

Although neither country had adequately prepared the logistical support needed for launching offensive operations, the cycle of action and reaction, domestic political posturing, and faulty communication between India and Pakistan appeared at the time to Ambassador Oakley to have many uncomfortable parallels with "Brass Tacks." Compounding his concern was the insurrection in Kashmir, which inflamed and sustained passions on both sides, and the weak leaders at the helm of both India (V. P. Singh) and Pakistan (Benazir Bhutto). Oakley was concerned that the two prime ministers did not have the type of personal authority or control needed to rein in their respective military establishments and walk away from the precipice.[33]

The situation inside Kashmir deteriorated through early spring. In mid-April, the United States publicly appealed for calm. As the violence in Kashmir continued, Indian officials and military officers discussed preemptive strikes against training camps in Pakistan.[34] In May 1990, Robert Gates was in Moscow preparing for a presidential summit between Bush and Boris Yeltsin. As the crisis in South Asia heated up, he flew to South Asia to try to defuse the tense situation.[35]

Joined by Ambassador Oakley, the U.S. team met with General Beg, his military staff, and President Ghulam Ishaq Khan. In his meeting with Beg and Khan, Gates said that he was not there to resolve the Kashmir issue, but he told Pakistan to stop sponsoring terrorism in Kashmir and explained the risks the United States believed Pakistan was running. Washington was concerned that the situation could erupt into a conventional war, which could then lead to a nuclear war.[36] To General Beg, Gates stated, "Our military has war-gamed every conceivable scenario between you and the Indians, and there isn't a single way you win."[37] The United States made it clear that it was not going to come to the rescue in the event of war.[38] Richard Haass, who accompanied Gates, recounted: "We told them, here's what we *think* is going to happen on the ground. Here's what we *know* is going to happen diplomatically"—meaning that in both contexts Pakistan would suffer.[39] The scenario Gates outlined sobered President Khan, and before Gates left for New Delhi, Khan assured him that Pakistan would close the training camps for Kashmiris in Azad Kashmir.[40]

Gates and his team had three rounds of talks in New Delhi, with the president, the prime minister, and the military. Gates explained that Washington believed that Indian strikes against Kashmiri training camps in Azad Kashmir would compel Pakistan to respond, if solely for internal political reasons. Knowing that Pakistan would certainly be defeated in a conventional war with India, Islamabad might then use nuclear weapons not as a last resort to preserve the regime, as had been previously thought, but "early" in a conflict.[41] During the next few days, the foreign secretaries in India and Pakistan guided the two sides away from the brink. Indian and Pakistani troops withdrew from border areas, and the crisis was gradually defused.[42]

There is consensus on these general developments (with the possible exception of the influence of the Gates mission), but many of the specific details of the 1990 crisis remain highly contentious. A close reading of Hersh's story, a careful parsing of a February 1994 roundtable discussion with some of the participants in the events of 1990, and personal interviews with senior U.S. government officials and members of the intelligence community suggest that there was a real, if relatively low, probability of nuclear war between India and Pakistan in spring 1990. Ironically, the crisis also offered a valuable lesson on how India and Pakistan could improve the prospects for future nuclear stability in South Asia.

In February 1994, the Henry L. Stimson Center, a research institution in Washington, D.C., convened a distinguished panel of U.S. and foreign experts on South Asia for an on-the-record roundtable discussion of the 1990 crisis.[43] The participants spent most of the session disputing what had actually occurred. Disagreement ranged from whether hot lines between India and Pakistan had been installed before the 1990 crisis, to the role played by Moscow, to the importance of the Gates mission, to why Washington had failed to certify Pakistan under the Pressler standard. Most intriguing, the participants often disagreed with each other, and sometimes contradicted themselves, on the risk of war.

However, there was broad consensus on at least one point. American officials had clearly feared that the situation in spring 1990 might spin out of control and that if it did, conventional hostilities would escalate to the nuclear level.[44] None of them had much faith that nonweaponized or even nuclear deterrence could have averted either the outbreak of conventional hostilities or something much worse.

Although South Asia was able to weather the 1990 war scare, it may not be so fortunate in the future. The Stimson Center roundtable debate also makes clear that despite excellent intelligence collection and constant information sharing, key American participants had different, and at times contrary, perceptions not only of the timing and meaning of the events that occurred during spring 1990 but also of the events themselves. Consequently, they drew diverse conclusions about the implications of these events for war and peace on the subcontinent. As one participant from the U.S. intelligence community observed, "There were a wide range of views, and there probably are today."[45] If members of the U.S. government intimately involved in the 1990 crisis could not fully comprehend a fast-moving and confusing situation, imagine how much more bewildering the events must have appeared to Indian and Pakistani leaders, who did not possess anywhere close to the same intelligence resources and who were not in constant communication with each other. The lesson is clear. Without closer bilateral contacts, ongoing dialogue, and a generally more normal relationship, New Delhi and Islamabad could find themselves locked in a crisis that, next time, could end in disaster.

PAKISTAN'S CURRENT NUCLEAR STATUS

Pakistan has reportedly frozen its nuclear program at either the 1989 or the 1990 level but as of early 1995 was still unable to escape the restrictions of the Pressler amendment. In 1993, Pakistani officials had cited their nuclear restraint as evidence of good faith that Washington should reward. They had also admitted that Pakistan already possessed all the nuclear material it needed.[46] In August 1994, former Prime Minister Nawaz Sharif declared, "Pakistan possesses the atomic bomb." This constituted the most unambiguous admission of the country's nuclear capability by a senior government official. Although this charge was seen as an attempt to embarrass Prime Minister Bhutto, who immediately condemned the "highly irresponsible statement," it reflected a larger immaturity in Pakistan's political system, one that handicaps Islamabad's ability to address the nuclear issue constructively with Washington and New Delhi.[47]

By January 1994, the State Department believed that Pakistan had enough bomb-grade material for six to eight nuclear weapons and that it could produce additional HEU for one or two nuclear devices a year. By the end of the 1990s, a senior diplomat stated, Pakistan could also produce enough plutonium for an additional one or two nuclear devices a year. Like India, Pakistan is trying to reduce the size and increase the reliability and yield of its nuclear devices without conducting a nuclear test.[48]

The Hot Peace: Building How Much Confidence?

Efforts to enhance stability and security in South Asia have been complicated by many factors. Indian hostility to discrimination by a few declared nuclear weapon states that impose nuclear restraints on other countries has led New Delhi to promote only global disarmament measures. It has resisted numerous bilateral and regional arms control measures that might jeopardize its "nuclear option." New Delhi has even challenged what constitutes the appropriate "region" for discussion; China's nuclear arsenal, it argues, is essential to the strategic calculus in South Asia.

The security concerns of Pakistan, the much smaller and weaker of the two countries and with little strategic depth, have been aggravated by Indian behavior during the last decade. Between 1987 and 1991, the Indian military, the fourth-largest in the world, imported over $17 billion worth of defense equipment, substantially more than any other country during this period.[49] At the same time, the end of the Afghan war and, more generally, of the Soviet threat to Southwest Asia severely reduced Pakistan's attractiveness as a strategic partner for the United States. Not completely unlike India, a more isolated Islamabad has tried to overcome its differences with Washington and revive its relationship.

Within this evolving regional context, two particular issues have been viewed as especially worrisome for regional peace and stability: competing claims to Kashmir and ongoing ballistic missile programs.

KASHMIR

In 1947, the Hindu maharaja of Kashmir lawfully, but belatedly, decided to join India, despite a predominantly Moslem population. Open military conflict between India and Pakistan ended only after UN intervention and the demarcation of a Line of Control that left roughly two-thirds of Kashmir in Indian hands and the western third with Pakistan. For India, Kashmir reinforces its secular mythology by providing living testimony of a sizable Moslem community coexisting peacefully in a larger Hindu state. Were Kashmir to secede, this would not only call into doubt the democratic nature of the Indian state but also encourage other ethnic groups to press their independence claims. For Pakistan, Kashmir represents an integral part of the historical justification for a homeland for Indian Moslems, a justification that later evolved into the perceived need for a distinctively Islamic state in South Asia. Kashmir's peaceful incorporation as part of India thus raises questions about the need for a separate Pakistan. Competition for this territory resulted in a second war in 1965 and today prompts constant small-arms fire and low-level violence. To preserve its grip on Kashmir, India has committed massive forces to pacify the Vale. To wrench Kashmir away, insurgents from Pakistan continue to infiltrate across the Line of Control. Kashmir remains the single largest irritant to better relations, and India and Pakistan remain far apart on resolving its fate.[50]

During the past few years the assertion by Kashmiri liberation movements, notably the Jammu and Kashmir Liberation Front (JKLF), of independence unrelated to either India or Pakistan has introduced a new variable into this equation. Although preventing this "third option" could align India and Pakistan, they are unlikely to transform this narrow common interest into a larger political settlement of the Kashmir problem.

BALLISTIC MISSILE CAPABILITIES

Both India and Pakistan have aircraft capable of carrying nuclear weapons. India could use Jaguars, Mirages, or Soviet-supplied MiG jets; Pakistan has Mirages, American-supplied F-16s, and C-130 transports. However, ongoing ballistic missile programs in each country have caused greater anxiety for regional stability, especially among U.S. experts. India has developed a short-range ballistic missile, named Prithvi, which had its maiden launch in February 1988. It reportedly can deliver a payload of 500 kilograms a distance of 250 kilometers with a 50 percent chance of landing within 250 meters of its intended target. U.S. government officials feared that the Prithvi could be deployed since early 1994; according to the Indian Embassy in Washington, New Delhi has agreed to notify Washington in advance of this decision. The missile is capable of delivering a nuclear weapon, assuming India can design one small enough to be placed on top.[51] As of January 1994, the State Department believed that India could deliver its nuclear weapons only by aircraft.[52]

India is also developing an intermediate-range ballistic missile, named Agni, which was first tested in May 1989. The Agni has a 2,000-kilometer range and will not be operational until 1995 at the earliest. Although New Delhi originally professed that the Agni was only a "technology demonstrator," Indian officials recently admitted its use for military purposes.[53] Indian officials privately suggest that this missile is designed to counter the nuclear threat from China.[54]

In May 1992, the United States moved to retard India's ballistic missile ambitions, as well as to express its displeasure at New Delhi's reluctance to embrace meaningful arms control measures. On May 4, the Indian Space Research Organization (ISRO) and the Russian Space Agency, Glavkosmos, signed a $250-million deal for a five-year joint project that included the transfer to India of three liquid hydrogen cryogenic rocket engines and the technology for their construction. Washington immediately slapped a two-year ban on commerce against both organizations, alleging that the deal violated the guidelines of the Missile Technology Control Regime (MTCR).[55] Both Russia and India claimed that the technology transfer agreement was intended solely to promote India's space program and therefore should be exempt from the MTCR export limits. The United States contended that the technology could also be used to assist India's development of intercontinental ballistic missiles.

Under strong pressure from the United States, and eager to exploit commercial opportunities in the U.S. satellite-launcher field and engage in joint Russian-American space activities, Moscow canceled its missile contract with India in July 1993. Russia's invocation of the force majeure clause of its contract prompted outrage in New Delhi, which alleged that Washington was using the MTCR as a political tool to prevent India and other Third World countries from modernizing their economies.[56] By early 1994, however, Moscow and New Delhi had restructured the original deal. Under the new agreement, New Delhi will receive seven rocket engines between 1996 and 1999.[57] Moscow will not transfer the associated technology for their construction.

Pakistan embarked on its ballistic missile development program during the 1980s. In 1989, it first tested the Hatf I, a surface-to-surface missile with an estimated range of eighty kilometers, and the follow-on Hatf II, with an estimated range of three hundred kilometers. As of August 1994, U.S. State Department analysts believed that the Hatf I was "probably operational" but that the Hatf II was not.

To rectify the ballistic missile imbalance with India, Pakistan turned to China to purchase the solid-fuel M-11 short-range ballistic missile. The missile has a reported range of under three hundred kilometers and is thought capable of carrying a nuclear warhead. In August 1993, the United States invoked trade sanctions against China and Pakistan for the sale and importation of M-11 technology; Washington argued that with a lighter payload, the M-11 would exceed the MTCR guidelines.[58] Pakistan admitted that it had acquired short-range missiles from China but denied that they were the M-11 or that they violated the MTCR guidelines.[59] China denounced the Clinton administration's decision as "entirely unjustifiable."[60] In October 1994, the United States and China reached an agreement on China's missile exports, with Beijing reportedly agreeing to abide by the MTCR guidelines in return for the lifting of the August 1993 trade sanctions.[61] Pakistan kept the unassembled M-11s in storage crates at the Sargodha air force base west of Lahore.[62] Pakistan's nuclear weapons are not small enough to be placed on top of its ballistic missiles, but they can be delivered by aircraft.[63]

Both India and Pakistan continue to make advances in the ballistic missile field, although they have so far exercised some restraint by not moving into full-scale production and deploying operational systems. Some South Asian analysts have queried why the United States should oppose the introduction of ballistic missiles in the region, given the fact that both India and Pakistan already possess advanced fighter jets that can deliver conventional and nuclear ordnance. Arguments that ballistic missiles are "fast fliers," are less likely than aircraft to be defeated by defenses, and cannot be recalled after launch are not fully persuasive given the short flight times for aircraft to reach targets.

More compelling is that deployed ballistic missile forces would strain suspect command and control links, thereby increasing the chances for accidental launch. Psychologically, ballistic missiles would make each side feel more vulnerable and less secure than before. To avoid a ruinous preemptive strike, each side would be tempted to adopt a launch-on-warning strategy that would require hair-trigger responses on the basis of inadequate information and under enormous pressure—a recipe for disaster. At the very least, ballistic missile deployments would introduce one more element of uncertainty into an already strained relationship. Worst-case analysis and mirror-imaging could also oblige each side to devote ever-greater resources to ballistic missile deployments and to increasing nuclear weapon stockpiles. With mutual deployments of ballistic missiles, pressure could mount to move from nonweaponized deterrence to each side openly acknowledging its nuclear weapons arsenal.

A ballistic missile arms race in South Asia would not by itself necessarily lead to war, but it would undoubtedly increase the level of mistrust and anxiety in an already tense region, would make the adoption of confidence-building measures (CBMs) between New Delhi and Islamabad more difficult, would fuel atavistic nationalism on the subcontinent, and would exponentially increase the degree of devastation should a fourth Indian-Pakistani war occur. The great challenge for India and Pakistan in the near term is whether they can transfer the restraint they have shown in the nuclear field to their competition in ballistic missiles.

EFFORTS TO BUILD CONFIDENCE IN SOUTH ASIA

Despite limited dialogue at the official level, and almost nonexistent informal interactions between Indians and Pakistanis, the two sides have so far unilaterally refrained from taking certain additional steps that would fuel a nuclear weapons and ballistic missile race on the subcontinent. Most obviously, neither Pakistan nor India (since 1974) has conducted a nuclear test. Neither has deployed operational nuclear weapons. Neither has developed thermonuclear weapons, although the U.S. government reports that India has continued its work in this area. It appears that neither has transferred sensitive nuclear technology or materials to other countries, although India was approached by Libya after its 1974 nuclear test and Pakistan has recently been approached by Iran.[64] Neither has integrated the use of nuclear weapons into their training exercises or military doctrines.

Attempts to codify this mutual restraint through confidence- and security-building measures to prevent or limit hostilities in South Asia actually predated partition and allowed Lord Mountbatten to communicate with both India and Pakistan when war broke out over Kashmir in October 1947. In 1965, Indian and Pakistani commanders agreed not to use aircraft to support skirmishing forces in the unprotected terrain of the Rann of Kutch. During the 1965 and 1971 conflicts, India and Pakistan tacitly agreed to not attack cities, dams, and irrigation works.[65]

Since 1974, Pakistan has proposed numerous arms control and nonproliferation measures, including a nuclear-weapon-free zone for South Asia, comprehensive bilateral or IAEA inspections, simultaneous Indian and Pakistani accession to the NPT, and a bilateral or regional nuclear test ban treaty.[66] India rejected all these proposals because they did not adequately address its stated objective of global nuclear disarmament.

The most significant arms control measure adopted by the two sides was an agreement not to attack each other's nuclear facilities. This issue first arose in 1982, when rumors of a preemptive Indian strike against nuclear installations in Pakistan appeared in the press.[67] In 1984 and 1985, additional reports stated that India was considering the destruction of the Kahuta enrichment facility.[68] During this period of acute Pakistani anxiety, Munir Khan, then the head of the Pakistan Atomic Energy Commission, told his Indian counterpart, Raja Ramanna, that Islamabad would respond to an attack on its nuclear facilities by striking the Bhabha Atomic Research Center (BARC), just outside Bombay. As Ramanna knew, India had more to lose from this exchange than Pakistan; the plutonium used by India for its weapons and research was far more toxic than any highly enriched uranium Pakistan might have produced at that point, and an attack on BARC would have catastrophic consequences for Bombay and surrounding areas. Khan believes that Ramanna relayed this message to Indian political leaders.[69] Pakistan also expressed its concern to the United States, which then approached the Indian government and received reassurances.[70]

In 1985, Pakistani President Mohammed Zia ul-Haq and Indian Prime Minister Indira Gandhi eased mutual concerns by reaching an understanding, which was later reduced to writing and finally signed in December 1988. Under this agreement, both states pledged to "refrain from undertaking, encouraging, or participating indirectly or directly in any action aimed at causing the destruction or damage to any such [nuclear] installations or facilities in the other country."[71] In January 1991, the two sides agreed to implement the treaty, and the following year they exchanged lists of facilities, although both lists were incomplete.[72]

India and Pakistan also agreed to two modest CBMs during this period. In 1987, after the Brass Tacks military exercise almost precipitated war, the two foreign secretaries and the chiefs of the army and air force revived "hot line" communication links to prevent future miscommunication and misunderstanding. Two years later, border officials agreed to meet biannually to review procedures for combating transborder smuggling, immigration, drug trafficking, and terrorism.[73]

The May 1990 Gates mission provided additional impetus to creating new CBMs. Gates left in both capitals a list of suggested CBMs.[74] Gates did not push for an American role but said that Washington was ready and willing to act as an honest-broker or mediator, as it had done for the Arabs and Israelis.

Immediately after the Gates mission, the two sides began discussing ways to prevent another cycle of action and reaction that might embroil the two countries in another war. During the next two years, they adopted the following measures: (1) prior notification of certain military exercises, maneuvers, and troop movements; (2) establishment of a hot line between the directors general for military operations (DGMOs); (3) regulations to prevent airspace violations; and (4) military-to-military exchanges.[75] These CBMs proved their value almost immediately. When India moved troops (without any heavy equipment) into the Punjab in late 1991 to maintain civil order during elections, it used the DGMO hot line to make sure that Pakistan knew its nonaggressive purpose.

Yet the record of implementing these measures has been spotty at best. CBMs have been used by both sides to jockey for tactical advantage. The DGMO hot line has at times been used *after* one side has initiated hostilities, in order to prevent the skirmish from spreading. The cease-fire agreement along the Line of Control has been ignored. Advance notice of military exercises and troop movements has not been given. Airspace violations have occurred.[76]

No greater evidence of this mutual folly exists than the dispute over the Siachen Glacier, which is located in the Karakoram mountain range, just beyond the end of the Line of Control that divides Indian from Pakistani Kashmir. As advanced mountaineering technology became available in the 1980s, the two sides engaged in military operations to stake claims to this barren and inhospitable bit of ice and rock. The American academic Stephen Cohen has likened the dispute to "two bald men fighting over a comb." In 1989, the two parties negotiated a draft agreement for a cease-fire and mutual withdrawal. However, nervousness over the domestic political ramifications prompted India to back away from signing it then and again in November 1992. By 1994, CBMs had become one more forum for the larger antagonisms, especially over Kashmir, that beset India and Pakistan.[77] According to one State Department official: "CBMs are used episodically. In fact, they both cheat."[78]

Concerned at the lack of progress toward peace in the region and wanting to avoid another confrontation, in 1990 Ambassadors William Clark and Robert Oakley formulated the idea of a four-power conference with the United States, the Soviet Union, India, and Pakistan; India requested that China be included in order to address the Chinese nuclear program, and Washington agreed. The five-power conference was formally proposed in June 1991 and was immediately appropriated by Prime Minister Sharif as a Pakistani initiative. India then refused to attend the conference, citing several reasons: the dissolution of the Soviet Union later that year; the agenda's failure to address China's nuclear weapons or those of the former Soviet republics that had inherited nuclear arms; and Pakistan's claiming credit for the conference. More to the point, India was primarily afraid that it would be pressured by the other four countries to limit or abandon its nuclear weapons program.[79] The proposal died stillborn.

However, India agreed to bilateral negotiations with the United States, and the two held meetings in June 1992 and again five months later. After the June meeting, statements to the press by the Indian foreign secretary, J. N. Dixit, led parliamentary critics to attack Prime Minister P. V. Narasimha Rao for conceding too much to the Americans. As a result, the Indian cabinet rejected the Foreign Ministry's initial paper for the follow-on November meeting because it was too conciliatory.[80] U.S. participants were so discouraged by their conversations with the Indian delegation at this meeting that they openly wondered whether New Delhi would ever be willing to accept less-than-universal constraints on its nuclear program.[81]

A third bilateral meeting took place in September 1993 with the Clinton administration. These talks were more promising and discussed gaining India's support for two of President Clinton's initiatives: a comprehensive test ban treaty and a global ban on the production of fissile material outside of safeguards. The Indian delegation also pledged "in principle" to look at regional solutions to nonproliferation and arms control matters.[82]

At this meeting, the United States and India also discussed the refueling of the Tarapur Atomic Power Stations (TAPS), an acrimonious issue that had previously divided the two countries. In October 1963, the United States and India had entered into a thirty-year nuclear cooperation agreement. Under its terms, Washington authorized General Electric to construct two light-water reactors at Tarapur, north of Bombay, and to supply the necessary low-enriched uranium (LEU) fuel; the reactors and the fuel were placed under IAEA safeguards. India's 1974 PNE spurred the U.S. Congress to pass the Nuclear Nonproliferation Act of 1978 (NNPA), which required countries to renegotiate their nuclear cooperation agreements with the United States, accept comprehensive IAEA safeguards, and renounce PNEs. In the case of India, Washington threatened to cut off the LEU fuel supply for Tarapur if it refused. New Delhi accused Washington (legitimately) of unilaterally and retroactively redrawing the rules and threatened to retaliate to any U.S. breach of the original contract by asserting that IAEA safeguards no longer covered the Tarapur reactors or the plutonium contained in their spent fuel. From 1978 to 1981, the United States and India remained at loggerheads. In July 1982, the Reagan administration allowed France to supply the Tarapur fuel, which along with the reactor would remain under safeguards. But India would not have to accept full-scope safeguards.

In the early 1990s, the pending expiration of the original nuclear cooperation agreement in October 1993 revived the dispute. The same issues divided India and the United States: sovereignty, the fuel supply for Tarapur, and full-scope safeguards. India had four options, none of them attractive. It could accept full-scope safeguards, which would severely compromise its forty-year history of nuclear independence; this option was out of the question. It could search for a new supplier that would not insist on comprehensive safeguards, but it was unlikely to find one. It could shut down TAPS, but this would eliminate the source of over 10 percent of the electricity for the states of Maharashtra and Gujarat, India's industrial heartland.

The last option was to indigenously fabricate a mixed uranium and plutonium oxide (MOX) fuel. This not only presented New Delhi with a formidable and perhaps insurmountable technical hurdle but also represented a potential diplomatic crisis with Washington. To obtain the necessary plutonium to refuel TAPS, India needed to reprocess Tarapur's spent fuel, an action that under the original 1963 agreement required prior U.S. consent.[83] Even though the agreement ended in 1993, Washington insisted that it retained its prior consent rights.

On expiration of the nuclear cooperation agreement in October 1993, India surprisingly agreed to voluntarily maintain IAEA safeguards on TAPS and the French-supplied nuclear fuel. France agreed to honor its existing fuel supply contracts, which could enable TAPS to continue operations at least until the end of 1994, but Paris refused to supply additional fuel unless India accepted comprehensive safeguards.[84] In February 1994, India formalized this arrangement with the IAEA to ensure that international safeguards would apply on any fuel irradiated in the Tarapur reactors.[85] This meant that India could not legally reprocess Tarapur's spent fuel and use the plutonium for building nuclear bombs. New Delhi promoted this compromise as a goodwill gesture. In reality, it also bought some time to figure out a long-term solution to the Tarapur fuel problem, since India wanted TAPS to operate for another ten to fifteen years. More important, Washington had informed New Delhi during the September 1993 bilateral talks that if the Tarapur facility was not covered by safeguards, the United States might terminate $5 billion of credits by the Overseas Private Investment Corporation (OPIC).

After its September 1993 talks with the United States, India redoubled its efforts to find an alternative fuel source. Its search quickly narrowed to China, which did not insist on comprehensive safeguards as a precondition for nuclear fuel sales. In January 1995, TAPS started receiving Chinese LEU. The deal pleased all the parties. It avoided a crisis in U.S.-Indian relations, generated goodwill (and money) for China, and permitted India to continue to run TAPS, under safeguards.[86]

Prodded by the United States and some of the largest aid donors to India and Pakistan, particularly Japan, Islamabad and New Delhi traded "nonpapers" on nonproliferation, regional security, and confidence-building measures in January 1994. Pakistan's two proposals called for a plebiscite in Kashmir and suggested ways to increase respect for human rights there. India rejected the plebiscite but stated its willingness to discuss measures to reduce tensions in Kashmir.

India's nonpapers were broader in scope and incorporated some of the State Department's suggestions on CBMs. They discussed ensuring peace along the Line of Control, withdrawing from Siachen Glacier, resolving border and water-use disputes, expanding the 1988 nonattack of nuclear installations agreement to cover population and economic centers, and reaching an agreement under which each country would pledge not to first use or threaten to use its nuclear "capability" against the other. Islamabad did not respond favorably, noting that Pakistan did not possess nuclear weapons and that the no-first-use proposal was therefore irrelevant.[87]

SPRING 1994: THE CLINTON ADMINISTRATION'S CAPPING STRATEGY

In April 1993, President Clinton issued the first public report to Congress outlining U.S. nonproliferation objectives in South Asia. The Clinton administration's strategy sought "to cap, then reduce over time, and finally eliminate weapons of mass destruction and their means of delivery from the region."[88] This strategy of capping nuclear weapons capabilities in the region, rather than seeking their elimination, represented a major shift in U.S. nonproliferation policy. It reflected the administration's belief that the Pressler amendment's restriction on U.S. aid to Pakistan was ineffective and perhaps even counterproductive, that the nuclear programs in India and Pakistan were too advanced to abolish outright, and that the challenge for Washington was therefore to manage a long-term process of regional denuclearization after first halting any further development.

Also driving the Clinton administration's efforts were fears of another crisis in South Asia. Memories of 1990 were still fresh, and the preconditions that had contributed to that flare-up—unrest in Kashmir, weak political leaders, an impoverished bilateral relationship, and mutual mistrust and suspicion—still existed. Moreover, many U.S. officials thought that India's deployment of the Prithvi would precipitate a dangerous ballistic missile arms race and might even spark a fourth round of war that could escalate to the nuclear level. Pakistani officials had informed the United States that should India start the Prithvi production line, Islamabad would respond by deploying the M-11 missile.[89] A 1993 U.S. National Intelligence Estimate allegedly placed the risk of conventional war between India and Pakistan at "up to 20 percent."[90]

During the first few months of 1994, the Clinton administration tried to craft a new approach to breaking the nuclear logjam in South Asia. In early March 1994, the State Department proposed that Islamabad accept the following conditions: (1) a verifiable cutoff of fissile material that was intended for nuclear explosive purposes or that was outside of safeguards; and (2) a credible system of safeguards on *all* its nuclear activities, including on-site inspections of the Kahuta uranium enrichment plant. The United States did not specify that these had to be IAEA safeguards. In return for taking these steps, Washington offered Islamabad a one-time waiver of the Pressler amendment. This would allow Pakistan to receive the thirty-eight F-16 fighter jets that the Lockheed Corporation had already manufactured and for which Pakistan had paid over $650 million.

The State Department proposed that New Delhi adopt (1) a verifiable cutoff of fissile material that was intended for nuclear explosive purposes or that was outside of safeguards; and (2) a credible system of safeguards on *less than all* its nuclear activities. Given the asymmetries in the nuclear programs of the two countries, the administration believed that "similar but not identical" constraints would be acceptable to Pakistan. To induce Indian agreement, Washington was willing to discuss a range of scientific and technological cooperation.

The administration also requested that both Pakistan and India adopt a ballistic missile regime that would prohibit the deployment, the development, and ultimately the possession of ballistic missiles by either party (a parallel to the three-phase nuclear policy of capping, reducing, and then eliminating nuclear weapons). As a final component of its policy, Washington proposed an international conference with the five permanent members of the UN Security Council, along with India, Pakistan, Germany, and Japan, to consider what regional and global arms control and disarmament policies they could collectively adopt, with particular focus on South Asia.[91]

Unfortunately, the Clinton administration stumbled badly before it even left the starting block. Washington seriously miscalculated the attractiveness of the proposal both at home and abroad, did not tie up all the loose ends of its diplomatic package, and then compounded its difficulties by inept public diplomacy.[92] U.S. lawmakers, particularly Senator Larry Pressler, expressed outrage that Washington would dilute U.S. nonproliferation policy and effectively reward Islamabad for repeatedly violating American laws during the 1980s in the course of developing nuclear weapons. Immediately after receiving a private State Department briefing on the new initiative, Pressler leaked the details to the U.S. press in order to publicly discredit the policy. Other critics questioned the wisdom of providing F-16s to Pakistan when its nuclear weapons program remained intact.[93]

The proposal proved even less popular in India. The Clinton administration had anticipated that India would raise the question of Chinese participation, but Washington could not obtain Beijing's support. In March, the deputy assistant secretary of state for political-military affairs, Robert Einhorn, and the under secretary of defense, Frank Wisner, had held talks with Chinese officials. They stressed that the U.S. initiative was in China's strategic interest because China might otherwise find itself encircled by countries that possessed both nuclear weapons and ballistic missiles by the end of the decade. The Chinese were unmoved and gave no indication that they would participate in multilateral negotiations.

Washington also did not brief Indian officials in Washington or New Delhi ahead of time; they naturally grew suspicious and resentful after hearing bits and pieces of the policy through the media. India publicly rejected the deal in late March, even before Deputy Secretary of State Strobe Talbott's scheduled visit to New Delhi the following month. A formal Indian protest stated that delivery of the F-16s would be a threat to the country's security, would fuel an expensive arms race, and would increase regional tensions.[94] New Delhi argued that given Pakistan's past history of nuclear subterfuge and deceit, Islamabad could not be trusted to keep its word on a nuclear capping arrangement. Critics also pointed out that India might respond to the shipment of F-16s by purchasing similar high-performance aircraft or deploying the Prithvi, precisely the result the Clinton administration hoped to prevent.

The weakest part of the package was the lack of incentives offered to India. The degree to which the Clinton administration could cooperate on science and technology with India was tightly constrained by U.S. domestic legislation and export controls. Multilateral security assurances, reportedly a part of the deal, assumed that China would lend its efforts to enhancing regional security. However, after agreement on confidence-building measures between India and China in September 1993, the value of these additional assurances was unclear; in the nuclear sphere, it was unlikely that they would do much more than reiterate Beijing's long-standing declaration not to use nuclear weapons first. Further, the prospect of pledges made by outside powers to preserve India's security might strike many Indian nationalists as compromising the country's nonaligned position and blocking its aspirations for great power status. It was unclear even to U.S. officials why India should accept the U.S. offer. As a State Department official conceded, this part of the initiative "was not fully fleshed out."[95] When asked what incentives the United States offered India to curb its ballistic missile activities, a former cabinet secretary to Prime Minister Rao exclaimed, "It offered nothing!"[96]

More generally, there was an inherent structural flaw to any American nonproliferation diplomacy in the region. Because Pakistan was constrained by domestic political factors from unilaterally rolling back its nuclear program, it required Indian cooperation to escape the confines of the Pressler amendment. New Delhi was naturally reluctant to help Islamabad achieve what Islamabad could not achieve for itself.

All this indicated that the U.S. plan was really designed to get Pakistan on board, isolate India diplomatically, and then pressure India to cap its nuclear and ballistic missile programs. But to the surprise of Clinton administration officials, Pakistan rejected the initiative as well.

The U.S. proposal recognized that Benazir Bhutto, who had been reelected as prime minister in October 1993, was unwilling to roll back the country's nuclear program.[97] Because the proposal did not call for a nuclear rollback, the State Department was convinced that Islamabad would accept some formal nuclear restraint in order to receive the F-16s. But what Washington failed to understand was that a one-time waiver of the Pressler amendment would do little to resolve Pakistan's underlying security concerns. No Pakistani government could permit on-site inspections of Kahuta unless India accepted similar obligations. Further, the Pakistani Air Force, which wanted the advanced aircraft, had little say over policy. The army, under Chief of Staff General Abdul Waheed, directly influenced the government and was far less interested in the American proposal. Also, Pakistani officials privately expressed their concern over the possible Indian reaction should Islamabad obtain the F-16s. They did not want to provoke an arms race with their larger and wealthier neighbor.[98]

Secret follow-on talks between the United States and India in London on April 27 yielded no progress as the Indian delegation trotted out the same tired nostrums about universal, nondiscriminatory disarmament.[99] By mid-1994, the Clinton administration initiative had hit a dead end. "We have a tough selling job in Delhi, Islamabad, and Washington," said one U.S. official. "Other than that, this thing is going great."[100] During Indian Prime Minister Rao's visit to Washington in late May, Clinton soft-pedaled the nuclear issue in favor of stressing trade issues and forging a warmer bilateral relationship.[101]

It may have been that the timing was not right for *any* U.S. policy proposal to succeed in South Asia. Without a commitment by China to end its nuclear tests and reduce its nuclear arsenal, India had a plausible excuse for resisting American entreaties. Also, India and Pakistan each might have calculated that it could afford to resist, or at least delay responding to, the Clinton administration's South Asia initiative in the hope that Washington would not sustain its interest. Further, prudence dictated waiting until after the April 1995 NPT review and extension conference to evaluate the status of the treaty and the future of the international nonproliferation regime before placing legal constraints on their nuclear weapons programs.

Conclusion: A Future Unlike the Past?

In his classic treatise *On War*, the Prussian military expert Carl von Clausewitz remarked that achieving even the most basic tasks in war is extraordinarily difficult. Attributing this phenomenon to "friction," he noted: "Everything in war is very simple, but the simplest thing is difficult. The difficulties accumulate and end by producing a kind of friction that is inconceivable unless one has experienced war. . . . Countless minor incidents—the kind you can never really foresee— combine to lower the general level of performance, so that one always falls short of the intended goal. . . . Friction . . . is the force that makes the apparently easy so difficult.[102] If "war is the continuation of politics by other means," in Clausewitz's most widely quoted phrase, it should not be surprising that politics has its own equivalent of friction that lowers "the general level of performance" and "makes the apparently easy so difficult."

Looking back on the past two decades of South Asian history, we see that India and Pakistan have clearly overcome this friction to place some important limits on their nuclear competition. But an examination of this same period also reveals that friction both within and between India and Pakistan has prevented the achievement of more substantial progress to codify and institutionalize this nuclear restraint.

Undoubtedly, it has been easier for India and Pakistan to indulge old animosities than to redirect their energies to more productive areas. Simmering religious tensions, lack of internal cohesion, weak leadership, multiplying domestic burdens, and underdeveloped democratic institutions have bedeviled the search for a stable peace in South Asia. Forty-eight years of relations, characterized by a zero-sum mentality that has favored confrontation over conciliation, recall the French statesman Talleyrand's summation of the Bourbons: "They have learned nothing, and forgotten nothing."

Most famously, this beggar-thy-neighbor approach has typified the enduring struggle over Kashmir, which remains the most likely flashpoint for a future war. Existing confidence-building measures have atrophied from abuse, and the two sides have been unwilling to explore new ideas, such as demilitarized zones, cooperative aerial observation ("Open Skies"), risk-reduction centers, or greater military-to-military contacts.[103]

Unofficial contacts have also been meager. All sorts of bureaucratic impediments and red tape have prevented the exchange of newspapers and magazines, family visits, and tourism (especially to religious shrines). Most significant, commercial ties between the two countries are virtually nonexistent.[104] This artificial segregation has blocked a more rounded understanding of each other and has inhibited greater balance and objectivity in their political interaction.

Despite continued fighting over Kashmir, the abandonment of CBMs, and a miserable bilateral dialogue, each country has refrained from taking certain provocative actions. Tensions that in other parts of the world might have triggered political crises or provoked widespread conflict have been kept in check; low-level violence has remained, if not under control, at least within manageable boundaries. It could even be claimed, somewhat counterintuitively, that the nuclear restraint demonstrated by India and Pakistan is all the more remarkable because it has operated in such a contaminated political environment.

Paradoxically, the state of nonweaponized deterrence that has prevailed in South Asia may actually have prevented the two sides from undertaking a broader political engagement. It may have convinced India and Pakistan that the time-consuming and arduous work of placing their overall political and economic relationship on a healthier footing is unnecessary. More dangerously, it may have permitted them to believe that there is a nuclear ceiling beneath which they can probe and joust without fear of events spiraling out of control. With the perception that stable nuclear deterrence is working, each may see little reason to make the psychological adjustment and to invest the necessary political capital to improve bilateral ties. The state of "no peace, no war" may be acceptable, and on occasion even handy, for scoring domestic political points. The risk, always present, is that deterrence might fail at some point in the future, whether by accident, inadvertence, or design.[105]

Yet international, regional, and domestic factors continue to restrain a more open or aggressive nuclear posture on the subcontinent. Although the international community has tolerated "nuclear ambiguity" in India and Pakistan, it likely would react harshly if either country tested a nuclear weapon, openly declared that it possessed nuclear weapons, or deployed nuclear arms. Any such action would vastly complicate Pakistan's attempts to revive a strategic relationship with the United States. It would place at risk the international largesse India still receives from the donor countries, particularly Japan, and could even jeopardize India's ability to attract foreign capital.

At the regional level, the nuclear status quo has been far preferable to the alternatives. Neither country has demonstrated much interest in moving from nonweaponized to weaponized deterrence or importing the strategic accoutrements of the United States and the Soviet Union, with the arcane concepts of escalation ladders, assured second-strike capabilities, and sophisticated targeting plans. Financial constraints prevent Pakistan from competing in an unchecked nuclear arms race with a much larger and wealthier adversary. For its part, India does not want to get into a similar spiral with a much larger and wealthier China. And there is no compelling strategic rationale for clarifying their nuclear ambiguity at this time. India and Pakistan seem to have recognized this. Repeated calls from Indian and Pakistani nuclear hawks for an open declaration of each country's nuclear capability have failed to convince governments in New Delhi or Islamabad.

In addition, many government officials and scholars in India and Pakistan have contended that they are perfectly capable of managing their own nuclear affairs. In fact, the two countries have behaved with greater restraint and more responsibility than the nuclear weapon states. Pakistan allegedly stopped producing highly enriched uranium since 1990, and both countries have quietly and only gradually enhanced their nuclear and ballistic missile capabilities. They are far short of the nuclear stockpiles many experts had recently predicted.[106]

Moreover, evidence suggests that New Delhi and Islamabad have absorbed some "nuclear lessons" during the past few years. The 1990 crisis appears to have been a seminal experience for both countries. Immediately after the Gates mission, both countries moved quickly to defuse the crisis. Within days, New Delhi presented Islamabad with a series of confidence-building measures. In July, the Indian and Pakistani foreign secretaries met in the first of six sessions that discussed how the two sides could prevent future military and political crises from leading to a conflict. Despite problems in developing and implementing confidence-building measures, there have been some positive signs. Since 1990, India and Pakistan have continued to run annual military exercises without coming close to the misunderstanding and anxiety of the 1987 and 1990 exercises. In January 1991, the two sides agreed to implement the nonattack of nuclear installations agreement, and they exchanged lists of facilities the following year.

Some political restraint has even extended to the struggle over Kashmir. In February 1992, over one thousand Kashmiri militants attempted to cross the Line of Control from Pakistan into Indian Kashmir, with the intention of stirring up a local insurgency against the Indian authorities. To keep the marchers from crossing the border, Pakistani forces fired directly into the crowd, reportedly killing 12 and wounding over 150. Pakistan's Prime Minister Sharif explained his government's action: "We've had three wars with India. We don't want to have a fourth war."[107]

The end of the cold war has also helped dampen the incentives for war in the region. India can no longer rely on the Soviet Union to counter the United States and cannot even depend on Russia to provide rocket technology to ISRO or vote with India in the United Nations against a proposal for a South Asian nuclear-weapon-free zone. New Delhi cannot simply defy Washington's insistence on maintaining international safeguards on the Tarapur reactors. Especially since the cutoff of U.S. military and economic assistance in 1990, Pakistan has not been in any shape for another war with India. International donors have increasingly asserted their preference for both parties to adopt formal nonproliferation measures. This gives the United States, in particular, an opening to quietly but consistently push India and Pakistan to honor existing CBMs and adopt new ones, as well as to broaden their commercial interaction.

Indian, Pakistani, and American scholars have all attributed the nonviolent resolution of the 1987 and 1990 crises to the presence of nuclear weapons capabilities by both countries.[108] The State Department believes that a conventional war between India and Pakistan would last three to five weeks and end in a stalemate. But should Pakistan's forces fare badly, the war might end very differently. "Pakistan would be more likely than India to initiate the use of nuclear weapons and might do so if Pakistani forces faced imminent defeat."[109] Should Pakistan strike first, Indian retaliation would be certain. It is likely that both parties understand this dynamic, even if they are reluctant to officially admit it. A state of nonweaponized deterrence, based on each country's possessing an unassembled, unannounced, and undeployed nuclear arsenal, has probably been operating in South Asia for some time now.[110]

The relationship between India and Pakistan is no longer solely a zero-sum game with only winners and losers. India and Pakistan have jointly, and successfully, borne the primary burden of ensuring that their differences have remained well below a threshold of catastrophic violence. By the mid-1990s, India and Pakistan appeared to have arrived at an ironic realization: the presence of nuclear arsenals in both countries, and the associated specter of nuclear devastation, have forced them to live together, if not in peace, then at least not in a state of open hostility. Like the United States and the Soviet Union during the cold war, India and Pakistan are now "two scorpions in a bottle." Their shared predicament appears to have produced a greater appreciation that what India and Pakistan have in common—mutual survival—far transcends the host of issues that have traditionally separated the two countries. If India and Pakistan can build on their record of tacit nuclear restraint, defer the deployment of ballistic missiles, and craft and implement meaningful confidence- and security-building measures, there is little reason why nonweaponized deterrence cannot continue to operate for the foreseeable future.

Chronology

AUGUST 1947 Partition and independence are declared for Pakistan and India.

OCTOBER Indian and Pakistani forces clash in Kashmir; the United Nations introduces peacekeeping forces.

OCTOBER–NOVEMBER 1962 China overwhelmingly defeats India in a border dispute.

1965 A second round of warfare erupts between India and Pakistan.

NOVEMBER–DECEMBER 1971 After almost ten million refugees stream into West Bengal, India sends troops into East Pakistan and with Bengali forces defeats the central government and creates an independent Bangladesh.

JANUARY 1972 Zulfikar Ali Bhutto initiates Pakistan's nuclear weapons program.

MAY 18, 1974 India detonates a self-proclaimed peaceful nuclear explosive.

DECEMBER 1979 The Soviet Union invades Afghanistan.

JUNE 1981 The Reagan administration reverses U.S. policy, providing Pakistan with a six-year, $3.2-billion aid package.

AUGUST 1985 The U.S. Congress adopts the Pressler amendment, which requires annual presidential certification for the continuation of U.S. aid to Pakistan.

DECEMBER Pakistani President Mohammed Zia ul-Haq and Indian Prime Minister Indira Gandhi verbally agree not to attack each other's nuclear facilities.

MARCH 1986 The United States and Pakistan sign a six-year, $4.02-billion military and economic assistance package, to begin in October 1987.

JANUARY 1987 India's "Brass Tacks" military exercise provokes a crisis between India and Pakistan.

FEBRUARY 1988 India tests the Prithvi short-range ballistic missile.

DECEMBER India and Pakistan formally agree not to attack each other's nuclear facilities.

JANUARY 1989 Pakistan tests the short-range Hatf I and II ballistic missiles.

FEBRUARY Soviet soldiers leave Afghanistan.

MAY India tests the intermediate-range Agni ballistic missile.

APRIL–MAY 1990 Crisis erupts over Kashmir.

OCTOBER President Bush does not certify Pakistan to Congress; U.S. economic and military assistance is terminated.

JUNE 1991 A five-power conference with the United States, the Soviet Union, China, India, and Pakistan is proposed; India refuses to participate.

OCTOBER 1993 The 1963 U.S.-India nuclear cooperation agreement for Tarapur ends; France refuses to resupply fuel; India agrees to maintain IAEA safeguards on the reactor fuel.

JANUARY 1994 India and Pakistan exchange "nonpapers" on Kashmir, arms control, and regional security matters.

MARCH–APRIL The Clinton administration launches its South Asia initiative to prevent a ballistic missile arms race on the subcontinent.

Notes

[1]See testimony of James Woolsey, in Senate Committee on Governmental Affairs, *Hearing on Proliferation Threats of the 1990s*, 103d Cong., 1st sess., February 24, 1993 (Washington D.C.: USGPO, 1993), and in House Committee on Foreign Affairs, Subcommittee on International Security, International Organizations, and Human Rights, *U.S. Security Policy toward Rogue Regimes*, 103d Cong., 1st sess., July 28, 1993 (Washington D.C.: USGPO, 1993).

[2]Ye. Primakov, *A New Challenge after the "Cold War": Proliferation of Weapons of Mass Destruction* (Moscow: Foreign Intelligence Service of the Russian Federation, 1993), draft translation reprinted by Joint Publications Research Service, undated, pp. 3–4. This report also stated that "India may be classified among the countries which unofficially possess nuclear weapons" (p. 52).

[3]See, for example, S. Rashid Naim, "Aadhi Raat Ke Baad ('After Midnight')," in Stephen P. Cohen, ed., *Nuclear Proliferation in South Asia* (Boulder, Colo.: Westview, 1990), pp. 32–61; Marc Dean Millot, Roger Molander, and Peter A. Wilson, *"The Day After . . ." Study: Nuclear Proliferation in the Post–Cold War World* (Santa Monica: RAND, 1993), pp. 111–27.

[4]See Sandy Gordon, "Resources and Instability in South Asia," and Sumit Ganguly, "Ethno-religious Conflict in South Asia," *Survival* 35, no. 2 (Summer 1993): 66–87, 88–109; Brahma Chellaney, "India," in Mitchell Reiss and Robert S. Litwak, eds., *Nuclear Proliferation after the Cold War* (Washington, D.C.: Woodrow Wilson Center Press, 1994), pp. 165–90.

[5]For a discussion of a nonweaponized deterrence regime for India and Pakistan, see George Perkovich, "A Nuclear Third Way in South Asia," *Foreign Policy*, no. 91 (Summer 1993), pp. 85–104. This concept differs from the "nuclear weapon safe zone" idea, which is promoted by some Indian and Pakistani experts and which calls for the open deployment of a small number of nuclear weapons by both sides.

[6]Personal interview, Washington, D.C., January 5, 1994. This information, as well as other information from this source subsequently cited in this chapter, was independently confirmed by at least two other State Department officials.

[7]For a comprehensive survey of India's nuclear program, see David Albright, Frans Berkhout, and William Walker, *World Inventory of Plutonium and Highly Enriched Uranium, 1992* (New York: Oxford University Press, 1993), pp. 157–62; Leonard S. Spector with Jacqueline R. Smith, *Nuclear Ambitions: The Spread of Nuclear Weapons, 1989–1990* (Boulder, Colo.: Westview, 1990), pp. 63–88.

[8]For background on this event, see Roberta Wohlstetter, *"The Buddha Smiles": Absent-Minded Peaceful Aid and the Indian Bomb* (Los Angeles: Pan Heuristics, 1977); Shyam Bhatia, *India's Nuclear Bomb* (New Delhi: Vikas, 1979). The dimensions of the 1974 device corresponded to the "Fat Man" nuclear bomb that the United States dropped on Nagasaki in August 1945.

It appears that New Delhi slightly miscalculated in May 1974. The explosion caused debris to vent into the atmosphere, a result that could be interpreted as a technical violation of India's obligations under the 1963 Partial Test Ban Treaty. U.S. government official, personal interview, Philadelphia, October 1993.

[9]Personal interview, Washington, D.C., January 5, 1994. A Defense Department official independently confirmed the size of India's nuclear weapons "stockpile." Personal interview, Washington, D.C., December 23, 1994. A U.S. government analysis entitled "Nuclear Power Production in India" examined India's nuclear complex. The 1993 study concluded that India had a plutonium inventory of 523 kilograms outside of IAEA safeguards. Assuming that a nuclear device uses 10 kilograms of weapons-grade plutonium, which the report stated is the amount that India used for its 1974 test, and assuming that India would not require the unsafeguarded plutonium for any other purposes, such as fuel for its research reactors, as fuel for its fast-breeder test reactor, or as mixed plutonium and uranium oxide (MOX) fuel for the Tarapur Atomic Power Station, New Delhi would appear to have a plutonium stockpile large enough for over fifty nuclear devices. If India used only 5 kilograms, then it could construct an arsenal of more than one hundred nuclear weapons.

[10]On India's work on thermonuclear weapons, see William Webster, director, Central Intelligence Agency, in Senate Committee on Governmental Affairs, *Hearing on Nuclear and Missile Proliferation,* 101st Cong., 1st sess., May 18, 1989 (Washington, D.C.: USGPO, 1990), p. 17.

[11]For a comprehensive survey of Pakistan's nuclear development, see David Albright and Mark Hibbs, "Pakistan's Bomb: Out of the Closet," *Bulletin of the Atomic Scientists* (July–August 1992), pp. 38–43; Spector with Smith, *Nuclear Ambitions,* pp. 89–117; Ashok Kapur, *Pakistan's Nuclear Development* (New York: Croom Helm, 1987); Zahid Malik, *Dr. A. Q. Khan and the Islamic Bomb* (Islamabad: Hurmat, 1992).

[12]See Spector with Smith, *Nuclear Ambitions,* p. 95.

[13]The Reagan administration argued in the early 1980s that massive U.S. military and economic assistance would also further the cause of nonproliferation by dissuading Islamabad from acquiring nuclear weapons. Two assumptions animated this thinking: (1) that Pakistan's desire to obtain nuclear weapons was driven primarily by its military insecurity vis-à-vis India; and (2) that conventional weapons could alleviate this insecurity.

Strictly speaking, the Carter administration had earlier tried to revive its relationship with Pakistan after it terminated U.S. assistance in May 1979 because of Islamabad's pursuit of a nuclear weapons capability. But Pakistan's president, General Mohammed Zia ul-Haq, rejected the Carter administration's offer of $400 million, terming it "peanuts."

[14]In 1981, 1987, and 1989, Congress waived the Symington amendment, which prohibits U.S. aid to any country that receives nuclear reprocessing or uranium enrichment equipment, materials, or technology unless such equipment, materials, or technology is subject to IAEA safeguards. In 1982, President Reagan waived the Glenn amendment, which modified the Symington amendment by prohibiting U.S. aid to any country that, inter alia, receives reprocessing technology, regardless of whether this technology is subject to international safeguards. In January 1988, President Reagan waived the Solarz amendment, which prohibits U.S. aid to any nonnuclear weapon state that illegally imports, or attempts to import, from the United States any technology or device that would contribute significantly to the

ability of that country to acquire nuclear weapons. The full text of the Symington amendment can be found at Public Law 94–329, 90 Stat. 729, 755–56, June 30, 1976; the Glenn amendment at Public Law 95–92, 91 Stat. 614, 620–21, August 4, 1977; and the Solarz amendment at Public Law 99–83, 99 Stat. 190, 277, August 8, 1985.

A good deal of confusion permeates the nonproliferation literature regarding the differences between the Symington and the Glenn amendments. The Symington amendment amended the Foreign Assistance Act of 1961 by adding section 669, which concerned nuclear transfers of both uranium enrichment and reprocessing equipment, materials, and technology. The Glenn amendment eliminated this section 669 and added (1) a new section 669 dealing only with uranium enrichment transfers, and (2) a new section 670 dealing with reprocessing transfers. The Symington amendment is generally invoked when discussing uranium enrichment transfers and the Glenn amendment when discussing reprocessing transfers, although technically the Glenn amendment is the appropriate citation for either type of transfer. As a compromise, and further complicating matters, the entire legislative package is sometimes referred to as the Glenn-Symington or Symington-Glenn amendment.

[15] The full text of the Pressler amendment can be found at Public Law 99–83, 99 Stat. 190, 268, August 8, 1985.

[16] The State Department's Office of the Legal Adviser interpreted the language of the Pressler amendment as follows: "A state may possess a nuclear explosive device, and yet maintain it in an unassembled form for safety reasons or to maintain effective command and control over its use or for other purposes. The fact that a state does not have an assembled device would not, therefore, necessarily mean that it does not possess a device under the statutory standard. A judgment concerning possession can only be made upon an evaluation of all relevant facts and circumstances of a particular case." House Committee on Foreign Affairs, Subcommittee on Asian and Pacific Affairs, *Hearings on Foreign Assistance Legislation, FY1988–89,* 100th Cong., 1st sess., March 5, 1987 (Washington, D.C.: USGPO, 1987), pp. 487–88.

This language was deemed necessary because states may not maintain fully assembled nuclear weapons for safety and security reasons. When asked in 1992 about the status of the nuclear arms race between India and Pakistan, CIA Director Robert Gates stated, "The view of our people is that they do not actually stockpile the weapons, for safety reasons." The director of the CIA's Nonproliferation Center, Gordon Oehler, added, "They could have nuclear devices in a very short period of time, but we believe that they would not want to assemble them for safety reasons." Senate Committee on Governmental Affairs, *Hearing on Weapons Proliferation and the New World Order,* 102d Cong., 2d sess., January 15, 1992 (Washington, D.C.: USGPO, 1992), pp. 24, 25. A year later, before the same committee, CIA Director Woolsey testified, "As far as assembly is concerned, it is our estimate . . . that at the present time both India and Pakistan have the capability to assemble the components of nuclear weapons, a small number of nuclear weapons within a very short period of time, and that the distinction between whether or not those weapons are, in fact, assembled or only able to be assembled within a few days is a very small distinction." Oehler again commented, "They should be kept apart for safety and security reasons." *Hearing on Proliferation Threats of the 1990s,* p. 29.

[17] This statement requires some qualification. Economic assistance that had been legally obligated from funding in previous years continued into early 1991; food

aid continued as well. See Richard P. Cronin, "Pakistan Aid Cutoff: U.S. Nonproliferation and Foreign Policy Considerations," *CRS Issue Brief* 90149 (December 28, 1990). Further U.S. food and developmental aid was restored in 1992 through section 562 of the Foreign Assistance Appropriations Act.

Also, the State Department granted export licenses for commercial sales of military equipment to Pakistan after decertification. The Bush administration explained that it interpreted the Pressler amendment as requiring the termination only of U.S. government-financed assistance. See Senate Committee on Foreign Relations, *Hearing on Interpreting the Pressler Amendment: Commercial Military Sales to Pakistan*, 102d Cong., 2d sess., July 30, 1992 (Washington, D.C.: USGPO, 1992).

[18]Quoted in Kuldip Nayar, "We Have the A-Bomb, Says Pakistan's 'Dr. Strangelove,'" *Observer* (London), March 1, 1987; see also Spector with Smith, *Nuclear Ambitions*, pp. 96–97. For the political context in which the Nayar interview occurred, see note 32. President Zia ul-Haq was quoted in a *Time* magazine interview in March 1987 as saying: "Pakistan has the capability of building the bomb. You can write today that Pakistan can build a bomb whenever it wishes. Once you have acquired the technology, which Pakistan has, you can do whatever you like." See Ross H. Munro, "Knocking at the Nuclear Door," *Time*, March 30, 1987, pp. 42–43; see also Hedrick Smith, "A Bomb Ticks in Pakistan," *New York Times Magazine*, March 6, 1988.

[19]See "Pakistan Reportedly Had Nuclear Bomb in '87," *New York Times*, July 25, 1993; William J. Broad, "Pakistani Denies A-Test," *New York Times*, July 26, 1993; *Le Monde*, July 25–26, 1993, reported in Joint Publications Research Service, *Proliferation Issues* (hereafter referred to as JPRS-TND), 93-025 (August 2, 1993), p. 11; "Bare All and Be Damned," *Far Eastern Economic Review*, May 5, 1994, p. 23. See especially Mirza Aslam Beg, "Who Will Press the Button?" *News* (Islamabad), April 23, 1994. In this last article, Beg reported that Zulfikar Ali Bhutto had established a National Nuclear Command Authority (NNCA) to institutionalize nuclear decision making. The NNCA instructed the Joint Operations Center at the Joint Staff Headquarters in Rawalpindi, who transmitted orders to the three services. General Beg retired from the military in August 1991.

Also, in a meeting with an American scholar in September 1992, Beg stated: "Concerning the so-called red line of the Pressler amendment, we crossed it in the Zia days. [Washington] could have applied Pressler then." George Perkovich, "Trip Report: Pakistan and India, September 10–22, 1992," copy in author's possession.

[20]Personal interview, Washington, D.C., 1993.

[21]Richard Barlow, telephone interview, July 20, 1994. Barlow was hired by the CIA in 1985. According to Richard Kerr, his "knowledge on Pakistan was greater than anyone else's in the agency." Quoted in Seymour M. Hersh, "On the Nuclear Edge," *New Yorker*, March 29, 1993, p. 73.

[22]Quoted in Hersh, "On the Nuclear Edge," p. 60. Kerr stated that he was quoted accurately in the Hersh article. Telephone interview, Washington, D.C., July 28, 1994.

In a February 1994 on-the-record roundtable discussion at the Henry L. Stimson Center in Washington, D.C., a member of the U.S. intelligence community strongly implied that Pakistan had a nuclear weapons capability in 1987. See comments of Doug Makeig, in Michael Krepon and Mishi Faruqee, eds., "Conflict Prevention and Confidence-Building Measures in South Asia: The 1990 Crisis," *Occasional Paper No. 17* (April 1994) (hereafter cited as Stimson Center Report), p. 41.

[23]Oakley, in Stimson Center Report, p. 40 (emphasis added). Oakley had stated earlier at the session: "Pakistan needed to make the proper precautions and take the proper precautions. . . . [A]t about that time [spring 1990] the freeze on the Pakistan nuclear program was also removed. And the program began to move forward again. This is what led eventually to the application of the Pressler amendment." Stimson Center Report, p. 7.

The United States had told Pakistan in June 1989 that the nuclear weapons program could not move forward "one inch" if it wanted to receive certification in the future. Former State Department official, personal interview, Washington, D.C., June 13, 1993. Pakistan agreed, and Bhutto pledged to a joint session of Congress, "We do not possess nor do we intend to make a nuclear device." See Warren Strobel, "Bhutto Tells Hill Pakistan Seeks No Nuclear Weapons," *Washington Times*, June 8, 1989; see also Robert Pear, "Bhutto Urges U.S. to Start Seeking Political Solution for Afghanistan," *New York Times*, June 8, 1989. It is unclear if the "red line" beyond which Pakistan could not go was a prohibition against enriching uranium to greater than 20 percent U-235 or against fully assembling a nuclear explosive device, or both. In an interview in 1994, a U.S. government official familiar with the Pakistan nuclear program stated: "We drew so many 'red lines' it would blow your mind. They became meaningless."

[24]Personal interview, Washington, D.C., June 29, 1994.

[25]Personal interview, Washington, D.C., July 14, 1994.

[26]Stimson Center Report, p. 42; see also Hersh, "On the Nuclear Edge," p. 62. In a personal interview in May 1993, Oakley said that Beg believed that Iran would lend Pakistan all-out support in the event of war with India. Oakley replied that Iran did not have the power-projection capabilities to deliver forces and weapons to the India-Pakistan border. Beg discounted this, arguing that the United States had always underestimated Iranian capabilities and that Iran would come to Pakistan's assistance. Oakley said this was incredible. This information was also confirmed by a former State Department official, personal interview, Washington, D.C., June 13, 1993. When asked how Pakistan could have jeopardized its most important relationship, Oakley said that this was a grand miscalculation by General Beg and others. He also attributed this error to the fact that very few Pakistani officials knew what was happening in the nuclear program. Personal interview, Washington, D.C., May 18, 1993.

[27]U.S. government officials, personal interviews, Islamabad, March 1 and 5, 1993; Munir Khan, personal interviews, Islamabad, February 27 and March 4, 1993. As part of these negotiations, Pakistan also gave Washington a written promise that it would not conduct any nuclear tests. A U.S. government official stated in a May 1993 interview in Washington, D.C., that there is some doubt within the U.S. intelligence community whether Pakistan has actually complied with the first two requirements. Another U.S. government official in Islamabad in March 1993 stated that it is difficult for Washington to independently verify Islamabad's compliance with the third requirement, that is, not to work the metal into bomb cores.

Pakistan's public rhetoric belies its behavior about not rolling back its nuclear program. If Islamabad assembled nuclear weapons in May 1990, as some U.S. intelligence analysts and Bush administration officials assert, and if Pakistan has not rolled back its nuclear program, then these weapons would still be fully assembled. Pakistani officials have consistently stated that their country does not possess nuclear weapons (as distinct from the dismantled components of weapons), but they are quick to add that they could acquire this capability in a short period of time if necessary. Thus, either Pakistan has not rolled back its program by disassembling assembled weapons, or its officials have publicly lied. Purely for safety and security reasons, it would be prudent for Pakistan to keep these weapons in unassembled form.

[28]Retired senior Pakistani official, personal interview, Washington, D.C., August 9, 1994. This pledge did not meet the Pressler standard.

According to a retired U.S. intelligence officer, a key difference between 1989 and 1990 was that after the war scare in spring 1990, senior CIA officials refused to continue to turn a blind eye to Pakistan's nuclear weapons program. Telephone interview, 1994.

[29]Hersh, "On the Nuclear Edge," pp. 56–73. At the time of the 1990 crisis, Gates was deputy national security adviser; he later became director of the CIA. Kerr was the CIA's deputy director for intelligence.

One curious aspect of the attention generated by the Hersh report is that some of the claims he made had been reported years earlier without any of the controversy that surrounded the 1993 piece. See James Adams, "Pakistan 'Nuclear War Threat,'" May 27, 1990, *Sunday Times* (London). See also Zahid Hussain, "The Bomb Controversy," *Newsline* (Karachi) (November 1991), pp. 22–29; Sharon Herbaugh, "Quiet Diplomacy to Restart Aid, Redefine Relations," *Associated Press*, December 5, 1990.

[30]Quoted in Hersh, "On the Nuclear Edge," pp. 66, 56. During the Cuban Missile Crisis, Kerr analyzed Soviet military forces in Cuba. Indian and Pakistani experts strongly disagree on the possibility of nuclear war in 1990. See K. Subrahmanyam: "Down Memory Lane," *Economic Times* (New Delhi), March 24, 1993 ("Whatever Mr. Gates may have discussed with the Pakistanis, no policy maker in India recalls his raising the issue of nuclear confrontation"); M. R. Srinivasan, "NPT and India's Case," *Hindu* (Madras), July 10, 1993 ("There was no truth whatever in the report that either Pakistan or India was on the point of deploying nuclear weapons against each other"); General K. M. Arif, personal interview, Rawalpindi, March 3, 1993 (the 1990 crisis was "something of a non-event"). General Arif was Pakistan's army chief of staff under Zia.

[31]Hersh's argument rested on four specific items and on the assumptions and inferences that could be drawn from them:

(1) In the early spring of 1990, U.S. intelligence data, "perhaps an NSA intercept," showed that Pakistan had assembled nuclear bombs.

(2) In May "some [U.S. intelligence] officials believed" that the Kahuta uranium enrichment plant was evacuated. The inference was that Pakistan was preparing for a retaliatory Indian nuclear strike after Pakistan first destroyed New Delhi.

(3) Also in May, a truck convoy under heavy security left a storage depot in Baluchistan in southwestern Pakistan and drove to an air force base where F-16 fighter jets were based. The assumptions here are that this was a nuclear storage base and that the trucks carried nuclear weapons.

(4) F-16s were "prepositioned and armed for delivery—on full alert, with pilots in the aircraft." One intelligence analyst is quoted as saying, "I believed that they were ready to launch on command." The inference is that the F-16s were armed with nuclear weapons.

As noted above, former Bush administration officials whom I interviewed confirmed that Pakistan had assembled at least one nuclear bomb in spring 1990. I was unable to obtain independent confirmation of the other three charges Hersh made, but they all seem plausible.

For commentary on the Hersh article, see, for example, Douglas Jehl, "Assertion India and Pakistan Faced Nuclear War Is Doubted," *New York Times*, March 23, 1993; Khalid Hassan, "The U.S. Should Accept the Fact That Pakistan and India Both Have Nuclear Capability," *Washington Report on Middle East Affairs* (July-August 1994), pp. 16–18. The controversy was rekindled in 1994 with the publication of William E. Burrows and Robert Windrem, *Critical Mass: The Dangerous Race for Superweapons in a Fragmenting World* (New York: Simon and Schuster, 1994). Burrows and Windrem generally supported Hersh's story and embellished it with many new details.

[32]For an analysis of the Brass Tacks exercise, see Steven R. Weisman, "On India's Border, a Huge Mock War," *New York Times*, March 6, 1987; Stephen Philip Cohen, "1990: South Asia's Useful Nuclear Crisis?" (paper presented to the American Association for the Advancement of Science, Chicago, February 6–7, 1992); Kanti P. Bajpai, et al., "Brasstacks and Beyond: Perception and Management of Crisis in South Asia," University of Illinois at Urbana-Champaign (January 1995).

On January 28, 1987, after the period of greatest tension during the Brass Tacks crisis, an Indian journalist, Kuldip Nayar, interviewed Dr. A. Q. Khan concerning Pakistan's nuclear program. Khan claimed that Pakistan could build a nuclear bomb and that the CIA was aware of this fact. If this was a case of nuclear signaling, Nayar may have flubbed his assigned role. Instead of publishing the exclusive immediately, he reportedly shopped it to the Western press, where the *Observer* (London) published it on March 1. However, soon after the interview Nayar allegedly relayed Khan's remarks to the Indian Ministry of External Affairs through the Indian Embassy in Pakistan. Cohen has written, "It is likely that these events [Brass Tacks and another military operation, codenamed Checkerboard] were intended to precipitate an overt Indian nuclear program." Cohen, "1990: South Asia's Useful Nuclear Crisis?" p. 7.

[33]Personal interview, Washington, D.C., May 18, 1993. Oakley is quoted by Hersh as saying: "I began to scream that what's going to happen is Brass Tacks all over again . . . and this time they won't stop." Hersh, "On the Nuclear Edge," pp. 64–65. During the 1986–87 Brass Tacks exercise, Oakley was senior director for the Near East and South Asia at the National Security Council.

[34]On this point Oakley and Ambassador William Clark, who was Oakley's counterpart in New Delhi in 1990, had the following exchange during the Stimson Center session. Oakley: "General Sharma was threatening to take out the training camps and saying that it was time to teach Pakistan a lesson, we'll put these upstarts in their place once and for all." Clark: "'A boot up their backside,' I think he called it." Stimson Center Report, p. 7.

[35]The original plan was for a senior KGB officer to accompany him, which would have made for a greater impact in the region. But Secretary of State James Baker was unable to convince the Soviet foreign minister, Eduard Shevardnadze, to go along. Gates speculated that Moscow may not have shared Washington's assessment of the threat (perhaps because of incomplete intelligence) or, more likely, that old-guard Soviet and KGB bureaucrats resisted this new brand of Soviet-American cooperation. Robert Gates, personal interview, Washington, D.C., March 28, 1994; see also Hersh, "On the Nuclear Edge," p. 66. Gates was joined by Richard Haass and John Kelly, the assistant secretary of state for Near East and South Asian affairs.

Regarding Soviet intelligence, according to Robert Windrem, the day before Gates departed for South Asia, Moscow maneuvered a Kosmos 2077 Soviet photo-reconnaissance satellite into low-earth orbit to pass over Pakistan's Chagai Hills, which is suspected of housing a nuclear storage depot. Personal correspondence with the author, July 15, 1994.

[36]Gates, personal interview, Washington, D.C., March 28, 1994. Gates gave a presentation on the maneuvers and deployments of each side's military forces, in some cases down to the company level. This gave the Pakistani officials a clearer picture of India's military preparations than the one they possessed from their own domestic intelligence efforts. It also enhanced Gates's credibility. Retired senior U.S. official, personal interview, Washington, D.C., 1994.

[37]Quoted in Hersh, "On the Nuclear Edge," p. 67; confirmed by a U.S. government official, personal interview, Washington, D.C., June 13, 1993. Gates said that he was quoted accurately in the Hersh article. Personal interview, Washington, D.C., March 28, 1994.

[38]Oakley, personal interview, Washington, D.C., May 18, 1993.

[39]Personal interview, Washington, D.C., July 14, 1994. At this meeting, Oakley is quoted by Hersh as saying to the Pakistanis, "Don't expect any help from us." Hersh, "On the Nuclear Edge," p. 67.

[40]Hersh, "On the Nuclear Edge," p. 68.

[41]Paul Wolfowitz, personal interview, Washington, D.C., June 29, 1994; Abdul Sattar, personal interview, Islamabad, March 4, 1993. Sattar, who was Pakistan's foreign secretary in 1990, said that his Indian counterparts repeated to him the briefing that Gates had provided to Delhi. The conventional military balance heavily favored India; according to Wolfowitz, the Pentagon had concluded that "India would make short work of the Pak army."

[42]Other countries also intervened in 1990, although none with such a high profile as the United States. Russia, China, Britain, and Japan gave both India and Pakistan essentially the same message: if hostilities occur, we will not get involved on your side. Oakley, personal interview, Washington, D.C., May 18, 1993; but see Stimson Center Report, pp. 9, 25–26. How much influence these diplomatic missives exerted is uncertain.

[43]In addition to Oakley and Clark, participants at the roundtable session included Abdul Sattar (the Pakistani foreign secretary in 1990), U.S. military officers who had served as defense attachés in Islamabad and Delhi in 1990, representatives from the Indian and Pakistani Embassies in Washington, D.C., and members of the U.S. intelligence community. See note 22 for the original citation of this transcript.

[44]See also Hersh, "On the Nuclear Edge," pp. 57, 65; *Hearing on Proliferation Threats of the 1990s*, p. 30. In June 1994, the *New York Times* reported that the U.S. intelligence community had issued, in summer 1990, a classified warning that there was a "'50–50' chance of a new Indian-Pakistan war." See Michael R. Gordon, "Iraq Played 'Catch Me If You Can.' North Korea Says, 'What If You Do?'" *New York Times*, June 5, 1994.

[45]Doug Makeig, Stimson Center Report, p. 27. Makeig's point is the one that should be emphasized. I am not implying or inferring that participants at the Stimson Center session made purposefully misleading statements or selectively interpreted the events of 1990. Makeig was working at the Defense Intelligence Agency in 1990.

[46]Munir Akram, Ministry of Foreign Affairs, Islamabad, personal interview, March 3, 1993; Munir Khan, personal interview, Islamabad, March 3, 1993. During an official visit to Washington in February 1992, Pakistani Foreign Secretary Shahryar Khan partially confirmed this. The foreign secretary declared that his country had the components and know-how to assemble at least one nuclear device. "The capability is there. . . . [Pakistan has the] elements, which if put together, would become a device." He stated that under pressure from the Bush administration Pakistan had refrained from producing additional weapons-grade uranium and converting the HEU gas into metal form and from building additional nuclear cores. But Pakistan would not destroy the nuclear cores that already existed without an equivalent step by India. Otherwise, he foresaw "no reversal" by Pakistan. R. Jeffrey Smith, "Pakistani Official Affirms Capacity for Nuclear Device," *Washington Post*, February 7, 1992. Although A. Q. Khan had made similar remarks about Pakistan's nuclear capabilities in January 1987, that interview was conducted under very different circumstances.

Caretaker Prime Minister Qureshi admitted in July 1993, "The program is in the stage where we can manufacture a nuclear device wherever [*sic*] we need it." Quoted in *Muslim* (Islamabad), August 1, 1993, reported in JPRS-TND-93-026, August 10, 1993, p. 14; see also the report of Qureshi's remarks on Pakistan's nuclear program in *Muslim*, August 30, 1993, reported in JPRS-TND-93-029 (September 17, 1993), pp. 27–28.

[47]See Alistair Lyon, "Pakistan's Bhutto Dismisses Nuclear Bomb Claim," *Reuters*, August 24, 1994; Shekhar Gupta, "Nawaz Sharif's Bombshell," *India Today*, September 15, 1994, pp. 44–50.

[48]Personal interview, Washington, D.C., January 5, 1994. See also note 6.

[49]Chris Smith, *India's Ad Hoc Arsenal: Direction or Drift in Defense Policy?* (New York: Oxford University Press, 1994), p. 1.

[50]See Sumit Ganguly and Kanti Bajpai, "India and the Crisis in Kashmir," *Asian Survey* 34, no. 5 (May 1994): 401–6; Sumit Ganguly, "Avoiding War in Kashmir," *Foreign Affairs* 69, no. 5 (Winter 1990–91): 57–73.

[51]It is unlikely that the Prithvi's guidance package can be upgraded to achieve a circular error probable (CEP) of less than 100 meters, which the Indian air force would prefer. Reportedly, Prithvi will have an initial production run of one hundred, with seventy-five missiles assigned to the army and twenty-five to the air force. *Foreign Report*, June 30, 1994, p. 7.

India is believed to have designed nuclear devices that are "smaller, lighter, and more deliverable" than its 1974 explosive. See David Albright and Mark Hibbs, "India's Silent Bomb," *Bulletin of the Atomic Scientists* (September 1992), p. 30.

[52]Senior State Department official, personal interview, Washington, D.C., January 5, 1994. See also note 6.

[53]"When we visualized the *Agni* program, it was meant to be a technology demonstrator. But now that it has proved its capabilities, we have the systems in place to make it operational within two years. . . . *Agni* has been developed to carry any type of warhead. . . . [W]e now have a carrier on which both conventional and non-conventional weapons can be delivered over a long range." A. P. J. Abdul Kalam, *India Today*, April 15, 1994, pp. 42, 43. Kalam was the head of India's ballistic missile development program.

⁵⁴Indian officials and analysts have at times tried to justify the Agni's development by alleging that China has positioned tactical nuclear weapons in Tibet. In separate interviews, three U.S. State Department officials independently declared that there are no Chinese nuclear weapons in Tibet. Personal interviews, Washington, D.C., May 11, 1993, May 10, 1994, and August 4, 1994.

⁵⁵The United States created the MTCR regime in 1987 with six other countries. Members drew up a list of guidelines designed to restrict the spread of missiles and unmanned airborne vehicles that could deliver a payload greater than 500 kilograms (1,100 pounds) to a distance greater than 300 kilometers (186 miles). By mid-1994, the MTCR had twenty-nine members. In 1990, the Soviet Union promised to abide by the MTCR export guidelines, but it did not formally become a member of the regime; India is not an MTCR member. No other MTCR member imposed sanctions on ISRO or Glavkosmos. A few weeks after U.S. sanctions on ISRO were announced, India conducted a test of the Agni.

⁵⁶See the following editorials: "Ugly American Again," *Times of India,* July 21, 1993; "Somber Outlook for India," *Indian Express,* July 19, 1993; "Of Cryogenic Fiasco," *Patriot* (Delhi), July 19, 1993. For a rebuttal, see Mitchell Reiss, "Rockets, Realpolitik, and the U.S. Relationship," *Hindu* (Delhi), August 4, 1993. On the Russian-American deal, see R. Jeffrey Smith, "U.S., Russia Near Accord on Technology for India," *Washington Post,* July 14, 1993; Elaine Sciolino, "U.S. Aides Say Compromise Near on Russia Arms Technology Sale," *New York Times,* July 16, 1993; Elaine Sciolino, "Russia Is Halting Arms-Linked Sale," *New York Times,* July 17, 1993.

⁵⁷*RFE/RL Daily Report,* no. 63 (March 31, 1994); *RFE/RL News Briefs,* April 28–31, 1994, p. 6; *Times of India* (Bombay), April 1, 1994, reported in JPRS-TND-94-012 (June 7, 1994), pp. 21–22.

⁵⁸According to *Arms Control Today* (January-February 1992), p. 46, the M-11 has a 290-kilometer range with an 800-kilogram payload; the IISS lists its range as 120–50 kilometers but does not account for payload. *Military Balance, 1993–1994* (London: IISS, 1993), p. 152.

China is not an MTCR member, but it had verbally promised the Bush administration in November 1991 that it would adopt a responsible policy on missile sales. Pakistan is not an MTCR member.

⁵⁹In March 1994, Abdul Sattar, who was Pakistan's foreign minister in August 1993, stated that China had promised to sell Pakistan the M-11 missile but that U.S. pressure caused Beijing to inform Islamabad that it was unable to transfer this technology. However, Beijing would transfer a modified version of the M-11, one whose range and payload limits fell within the MTCR guidelines.

According to Sattar, the United States later claimed that China delivered to Pakistan, by ship in 1992, technology that would permit the modified M-11 to be upgraded. Washington asked Beijing to disclose the ship's manifest; the Chinese refused but said that the suspect technology was not on board. Washington then asked Islamabad to disclose the ship's manifest. Pakistan replied that it did not have a copy. Washington then asked to inspect the M-11 missile sites. Pakistan refused, after conferring with China. Washington subsequently decided to impose sanctions. Personal interview, Washington, D.C., March 29, 1994. This account was corroborated by a U.S. State Department official, personal interview, Washington, D.C., August 4, 1994.

[60]The U.S. sanctions banned the sale of $1 billion in advanced technology for China's space and military programs. Patrick E. Tyler, "China Calls American Sanctions Unjustifiable," *New York Times*, August 27, 1993.

[61]See Elaine Sciolino, "U.S. And Chinese Reach Agreement on Missile Export," *New York Times*, October 5, 1994; Daniel Williams, "U.S. Deal with China Allows High-Tech Sales in Exchange for Pledge," *Washington Post*, October 5, 1994. In November 1994, it was reported that the United States had told China that if it fully disclosed its past exports of M-11 missile technology to Pakistan, Washington would waive U.S. economic sanctions that would be imposed if Washington later concluded that Beijing had exported complete M-11 missile systems. Strong U.S. suspicions that China had exported such systems, coupled with a reluctance to impose sweeping economic sanctions on China, prompted this overture. See Elaine Sciolino, "U.S. Offers China Deal to Resolve a Missile Dispute," *New York Times*, November 14, 1994. For an examination of China's nonproliferation policies, see Shirley Kan and Zachary Davis, "China," in Reiss and Litwak, eds., *Nuclear Proliferation after the Cold War*, pp. 145–64.

[62]State Department official, personal interview, Washington, D.C., August 4, 1994. In September 1994, it was reported that Pakistan was moving ahead with its plans to purchase M-11 missiles. See Bill Gertz, "Pakistan-China Deal for Missiles Exposed," *Washington Times*, September 7, 1994; R. Jeffrey Smith and Thomas W. Lippman, "Pakistan M-11 Funding Is Reported," *Washington Post*, September 8, 1994.

[63]Senior State Department official, personal interview, Washington, D.C., January 5, 1994. See also note 6.

[64]Immediately after its 1974 nuclear test, Libya suggested to India that the two countries sign a bilateral nuclear cooperation agreement. Libya was rebuffed. Retired senior Indian atomic energy official, personal interview, Bombay, June 4, 1986. See also Keith Bradsher, "India Official Says Qaddafi Sought Atom-Arms Technology in 70's," *New York Times*, October 10, 1991.

Pakistan informed the U.S. government that it refused Iranian offers to engage in "nuclear cooperation" in return for meeting Pakistan's $3.5-billion defense budget. U.S. government officials, personal interviews, Islamabad, February 27 and March 1, 1993. See also David Albright and Mark Hibbs, "Spotlight Shifts to Iran," *Bulletin of the Atomic Scientists* (March 1992), p. 11; "The Temptation of Pakistan," *Foreign Report* (London), March 25, 1993, pp. 1–2.

[65]These examples are drawn from Sumit Ganguly, "Mending Fences: Confidence-Building Measures between India and Pakistan," Stimson Center monograph, forthcoming.

[66]For a complete listing of Pakistan's arms control and nonproliferation proposals, see Warren H. Donnelly and Zachary Davis, "Pakistan's Nuclear Status," *CRS Issue Brief* 91142 (July 10, 1992), p. 4; see also Zafar Iqbal Cheema, "Nuclear Diplomacy in South Asia during the 1980s," *Regional Studies* (Islamabad) 10, no. 3 (Summer 1992): 53–66.

[67]Milton R. Benjamin, "India Said to Eye Raid on Pakistani A-Plants," *Washington Post*, December 20, 1982. It is likely that Israel's destruction of the Osiraq nuclear reactor in June 1981 stimulated Indian thinking about a preemptive strike against Pakistan. On using the Osiraq raid as a model for destroying nuclear programs in other countries, see Avner Cohen, "The Lessons of Osiraq and the American Counterproliferation Debate," in Mitchell Reiss and Harald Müller, eds., "In-

ternational Perspectives on Counterproliferation," Woodrow Wilson Center Working Paper No. 99 (January 1995), pp. 75–104.

⁶⁸See Spector with Smith, *Nuclear Ambitions,* pp. 66–67; Burrows and Windrem, *Critical Mass,* pp. 349–50. These stories reappeared after the Brass Tacks military exercise, with the Ministry of External Affairs denying that India and Israel had discussed how to destroy Kahuta. See *Times of India,* February 25, 1987. Reportedly, a few years earlier the United States had debated sabotaging Pakistan's then-nascent nuclear program. See Richard Burt, "U.S. Will Press Pakistan to Halt A-Arms Project," *New York Times,* August 12, 1979.

⁶⁹Khan, personal interviews, Islamabad, February 27 and March 4, 1993. Khan believed that Israel was concerned with Pakistan's nuclear program in the early 1980s, in part because of Islamabad's ties to some of Israel's Arab neighbors, and that Israel approached India to discuss the idea of destroying Kahuta.

⁷⁰Cohen, "1990: South Asia's Useful Nuclear Crisis?" pp. 5–6. The United States was instrumental in deterring an Indian attack on Pakistan's nuclear facilities during the 1980s, the time of its greatest vulnerability. Massive U.S. military and economic assistance created the impression of strong and durable ties between the two countries, in effect a de facto security relationship. Washington's acquiescence to Pakistan's progressive accumulation of nuclear competence reinforced this impression by suggesting that close bilateral ties not only took precedence over nonproliferation concerns but completely eclipsed them. Each waiver of U.S. nonproliferation laws underscored this point. See Mitchell Reiss, "The Illusion of Influence: The United States and Pakistan's Nuclear Program," *RUSI Journal* (Summer 1991), pp. 47–50.

⁷¹"The Agreement on the Prohibition of Attack against Nuclear Installations and Facilities between Pakistan and India" was signed by Prime Ministers Rajiv Gandhi and Benazir Bhutto and is described in "Pakistan and India Sign Pact," *Washington Post,* January 1, 1989. This idea originated with the leading strategist in India, K. Subrahmanyam, who was director of the Institute for Defense Studies and Analyses in New Delhi at the time. See "Building Trust on the Bomb: What India and Pakistan Can Do," *Times of India,* July 30, 1985.

⁷²U.S. government officials, personal interviews, Islamabad, March 1, 1993, and Arlington, Virginia, July 10, 1993. See also *Nucleonics Week,* January 9, 1992. The agreement calls for these lists to be updated annually. According to Brahma Chellaney, India did not originally list a small gas centrifuge enrichment facility at Ratnahalli, near Mysore in the southern state of Karnataka. Pakistan did not originally list its uranium enrichment plant at Golra. Chellaney, "India," p. 189.

⁷³Ganguly, "Mending Fences"; S. Shafqat Kakakhel, "Pak-India Confidence and Security Measures: Recent Developments and Future Prospects" (paper presented at the Conference on Confidence- and Security-Building Measures in South Asia, New Delhi and Islamabad, May 24–30, 1993), p. 7. See also Douglas C. Makeig, "War, No War, and the India-Pakistan Negotiating Process," *Pacific Affairs* 60, no. 2 (Summer 1987): 271–94.

⁷⁴Many of these CBMs can be found in President Clinton's "Report to Congress on Progress toward Regional Nonproliferation in South Asia," April 1993, pp. 5–6, copy in author's possession.

⁷⁵U.S. government officials, personal interviews, New Delhi, February 1993; Ganguly, "Mending Fences"; Kakakhel, "Pak-India Confidence and Security Measures." India and Pakistan also signed in August 1992 a "Joint Declaration on the Complete Prohibition of Chemical Weapons."

[76]State Department officials, personal interviews, April 15 and August 4, 1994.

[77]See Michael Krepon's three South Asia trip reports, March 7–19, 1993, May 17–25, 1993, and May 7–21, 1994. Copies provided to the author by Michael Krepon. On the Siachen Glacier dispute, see Robert G. Wirsing, *Pakistan's Security under Zia, 1977–1988: The Policy Imperative of a Peripheral Asian State* (New York: St. Martin's, 1991).

India and China have had more success in adopting and implementing CBMs. By 1994, they had agreed to an equal ceiling on border troop deployments, a clearer demarcation of the MacMahon Line, a pledge not to use force to change border positions and to give prior notice of troop movements and maneuvers, steps to prevent airspace violations, and a hot line between and regular meetings of border commanders. See Michael Krepon, Dominique M. McCoy, and Matthew C. J. Rudolph, eds., "A Handbook of Confidence-Building Measures for Regional Security," Henry L. Stimson Center, September 1993, p. 49; Lena H. Sun, "China, India Sign Accord to Ease Border Dispute," *Washington Post,* September 8, 1993; more generally, Surjit Mansingh, "India-China Relations in the Post–Cold War Era," *Asian Survey* 34, no. 3 (March 1994): 285–300.

[78]Personal interview, Washington, D.C., August 4, 1994.

[79]U.S. government official, personal interview, New Delhi, February 1993.

[80]The ministry was ordered to draft a new paper, which was then approved. The head of the Indian delegation was later forced to rehearse his answers in front of the prime minister before being dispatched to Washington. U.S. government official, personal interview, New Delhi, February 23, 1993. This story was recounted to this U.S. official by an Indian official present at the Rao meeting.

[81]U.S. government official, personal interview, Washington, D.C., November 1992. In November 1992, the United States proposed separate but parallel talks between the United States and India and between the United States and Pakistan, but Pakistan refused to enter into these "proximity negotiations," probably because it still clung to the idea of a five-power conference.

[82]India may have been more flexible during these negotiations because Washington had quietly assisted New Delhi on two sensitive matters within the previous twelve months. First, after the destruction of the Babri mosque, the United States issued a demarche to Moslem oil-producing countries to request that they not publicly criticize the Rao government and not delay or suspend oil supplies to India. Second, in March 1993, the United States reacted promptly to calm tensions in the region after the Bombay bombings that killed over two hundred people. See John M. Goshko and Don Oberdorfer, "U.S. Moved Quickly to Calm Pakistan and India after Bombay Bombings," *Washington Post,* April 15, 1993.

[83]A 1993 U.S. government study entitled "Nuclear Power Production in India" concluded (1) that TAPS required about 600 kilograms of plutonium annually for MOX fuel rods and (2) that four years would be needed to fully reload the two Tarapur reactors. At the end of 1993, India's plutonium inventory totaled approximately 1,480 kilograms, and it could extract an additional 190 kilograms of plutonium per year. If Delhi used only this plutonium for refueling TAPS, it would have exhausted its stocks in less than four years, or before TAPS was completely refueled. In other words, without reprocessing Tarapur's spent fuel, Delhi could not operate TAPS.

As a possible indication that India wanted to rectify its difficult fuel situation, A. N. Prasad, formerly the head of the Fuel Reprocessing and Nuclear Waste Man-

agement Division, was selected in 1994 as the new head of the Bhabha Atomic Research Center.

The most comprehensive analysis of the Tarapur issue is Brahma Chellaney,
Nuclear Proliferation: The U.S.-Indian Conflict (New Delhi: Orient Longman, 1993);
see also Satu Limaye, *US-Indian Relations: The Pursuit of Accommodation* (Boulder,
Colo.: Westview, 1993), and Wohlstetter, "The Buddha Smiles." For an excellent
analysis of India's dilapidated nuclear power program, see Thomas B. Smith,
"India's Electric Power Crisis: Why Do the Lights Go Out?" *Asian Survey* 33, no. 4
(April 1994): 376–92.

[84]Personal correspondence, French Foreign Ministry official, July 1994. In September 1991, French Foreign Minister Roland Dumas had announced before the
UN General Assembly that France would require full-scope safeguards as a condition of nuclear transfers. France joined the NPT in August 1992.

[85]The Indian-IAEA safeguards agreement entered into force on March 1, 1994.
The agreement is of indefinite duration and will be in effect until it is terminated
by mutual agreement of the parties. See INFCIRC/433, May 1994.

This safeguards agreement did not cover the Tarapur facility itself. Theoretically, this "loophole" would permit India to unload the entire reactor core and replace it with unsafeguarded low-enriched uranium (LEU). Spent fuel from this
core would not be covered by safeguards and could then be reprocessed to obtain
bomb-grade plutonium. In practice, all possible suppliers of LEU belong to the
NPT. India thus cannot obtain unsafeguarded LEU for Tarapur unless the supplier
is willing to violate its NPT obligations.

[86]On the fall 1993 negotiations, see U.S. government officials, telephone interviews, Washington, D.C., July 20, 1994, and August 5, 1994. OPIC is a U.S. government agency that encourages private-sector investment in the developing world
largely by providing U.S. companies with insurance against political risks, such as
expropriation of assets. The $5-billion figure was the amount of prospective invest-
ment registered by U.S. companies with OPIC; it did not commit these companies
to actually investing in India or obtaining OPIC financing.

On the Chinese LEU sale, see *Financial Times*, January 6, 1995; State Department
officials, personal interviews, February 10, 1995. One of these officials stated that
"India would have used the spent fuel from the Tarapur reactors if necessary. They
couldn't afford to shut TAPS down for domestic political reasons."

[87]On the Indian proposals, see K. K. Katyal, "India Conveys Six Proposals to
Pak.," *Hindu,* January 25, 1994; "6 Proposals India Sends to Pakistan," *Times of
India,* January 25, 1994; "India Sends Proposals to Pak on Ties Improvement," *Hin-
dustan Times,* January 25, 1994. For Pakistan's response, see President Clinton, "Re-
port to Congress: Update on Progress toward Regional Nonproliferation in South
Asia," April 1994, copy in author's possession.

[88]Clinton, "Report to Congress," April 1993. According to Oakley, the classified
version of the State Department's report contained information on the nuclear
weapons potential of both countries, on how quickly they could assemble nuclear
weapons, and on the fact that India had little incentive to cooperate on nonproliferation matters as long as the Pressler amendment was in place. Personal interview, Washington, D.C., May 18, 1993.

In 1991, the Carnegie Endowment for International Peace convened a study
group to undertake a fundamental reassessment of U.S. policy toward India. The

resulting report, prepared by Selig S. Harrison and Geoffrey Kemp and entitled *India and America: After the Cold War*, was published in early 1993 and influenced the Clinton administration's approach to the region.

[89]U.S. State Department official, personal interview, Washington, D.C., August 4, 1994.

[90]U.S. State Department officials, personal interviews, Washington, D.C., April 15 and August 4, 1994. The National Intelligence Estimate gauged that the risk of nuclear war was lower than the risk of conventional war. The Bureau of Intelligence and Research opposed assigning a specific percentage estimate for the risk of war because (1) it disagreed with the 20 percent figure, thinking this far too high, and (2) it feared that the figure would be misinterpreted by U.S. arms control officials who were not familiar with the region.

[91]U.S. State Department official, personal interview, Washington, D.C., May 10, 1994. For press coverage, see Eric Schmitt, "Lifting Ban on Pakistan Aid Is Seen as Way to Curb Arms," *New York Times*, March 13, 1994; Michael R. Gordon, "South Asian Lands Pressed on Arms," *New York Times*, March 23, 1994; R. Jeffrey Smith, "U.S. Proposes Sale of F-16s to Pakistan," *Washington Post*, March 23, 1994.

[92]The Clinton administration had partially tipped its hand earlier. In November 1993, it had proposed revising the Pressler amendment—as part of an overhaul of the 1961 Foreign Aid Act—by applying its limitations to all nonnuclear weapon states that have reprocessing or uranium enrichment capabilities and by permitting the president to exempt Pakistan (and any other country) from U.S. sanctions if he determined that this was in the U.S. national interest. See R. Jeffrey Smith, "Clinton Moves to Ease Pakistan Nuclear Curb," *Washington Post*, November 25, 1993; Steven A. Holmes, "Clinton Plans Change in the Law Banning Military Aid to Pakistan," *New York Times*, November 27, 1993. The administration withdrew its proposal in the face of strong congressional opposition.

[93]See especially Nathan Glazer, "Why Arm Pakistan?" *New York Times*, April 13, 1994. The administration made virtually no effort to publicly defend its policy, holding only one off-the-record meeting at the Washington-based Henry L. Stimson Center.

The capping proposal undermined a number of long-standing U.S. nonproliferation principles by abandoning the traditional U.S. policy opposing nuclear proliferation in exchange for one that "managed" the problem. At a time when the United States was negotiating with North Korea over its nuclear activities, its message was that if threshold states could be patient, eventually Washington would tolerate their nuclear ambitions. In addition, by not insisting on full-scope safeguards for India, Washington undercut the policy of the Nuclear Suppliers Group, which required states to accept comprehensive safeguards as a condition of sale for certain nuclear technologies.

The capping strategy also called for both India and Pakistan to halt the production of fissile material that was intended for nuclear explosive purposes or that was outside of safeguards, a proposal that President Clinton had first suggested as a global initiative before the UN General Assembly on September 27, 1993. A cutoff convention risks creating a discriminatory system that perversely favors those nuclear threshold countries, such as India and Pakistan, that are not NPT members at the expense of those countries that are. Under such a convention, nuclear material previously produced by threshold nuclear powers would be "grandfathered" and not subject to IAEA safeguards. Because this material could be used to make nuclear weapons, the convention would legitimize these countries as de facto nuclear weapon states. In contrast, all nonnuclear weapon state parties to the NPT are required to place all their nuclear material under safeguards. This was not the best message to send the international community just before the 1995 NPT review and extension conference, where the treaty's future will be debated. See Mitchell Reiss, "April 1995: The Last Nuclear Summit?" *Washington Quarterly* 17, no. 3 (Summer 1994): 5–15.

[94]See John-Thor Dahlberg, "Plan to Ship F-16s to Pakistan Raises India's Ire," *Los Angeles Times*, March 17, 1994; John F. Burns, "India Rejects U.S. Bid for Nuclear Pact with Pakistan," *New York Times*, March 26, 1994, and "India Unmoved in Arms Talks with U.S.," *New York Times*, April 9, 1994; editorials and commentary in Indian newspapers, in JPRS-TND-94-010 (May 5, 1994), pp. 17–21; Thomas W. Lippman, "Anti-Nuclear Initiative Gets Cold Shoulder," *Washington Post*, May 8, 1994. The United States never formally presented the initiative to India. U.S. State Department official, personal interview, Washington, D.C., August 4, 1994.

[95]Senior State Department official, personal interview, Washington, D.C., May 10, 1994. The larger issue raised by the U.S. proposal was how Washington could increase its influence with New Delhi. George Perkovich has suggested that Washington could use the prospect of lifting the Pressler amendment as a type of "reverse leverage" with India. For example, Washington could indicate that it would lift the Pressler amendment restrictions on Pakistan should India deploy the Prithvi.

[96]Naresh Chandra, personal interview, Washington, D.C., June 8, 1994.

[97]Bhutto was quoted soon after taking office as saying, "We will protect Pakistan's nuclear program and will not allow our national interest to be sacrificed." See Edward A. Gargan, "Bhutto Pledges to Maintain Pakistan's Nuclear Program," *International Herald Tribune*, October 21, 1993; Molly Moore, "A Hardened Bhutto Returns to Face a Daunting Array of New Problems," *Washington Post*, October 21, 1993. The following month Bhutto added, "Rolling back the nuclear program is not feasible." See "Pakistan Holds Firm to Nuclear Arms Plan," *New York Times*, November 21, 1993.

[98]U.S. State Department official, personal interview, Washington, D.C., April 15, 1994. In April 1994, President Clinton's "Report to Congress: Update," pp. 4–5, stated, "It is our assessment that the contemplated delivery of these F-16s would not materially change the existing military balance, which remains in India's favor."

Some flexibility may have been signaled by the way Benazir Bhutto characterized Pakistan's opposition to the U.S. plan: "There is no question of rolling back the nuclear program. If we are unilaterally pressed for capping, it will be discriminatory." Quoted in John F. Burns, "India Unmoved in Arms Talks with U.S.," *New York Times*, April 9, 1994. Washington had not asked Islamabad either to roll back or to unilaterally cap the program—suggesting that a deal might be possible. See Ahmed Rashid, "Breaking the Ice," *Herald* (Islamabad) (April 1994), pp. 36–43.

[99]The Indian side repeated Rajiv Gandhi's proposal for universal disarmament by 2010, a proposal that Gandhi had first announced before the Third UN Special Session on Disarmament in New York in May 1988. The Indian delegation was led by Foreign Secretary Krishnan Srinivasan, who had no expertise in arms control matters. Further, he had eliminated from the delegation the two arms control experts from the Foreign Ministry, Hardeep Puri and Rakesh Sood, who had attended the previous bilateral negotiations with the United States. Some U.S. State Department officials saw this gesture as a deliberate attempt by New Delhi to sub-

vert the April meeting. For a critical examination of the Indian approach to this meeting, see the extraordinary interview with J. N. Dixit, *Sunday*, July 3–9, 1994, pp. 25–29.

An astute Indian arms control expert, C. Raja Mohan, has criticized New Delhi for viewing nuclear matters in moral terms, rather than in national security terms. "India [has been] tied down by three unsustainable nuclear propositions: no political decision on acquiring nuclear weapons; a ritualistic opposition to the NPT and the nonproliferation regime; and a refusal to discuss the nuclear issue with Pakistan. Together the three propositions were designed to engineer the worst of all possible outcomes: refusal to come to terms with the reality of a nuclear Pakistan; conflict with great powers on nonproliferation; and yielding an uncontested victory to Pakistan on arms control propaganda." Paper presented at the Center for Security and Technology Studies, Lawrence Livermore National Laboratory, April 20, 1993, p. 10.

[100]Quoted in Molly Moore, "Indian Leaders Skeptical of U.S. Nuclear Plan," *Washington Post*, April 9, 1994.

For an alternative U.S. policy toward India, see Mitchell Reiss, "Arms Control Failure: The Washington Naval Treaty and Lessons for the NPT Review Conference," in Francine Frankel, ed., *Bridging the Nonproliferation Divide: The United States and India* (Lanham, Md.: University Press of America, 1995).

[101]See John M. Goshko, "Clinton Moves to Ease Relationship with India," *Washington Post*, May 20, 1994; Dilip Bobb, "Rao's US Visit: A Quiet Triumph," *India Today*, June 15, 1994.

[102]Carl von Clausewitz, *On War*, ed. and trans. Michael Howard and Peter Paret (Princeton, N.J.: Princeton University Press, 1976), pp. 119, 121.

[103]Reasons for opposing CBMs exist in both India and Pakistan. They include political fatigue from coping with more pressing internal problems and resistance from the intelligence communities—the Research and Analysis Wing (RAW) in India and ISI in Pakistan. Ganguly, "Mending Fences."

Lest India and Pakistan be judged too harshly, it should be remembered that the Soviet-American nuclear competition, often cited as an example of successful bilateral deterrence, offers a useful frame of reference for evaluating the pace of arms control in South Asia. After both the Soviet Union and the United States acquired nuclear weapons, it took them another fourteen years and the Cuban Missile Crisis before they instituted their first confidence-building measure—the 1963 Hotline Agreement. India and Pakistan are well ahead of this schedule. Although they have jointly possessed unassembled nuclear weapons for less than ten years, they weathered the 1990 nuclear crisis and established multiple hot lines. They have a real chance to benefit from, and thus avoid, the errors and dangers of the first few decades of the superpower nuclear rivalry.

[104]In 1992–93, according to official Indian statistics, India's exports to Pakistan constituted less than one-third of 1 percent of its global exports. Only 0.06 percent of all goods imported into India during this same time period came from Pakistan. Trade statistics provided to the author by the Indian Embassy, Washington, D.C., June 29, 1994; see also International Monetary Fund, *Direction of Trade Statistics Yearbook, 1993* (Washington, D.C.: International Monetary Fund, 1993), pp. 222, 312. On trade problems between India and Pakistan, see Sunil Dasgupta, "Private Initiatives," *India Today*, March 31, 1993. There is little doubt that greater interaction between Indians and Pakistanis would help counter the hostile propaganda, dis-

torted images, and demonization of the other country promoted through official and unofficial channels.

[105]Some analysts in South Asia assert that the inference from this type of statement—that India and Pakistan are incapable of responsible nuclear behavior—is not just condescending but implicitly racist. Because this allegation is so serious and widely believed in Pakistan and especially in India, it deserves to be taken seriously by Americans. The point here is that managing nuclear weapons, whether assembled or unassembled, inherently presents formidable challenges for secure command and control and for nuclear safety. The American strategic literature is replete with examples from the U.S. experience in which miscommunication or faulty technology almost precipitated disaster. For excellent examinations of this important subject, see Scott D. Sagan, *The Limits of Safety: Organizations, Accidents, and Nuclear Weapons* (Princeton, N.J.: Princeton University Press, 1993); Scott D. Sagan, "The Perils of Proliferation: Organization Theory, Deterrence Theory, and the Spread of Nuclear Weapons," *International Security* 18, no. 4 (Spring 1994): 66–107; Bruce Blair, *The Logic of Accidental Nuclear War* (Washington, D.C.: Brookings, 1993); Peter Douglas Feaver, *Guarding the Guardians: Civilian Control of Nuclear Weapons in the United States* (Ithaca, N.Y.: Cornell University Press, 1992); Peter Douglas Feaver, "Proliferation Optimism and Theories of Nuclear Operations," in Zachary S. Davis and Benjamin Frankel, eds., *The Proliferation Puzzle: Why Nuclear Weapons Spread (and What Results)* (London: Frank Cass, 1993), pp. 159–91; more generally, Robert Jervis, *Perception and Misperception in International Politics* (Princeton, N.J.: Princeton University Press, 1976).

[106]See, for example, a 1988 "Report of the Carnegie Task Force on Nonproliferation and South Asian Security," which estimated that by 1991 Pakistan might have fifteen nuclear weapons and India might have one hundred. *Nuclear Weapons and South Asian Security* (Washington, D.C.: Carnegie Endowment for International Peace, 1988), p. 55.

[107]See Devin T. Hagerty, "The Power of Suggestion: Opaque Proliferation, Existential Deterrence, and the South Asian Nuclear Arms Competition," *Security Studies* 2, nos. 3–4 (Spring-Summer 1993): 277. According to Hagerty: "Indian and Pakistani leaders worked *together* to defuse the crisis, suggesting, again, that neither side wanted it to escalate to the nuclear level. Indian and Pakistani military leaders were reportedly in close touch during the crisis via a 'hot line'" (emphasis in original).

[108]See, for example, Brahma Chellaney, "South Asia's Passage to Nuclear Power," *International Security* 16, no. 1 (Summer 1991): 68–69; Mushahid Hussain, "A Bomb for Security," *Newsline* (Karachi) (November 1991), p. 32; Shireen M. Mazari, "Nuclear Weapons and Structures of Conflict in the Developing World," in W. Thomas Wander and Eric H. Arnett, eds., *The Proliferation of Advanced Weaponry: Technology, Motivations, and Responses* (Washington, D.C.: AAAS, 1992), p. 48. Stephen Cohen wrote in 1990 that proliferation in South Asia "will stabilize the Indo-Pakistani relationship" and "may have a calming, even stabilizing regional effect." See "Solving Proliferation Problems in a Regional Context: South Asia," in Aspen Strategy Group, *New Threats: Responding to the Proliferation of Nuclear, Chemical, and Delivery Capabilities in the Third World* (Lanham, Md.: United Press of America, 1990), p. 177.

[109]Senior State Department official, personal interview, Washington, D.C., January 5, 1994. See also note 6.

[110]One American expert on South Asia has written: "There is a false impression that India and Pakistan are hurtling, uncontrolled, toward a nuclear-armed confrontation. . . . [U]nderneath this ostensibly turbulent surface, the leaders of both India and Pakistan are quite consciously and cautiously attempting to prevent that from happening." Neil Joeck, "Tacit Bargaining and Stable Proliferation in South Asia," *Journal of Strategic Studies* 13, no. 3 (September 1990): 89. It should be noted that Indian and Pakistani restraint may be motivated by factors other than nonweaponized deterrence, including conventional deterrence and external pressures. If this is the case, unassembled nuclear weapons are arguably still the most powerful deterrent factor. Should the two sides successfully sustain nonweaponized deterrence, they will have achieved something far more important than increased security and stability in South Asia, as valuable as that will be. They will have provided a model for the nuclear weapon states to emulate.

Chapter 6

North Korea: Living with Uncertainty

The end of the cold war in Asia introduced new opportunities, as well as new impediments, for countries to rethink their strategic interests and enhance their national security. No country was a bigger loser in this evolving diplomatic landscape than the Democratic People's Republic of Korea (DPRK), the xenophobic, heavily armed "Hermit Kingdom" ruled at that time by the "Great Leader" Kim Il Sung and his reclusive son, the "Dear Leader" Kim Jong Il.

As North Korea confronted the 1990s, it found itself more isolated than at any other time in its brief history. The Soviet Union, Pyongyang's single largest source of advanced military equipment, was no more. China, Pyongyang's other strategic partner, moved to advance its national interests by engaging in a prosperous trade with the Republic of Korea (ROK) and by allowing the simultaneous admission of both Koreas into the United Nations. South Korea during this period skillfully obtained diplomatic recognition from Russia and China, but North Korea did not win "cross-recognition" from Japan and the United States. By this time, the DPRK's fraternal allies in Eastern Europe had all been toppled by internal revolutions, with East Germany swallowed up by a more prosperous West Germany, a scenario Pyongyang wanted to avoid at all costs.

What was the impact of these events on North Korea? Did the country's diplomatic isolation and general insecurity translate into a greater willingness to engage in a dialogue, albeit cautiously and gradually, with the outside world? Or did this vulnerability promote a defensiveness that called for greater resistance to outside pressures?

Specifically, did North Korea believe that nuclear weapons were of no lasting benefit to the regime and that the nuclear program should be traded for diplomatic recognition and financial assistance? Was the country's nuclear program designed to generate this bargaining leverage by deliberately arousing the concern of South Korea, the United

231

States, and the international community so that Pyongyang could dictate the pace and terms on which it entered the world?

Or was the North Korean nuclear program a serious, dedicated effort to acquire a nuclear arsenal to counter the South's booming economy and growing conventional military strength so that the North Korean regime might be preserved? Was North Korea attempting to stonewall the United States and the international community for as long as possible to give it time to acquire a nuclear stockpile as a hedge against an uncertain future in a hostile world?[1] In other words, was it playing what former CIA Director Robert Gates called "the wallet-on-the-string trick"?

No one outside North Korea, and perhaps even in North Korea, could answer these questions with certainty. The answers probably changed over time and depended on which DPRK official was asked. The dilemma for the world was that much of the North's behavior could be used to satisfy both sets of questions. Depending on which prism you looked through, the North's behavior could have indicated a masterly diplomacy aimed at extracting concessions from the United States, or it could have suggested a committed effort to avoid comprehensive inspections and to acquire nuclear weapons. North Korea was either trying to build a bomb or trying to gain international legitimacy through a dangerous game of nuclear brinkmanship, *or both*—but who could tell?

If Pyongyang's nuclear intentions were difficult to divine, the stakes for peace on the Korean peninsula, stability in Northeast Asia, and the viability of the international nonproliferation regime could not have been more clear. A nuclear North Korea, with its history of belligerence and terrorist acts, would have posed an even greater threat to its neighbors. It would have vastly increased South Korea's insecurity and likely prompted a similar effort to build nuclear weapons, thereby triggering a nuclear arms race on the Korean peninsula. Although Japan's antinuclear culture and domestic laws would most likely have inhibited a response in kind, Tokyo would have invested greater sums on conventional defense (and probably bought a measure of security by appeasing North Korea). A second Korean war, even without the use of nuclear weapons, would have overturned four decades of remarkable economic strides by the South and resulted in enormous military and civilian casualties.

The stakes in North Korea extended well beyond the region. The possibility that Pyongyang could export its nuclear know-how and bomb material around the world, especially to the volatile Middle East, was unnerving. Pyongyang already conducted a flourishing arms trade by peddling its ballistic missile technology; these sales, to-taling an estimated $500 million a year, were the leading source of hard currency for the Kim Il Sung regime. Nuclear material and technology would have brought a premium price.

Also at risk was the credibility of the IAEA and its system of safeguards to monitor the nuclear activities of its members. Revelations after the Persian Gulf war of Iraq's covert nuclear weapons program greatly embarrassed the IAEA. The IAEA had a similar responsibility in North Korea, which had (belatedly) agreed in 1992 to allow international inspections.

Coming on the heels of the discovery in Iraq, a failure by North Korea to fully live up to its safeguards obligations would severely undermine the IAEA's role as the world's nuclear watchdog. Further, it would raise doubts about the future of the international nonproliferation regime on the eve of the NPT review and extension conference in April 1995. It would vastly complicate U.S. efforts to persuade a majority of NPT members at the conference to endorse the unconditional and indefinite extension of the treaty, the centerpiece of global efforts to halt the spread of nuclear arms. And it would increase the threat that other NPT members whose commitment to nonproliferation was uncertain at best—Iraq, Iran, and Libya—might follow North Korea's lead and leave the treaty.

North Korea's Nuclear Program

The United States—because of its long-standing commitment to non-proliferation, its strategic interests in Asia, and its support for South Korea, evidenced most visibly by the stationing of U.S. troops in the country—had primary responsibility for dealing with the North Korean nuclear problem. Washington had long monitored North Korea's nuclear activities, which dated from the mid-1950s.[2] But it was not until the early 1980s that the United States became troubled by the North's nuclear program. At that time, Washington identified the construction of a small, 30MW(t) nuclear reactor[3] at Yongbyon, sixty miles north of Pyongyang and one hundred miles north of the demilitarized zone dividing North and South. The United States asked Moscow to lean on North Korea to join the NPT and place this facility under international safeguards. North Korea duly joined the NPT on December 12, 1985, partially motivated by Moscow's promise of four nuclear power reactors.[4] A safeguards agreement with the IAEA should have been signed within eighteen months, by mid-1987, but the IAEA sent the wrong document, and it was not until June 1987 that Pyongyang obtained the correct version. Nonetheless, the DPRK still failed to conclude the agreement.

In January 1986, North Korea had begun operating the 30MW Yongbyon reactor.[5] From U.S. reconnaissance photographs, the reactor appeared ambitious for the type of research program thought most suitable for North Korea; it looked like a scale model of the Calder Hall reactor in Britain, a natural-uranium, graphite-moderated reactor whose low burn-up rate could produce a high proportion of plutonium–239 in its spent fuel.[6] North Korea could obtain the natural uranium and graphite for the reactor locally; there was no need for imported heavy water or enriched uranium.

The North also began construction of a 200MW(t) reactor at Yongbyon and a 600–800MW(t) reactor near Taechon in the northwestern corner of the country. When completed, the 200MW reactor could produce enough spent fuel for 40 to 55 kilograms of plutonium per year; the 600–800MW reactor could produce annually between 140 and 180 kilograms of plutonium. Together, this was enough plutonium for up to forty-five nuclear bombs a year.

To build nuclear bombs, North Korea also needed a way to chemically extract the plutonium from the spent nuclear fuel. In 1988, the United States saw evidence of a new facility at Yongbyon. Extrapolating from its size, Washington estimated that when fully operational, this reprocessing plant would be able to treat up to several hundred tons of spent fuel per year, a capacity that could handle all the spent fuel from the North's three indigenously built reactors.[7] The identification of a high-explosive testing range near the Yongbyon nuclear complex completed the picture. After the demise of the Soviet Union, U.S. intelligence also uncovered evidence of a systematic North Korean effort to recruit nuclear scientists and engineers from the former Soviet Union.[8]

Putting the pieces of the North Korean nuclear puzzle together had been the easy part. The real challenge was how to block North Korea from acquiring nuclear weapons.

Diplomatic Maneuvering, 1988–1991

From the very beginning, the North Korean nuclear problem could not be settled simply as a discrete issue divorced from larger considerations. With the changing political dynamics of Northeast Asia after the cold war and with the increasing focus of the outside world, especially the United States, on the North's nuclear activities, Pyongyang realized that it could play its nuclear card to fashion the larger political engagement it sought.

THE BUSH ADMINISTRATION'S STRATEGY

After one war and decades of mutual hatred and recriminations, on July 7, 1988, South Korean President Roh Tae Woo extended an olive branch to North Korea. Roh announced that Seoul would cooperate with Pyongyang in helping it improve relations with the United States and Japan and would not oppose trade with the North by the South's allies, as long as this trade excluded military equipment. The immediate motivation behind Roh's "Nordpolitik" was his desire that North Korea not upstage the Olympic Games that Seoul was about to host that summer.

That fall the United States, in close coordination with South Korea, quietly undertook small steps to increase the overall level of engagement between two countries that were technically still at war. In October 1988, Washington encouraged visits to the United States by North Korean academics and eased restrictions on visits to the DPRK by U.S. citizens. It also permitted the export to North Korea of U.S. goods that met "basic human needs."

The most important step was opening diplomatic contacts with North Korea in Beijing. From these meetings, the Bush administration decided to move forward by outlining five "conditions" that North Korea needed to satisfy before bilateral relations could improve further: (1) tone down the anti-U.S. rhetoric; (2) halt all terrorist activities; (3) help with returning the remains of the more than eight thousand U.S. servicemen missing in action (MIAs) from the Korean War; (4) engage in a dialogue with the South; and (5) agree to IAEA safeguards on all its nuclear activities. [9] The U.S. strategy was intended to slowly coax North Korea into a broader engagement with the outside world and compel Pyongyang to be a reasonable and responsible international actor.

During the next few years, the DPRK responded positively. Pyongyang cooled down its anti-U.S. diatribes. In 1991, the North publicly stated that it opposed all forms of terrorism and would cooperate with international efforts to stop terrorist acts. [10] The first remains of MIAs had been returned the year before. In a significant step, North-South talks between the prime ministers had begun in September 1988; these implied Pyongyang's recognition of the legitimacy of the South Korean government, which it had previously ridiculed as a puppet and colonial appendage of the United States. [11]

The nuclear issue was more problematic. North Korea insisted on two preconditions before it would sign a safeguards agreement: the removal of U.S. nuclear weapons from South Korea; and a "negative security assurance" that the United States would not use nuclear weapons against it. This linkage suggested that Pyongyang understood that the value Washington attached to independent certification of North Korea's nuclear bona fides gave it some bargaining leverage. [12]

In fact, Washington had grown increasingly worried over the North's nuclear program. In spring 1989, North Korea shut down the 30MW reactor for approximately three months, and anxieties multiplied that Pyongyang had removed some nuclear fuel rods from the core. A National Intelligence Estimate at the time concluded that North Korea was trying to develop nuclear weapons, a judgment that South Korean authorities had already made. New satellite photographs showed a building that looked suspiciously like a spent-fuel reprocessing facility at the Yongbyon nuclear complex. [13]

During the next two years, Washington watched as the Yongbyon nuclear complex expanded to more than one hundred buildings. By 1991, the nuclear issue overwhelmed all the other issues on the U.S. agenda with North Korea. From analyzing satellite photos of the Yongbyon nuclear complex, the United States thought that Pyongyang could separate significant amounts of weapons-grade plutonium within a few years, and it delivered this message to U.S. allies. In June 1991, ROK President Roh stated that the North had conducted tests of the nonnuclear components of nuclear devices at Yongbyon. North Korea denied these charges and explained that its 30MW reactor was part of its civilian energy program. The justification rang hollow, since the Yongbyon reactor contained no electrical lines or transformers.

This unwanted attention coincided with a number of setbacks to Pyongyang's diplomacy in 1990 and 1991. The historic meeting between Mikhail Gorbachev and South Korean President Roh in San Francisco in June 1990 quickened the downturn in Soviet–North Korean relations. [14] In September 1990, Soviet Foreign Minister Eduard Shevardnadze pressured Pyongyang to sign the safeguards agreement. At this meeting, DPRK Foreign Minister Kim Young-nam darkly warned that North Korea would embark on a "nuclear development" program if Moscow further improved ties to Seoul and that it would recognize Japan's claims to four northern islands occupied by the So-

viet Union.[15] Moscow, in turn, threatened to cut off all nuclear cooperation if the North's nuclear facilities were not placed under IAEA safeguards, a threat it repeated during the coming months.[16] Despite
North Korea's bluster, Moscow and Seoul established diplomatic relations at the end of September. Adding insult to injury, three weeks
later, China and South Korea agreed to open trade offices in each
other's capitals.

In early 1991, after receiving word from Moscow and Beijing that
they would no longer block South Korea from entering the United Nations, Pyongyang announced that it would "reluctantly" seek separate
UN membership with South Korea, reversing its previous insistence
that there was only one Korea. At this time, Japan informed the DPRK
that it would not establish diplomatic relations, provide reparations
for its occupation of Korea before World War II, offer financial assistance, or permit Japanese investment until the North implemented
IAEA inspections.[17]

In mid-July 1991, North Korea finally initialed a safeguards agreement in Vienna and was expected to formally sign it at the IAEA's
General Conference that September. But a conference resolution urging North Korea to sign and implement the agreement upset this plan,
since Pyongyang refused to "lose face" by appearing to publicly succumb to international pressure.

It was not pressure but rather the Bush administration's unilateral
"inducement" that moved the process forward again. On September 27,
1991, President Bush declared that the United States would withdraw
from overseas all deployments of ground- and sea-launched tactical nuclear weapons. The policy was primarily aimed at influencing Moscow
to collect all the tactical nuclear weapons from the non-Russian Soviet
republics, but it also captured U.S. nuclear weapons stationed in South
Korea, long a central concern of the North. When Pyongyang continued
to delay signing the safeguards agreement, Washington sweetened the
deal in mid-October by announcing that it would remove all air-
launched nuclear weapons from South Korea.[18]

South Korea did not stand still waiting for the North's decision. In a
move that would have important implications during the next year,
Washington at this time recommended that South Korea raise in the
ongoing prime ministerial talks the issue of "trial inspections" of nuclear facilities. The idea of a highly intrusive bilateral inspection
regime, with short-notice "challenge" inspections, quickly gained a
life of its own.[19] Washington promoted this regime as a complement,
or alternative, to IAEA safeguards. In Washington's eyes, the IAEA
had been discredited by the disclosures of Iraq's secret nuclear

weapons effort. A North-South inspection regime, with powers like those that the UN Special Commission used to expose and eliminate Baghdad's nuclear weapons capabilities, had much more appeal.

In addition, Roh decided to remove another reason the DPRK had cited for resisting a safeguards agreement. On November 8, the South Korean president stated that Seoul would "use nuclear energy strictly for peaceful purposes" and would not "manufacture, possess, store, deploy, or use nuclear weapons" or "possess nuclear fuel reprocessing and uranium enrichment facilities."[20] Roh called on the North to do likewise.

By offering these inducements at a time when fears over Pyongyang's nuclear ambitions were coming into sharper focus, Washington and Seoul were acting with great confidence. But within the Bush administration there were also skeptical voices arguing that the United States and South Korea were moving too far, too fast. Partly for that reason, on November 21, Secretary of Defense Richard Cheney decided to suspend the second phase of U.S. troop reductions in Korea, which were scheduled to start in 1993, "until the dangers and uncertainties of the North Korean nuclear program" had been "thoroughly addressed."[21]

THE FALSE DAWN: DECEMBER 1991–JANUARY 1992

The pace of nuclear diplomacy accelerated in December. On December 11, the United States and the ROK said that they would allow the North to inspect any civilian or military sites in South Korea in return for reciprocal inspection rights.[22] Two days later, the North-South prime ministerial meetings finally bore fruit when the two parties signed an Agreement on Reconciliation, Nonaggression, and Exchanges and Cooperation between the South and the North.[23] This agreement consisted of a number of sweeping and quite general statements calling for unprecedented cooperation across a range of issues. At a time when citizens in both countries could not even exchange postcards, the agreement was more a goodwill gesture than a road map for the future of the peninsula. Notably, it did not cover the nuclear issue.

On December 18, in a nationally televised speech, Roh announced, "There do not exist any nuclear weapons whatsoever, anywhere in the Republic of Korea."[24] At a later press conference with Roh, President Bush stated that the United States had a "neither confirm nor deny" policy. But he added, "[I] heard what Roh said and I'm not about to argue with him." The message was clear: there were no longer any U.S. nuclear weapons in South Korea.

On December 31, North and South Korea reached an agreement on a Joint Declaration on a Non-Nuclear Korean Peninsula. This "Joint Denuclearization Declaration" stipulated that the two parties would "not test, manufacture, produce, introduce, possess, store, deploy, or use nuclear weapons" and that they would "not possess facilities for nuclear reprocessing and uranium enrichment." These pledges went further than any other arms control agreement in history and far exceeded what was required by the NPT and the IAEA safeguards agreement.[25] The two Koreas deferred the thorny details of an inspection regime to a Joint Nuclear Control Commission (JNCC), which would be established one month after the declaration entered into force.

In early January 1992, after consultations with Washington, the ROK informed the North that it was prepared to suspend the annual Team Spirit '92 joint military exercise with the United States if Pyongyang signed the IAEA safeguards agreement. The South explained that suspension the following year depended on establishing and implementing an effective bilateral inspection regime.[26] On January 7, the South Korean Defense Ministry announced that Team Spirit '92 was canceled; North Korea that same day announced only that it would sign the IAEA safeguards agreement "in the near future."[27]

Even though Pyongyang had not yet signed the safeguards agreement, the Bush administration decided that it would also grant North Korea one meeting with a senior U.S. official, a goal that Pyongyang had long sought. On January 22, Arnold Kanter, the under secretary of state for political affairs, met in New York, at the U.S. Mission to the United Nations, with Kim Yong Sun, the Korean Workers Party (KWP) secretary for international affairs. Kanter's assignment was to clarify to North Korea the preconditions for normalization of U.S.-DPRK relations.[28] These preconditions included the implementation of the IAEA safeguards agreement *and* the bilateral inspection regime; both were required because of Washington's qualms over the effectiveness of IAEA safeguards. Kim promised that North Korea would sign the safeguards agreement by the end of January and would also implement a bilateral inspection regime in accordance with the Joint Denuclearization Declaration.[29]

On January 30, North Korea signed the IAEA safeguards agreement. As if to prove that nothing could come easily, Pyongyang warned that inspections might be delayed because ratification of the agreement by the Supreme People's Assembly (the DPRK's parliament) could take several months.[30] The assembly finally gave its consent on April 9, 1992, and the agreement entered into force the next day. The IAEA and, by extension, the international community now had a more solid legal basis against which North Korea's compliance with its nuclear obligations could be measured. Whether Pyongyang's commitments were firm enough to actually permit inspections would be severely tested in the years ahead.

With the Joint Denuclearization Declaration, South Korea also had an agreement with the North for a nonnuclear Korean peninsula. But the Roh government wanted to move beyond a narrow focus on this issue and discuss a larger agenda with Pyongyang, especially commercial ties. Nuclear matters should not hold hostage the broad range of issues the two Koreas needed to discuss, Seoul argued. Besides, the nuclear issue could be resolved more readily as part of a broader political and economic engagement with Pyongyang. In early 1992, South Korea quietly began taking preliminary steps for what would have been an unprecedented summit between Presidents Roh and Kim Il Sung.

Preparations did not advance far, largely because of opposition to Roh's idea within his own government. Roh pushed harder a few months later, after some of the North-South mechanisms envisioned in the December agreements, such as the JNCC, had taken shape. But the Bush administration strongly objected. Despite its own successful track record of making unilateral inducements to stimulate progress with North Korea—modifying its "neither confirm nor deny" nuclear stance, canceling Team Spirit '92, and arranging a high-level meeting in New York with North Korea, all before the DPRK had signed the IAEA safeguards agreement—the United States insisted that South Korea should craft a bilateral inspection regime before moving on to other matters. Washington "put tremendous pressure" on Seoul to end its summit plans and stick to the script. Reluctantly, Seoul complied.[31]

Within two years, however, the United States and South Korea would swap positions, with Washington wanting a broader dialogue between the two Koreas and with Seoul resisting.

Inspection Regimes: Walking down a Dual Track

By spring 1992, North Korea's nuclear diplomacy was clearly part of a larger political engagement with the outside world. Its initiative to normalize relations with Japan, the reconciliation agreement with the South, the denuclearization pledge and establishment of the JNCC to implement bilateral inspections, the signing of the IAEA safeguards agreement, and its eagerness to deal directly with the United States were all striking departures from its previous habitual practice of hostility and paranoia.

The reasons for this change went beyond Pyongyang's eroding position on the diplomatic chess board. Indicators suggested that the North's economy was in dire straits. From 1990 to 1992, North Korea's GNP contracted annually between 3 and 5 percent. During this same period, its trade volume declined by almost 50 percent. Hampered by a severe energy shortage, factories were operating at half-speed. Pyongyang reasoned that greater openness and flexibility could result in financial assistance from the United States, South Korea, and Japan to revive the flagging economy.[32]

Yet this did not necessarily mean that the DPRK was on its last legs and could be squeezed economically into making concessions on its nuclear program. According to one experienced North Korea watcher at the American embassy in Seoul: "There are a lot more notches on their belt. Their entire economy was set up to be independent, which it largely is. There may have been a dip lately, but the people are still better off now than they were ten, twenty, or thirty years ago."[33]

The Bush administration decided at this time not to talk further with the North until there was measurable progress on nuclear inspections. Influencing this stance was increasing alarm over the North's nuclear weapons program,[34] Washington's belief that it had already made too many concessions or that North Korea had not responded adequately or quickly enough to them, and the sense that the North's need for outside assistance suggested that time was on the side of the United States. For now, Washington was content to let the IAEA and Seoul carry the ball.

THE BLIX VISIT

On May 4, 1992, North Korea handed to the IAEA's director general, Hans Blix, its initial declaration of nuclear materials and facilities. This document, which was required by the safeguards agreement it had ratified the previous month, listed the country's nuclear reactors and the reprocessing plant at Yongbyon. In an encouraging sign, Pyongyang provided more information than was technically required (including over a dozen nuclear sites that had been previously unknown) and provided the document well before the deadline.

The IAEA's mission was to confirm that the initial declaration was accurate and complete. The agency would conduct what amounted to a nuclear audit by inspecting the nuclear facilities on the list and obtaining an inventory of all nuclear materials. This type of inspection was termed "ad hoc." Once the agency verified that nuclear activities conformed to the initial declaration, the IAEA would conduct less intrusive "routine" inspections according to specific "facility attachments." A third type of procedure, termed "special" inspections, could be invoked to grant the IAEA access to sites not identified in a state's initial declaration. Only rarely had the IAEA used this extraordinary measure—in effect, a nuclear hunting license.[35]

Before the first ad hoc inspections took place, Blix accepted Pyongyang's invitation to visit North Korea in mid-May. Blix toured extensively and was the first Western visitor to the Yongbyon reprocessing plant, a massive structure six hundred feet long and six stories high. The North Koreans told him that the plant was 80 percent completed but that only 40 percent of the equipment had been installed. They called it a "radiochemical laboratory" and said that it did not violate the terms of the December 1991 Joint Denuclearization Declaration because it had been used only on a limited test basis and was not a fully fledged reprocessing plant.[36]

During Blix's visit, North Korean officials admitted that they had reprocessed about ninety grams of plutonium in "hot tests" at this lab in March 1990. This plutonium had allegedly come from damaged fuel rods that had been removed from the 30MW reactor and then chemically dissolved; according to the IAEA, the rods did not contain enough fissile material for a nuclear device.[37]

More disconcerting to Blix was the progression of North Korea's reprocessing capabilities. Countries typically advance from hot cells (lead-shielded rooms with remote-handling equipment) to a larger "pilot plant" facility to an industrial-scale plant, such as the Yongbyon "radiochemical laboratory." Blix commented: "The timetable of the operations and the industrial logic seemed to suggest that a small pilot plant should have preceded the 'Radiological Laboratory.' The existence of any such pilot plant was categorically denied by the DPRK."[38] Still, the possibility of a secret reprocessing facility in North Korea would continue to trouble the IAEA and the United States.[39]

Blix also requested the right to conduct inspections at sites that were not on the DPRK's initial declaration. The North Koreans balked at the word "inspections," so Blix asked for "visits," which were granted. Blix was subsequently allowed to tour a military site.[40] The director general suggested that granting this right to IAEA inspectors would create greater transparency and defuse international suspicions. North Korean officials protested this infringement of their sovereignty, so Blix then proposed that the DPRK issue a standing invitation, perhaps not to "inspectors" but to "officials" of the IAEA, to visit any site or installation. Pyongyang agreed. The press release issued on Blix's departure stated, "With a view to creating transparency and confidence, officials of the agency are invited to visit any site and installation they wish to see, irrespective of whether it was found on the initial list submitted to the IAEA."[41] International inspections, which began at the end of May, would test that proposition.

THE NORTH'S INTERNATIONAL POSITION WORSENS

Meanwhile, international pressure on North Korea to adhere to its nuclear obligations continued. At the June 1992 summit between Russian President Yeltsin and U.S. President Bush, the two sides issued a joint statement calling on the DPRK to fully comply with "its obligations under the NPT and Joint Declaration, including IAEA safeguards as well as credible and effective bilateral nuclear inspections."[42] The twelve member states of the European Community informed North Korea in June that preconditions for improving relations were IAEA inspections and a bilateral inspection regime.[43] This message was repeated in July in the final statement of the G-7 members at the Munich summit and again later that month by the foreign ministers of the Association of Southeast Asian Nations (ASEAN).[44]

On August 24, 1992, China and South Korea established diplomatic relations, a heavy blow that eliminated any remaining chance that North Korea could engineer cross-recognition with the United States and Japan. Before taking this step, Beijing had told Pyongyang that recognition of South Korea would not affect their 1961 friendship and cooperation agreement and that China would guarantee the continued existence of North Korea. But North Korea would have to abandon its nuclear weapons development program, a move that it reportedly promised to make.[45]

Pyongyang received more bad news three months later. During a visit to Seoul, Yeltsin declared that Russia would halt all military assistance to North Korea. He also stated that the 1961 Russia-DPRK defense pact, which called for automatic intervention in the case of war, needed to be "either canceled completely or drastically revised." He added bluntly, "We do not intend to render such military assistance."[46] It was also announced that Russia would not resume nuclear cooperation with the North until Pyongyang fully implemented IAEA safeguards. Pyongyang denounced the policy change as a "foolish and despicable act."[47]

THE JNCC TALKS—GOING NOWHERE

While IAEA inspections continued, Washington pushed Seoul to conclude the bilateral inspection regime. The two Koreas had established
the Joint Nuclear Control Commission (JNCC) in March 1992 with a
mandate to create an inspection regime that could "verify the denuclearization of the Korean peninsula." They quickly agreed to conduct
the first bilateral inspections by mid-June.[48]

Given that the two sides had absolutely no experience in creating
and implementing any form of inspection regime, that the agreements
they had signed provided little guidance, and that their relationship
was still characterized by mutual suspicion, if not rampant hostility, it
was hardly surprising that discussions soon bogged down.[49] But signs
of progress occurred in September 1992. By this time, moderate elements in the Roh government had realized that settlement of the nuclear issue should precede any movement on the economic front. The
North-South prime ministerial talks in mid-month went well, resulting in three agreements implementing their December 13 Nonaggression and Reconciliation Agreement. President Roh publicly downgraded the threat posed by the North's nuclear program, saying on
September 17 that the North's "determination to develop nuclear
weapons" had "become weaker."[50] In the JNCC talks, the two sides
outlined an organizational format for the inspection regime and
agreed to discuss treaty language at their next meeting in October. The
South also indicated greater flexibility on challenge inspections.[51]

The hard-liners in Seoul (and Washington) had been chased from
the field—but not for long. At the end of September, South Korea's
Agency for National Security Planning (the successor to the Korean
CIA) uncovered a North Korean spy ring operating in the ROK.[52] The
brief warming trend in North-South relations abruptly cooled.

More permanent damage, though, occurred a week later. On October 8, a communiqué issued at the end of the annual ROK-U.S. Security Consultative Meeting (SCM) declared that the two countries had
agreed in principle to conduct the Team Spirit '93 military exercise.
Seoul calculated that the announcement would give it added bargaining leverage in the JNCC talks, especially on challenge inspections.[53]
Pyongyang reacted harshly, despite assurances that a final decision on
Team Spirit would depend on whether bilateral inspections took place
by the end of the year. The DPRK threatened "to suspend the peace
process" if this military exercise was conducted. Discussions in the
JNCC during the next three months failed to resolve any of the outstanding issues.

Until the end of January 1993, Washington and Seoul remained willing to cancel Team Spirit in return for progress on bilateral inspections. While IAEA officials were conducting ad hoc inspections, including visits to facilities not even listed on North Korea's initial declaration, the United States had started to rethink the wisdom of a policy that featured the North-South regime as its centerpiece. To officials at the Pentagon, the State Department, and the White House, insistence on a highly intrusive bilateral regime as a first step now seemed like overreaching. They also acknowledged that bilateral inspections would not provide much confidence on a technical basis because of the inadequate training and inexperience of South Korean inspectors and predicted that Washington would abandon the policy within a few months.[54] With the JNCC talks going nowhere, the IAEA inspections that Washington had belittled during the past two years now started to look more promising.

The North Ups the Ante

Kim Il Sung's address on New Year's Day 1993 was notable for what it did not say: nothing about the country's anti-Fascist campaign, nothing about the newly elected South Korean president, and nothing about the United States, even though 1993 marked the fortieth anniversary of the end of the Korean War. Overall, the speech was designed to send a conciliatory message to both Seoul and Washington. Not even the "Great Leader" could have anticipated the turmoil the coming year would bring.

IAEA INSPECTIONS: TENSIONS BREW

During much of 1992, the IAEA quietly went about its business in North Korea. Construction at the "radiochemical laboratory" had halted. The North responded positively to the IAEA's request for permission to visit any site, even ones not listed on the initial declaration; in other words, it granted permission to conduct special inspections. In September, inspection of one such site was "limited to the visible part of what appeared to be a one-story building under military control," according to a later IAEA report. This site had "an additional below-ground level which was not visited."[55]

"Building 500," as U.S. intelligence labeled it, was in fact one of two sites that Pyongyang had tried to hide from international inspectors. In winter 1991, satellite photographs had shown North Korean workers digging trenches and laying pipes in the frozen earth between the reprocessing plant and the lower level of Building 500. The fear was that North Korea could secretly remove nuclear waste and store it here, beyond the prying eyes of international inspectors. Pyongyang also tried to disguise the location of an older nuclear storage site by covering it over with dirt and landscaping the area. The IAEA estimated that the two sites contained four thousand cubic meters of liquid nuclear waste.[56]

The IAEA had also been disturbed by the results of its laboratory analysis of the few grams of plutonium that the DPRK had admitted separating in 1990. An isotopic examination of the nuclear waste generated in separating this plutonium showed discrepancies with the timing and the number of batches processed. As an IAEA report later explained, "Impurities in the plutonium actually showed that it had been produced in three separate batches over three years."[57] This proved not only that North Korea had lied about its nuclear activities but, more important, that it had accumulated more plutonium than it had acknowledged.

To confirm its suspicions, the IAEA took smear samples from the glove boxes inside the hot cells to find a decay product of one of the plutonium isotopes. Over time, a plutonium isotope, plutonium-241, decays into americium-241, which should not have been present in the glove box when the plutonium given to the IAEA was originally separated. The americium-241 therefore acted as a clock that could indicate when the separation had happened. In analyzing these samples, the IAEA found evidence that North Korea had conducted three separate processing campaigns: in 1989, 1990, and 1991.[58]

The IAEA was still operating under a cloud because of its perceived failures in Iraq, and it was going to make sure that its handling of North Korea was beyond reproach. Its experience with South Africa, which had cooperated fully on over seventy-five inspections since signing a safeguards agreement in September 1991, also provided a standard of cooperation against which the North would be judged.

In late November 1992, the IAEA started to turn up the pressure. Blix accused North Korea of not declaring all of its nuclear facilities. At the December Board of Governors meeting, the IAEA refused to accept Pyongyang's excuse that inspections could not go forward if the Team Spirit military exercise was held. Blix requested that the IAEA be allowed to "'visit,' drill, and take samples" (he was careful not to use the word "inspect") at the two undeclared sites. He promised to handle the matter quietly. The DPRK rejected his request.

A sixth ad hoc inspection took place in January 1993, however. During this visit, IAEA inspectors requested clarifications regarding the inconsistencies that had turned up during their previous inspections. They again requested permission to visit the two nuclear waste sites at Yongbyon.[59] Once more, both requests were turned down.

After months of DPRK denials and obstruction, Blix and the IAEA had run out of patience. On February 9, 1993, Blix issued an unprecedented request to conduct special inspections and gave North Korea ten days to respond before he would refer the matter to the Board of Governors. He did not have to wait that long. Four days later, Pyongyang officially refused, saying that these sites were nonnuclear military facilities and off-limits to inspections. Blix now referred the matter to the Board of Governors, which was scheduled to meet on February 21.

TAKING STOCK IN PYONGYANG

Complicating the IAEA's diplomacy was the opaque nature of the North Korean regime and the difficulty in understanding not only how decisions were made but also who made them. Most observers perceived a rough division of North Korean policy elites into two factions: "hard-liners" and "pragmatists." The hard-liners included leading elements from the armed services and perhaps Kim Il Sung and Kim Jong Il. They were thought to be the primary backers of the nuclear weapons program, which they viewed not as a bargaining chip but as a symbol of the country's independence and a guarantee that the regime would not perish.[60]

On the other side, the pragmatists consisted of those posted abroad or studying overseas in the late 1980s during the revolutions in Eastern Europe and the Soviet Union, as well as those who had visited South Korea on diplomatic missions during the past few years of warming North-South relations. (In a masterly propaganda stroke, Seoul gave visiting North Korean delegations cameras and video camcorders as welcoming gifts so that they could record the sights and sounds of the South to show their friends and colleagues when they returned home.) These North Korean elites fully appreciated the dynamism in the South as compared with their own economic straits. This group reportedly viewed the nuclear weapons program as an obstacle to better relations with the outside world and was willing to discard it for the right price. Which of these two groups was more influential at any one time was difficult to know.[61]

The diplomatic engagement North Korea had embarked on in late 1990 suggested that the pragmatists had assumed the upper hand. Yet by the beginning of 1993, what could they point to as a result of their efforts? To be sure, the United States had withdrawn all nuclear weapons from South Korea, and the Team Spirit '92 exercise had been canceled. But the U.S. nuclear umbrella was still in place, and the second phase of the planned U.S. troop reductions had been suspended. The JNCC talks had broken down. And the dispute with the IAEA had reached an impasse. Further, Team Spirit '93 was going forward. South Korea cited the inspection issue when it announced on January 25, 1993, that the joint military training exercise would take place in mid-March with 120,000 troops, including 50,000 from United States.[62] North Korea was stunned by the announcement.[63]

The other side of the ledger looked no better. North Korea had been unable to normalize relations with either Japan or the United States and had been unable to stop the Soviet Union and China from establishing diplomatic relations with South Korea. The anticipated flow of foreign investments and loans had so far completely failed to materialize. Worse, Japan, the United States, and South Korea had tied diplomatic normalization and financial assistance to the North's first establishing a bilateral inspection regime and receiving a clean bill of health from the IAEA. Pyongyang suspected that even if these issues could be settled, others lurked in the wings—ballistic missile exports, chemical weapons, and human rights.[64] Some may have thought that nothing short of a fundamental transformation of the North Korean regime would satisfy the United States. When viewed from Pyongyang, the realization of North Korea's objectives remained as distant as ever. It was about to recede further.

FEBRUARY 1993: TENSIONS SIMMER

On January 20, 1993, President Bush handed the North Korean nuclear problem off to Bill Clinton. The new Clinton administration, more interested in the economy and a sweeping domestic agenda, inherited a diplomatic strategy toward the North that was stuck in midstream. The preferred course, a tough bilateral inspection regime, had failed. The second choice, the IAEA, had succeeded in uncovering unambiguous evidence that North Korea had cheated, but it was unable to force Pyongyang to come clean about its nuclear activities.

The negotiations with North Korea were entering a new and much more complex phase. The problem was about to become a crisis, and Clinton's national security team was almost completely unprepared for the challenges ahead. During the next few years, the United States not only had to bring North Korea back into the fold but also had to keep on board key countries—such as South Korea, Japan, and China—that had similar but not necessarily identical interests on the

Korean peninsula. At times, discussions among all these parties were taking place simultaneously. More than once, this resulted in missed signals, botched communications, and more than a little confusion among the thirty different sets of ongoing negotiations and consultations.

This Rube Goldberg diplomatic process severely taxed the Clinton administration and at times overwhelmed it. As its lodestar, three fundamental assumptions guided Washington. First, there was a mutually acceptable deal out there: if only the right incentives could be found, the United States and North Korea could "get to yes." Second, the Clinton administration had the credibility and resourcefulness to keep its allies in line and win China's backing for U.S. diplomatic efforts. And third, North Korea would stick to any deal that was negotiated. The next few years would raise doubts about all three assumptions.

With North Korea's refusal to accept special inspections, the Clinton administration's first decision centered on the IAEA Board of Governors meeting in late February. Not only had the Blix visit in May 1992 and six subsequent ad hoc inspections failed to eliminate suspicions surrounding North Korea's nuclear program, but information from these inspections and other sources cast further doubt on the benign nature of Pyongyang's nuclear activities. For some time, the IAEA had been directed in its sleuthing by intelligence information provided by the United States. Blix now requested, from Washington, slides of overhead reconnaissance photos of the Yongbyon nuclear complex to show the governors. Blix saw this evidence as essential to convince the board members, a group of technically unsophisticated career diplomats and political appointees, that North Korea was cheating. The first set of U.S. slides of Yongbyon were too fuzzy to be useful (due to objections from the U.S. intelligence community about revealing its snooping capabilities), but the second set improved after the U.S. Mission to the IAEA and the IAEA itself requested that Washington provide the same degree of resolution as in commercially available Landsat photos.

Blix choreographed the February 22 meeting beautifully.[65] First, an analyst presented the IAEA's technical findings. Then Blix announced that there would be a slide show, which started immediately. Sven Thorstensen, one of the senior officials in the IAEA's Safeguards Division, interpreted each slide as it flashed on the screen. Especially valuable was his comment that early photos of Building 500 looked exactly like those of a nuclear waste site he had personally visited in Europe. The slides showed that Building 500 had been constructed from scratch only a year before the inspectors' first visits, and they refuted the North Korean claim that the building had served as a military installation for the past fifteen years. The photographs also documented other efforts by Pyongyang to deceive the inspectors.

There was total silence when the slide show was finished. The first to speak was the DPRK representative to the IAEA. He claimed that the slides had been fabricated by the United States and cited the movie *Star Wars* as evidence of American high-tech sleight-of-hand. The sites were military and nonnuclear and would not be opened for inspection, he asserted. The North Korean response impressed no one.[66]

On February 25, the Board of Governors adopted by consensus a mild resolution that called on North Korea "without delay" to permit the "full and prompt implementation of the safeguards agreement," including the information and access Blix had requested on February 9.[67] The board decided not to refer the matter to the UN Security Council, a much more serious step that could have led to economic sanctions. Due largely to China's position that the North ought not to be cornered, the board asked the director general to report back within thirty days, effectively giving North Korea that period to comply with the resolution.[68] North Korea rejected the board's demand the very next day, labeling the resolution an infringement of its sovereignty and stating ominously that it might have to adopt "self-defensive measures" to safeguard its sovereignty.[69]

The North may have thought that it could intimidate two newcomers on the international scene: Kim Young Sam, a former dissident who had recently been elected South Korea's first civilian prime minister and who assumed the presidency on February 25, 1993;[70] and Bill Clinton, the first Democrat in the White House since Jimmy Carter, who had proposed the unilateral withdrawal of U.S. troops from South Korea in his first few months in office. The North probably wanted to take the measure of the new presidents, especially Clinton, and see if Washington would now be more pliable than before. As a first test, it soon raised the stakes.

THE NPT WITHDRAWAL SCARE

Team Spirit '93 started on March 9. Pyongyang reacted as it had before, ritually denouncing the exercise as "nuclear war maneuvers" and placing the country on "semi–war alert status."[71] What was not traditional was the North's surprising announcement three days later. On March 12, North Korea declared that it was withdrawing from the NPT.[72] Citing the "grave situation" created by Team Spirit and the

February 25 resolution demanding special inspections "on the basis of the intelligence information fabricated by the United States," the DPRK gave three months' notice, in accordance with NPT procedures.[73] That same day, the North Korean ambassador in China warned that his country would adopt a "strong defensive counter-measure" if sanctions were imposed.[74]

The North's unprecedented move shocked the international community. South Korean President Kim immediately placed his military on high-level alert. Yet neither President Clinton nor Secretary of State Warren Christopher made any public gesture of support to calm Seoul's jitters.[75]

North Korea was playing a high-stakes game of nuclear brinkmanship and seemed to have gauged the situation perfectly. Instead of being on the defensive and under the shadow of an IAEA deadline, overnight it had generated substantial bargaining leverage for itself. It gambled that the importance the international community, especially the United States, attached to the NPT would force Washington and Seoul to begin addressing the North's agenda of political and economic issues. Insisting on special inspections and clarifying "inconsistencies" in the North Korean nuclear program had now become secondary to keeping Pyongyang in the treaty.

The world had ninety days to persuade North Korea to return to the NPT. But the "sticks" in a "carrots-and-sticks" approach were problematic. For all its nervousness over the North's nuclear program, South Korea was even more nervous about pushing Pyongyang too far. The dual nature of South Korean behavior—unyielding when the U.S. dialogue with North Korea went well and compliant when the situation deteriorated—would become a familiar and frustrating fact of life to American diplomats.[76]

Further, China publicly opposed instituting harsh measures against North Korea or even bringing the matter before the UN Security Council, where China could veto any sanctions resolution. More generally, at a time when the Clinton administration was trumpeting the link between the extension of most-favored-nation (MFN) trading status and China's human rights practices, Beijing was reluctant to endorse the legitimacy of any outside actor's using sanctions to coerce another state. In late March, Chinese Foreign Minister Qian Qichen made clear Beijing's position: "We support patient consultations to reach an appropriate solution. If the matter goes before the Security Council, that will only complicate things."[77]

The primary question was what carrots would be offered, and North Korea did not have to wait very long to find out. On March 30, the

Washington Post reported that the United States and South Korea had agreed to a conciliatory approach. ROK Foreign Minister Han Sung Joo said, "Pressure alone will not work." The North should be offered tangible benefits in return for its cooperation. Possible carrots included conducting nuclear inspections of ROK military installations, downsizing the annual Team Spirit exercise, providing security guarantees, and—Seoul's favorite—increasing trade and improving relations between the North and the United States, South Korea, and Japan.[78]

On April 1, 1993, two days after Pyongyang again denied the IAEA access to two sites, the IAEA Board of Governors declared, "The Agency is not able to verify that there has been no diversion of nuclear material required to be safeguarded." It directed Blix to report this finding to the UN Security Council, marking the first time that this body would discuss matters of war and peace on the peninsula since the end of the Korean War.[79] China voted against the board resolution—implying that it would also oppose UN sanctions.

No one wanted to see North Korea leave the NPT, but it also appeared that North Korea did not want to abandon the treaty either. The North's official March statement of withdrawal had hinted at a compromise. It had stated that the North would leave the NPT until the United States stopped "its nuclear threats against the DPRK" and until the IAEA Secretariat returned "to its principle of independence and impartiality." On March 30, the DPRK minister for atomic energy telexed Blix, "We are always ready to respond if the agency's Secretariat wishes to consult with us on the implementation of the safeguards agreement." Another telex three weeks later asked the IAEA for suggestions on how to resolve the inspection problem, requested consultations, and reminded the agency that North Korea had never rejected visits for maintenance and replacement of safeguards equipment.

In mid-April, the Clinton administration said that it was willing to hold direct high-level talks with the North to prevent it from leaving the NPT. Pyongyang signaled its interest, and Washington then formally extended the offer. The first high-level talks since January 1992 were scheduled for early June. If there was a moment when the bilateral inspection regime and, more generally, the North-South dialogue took a backseat, this was it. From now on, Washington would drive the negotiations.

In late April, North Korea informed the IAEA that inspections could resume. The next week, Pyongyang granted visas to IAEA inspectors for "technical checks"—routine maintenance on surveillance and containment equipment, such as replacing batteries and film and examining seals—at the 30MW reactor and the spent-fuel reprocessing facility at Yongbyon. This step, which would have unforeseen and far-reaching implications, was designed to preserve what the IAEA called the "continuity of safeguards."

In mid-May, American officials suggested that the Clinton administration was willing to "speak to" the North's demands concerning security assurances, inspections of U.S. military bases in the South, and the cancellation of Team Spirit. Washington was careful to avoid suggesting that it would reward the North for what Pyongyang had already been obligated to do—permit comprehensive IAEA inspections—but the scheduled June meeting was already a reward of sorts. The administration bravely insisted that Pyongyang would first have to change its nuclear behavior before the United States would negotiate on these other issues.[80] Within the U.S. government, this became known as the step-by-step approach. Washington and Pyongyang would take the first baby steps in New York on June 2.

Renewed Hope: Direct U.S.-DPRK Talks

By mid-1993, North Korea had won three tactical victories. First, face-to-face high-level talks with the United States constituted a move toward the cherished goal of diplomatic recognition. Unlike the one-time meeting in January 1992, these nuclear discussions promised to begin an ongoing diplomatic process. Second, the IAEA had been marginalized, since Pyongyang would now discuss safeguards matters with Washington, not the agency. And third, the bilateral inspection regime was dead. From now on, the North not only could speak directly to Washington but also would use this channel to try to play the sometimes competing interests of the United States, South Korea, and the IAEA against each other to its own advantage. Its confrontational nuclear diplomacy had paid off.

THE FIRST ROUND: JUNE 1993

Kang Sok Ju, first vice foreign minister of the DPRK, and U.S. Assistant Secretary of State Robert Gallucci, a nuclear arms control expert and seasoned negotiator, met at the U.S. Mission to the United Nations in New York on June 2. Kang's opening remarks, in which he expressed a desire "to obtain quid pro quo," signaled that the North was willing to cut a deal.[81]

The talks went down to the wire before the two sides reached agreement on June 11, one day before the North's withdrawal from the NPT was to take effect. In the brief joint statement, the parties agreed to the following principles: "assurances against the threat and use of force"; "peace and security in [a] nuclear-free Korean peninsula"; and the "impartial application of full-scope safeguards." On the question of NPT membership, the DPRK "decided unilaterally to suspend as long as it consider[ed] necessary the effectuation of its withdrawal."[82] At the press conference immediately afterward, Kang emphasized the symbolism of the joint U.S.-DPRK statement, which he referred to as a "very historic agreement."[83]

But issues of substance remained. The DPRK had still not agreed to special inspections at the two undeclared sites. Also, North Korea was still in the NPT, but apparently just barely. Because it had only suspended its withdrawal, it argued that it was in a "unique" situation in which it did not have to fulfill all of its NPT and IAEA safeguards obligations. The NPT's clock was not reset at three months' notice. Should Pyongyang again decide to leave the NPT, it claimed it could do so within a day.[84]

The United States had bought some time in New York to put the mutually agreed-upon principles into practice, but perhaps not very much time.

THE SECOND ROUND: JULY 1993

Kang and Gallucci met in Geneva in mid-July, and the two issued a joint statement on July 19.[85] The United States agreed to help North Korea obtain light-water reactors (LWRs) to replace its graphite-moderated reactors "as part of a final resolution of the nuclear issue." North Korea agreed to begin talks with the IAEA to review safeguards and with South Korea to discuss the bilateral inspection regime and other issues. If Pyongyang held up its part of the bargain, the statement added, the two sides would meet again within two months "to lay a basis for improving overall relations," which suggested steps toward normalization.[86]

At the ensuing press conference, Gallucci characterized the meeting as "a small but significant step." He emphasized that the next round of talks would not take place until the North had resumed talks with the IAEA and South Korea. Gallucci asserted that the United States would not help the North obtain LWR technology until it had "unambiguously complied" with its IAEA safeguards obligations. As in June, the joint statement did not mention the question of special inspections. But Gallucci's comments suggested that these inspections would have to take place if the North wanted light-water reactors.[87]

The preconditions for the third round were minimal—more talks with the IAEA and the South. But Washington had also insisted that the IAEA be allowed to perform another technical check to ensure continuity of safeguards. Without first consulting the IAEA, the American delegation assured the North Koreans that this visit would be just like the one conducted in May.[88]

The two sides agreed to reconvene in Geneva in mid-September 1993 for the third round. Neither side could have foreseen the passage of another year and a major escalation of tensions on the Korean peninsula before they would meet again.

Groping toward a "Broad and Thorough" Approach

North Korea permitted the IAEA to visit the Yongbyon nuclear center in early August. Problems arose immediately, when the inspectors insisted on access to more sites than they had seen in May. To Pyongyang, it appeared that the IAEA was trying surreptitiously to conduct an ad hoc inspection, which was inconsistent with the North's self-declared "unique" NPT status and contrary to what the Americans had promised. The North Koreans prevented the inspection team from installing new film and replacing batteries in monitoring equipment or replacing a broken seal. Contrary to subsequent news reports, the North Koreans did not "force" the inspectors, armed only with flash-lights, to investigate buildings at night.[89] Nonetheless, the inspectors returned to Vienna with their mission incomplete. It would be a while before the IAEA would return to Yongbyon.

FINESSING THE SAFEGUARDS ISSUE

Despite the complications of the August technical check, at the end of the month North Korea invited a five-member IAEA delegation to Pyongyang to resume talks on the ad hoc inspections that had been suspended since February. No progress resulted from these meetings, and the North Koreans continued to complain about the IAEA's "misconduct and partiality."[90] The North indicated, however, that it wanted the discussions to continue, if only to get to a third round with the United States.

The North-South talks did not go much better. Seoul agreed to the North's proposal for an exchange of special envoys (rather than lower-level officials), but Pyongyang then demanded that Seoul first scrap some ROK military maneuvers planned for October. It also refused to discuss the nuclear issue in the JNCC, hoping to drive a wedge between South Korea (and the United States) and the IAEA. With the U.S. conditions unfulfilled, Gallucci had no choice but to announce in mid-September that the third round was indefinitely postponed.

By this time, Blix and the IAEA had grown increasingly irritated with the North's evasion of its safeguards obligations. North Korea had never clarified the technical discrepancies presented to the Board of Governors in February and had never discussed ways to resolve the dispute over the two nuclear waste sites. In early September, the IAEA informed the North Koreans that it had to conduct ad hoc inspections before September 28 "in order for the agency to meet its inspection goals." Pyongyang telexed back that the inspectors could perform the same limited activities as they had in August "for maintaining continuity of safeguards information."[91]

The Clinton administration pressed the IAEA to accept this offer, on the theory that access to the two key facilities—the nuclear reactor and the reprocessing plant—was all that was required to verify that there had been no diversion of nuclear material. But with the Iraq inspection debacle still a fresh memory, the IAEA refused to budge.[92]

At the IAEA's General Conference on September 27, Blix reported that "the readiness of the DPRK to implement the safeguards agreement" had "diminished rather than grown" since the spring. He noted, "The area of non-compliance with the comprehensive safeguards agreement is widening." Blix rejected "token safeguards measures" and emphasized the need for full nuclear transparency.[93] Blix had refused to compromise the integrity of the IAEA, but the United States, South Korea, and Japan, not to mention China, had no desire to take this issue to the United Nations. A General Conference draft resolution temporarily papered over the difference; it urged North Korea to "cooperate immediately" with the IAEA but did not set a deadline and did not refer the matter to the UN Security Council.[94]

In mid-October, the director general toured Northeast Asia, where he took a harder, but also narrower, line. The immediate concern was ad hoc, not special, inspections. In Seoul, Blix declared: "Some safeguards activities are already being damaged in their continuity. . . . Today, increasingly the concern is that the *declared facilities and declared material* could also be diverted from peaceful purposes." Blix ruled out limited inspections. "Safeguards are not anything you have à la carte, where a customer orders hors d'oeuvres and dessert. It is a whole menu."[95] But IAEA spokesman David Kyd admitted that the monitoring equipment at two key facilities—the nuclear reactor and the reprocessing plant—would remain operable until the end of the year.[96]

At this time, Pyongyang privately stepped up its calls for immediate face-to-face talks with the United States, talks that it hoped could resolve the nuclear and other divisive issues. In other words, the North wanted Washington to reverse the order of events it had stipulated back in July. To show good faith, North Korea resumed "working-level" discussions with the South on a special envoy exchange. Pyongyang also entertained Congressman Gary Ackerman and let him cross the demilitarized zone (DMZ) into South Korea, the first U.S. official to do so since the end of the Korean War. During the Ackerman visit, the North Koreans presented to a U.S. foreign service officer who had accompanied the congressman a detailed "package deal" that linked the inspection dispute with diplomatic recognition, cancellation of Team Spirit, and other issues. On the officer's return to Washington, the North Korean proposal was circulated throughout the Clinton administration. Only the State Department treated the proposal seriously; it could not persuade the National Security Council or the Defense Department, which did not want to bargain away Team Spirit, to explore the idea further.[97]

With the IAEA refusing to compromise, Washington informed the DPRK Mission to the United Nations in New York (where it had been regularly holding working-level meetings) that unless Pyongyang allowed ad hoc inspections by the end of the month, Blix would report the matter to the UN Security Council.[98] The warning provoked an immediate response. Two articles in mid-October in the DPRK party organ, *Nodong Sinmun*, cautioned that the United Nations and the IAEA should act "with discretion" or else risk bringing "irrevocable disgrace and setback to themselves." But the articles repeated some elements of the "package deal" that had been presented earlier in the month in Pyongyang, asserting that the nuclear issue could best be settled by direct U.S.-DPRK talks.[99] North Korea also pursued this tack in meetings in New York for the remainder of the month.[100]

Seoul prodded the talks along by helpfully offering a "carrot" to the North. Despite the opposition of the Joint Chiefs of Staff, South Korea leaked to the press in late October that if North Korea agreed to an exchange of special envoys and accepted ad hoc inspections, it would suspend Team Spirit '94.[101] Any UN "stick" was publicly removed a few days later when the Chinese ambassador to Japan announced that Beijing would strongly oppose UN sanctions against North Korea and repeated China's view that the issue should be resolved through dialogue.[102]

Only days before Blix was scheduled to address the United Nations on November 1, the DPRK Ministry of Atomic Energy telexed the IAEA that it had "decided now to agree to accept agency inspections for the purpose of maintenance and replacement of the safeguards equipment," with the additional caveat that inspections be conducted "on such scope as they were carried out last August."[103] The North's message not only rejected ad hoc inspections but also limited IAEA technical checks to the nuclear reactor and the reprocessing plant at Yongbyon.

The DPRK had placed the IAEA in a bind. Blix could reject the offer, preserve the principle that members could not dictate inspection terms, and uphold the integrity of the IAEA safeguards system. But the price was high: the further erosion of the continuity of safeguards and of his own position with Washington, Seoul, Tokyo, and Beijing, none of which wanted to turn the matter into a possible crisis by seeking UN sanctions. He would also be acquiescing to what another senior IAEA official called the North's "frantic effort to cheat."[104]

On November 1, Blix bought the IAEA some time. He told the UN General Assembly, "The area of non-compliance with the comprehensive safeguards agreement has been widening." And he warned, "Continuity of some safeguards-relevant data has been damaged."[105] But Blix refrained from saying that continuity of safeguards had been *broken*. That same day, the UN General Assembly passed another resolution criticizing the North's failure "to discharge its safeguards obligations" and urging it "to cooperate immediately" with the IAEA.[106] The assembly did not call for sanctions and did not set a deadline for compliance. The DPRK cast the lone vote against the resolution, demonstrating the extent of its isolation. The situation had again reached an impasse.

The Preemption Option

The maddening cat-and-mouse game with North Korea and the inadequacy of the diplomatic track had long prompted commentators to call for a preemptive military strike on the Yongbyon nuclear complex.[107] The ROK defense minister, Lee Jong Koo, had twice suggested that South Korea launch Entebbe-style commando raids to destroy Yongbyon.[108] In spring 1993, South Korean intelligence officials reportedly visited Israel for briefings on the details of Tel Aviv's successful June 1981 raid on Iraq's Tammuz nuclear reactor.[109]

No one in the Clinton administration publicly advocated this policy. But in early November, the London *Sunday Times* reported that the

United States had prepared plans and briefed the president for a cruise missile strike on the Yongbyon nuclear complex.[110]

A military strike made little sense. If North Korea had acquired nuclear weapons, or had even separated the plutonium to build such weapons, it was highly unlikely that they would have been stored at Yongbyon. As good as U.S. intelligence may have been, it was hard to identify all of the North's possible nuclear sites and even harder to destroy them.

Further, a preemptive strike would risk a second Korean war. A 1992 RAND study for the Defense Department advised undertaking preemptive military strikes against the DPRK's nuclear facilities only if South Korea and the United States were "willing and able to wage a full-scale war against North Korea."[111] Classified Pentagon planning estimates showed that such a war would result in an estimated 300,000 to 500,000 military casualties in the first ninety days. No figures were given for civilian deaths.[112]

In addition, a preemptive strike might invite the real, if low, possibility of a nuclear response from Pyongyang. But even conventional attacks on South Korea's nuclear power stations could be devastating, scattering deadly radioactivity over the peninsula and throughout the region. Preemptive military action would be vehemently opposed by South Korea and Japan, without whose support the United States could not wage a war.[113] Nothing less than the military defeat, occupation, and inspection of the entire country would eliminate the North's nuclear weapons program. For better or worse, diplomacy was the only option available.

DISARRAY IN THE CLINTON ADMINISTRATION

As the rhetoric heated up and tensions mounted during the fall, the Clinton administration continued to stumble in foreign affairs. The meandering U.S. policy on Bosnia, the deaths of eighteen servicemen in Somalia in October, and the rebuff of the USS *Harlan County* by a gang of Haitian thugs that same month raised questions about the administration's competence to manage American foreign policy.

These missteps continued in early November. A senior Defense Department official traveling with Secretary Les Aspin to Japan and South Korea informed reporters that North Korea was reinforcing its troops near the demilitarized zone; these comments were interpreted (incorrectly) by some news organizations as indicating an imminent military conflict on the peninsula. Aspin's public musings in Tokyo on the efficacy of international economic sanctions may have convinced

Pyongyang that Washington could be pressured to agree to further concessions before North Korea permitted IAEA inspections.[114] Betraying a sensitivity to domestic critics, the defense secretary remarked in early November that for political reasons, the Clinton administration should not "look weak" on this issue.[115] On November 7 on NBC's *Meet the Press,* Clinton proclaimed: "North Korea cannot be allowed to develop a nuclear bomb. We have to be very firm about it."[116] At a time when the U.S. intelligence community had concluded that Pyongyang could possess a nuclear device, the president publicly drew a line in the sand, one that the North might already have stepped over.

These outward signs of disarray mirrored disorganization within the government. The Clinton administration conveyed the impression that North Korea was an intermittent nuisance, not a foreign policy priority. No single official had responsibility for the issue. When U.S. negotiators had met in July 1993 with DPRK officials in Geneva, they had not properly thought through the U.S. position, according to one State Department official involved in the talks. The delegation also did not have the normal "backstopping committee" in Washington to support it. As a result, the U.S. team received conflicting instructions from the State Department, the National Security Council, and the Pentagon.

Further, the Clinton administration had never undertaken a thorough analysis of North Korea's negotiating style to learn more about its adversary. Given that the North spent an enormous amount of time and effort carefully signaling its intentions and policy shifts, researching the North's use of certain key words and phrases would have been prudent. Yet this was never done.[117] Some of these organizational shortcomings would begin to be rectified at the end of March 1994, when U.S. negotiator Gallucci was designated ambassador-at-large and appointed chairman of the Senior Policy Steering Group on Korea.

THE "BROAD AND THOROUGH" APPROACH

With the Clinton administration split internally, frustrated with the IAEA's safeguards stance, unable to get China on board for UN sanctions, and boxed in by its anxious allies, North Korea took the initiative. On November 11, 1993, the DPRK's negotiator at the first two rounds, Kang Sok Ju, now publicly called for the United States to accept a "package solution" to the nuclear problem and renounce "the nuclear threat and hostile policy" against Pyongyang, a reference to Team Spirit. He also repeated the North's willingness to "allow the readjustment and replacement of the inspection cameras" for the nuclear reactor and the spent-fuel reprocessing facility. He assured Washington, "We totally froze the movement of nuclear material within the DPRK."[118] In other words, North Korea had not used the time since the August inspection to improve its nuclear weapon capabilities.

The Kang statement suggested flexibility, but a closer reading revealed that Pyongyang had toughened its bargaining stance by turning the tables on the United States. Back in spring 1993, the Clinton administration had said that it would not cancel Team Spirit unless the North first agreed to comprehensive inspections, including access to the two nuclear waste sites, inspections that would establish whether Pyongyang had cheated by separating more plutonium than it had declared to the IAEA. Indeed, the agency's demand for access to these two sites had precipitated the March crisis. In October, South Korea had said that it would cancel Team Spirit if the North first agreed only to ad hoc inspections and the exchange of special envoys. Now Kang was proposing that Team Spirit be canceled *before* IAEA inspections, limited to the nuclear reactor and the reprocessing facility only.

The idea of a package deal that included nuclear matters, military exercises, economic aid, and normalization of relations intrigued the Clinton administration, however, especially officials at the State Department. For some time, it had been clear to both the American and the North Korean negotiators that the step-by-step approach would not succeed. North Korea had repeatedly urged a comprehensive approach throughout the fall, and the two sides had explored the subject in their New York meetings.

For Washington, the question now became what political and economic incentives should be part of a package deal that would be spelled out to Pyongyang at a third round of talks. The idea was to show the North a road map to achieving these objectives. The political difficulty for the Clinton administration was that it would have to go first. But canceling Team Spirit seemed a small concession, as Kang knew, because Washington had decided in August not to budget funds for the exercise.

In mid-November 1993, the Clinton administration decided to switch its policy. Washington would cancel Team Spirit and meet for a third round in return for the North's satisfying three conditions: (1) ad hoc inspections; (2) direct talks with South Korea; and (3) agreement in principle to resolving all outstanding nuclear issues, including access to the two waste sites.[119] Perhaps anticipating the IAEA's objections, Washington rejected Kang's proposal and insisted on the broader ad hoc inspections. But it deferred the intractable issue of special inspections. Rather than being a precondition, special inspections would now be part of the package deal's endgame.

After consulting with foreign leaders at the Asia-Pacific Economic Cooperation (APEC) meeting in Seattle in mid-November, the United States formally disclosed the new approach at a November 23 White House press conference by Presidents Clinton and Kim Young Sam. Kim said that Washington and Seoul would make "thorough and broad efforts to bring about a final solution." The idea was to give the North Koreans "the chance to broaden the dialogue." Clinton denied that he was rewarding North Korea's bad behavior by offering concessions for its living up to its nuclear obligations.[120]

But the Clinton administration remained fuzzy on the details. In an off-the-record White House briefing for reporters after the press conference, senior administration officials explained, "We will in the weeks ahead be trying to refine exactly what those options are so we know what to present."[121] Conceded another administration official, "This is a work in progress."[122] There was no explicit deadline, perhaps in the belief that the IAEA would provide one when Blix determined that the continuity of safeguards was finally broken. Why this "broad and thorough" approach would be any more successful than earlier administration efforts was unclear. The administration could not even agree internally, or with South Korea, on what measures to offer the North and when they should be offered. The Pentagon refused to put Team Spirit '94 on the table, even though during the summit Kim had told Clinton that this decision would be made by Seoul, not Washington.[123] The administration had changed course but did not know where it was going or how to get there.

The lack of genuine policy options had driven the Clinton administration to adopt the broad and thorough approach. Washington could have refused to compromise further with North Korea, abandoned the UN route, beefed up its military presence in South Korea and the region, and perhaps reinserted U.S. tactical nuclear weapons. In other words, it could have relied on the deterrence policy that had operated successfully on the peninsula for the previous four decades.

But deterrence had its limitations. Although the U.S.-ROK forces could almost certainly deter the North from attacking the South, or from using nuclear weapons, it was far less clear that they could prevent North Korea from forming a sizable nuclear arsenal by reprocessing the nuclear fuel in the 30MW reactor. Further, once the 200MW and 800MW reactors came on-line in a few years, Pyongyang could produce a much larger nuclear stockpile. Even more alarming, it was doubtful whether the United States could deter (or even detect) North

Korean exports of weapons-grade plutonium to other countries, especially in the Middle East.

North Korea's strategic nuclear potential thus led Washington in a policy direction—continued dialogue with the North at almost any cost—that discomforted many Clinton administration officials. It provided the rationalization for repeated incremental compromises, each one easing the way for the next, until the administration found itself in a position no one could have imagined only months before.

The decision made in November—to postpone special inspections until the end of the negotiating process rather than make them a precondition for bilateral talks—was more momentous than anyone in the Clinton administration realized at the time. Although no one in the administration publicly stated, or perhaps even privately thought, that the United States was going to discount the North's nuclear history, deferring the issue of special inspections to the final stages of a long negotiating process made that step much easier to rationalize later on. It shortened the conceptual distance between holding fast to a strict interpretation of North Korea's international legal obligations—a policy the Clinton administration had adopted in February 1993—and displaying a willingness to tolerate "one or two" North Korean nuclear weapons in the attempt to "cap" the nuclear weapons program, a policy it would adopt a year later. Within months, the Clinton administration would move from a policy of prevention to one of containment.

Getting to the Third Round—Almost

At the beginning of December, one State Department official characterized the new strategy: "Walk softly and carry a big carrot." But even he probably did not anticipate how difficult it would be to persuade North Korea to take a bite.

The IAEA could derail the entire approach at any moment. At the December 2 Board of Governors meeting, Blix did not utter the magic words that the continuity of safeguards had been broken, perhaps in fear that the resulting uproar would drive the North Koreans completely out of the NPT, or worse. But he inched closer, stating that safeguards in the DPRK could not "provide any meaningful assurance of peaceful use of these installations and this material."[124] The day before the meeting, Pyongyang had again offered to allow inspectors to replace camera film and batteries at the nuclear reactor and the reprocessing plant, and again, the IAEA had declined.

Meanwhile, U.S. and North Korean negotiators continued to meet in New York against a background of rising tensions. Leaks and mis-statements by U.S. officials on the status of the North's nuclear weapons program narrowed the political maneuvering room for an administration that was already weighted down by heavy domestic criticism. In early December, the media reported that a Special National Intelligence Estimate had predicted that efforts to get the DPRK to allow inspections at the two nuclear waste sites would fail.[125] Defense Secretary Aspin twice commented that North Korea might have enough plutonium for "a bomb, maybe a bomb and a half," and U.S. intelligence sources reported that there was a "better than even" chance that North Korea had two nuclear weapons.[126] These remarks contradicted Clinton's unequivocal declaration, made the month before, that North Korea could not be allowed to have even one bomb.

On December 29, 1993, the United States finally persuaded North Korea to expand the scope of IAEA inspections it would permit. Washington first had to change its tactics on ad hoc inspections, which the North Koreans had resisted because of their self-proclaimed "unique" NPT status. After the administration stopped labeling these activities inspections and emphasized instead their necessity for international credibility (in effect, taking a regional security rather than a strict nonproliferation approach to the issue), Pyongyang agreed "immediately."[127] North Korea conceded by accepting, in principle, IAEA access to the seven (not just two) declared nuclear sites at Yong-byon. The DPRK would work out the procedural details with the agency. In return, the United States was prepared to suspend Team Spirit (a move the Pentagon had resisted for over two months) and move to a third high-level meeting with the North. Special inspections would be dealt with then.[128] The official DPRK news agency called the agreement a "breakthrough."

But problems remained. When the deal was announced in early January 1994, the administration's domestic critics wondered whether there was *any* concession the Clinton administration would not make to keep the North Koreans at the negotiating table. They noted that the latest arrangement was hardly the diplomatic triumph cited by the administration; in return for suspending Team Spirit, the United States, the IAEA, and North Korea had merely returned to where they had been in February 1993.[129]

The IAEA and North Korea resumed discussions of procedural details in early January. Pyongyang took the activities list that the IAEA had compiled the previous spring for conducting ad hoc inspections at the seven declared sites, and it deleted certain items that would be out-of-bounds for the next inspection visit.[130] North Korea also appeared in no hurry; it repeatedly requested additional information about what, precisely, the IAEA intended to do. Frustrated with the North's delays, the United States announced on January 31 that it planned to proceed with Team Spirit if Pyongyang did not permit inspections.[131] North Korea reacted by accusing the United States of breaking its promises and threatened to tear up "all the goodwill measures and commitments" the North had "taken so far"—a reference to Pyongyang's unfreezing its nuclear program and withdrawing from the NPT.[132] The new deadline became the IAEA Board of Governors meeting on February 21, when the matter might again be referred to the UN Security Council.[133]

With Blix already preparing a report that the continuity of safeguards had been broken, North Korea and the agency reached agreement on February 15 on inspections at Yongbyon.[134] In reality, these were "continuity of safeguards," not ad hoc, inspections, since the IAEA had actually acquiesced to North Korea's demands to remove certain sites from the inspection list. The IAEA had reversed its firm stance against inspections "à la carte"—a stance on which it had insisted only weeks earlier.[135]

But there was more ground to cover, and American and North Korean negotiators continued their diplomatic tango during the last few days of February, when they finally clarified the exact timetable. As soon as IAEA inspections started and North-South talks resumed to schedule an exchange of special envoys, Seoul would announce the suspension of the Team Spirit military exercise, and Pyongyang and Washington would announce the March 21 date of a third round of bilateral talks to take place in Geneva.[136] By March 3, all of these events had taken place as planned.

After months of tense negotiations, Washington thought that it was finally about to reach the third round it had originally scheduled for mid-September 1993. It was wrong.

MARCH 1994: TENSIONS BOIL

Problems arose almost as soon as the North-South talks resumed at Panmunjom, which in turn created difficulties for the IAEA inspectors at Yongbyon.[137] In New York the previous week, American negotiators had "guaranteed" to the North Koreans that the North-South talks would be smooth sailing. The South Koreans soon dashed these expectations. Pyongyang reacted to Seoul's aggressive bargaining by impeding the inspections. As the North-South talks deteriorated, the

North made the worst possible move it could have: it denied the IAEA inspectors access to the hot cell area. A furious IAEA immediately pulled the inspection team. The agency ignored a U.S. request to keep the inspectors there until Washington could consult with Seoul and see if the North-South talks could be put back on track.

On March 16, 1994, the IAEA stated that it could not verify that diversion of nuclear material had not occurred at the reprocessing facility. Despite being denied access to certain sites, the inspectors described ways in which the North was advancing its nuclear program. Pyongyang had almost finished a second reprocessing line that would double North Korea's plutonium production capacity. The DPRK had also fabricated a replacement fuel load for the 30MW reactor and was continuing construction of and fabricating the fuel for the 200MW reactor.[138]

On March 19, North Korea dropped all of its preconditions for the exchange of special envoys, but Seoul continued to insist that the North completely accept its draft agenda.[139] The talks immediately collapsed. The North Korean delegate at Panmunjom stormed out, threatening: "Seoul is not very far from here. If a war breaks out, it will be a sea of fire." Two days later, the IAEA Board of Governors found that the DPRK was "in further noncompliance with its safeguards agreement" and requested that Blix inform the UN Security Council and General Assembly.[140] Because its preconditions had not been met, Washington had no choice but to cancel the March 21 meeting. Republican Senator John McCain declared that the Clinton administration's Korean strategy had "failed miserably."[141]

The Clinton administration now moved from carrot to stick. It shipped the Patriot antimissile batteries that General Gary E. Luck, the senior U.S. military commander in South Korea, had requested back in December to bolster his forces against possible missile attacks from the North.[142] Secretary of Defense William Perry instructed the U.S. Air Force to stockpile a supply of munitions and spare parts for F-117 Stealth fighters and F-15E jets and the U.S. Army to replace antiquated helicopters with newer Apache attack helicopters.

Once more, the United States tried to muster support for UN sanctions. Yet Seoul, Tokyo, and Beijing had no enthusiasm for such a move, as Secretary of State Christopher had learned during his trip to the region in mid-March. The primary purpose of his visit had been to compel China to alter its human rights record; the United States planned to influence China by threatening to revoke the extension of MFN trading benefits. The Clinton administration apparently thought that human rights and the DPRK nuclear program could be placed in separate compartments. At the same time Christopher was washing China's dirty laundry in public, he was privately petitioning Beijing to pressure the North on the nuclear issue and to support UN sanctions. Yet how could the Chinese have agreed to economic sanctions with MFN dangling over their heads? Approving sanctions would have undermined their argument against holding MFN hostage to their internal practices.

The Clinton administration also believed that China shared the U.S. interest in seeing a nonnuclear Korean peninsula. Although China most likely did not want North Korea to acquire a nuclear option or even a small nuclear arsenal, it may not have been willing to invest much diplomatic capital to prevent that outcome. Pyongyang did not pose a security threat to Beijing, which had lived since 1949 with a much larger and at times more menacing nuclear neighbor. Also, the North Korean nuclear dispute elevated Beijing as the key interlocutor with the DPRK and thus provided a source of leverage with the United States and countries in the region. And the nuclear dispute frustrated Washington, thereby diminishing U.S. standing and influence in Northeast Asia. Beijing's primary interest was to avoid a second Korean war, which would cause millions of Korean refugees to spill over into China. Beijing would not support any measure, such as UN sanctions, that increased that possibility.

Christopher predicted on March 20 that the Chinese would abstain on a UN Security Council resolution aimed at North Korea.[143] But that same day, the Chinese ambassador to South Korea stated: "It's an international rule now to solve all issues through dialogue. Why should the North Korean nuclear problem be an exception? China cannot agree to sanctions or any other stringent measure."[144] A few days later, China's prime minister, Li Peng, cautioned, "If pressure is applied on this issue, that can only complicate the situation on the Korean peninsula and it will add to the tension there."[145]

At the United Nations, the Clinton administration submitted a resolution with language almost identical to that of the May 1993 resolution requesting North Korea to comply with its NPT obligations.[146] But China suggested an even weaker step, which resulted in a nonbinding statement on March 31 by the president of the UN Security Council. It did not mention economic sanctions but implied a six-week deadline before further UN Security Council "consideration."[147]

Carrots had not worked, and sticks had priced themselves out of the market. The United States and North Korea had failed to get to a third round. Just when it looked as if the situation could not get worse, it did.

Crossing the Nuclear Rubicon

On April 1, North Korea shut off the 30MW reactor at Yongbyon. Since spring 1993, North Korea had held off taking this step. The nuclear reactor fuel contained enough plutonium to make four to six bombs.

The prospect that North Korea could extract plutonium from the spent fuel in this reactor core posed a new nuclear nightmare: a North Korea armed with a stockpile of nuclear bombs to either keep or sell around the world. As Defense Secretary Perry admitted in early April, "Our policy right along has been oriented to try to keep North Korea from getting a *significant* nuclear-weapon capability."[148] Senior Pentagon officials now downplayed whatever Pyongyang had done in the past, calling any bomb material it had already produced "Bush's plutonium." One or two nuclear weapons would be tolerated, as long as the North did not acquire any more.

With the Patriot missiles having arrived at Pusan and with tough talk emanating from Washington, South Korea announced in mid-April that it would no longer insist that special envoys be exchanged before a third round of U.S.-DPRK talks, a major concession that it had refused to make the month before.[149] Further reflecting Seoul's sensitivities, Defense Secretary Perry and ROK Defense Minister Rhee Byong-tae announced on April 20 that the Team Spirit '94 military exercise would be deferred until "the November time frame" and that it would be canceled altogether if North Korea agreed to IAEA inspections.[150]

Meanwhile, North Korea had informed the IAEA that it intended to refuel the 30MW reactor "at an early date," meaning that the nuclear fuel would soon be removed. It would allow inspectors to observe and count the fuel rods as they were removed, but inspectors would not be able to take samples for testing. The IAEA demanded to examine the fuel rods, a standard IAEA practice that would reveal their age and whether they were part of the original fuel load, as North Korea claimed, or had been replaced since the reactor began operations in 1987, as the United States and others believed. This examination would confirm whether Pyongyang had extracted the plutonium it had provided to the IAEA from this spent fuel and, if so, would determine how much might have been diverted for nuclear bombs. Pyongyang and the IAEA continued to dicker on this issue for the next month.[151]

But North Korea and the IAEA had reached one agreement—on completing the March inspection. These inspections were performed in mid-May. They were soon overshadowed by a much more disturbing development.

NORTH KOREA PULLS THE FUEL

On May 12, North Korea telexed the IAEA that it had already begun removing the fuel from the nuclear reactor for "safety reasons." The letter invited IAEA inspectors to select and secure the fuel rods. But testing would be permitted only after the third round of talks with the United States.[152] Further discharge of the fuel would destroy the ability of the IAEA to reconstruct the North's nuclear history. Moreover, without international monitoring, North Korea could divert the spent fuel and later extract plutonium for nuclear bombs.

Because only about 5 percent of the 7,700 fuel rods had been removed, the situation in mid-May remained salvageable. After the IAEA inspectors completed their final checks from the March inspection, the Clinton administration decided, on May 20, that it would go to the third round, despite the North's flagrant behavior.[153] The next day, North Korea agreed to discuss safeguards arrangements with the IAEA.

The administration had held off formally announcing a date for the third round until after these negotiations. But three days of IAEA-DPRK talks failed to produce an agreement, and Washington learned that Pyongyang had accelerated unloading its fuel. By late May, half of the fuel had already been removed, including some of the three hundred strategically positioned rods that the IAEA had wanted to sample. Worse, they were stored haphazardly in baskets in the cooling pond, vastly complicating (and perhaps making impossible) the IAEA's task of determining the North's nuclear history.[154] North Korean negotiators in New York surprised State Department diplomats by rejecting a proposed early June meeting for the third round. "The fact of the matter is," said one U.S. official, "we don't really understand what they are doing."[155]

BACK TO THE UNITED NATIONS

On June 2, Blix wrote to UN Secretary General Boutros Boutros-Ghali that the agency had lost the ability to verify that nuclear material from the reactor had not been diverted. "The situation resulting from the core discharge is irreversible."[156]

Still, the United States had a formidable diplomatic challenge to persuade key international players to enact UN sanctions, especially since North Korea had repeatedly threatened that such a step would be tantamount to "an act of war" and since Pyongyang had not (yet) diverted any of the withdrawn spent fuel for reprocessing. In addition, sanctions could not reconstruct the nuclear history that the North had already destroyed.

At this time, Russia voiced its reservations over the sanctions route. Moscow wanted to force the United States to take seriously a proposal for an international conference of Russia, the United States, Japan, China, and the two Koreas, a proposal that it had aired back in March.[157] A conference would mollify the key actors in the region (especially a very nervous Japan) and could also now provide much-needed political cover for the White House if it succeeded in "capping" (rather than eliminating) the North's nuclear weapons program. By June 8, Washington had agreed in principle to the conference but needed to coordinate the details and timing with its continued push for UN sanctions.

By mid-June, after close consultations with South Korea, Japan, Britain, France, Russia, and China, the United States had formalized a two-phase strategy for UN sanctions against North Korea. All the parties except the Chinese had approved Washington's draft resolution. The plan called for the UN Security Council to endorse a first tranche of modest sanctions, which would start in thirty days. Before that period elapsed, Moscow would convene an international conference on the Korean problem. This was intended to give the North Koreans a last, face-saving chance to resolve the crisis before the initial sanctions took effect. These sanctions would then be followed by a second tranche of harsher sanctions, which would include terminating remittance payments from Koreans living in Japan. State Department officials admitted, however, that there was no guarantee that China would support the resolution.[158]

It was unclear whether these diplomatic maneuvers would come in time to prevent tensions from erupting into war or would inflame them further. In early June, Pyongyang threatened to expel the two IAEA inspectors who were babysitting the fuel rods at Yongbyon. On June 13, North Korea left the IAEA, three days after the agency had ended all technical assistance.[159] Defense Secretary Perry had ordered the reinforcement of U.S. troops and had intensified intelligence-gathering operations on the peninsula. Loose talk of preemptive U.S. military strikes against North Korea became more prevalent. Washington proposed a voluntary arms embargo against North Korea. South Korea announced that it would call up 6.6 million reservists for a defense drill. In Seoul, the war scare triggered a frantic search for gas masks and caused a run on essential items. *Time* magazine diagrammed a glossy, multicolored "war game" on the next Korean conflict.

Ominously, U.S. satellite photos showed that the North Korean military was moving to a war footing, perhaps because it interpreted U.S. reinforcement efforts (especially the Patriot deployments) as a replay of the run-up to Operation Desert Storm. Pyongyang increased training exercises, including the use of tanks and aircraft that devoured a lot of scarce fuel. These maneuvers were far different from the North's annual "semi–war alert" response to the Team Spirit exercise. "They were not provocative, but prudent if you were a North Korean military commander," was how one U.S. official characterized the North's preparations. Still, the Pentagon dusted off its plans to destroy the Yongbyon nuclear complex in the event that the North started to reprocess the spent fuel. "This is what it looks like when two countries blunder into war."[160]

THE CARTER VISIT: "THE CRISIS IS OVER"

At this precise moment, Jimmy Carter arrived in Pyongyang for meetings with North Korean officials, including the eighty-two-year-old Kim Il Sung. The former U.S. president had a standing invitation to visit North Korea but twice had been told by the Bush administration not to go. Senior Clinton administration officials also tried to dissuade Carter, who had publicly criticized the UN sanctions approach and warned about a descent into another Korean conflict. They also feared that he would independently try to strike with Pyongyang a deal that could compromise the administration's efforts in the United Nations. But Vice President Al Gore reportedly favored the trip. After Clinton spoke directly with Carter, he approved. Clinton's consent evidenced not only a disdain for his foreign policy team but also his doubts about the wisdom of a strategy—UN sanctions in response to the North's nuclear stonewalling—that he had approved and directed since his first days in office.

From the start of the three-day visit, it appeared that Carter had his own agenda for preventing the outbreak of hostilities in Korea. Accompanied by a crew from Cable News Network (CNN), which instantly broadcast his mediation efforts around the world, Carter said that Kim Il Sung had agreed during their first meeting to allow the two IAEA inspectors to remain at Yongbyon. Kim also told Carter that North Korea would permit the IAEA to maintain its monitoring equipment, would not refuel the 30MW reactor, and would not reprocess the spent fuel it had just unloaded—in return for high-level talks with the United States. In other words, Pyongyang would freeze its nuclear program in anticipation of a third round. At the end of his first day in Pyongyang, Carter conveyed this offer to Clinton's national security adviser, Anthony Lake, over an open telephone line. Lake asked Carter to try to clarify Kim's offer of a freeze. When he explained that the administration was continuing to seek UN sanctions, Carter heatedly objected.

During his second day of meetings in Pyongyang, Carter apparently decided to engage in some creative diplomacy. He told the North Koreans that the Clinton administration had stopped "the sanctions activity in the United Nations" and had already agreed to hold a third round of bilateral talks. Caught unawares, the White House publicly disavowed Carter's remarks and hustled to undo the damage to its UN strategy and its relations with key allies. Administration officials privately were scathing in their attacks on Carter's free-lancing.[161]

In his bewildering diplomatic foray, televised live before a global audience, Carter had tried to create a new diplomatic reality on the Korean peninsula. In the process, he had embarrassed a president who was already perceived as having a poor grasp of foreign policy. He had weakened the IAEA by suggesting that the United States should not press the North to talk with the agency because there was too much bad blood between them. More important, he had fatally undermined U.S. efforts in the United Nations. But that had been his intention all along, as his remarks after his trip made clear. "The declaration of sanctions by the U.N. would be regarded as an insult by them, branding it as an outlaw country," Carter said. "It would also be viewed as a personal insult to their so-called Great Leader by branding him as a liar and a criminal. This is something in my opinion which would be impossible for them to accept."[162]

Letting himself be used by the North Koreans, at considerable risk to his personal stature, was a small price to pay for successfully heading off what he feared was a possible second Korean war. On returning to Washington to debrief the Clinton administration about his trip, the former president declared, "I personally believe that the crisis is over."[163]

Carter's instincts were right on the mark, at least for the short term. Faced with an uncertain vote in the United Nations, especially after Carter's trip, and wary that any sanctions might provoke North Korea into launching a war, the Clinton administration again changed its policy, literally overnight. Washington now announced that it would agree to high-level talks if Pyongyang confirmed the three conditions Kim Il Sung had already offered Carter: (1) IAEA inspectors would remain at Yongbyon; (2) North Korea would not refuel the reactor; and (3) the North would not reprocess the spent fuel it had just unloaded.[164] Washington would now follow up to see if the North's proposal was genuine.

This policy change meant backsliding from a key element of the administration's previous stance, namely, that it would not talk with the North unless the IAEA was allowed to determine that fuel had not been diverted from the Yongbyon reactor. But the DPRK had made reconstructing its nuclear history almost impossible when it had unloaded the fuel and deliberately scattered the fuel rods in the cooling pond baskets only weeks earlier. In other words, that horse had already left the barn. The administration's new position reflected this new reality. In response to a question on North Korea's nuclear program, President Clinton remarked, "I think what we have to do is look to the present and the future."[165]

On June 22, Clinton announced "a very positive development": North Korea had formally agreed to freeze temporarily its nuclear program, and the two sides would meet for a third round of talks on July 8 in Geneva.[166] Short-circuiting the administration's strategy, Carter had nevertheless taken the administration where it wanted to go—back to the negotiating table with the North Koreans. Yet the spectacle of the Clinton administration's apparently endless patience as the North Korean regime advanced its nuclear weapons program troubled many observers. Washington's track record was not impressive. By July 1994, North Korea had won a number of tactical victories: (1) it had dodged UN sanctions, as well as diminished the likelihood of any future sanctions; (2) it had stalled U.S. plans for reinforcing American forces in the South; (3) it had prevented a full and independent accounting of its nuclear history; (4) it had continued to defy the IAEA and not permit special inspections; (5) it had turned its claim of "unique" NPT status into reality by obtaining special treatment on IAEA inspections; (6) it had reengaged the United States in high-level talks on its terms; and (7) it had not foreclosed its nuclear weapons option, since the highly radioactive fuel rods needed to cool before they could be reprocessed and the plutonium extracted.

Before mid-1994, it had been possible to arrive at an outcome consistent with traditional U.S. nonproliferation principles, with the established practice of the IAEA, and with the Clinton administration's own declared policy objectives. After mid-1994, not one of these outcomes was possible any longer. The Clinton administration had lost a battle. But it had not lost the war.

THE THIRD ROUND: AUGUST 1994

The third round of talks began in Geneva on July 8, 1994. They were only a day old when the North Korean delegation learned that Kim Il Sung had died of a heart attack. News of his death plunged his countrymen into hysterical displays of grief as the DPRK announced a nine-day period of mourning.

Kim Il Sung's death immediately raised questions about the path his country would take under his son and heir apparent, fifty-two-year-old Kim Jong Il.[167] A wild card had now been introduced, but whether it was a joker or a king no one knew for sure. An inscrutable country had just become more so.

The reaction in Geneva was evident in the faces of the North Koreans. One American negotiator said that his counterparts were "very insecure, really thrown by Kim's death." The head of the DPRK delegation informed the U.S. delegation that he had been recalled to Pyongyang as a member of the state funeral committee. Before leaving, he informally assured the U.S. side that North Korea would continue its current nuclear policies.[168] The U.S.-DPRK talks were rescheduled for early August.

The two parties reconvened in early August, and after a week of negotiations, they issued a statement on August 12. North Korea pledged to freeze work on the two graphite-moderated reactors and abandon reprocessing if the United States provided assurances that Pyongyang would receive light-water reactors. The DPRK also agreed to remain an NPT party, which meant accepting full-scope safeguards, including special inspections if necessary.[169] The North had rejected a U.S. proposal to store in a third country the fuel rods it had recently removed from the 30MW reactor (with enough plutonium for four or five bombs), but an alternative offer to stabilize the pond water containing the fuel rods remained on the table.[170] Consistent with the broad and thorough approach, the two sides were prepared to set up "diplomatic representation in each other's capital," which could eventually lead to full diplomatic recognition. The head of the U.S. team, Robert Gallucci, summed up, "The most important thing to say about the agreement is that it is a first step, a basis upon which we can build and go farther."

Although there was no indication when the North would permit special inspections, it appeared that they would now be tied to receipt of costly LWR technology, an event that could be years away. The United States had kicked the can down the road on special inspections in order to get to the third round. It had now kicked the can even farther down the road. But it now also had the outline of a workable deal.

THE FOURTH ROUND: SEPTEMBER 1994

Amid all this diplomatic activity between the United States and North Korea, South Korea scrambled not to be left out. In what the South Korean president characterized as "the very first joint project for national development," Kim Young Sam offered in mid-August to provide technology and financing for the construction of two light-water reactors in North Korea. The only condition was that Pyongyang first allow comprehensive inspections.[171] The gesture could have resolved a dilemma over financing the deal, since Russia was unwilling to foot the reactor bill and the United States was currently barred by domestic law from providing either the technology or the funding. In addition, the move would have reinserted Seoul more centrally into Washington's ongoing dialogue with the North.[172] But North Korea's objections to South Korea's building the two reactors, as well as the absence of any other nuclear vendors willing to finance the bulk of the project and the North's insistence on "several billion dollars" as compensation for forgoing its two graphite-moderated reactors, lowered hopes that Washington and Pyongyang would easily or speedily resolve the nuclear dispute in the fourth round of talks scheduled for September 23 in Geneva.[173]

After a week of difficult negotiating, the two sides announced a brief suspension on September 29, and Gallucci flew back to Washington for further consultations. The two main areas of disagreement were North Korea's insistence on refueling the 30MW reactor and its firm stance on keeping the fuel rods in the country. On the refueling question, Kang, apparently under pressure from Pyongyang, had told Gallucci that the North needed to refuel the reactor "for a very brief period," perhaps no longer than six months, which would not produce any significant amounts of plutonium. Gallucci told him that this was a deal-breaker and that the United States would walk away from the table.[174] Other divisive issues included the central role of South Korea in the LWR project and the question of when North Korea would halt construction on two graphite-moderated reactors and permit IAEA inspections of the two nuclear waste sites at Yongbyon.[175]

The talks resumed in Geneva on October 6 amid speculation that the two sides would be unable to resolve their differences. The first signal that a settlement might be possible came from Seoul. Despite the Clinton administration's assertions that it would not sweeten the deal, South Korean President Kim Young Sam's strong public rebuke that Washington was too eager to compromise suggested that the United States had altered its bargaining position to accommodate the North.[176]

On October 17, it was announced that the two sides had reached agreement on all outstanding disputes. After further consultations with their home governments, Gallucci and Kang formally signed the "Agreed Framework" on October 21. Clinton hailed the deal as "good for the United States, good for [its] allies, and good for the safety of the entire world." Significantly, the IAEA, South Korea, and Japan immediately endorsed the agreement.[177]

THE FRAMEWORK AGREEMENT

Given the inherent complexity of the issues, the agreement was remarkably brief, only four pages with a two-page confidential minute. The agreement outlined a carefully calibrated, step-by-step process over a ten-to-twelve-year period, during which time all of Washington's (and presumably Pyongyang's) concerns would be addressed. As a first step, North Korea would shut down the 30MW reactor and seal the reprocessing facility; the spent fuel rods would remain in the cooling pond. The IAEA would monitor this freeze (as would the United States by National Technical Means). These actions would ensure that the research reactor would not produce any more plutonium and that the North would not reprocess spent fuel from any source. Construction on the two graphite-moderated reactors would halt.

A multilateral consortium of nuclear vendors, the Korean Energy Development Organization (KEDO), would be formed to provide the North with two light-water reactors with a combined generating capacity of 2,000MW at an estimated cost of $4 billion.[178] Sensitive nuclear technology (understood as those items on the Nuclear Suppliers Group "trigger list") would not be transferred until Pyongyang came into "full compliance" with its IAEA safeguards obligations. In other words, it had to permit special inspections of the two nuclear waste sites at Yongbyon. According to Gallucci, should the IAEA uncover evidence that the North had reprocessed more spent fuel than it had previously disclosed, Pyongyang would have to identify where the resulting plutonium was located and place it under IAEA safeguards.[179]

At the same time that sensitive nuclear components would be transferred for the first LWR, the spent fuel rods would be shipped out of the North.[180] As soon as the first LWR came on-line, Pyongyang would begin to dismantle the research reactor, the two graphite-moderated reactors, and the reprocessing plant. Dismantlement would be completed when the second LWR was finished. The timetable for special inspections, delivery of sensitive LWR technology, removal of the fuel rods, and dismantlement activities was spelled out in the confidential minute.[181] To compensate the DPRK for the projected loss of electricity during the interim period from when the research reactor was shut down and the two graphite-moderated reactors would have started operating to when the two LWRs came on-line, KEDO would supply up to five hundred thousand tons of heavy oil annually.[182] It was expected that South Korea would provide roughly 70 percent of the financing for the deal, Japan 25 percent, and other countries, including the United States, the remaining 5 percent.[183] The total U.S. contribution would amount to $20 million to $30 million a year.[184]

Consistent with the broad and thorough approach, the United States and North Korea also pledged to take initial steps toward a more normal political and economic relationship, including removing trade and investment barriers and discussing the creation of liaison offices in each other's capitals. The North would engage in dialogue with South Korea and take steps to implement the December 1991 Joint Denuclearization Declaration.[185]

Even while the ink on the framework agreement was still wet, a number of criticisms by Republican lawmakers and others could be heard. Pervading these protests was a general frustration at rewarding North Korea for now agreeing to honor its existing international legal obligations.

There were five main areas of concern. First, the spent fuel rods, the source of the rising tensions on the peninsula only months before, would remain in the cooling pond for perhaps five years or longer. It was argued that the North could use the heavy oil and then reprocess this fuel to obtain enough plutonium to build four or five nuclear weapons. A not altogether satisfying response from the administration was that Pyongyang could have done just this, under IAEA safeguards, without the framework agreement, which at least committed the North to shipping the fuel rods out of the country.

Second, the estimated five-year delay in special inspections undermined the IAEA safeguards system and eroded the NPT regime; critics, such as Senators Robert Dole, John McCain, and Frank Murkowski, argued that the United States had codified the North's noncompliance.[186] Although this was true, it was also true that the radioactive isotopes in the nuclear waste had a half-life of thousands of years. A delay would not harm the IAEA's eventual analysis of the waste.[187] Any attempt at diversion would most likely be detected by the international inspectors at Yongbyon or by U.S. National Technical Means. Should the DPRK refuse to ship the spent fuel rods out of the country or to allow special inspections, thereby terminating the agreement, all it would have received would be some oil and a partially built light-water reactor that it would be unable to complete.

The framework agreement also allegedly set a poor precedent for other countries that harbored nuclear ambitions, countries such as Iran and Iraq. These states might also engage in nuclear brinkmanship to win similar benefits.[188] The Clinton administration claimed, on the other hand, that the lesson of North Korea was that the United States would not walk away when a country breached its safeguards obligations.[189] The North Korean nuclear problem had its own characteristic features—a country that could soon produce enough weapons-grade material for a sizable nuclear arsenal, allies that did not want to go to war to enforce the NPT regime and were willing to pay billions of dollars to "buy out" the North's nuclear program—and these features did not translate easily or at all to other countries of proliferation concern.[190] Moreover, the framework agreement required the DPRK to go well beyond its NPT obligations. Under the NPT, North Korea would be allowed to run its research reactor, complete and operate its two larger reactors (which could produce hundreds of kilograms of plutonium by the end of the decade), keep the spent fuel rods in the country, and operate the reprocessing plant to extract plutonium. The framework agreement promised to eliminate all these activities.

Fourth, many observers were troubled that the agreement did not define key terms and phrases, such as "freeze," "dismantle," and "key nuclear components." It did not specifically mention the term "reprocessing plant" but instead used the phrase "graphite-moderated reactors *and related facilities.*"[191] Many, though not all, of these terms were defined in the confidential minute, however.[192]

Finally, given the litany of North Korean lies, deceptions, and broken promises during the previous two years, Pyongyang simply could not be trusted to keep its part of the bargain. The Clinton administration responded to this criticism by claiming that the agreement did not rely on trust; indeed, it was structured on a series of conditional tit-for-tat steps. The operating principle was "mistrust, and verify."[193] As insurance against a North Korean breach, Pyongyang was completely dependent on foreign supplies of low-enriched uranium to fuel the two LWRs.[194]

The framework agreement was far from perfect, but the Clinton administration believed that it would cap the North Korean nuclear weapons program in the near term and would abolish the program completely in the long term. The agreement was far preferable to returning to the UN Security Council, walking away from the table, or going to war.

In a larger sense, the framework agreement would pierce the veil of North Korean secrecy and totalitarian control; one of its most attractive consequences was that construction of the LWRs would require thousands of South Korean engineers, technicians, and laborers to work, live, and socialize in the North for a decade. Normal diplomatic relations between the DPRK and its neighbors, the United States, and other Western countries would create greater transparency and openness. Foreign investment would open the country wider still. There was a real possibility that the North Korean regime would gradually wither away under these outside influences and be absorbed by South Korea.

Other factors also influenced the U.S. decision to accept the deal at this time. During the fourth round, North Korea had threatened to refuel the 30MW reactor, for which it had already fabricated the nuclear fuel. Although this would not have immediately changed the situation (it would have taken a while for the fuel to be irradiated and even longer for it to be withdrawn and then separated to obtain weapons-grade plutonium), refueling would have been unacceptable politically for the United States. In June, Clinton's list of conditions for resuming the bilateral talks had included the North's not refueling the reactor, a point that had been repeated by U.S. negotiators. And although Washington had retreated from ultimatums before, the withering domestic criticism such behavior invited had by fall 1994 made the administration extremely reluctant to retreat again.

Washington was also concerned about the safety of the spent fuel rods in the cooling pond. The metal jacket, or "cladding," around the fuel rods was corroding, which could lead to a radiation accident.[195] This meant that Pyongyang had legitimate grounds for fuel reprocessing, which it had earlier maintained it must do by late August. Any reprocessing would have ended the negotiations and rapidly increased tensions on the Korean peninsula.

In addition, the United States was feeling pressure from the ROK military. Back in April, Washington and Seoul had decided to defer Team Spirit until November. With that date rapidly approaching, some elements in South Korea wanted to schedule the military exercise; the announcement would likely have derailed the Geneva talks.

Finally, U.S. midterm elections were only weeks away, and numerous polls showed the president's party losing a raft of seats in the House and control of the Senate to the Republicans. After numerous foreign policy debacles, the Clinton White House was eager to showcase a success.[196]

By the beginning of 1995, both parties had so far fulfilled their obligations under the framework agreement. Pyongyang had frozen its nuclear program, allowed IAEA inspections, and even permitted U.S. officials to visit the Yongbyon nuclear complex for the first time. U.S. and North Korean officials had met in Beijing to discuss the transfer of LWR technology, in Pyongyang to determine how to safely store the spent fuel rods, and in Washington to work out the details on setting up liaison offices. These moves were a promising start. But there was still a very long road ahead.[197]

Conclusion

During 1993 and 1994, the United States and North Korea engaged in an extraordinary and tortuous diplomatic dance that wavered between capitulation and crisis before finally settling on the compromise outlined in the October 21, 1994, framework agreement. The United States and North Korea had finally "gotten to yes." But it remained uncertain whether Pyongyang would honor the framework agreement—a question that might not be fully answered for more than a decade. Whatever the ultimate outcome of the agreement, the North Korean nuclear dispute provided a wealth of lessons for the formulation and conduct of American foreign policy and for the future of the international nonproliferation regime.

U.S. POLICY TOWARD NORTH KOREA

The Clinton administration's North Korean policy was handicapped by a number of shortcomings, many of its own making. As a purely procedural matter, the administration simply did not organize itself well internally to deal with an issue of this magnitude. That this was neither a proliferation problem nor a regional security problem—it was a combination of the two—also hampered policy formulation. For a long time, there was no connection inside the administration between the arms control experts, who concentrated on IAEA safeguards and the NPT, and the regional experts, who emphasized the nuances of East Asian politics. Bluntly put, until spring 1994, no one was in charge. The result was indecision and drift. One example was President Clinton's announcement of the "broad and thorough" approach in November 1993, when neither he nor his advisers were able to explain what it meant. Another was the administration's inability to get to a third round with the North Koreans. From July 1993, when the second round of talks ended, until late February 1994, when Washington and Pyongyang hammered out a formula to reach the third round, negotiations were stalled in "eight months of absolute absurdity," according to one State Department official closely involved with these issues.[198]

A fundamental U.S. error during 1993 and 1994 (and ironically, one shared by Clinton administration critics) was thinking that Washington had a strong hand to play and that small, isolated, and impoverished North Korea had a weak one. In fact, the opposite was closer to the truth. U.S. policy labored under a powerful "disadvantage"—its traditional opposition to nuclear proliferation and its long-standing support for the integrity of the IAEA and the NPT regime. North Korea, needless to say, suffered from none of these constraints. As one State Department official noted when preparing for the third round of talks scheduled for July 1994, "It would be a lot easier to write their talking points than ours."

Further, the quality of U.S. diplomacy suffered from the opacity of the North Korean regime. Washington found itself staring into a diplomatic black hole; it could not see how decisions were made in Pyongyang or who made them. Despite the efforts of the U.S. intelligence community to track key North Korean officials and divine their genuine views and opinions, it was unable to provide much useful information to State Department negotiators.[199]

When necessary, Pyongyang could also play certain high cards to generate new bargaining leverage by raising Washington's fears about a new nuclear weapon state and a full-blown international crisis, as well as about the erosion of the NPT regime and the IAEA safeguards system. The North's threatened withdrawal from the NPT in March 1993 and its unmonitored unloading of the reactor fuel in May–June 1994 were the two most prominent examples.

In response to these provocations, the Clinton administration had unfortunately limited its diplomatic maneuvering room. It had only two narrow options: either negotiating with the North Koreans in Geneva or seeking UN Security Council sanctions against them in New York (which Pyongyang warned would lead to war). But the UN sanctions route was a particularly unattractive option for Washington. Unlike Operation Desert Shield/Storm, which addressed a clear-cut, immediate threat to a vital national interest easily understood by most Americans—oil supplies—the North Korean dispute was in many ways much harder to comprehend. The DPRK had violated an international agreement that was virtually unknown to the American people. If Pyongyang posed a longer-term risk to stability in Northeast Asia and more generally to international security by its export of nuclear technology and materials to countries around the world, this was but a distant and still hypothetical threat. The Clinton administration correctly calculated that the American people would not go to war over the integrity of the IAEA or even over one or two nuclear weapons in North Korea. Moreover, the ROK and Japan had no stomach for war, short of an unprovoked North Korean attack on the South. Consequently, Washington had little choice but to continue negotiating with the North at almost any price, thereby losing valuable diplomatic flexibility.

A single, senior official invested with presidential authority could have disciplined the unwieldy bureaucracy, set strict policy priorities, and shaped a more consistent U.S. approach. Although Gallucci never really had this power, his appointment as ambassador-at-large for Korea in late March 1994 brought greater order to the interagency process and for the first time provided the administration with a clear, articulate voice.

There were some inherent structural shortcomings, such as coalition management, however, that no single person could correct. The United States could never say or do enough to reassure South Korea and Japan. "When you're tough with North Korea," said a State Department official involved in the negotiations, "they are afraid that you're going to provoke a war that will be fought on their territory. If you are conciliatory, they are afraid that you're going to establish a condominium over their heads."[200] Despite constant consultations, an insecure Seoul and an apprehensive Tokyo countered Washington's attempts to take stronger measures against the North, even lobbying Beijing at times (such as in March 1994) to rein in the United States in the UN Security Council. On other occasions, South Korea sounded belligerent when it viewed the United States as being overly conciliatory to North Korea. None of this helped send a clear signal to Pyongyang.

Still, the Clinton administration could have done better. The countries in the region saw the North Korean nuclear dispute as a regional problem, not as an NPT or IAEA issue. Until mid-1994, Washington could not explain to these countries what a "regional solution" to the dispute might look like because the Clinton administration either did not see the dispute in these terms or did not know itself the type of solution it could live with.[201]

Even less excusable was the Clinton administration's mishandling of China. By virtue of its relationship with North Korea and its UN Security Council veto, Beijing was central to any U.S. strategy to halt Pyongyang's nuclear weapons program. Yet Washington's North Korean policy consistently took a backseat to a very public crusade link-

ing China's human rights practices with the extension of MFN benefits. How the administration believed that it could bash the Chinese
on human rights in the morning and then gain their support for UN
economic sanctions in the afternoon was unclear. What was clear was
that this compartmentalized approach aggravated Sino-American relations and was salvaged at the last minute only by an embarrassing
American climb-down in late May 1994.[202] This sordid maneuvering
came too late in the day to win much Chinese goodwill. More important, it could only have convinced the North Koreans that the administration did not know where it was headed and hence could be led in
a direction more to their liking.

Even after the October 1994 framework agreement, the administration did not appear to have a larger strategy for promoting peace and
stability in Korea and throughout the region. In other words, Washington did not have a game plan for exploiting the diplomatic opening
with North Korea that the agreement had won.[203] A number of divisive issues remained: the DPRK's million-man army and its forward
deployment near the demilitarized zone dividing the two Koreas;
Pyongyang's development of ballistic missiles (and their export
around the globe); the North's chemical (and probable biological)
weapons programs; and the DPRK's record on human rights. How, or
even whether, Washington would coordinate its North Korean policy
with Seoul and Tokyo to address these mutual concerns and avoid
propping up an enfeebled, but still dangerous, regime was unclear.

In general, a more competent, experienced, and self-confident national security team might have better managed this issue. As a result, the United States may have been able to successfully seek a
tough sanctions resolution against North Korea earlier in the game,
certainly before North Korea had removed the fuel rods from the
Yongbyon reactor and destroyed its nuclear history. The ability to
credibly go down this route would have infused U.S. diplomacy with
an option it never really had and raised questions in North Korea as
to how long it could resist IAEA inspections and thumb its nose at
the world community. In 1993–94, whenever economic sanctions even
appeared on the horizon, North Korea found some way to reengage
the United States. If this option had been pursued sooner, it is possible that the North would have been forthcoming sooner as well. At
the very least, this approach would have been more faithful to U.S.
nonproliferation principles.

The larger foreign policy problems that plagued the Clinton administration also impaired U.S. diplomacy toward the DPRK. The president and his senior advisers were widely perceived as too conciliatory

and lacking in credibility. After early setbacks in Bosnia, Somalia, and Haiti, Washington never had the tactical flexibility to make the type of productive unilateral concessions to the North that the Bush administration had offered; indeed, the Clinton administration was crucified in the press and on Capitol Hill for doing far less. But with an enormous reservoir of credibility from the defeat of Saddam Hussein, a coherent strategy for the region, and the forceful personality of Secretary of State James Baker, the Bush administration had been able to stay the course long enough to achieve two of its main goals: North Korea's signing of an IAEA safeguards agreement and the beginning of ad hoc inspections. More impressive is that the inducements offered by the Bush administration (removal of all U.S. nuclear weapons from South Korea, cancellation of Team Spirit '92, and the Kanter high-level meeting) came at a time of increasing U.S. anxiety over North Korea's nuclear weapons activities.[204] Yet few questioned the Bush administration's competence, judgment, or strategy.

The International Nonproliferation Regime

After the embarrassment of Iraq, the IAEA received vindication in North Korea, where it performed a remarkable job of nuclear detective work. The agency uncovered (with U.S. assistance) unmistakable evidence that North Korea had cheated on its safeguards obligations. This evidence prompted the request for special inspections, and it was the North's subsequent refusal that provided the legal justification for possible UN Security Council action. If the UN Security Council failed to act after the IAEA referred the matter to it, that was hardly the agency's fault. As one American nonproliferation veteran wisely wrote, "The role of safeguards in the current circumstances is to support the political process, not to compensate for its perceived deficiencies."[205] The North Korean nuclear dispute thus proved to many skeptics, in the United States and abroad, that the IAEA has a vital role to play in supporting nonproliferation efforts worldwide. Because of the framework agreement, it will continue to play that role in the DPRK.

Although the stature of the IAEA has been restored and even enhanced, less clear is the influence the dispute has had on the NPT and on future prospects for controlling the spread of nuclear weapons. Much will depend, of course, on whether Pyongyang fully honors the nonproliferation obligations it has assumed in the framework agreement. If the agreement fails and the North resumes its nuclear weapons program, the harm to the NPT could be both local and global, immediate and lasting. The North's nuclear recidivism would once again raise tensions on the Korean peninsula and have a ripple effect on regional security and stability. The international nonproliferation regime would be discredited. With the failure of the diplomatic approach now painfully demonstrated, pressures would grow in South Korea (and perhaps elsewhere in East Asia) to meet the renewed North Korean nuclear threat by military means, which could include abandoning the NPT and acquiring independent nuclear arsenals. Any or all of these steps would reduce confidence in the NPT and would damage, perhaps critically, the international nonproliferation regime.

In a deal of the framework agreement's size and complexity, between parties that still harbor deep fears and suspicions of each other, disagreements and misunderstandings will undoubtedly arise. The two most likely periods when the framework agreement could unravel are during 1995, when KEDO will undergo substantial start-up pains, and approximately five years later, when the North must permit special inspections and allow the spent fuel rods to leave the country in return for receiving sensitive LWR technology. Should these hurdles be surmounted, however, the agreement stands a good chance of ending North Korea's nuclear weapons program. Such a result would peacefully resolve a difficult and dangerous proliferation problem, enhance security on the Korean peninsula and within the region, and strengthen the NPT regime.

Chronology

DECEMBER 1985 North Korea signs the NPT; the Soviet Union agrees to construct four 440MW nuclear power plants in North Korea.

JANUARY 1986 The 30MW Yongbyon reactor starts operations.

JULY 7, 1988 South Korean President Roh Tae Woo launches "Nordpolitik" to explore a political and economic opening with North Korea.

OCTOBER The United States broadens its contacts with North Korea, including low-level, bilateral talks in Beijing.

SPRING 1989 The Yongbyon reactor shuts down for three months; it is suspected that some fuel rods are removed.

SEPTEMBER 1990 Pyongyang tells Moscow that it will embark on its own "nuclear development" if Moscow further improves relations with Seoul; nevertheless, the Soviet Union and South Korea establish diplomatic relations at the end of the month.

SEPTEMBER 17, 1991 North and South Korea simultaneously enter the United Nations.

SEPTEMBER 27 President George Bush announces the withdrawal of all U.S. ground- and sea-based tactical nuclear weapons that are deployed overseas or on ships.

NOVEMBER 8 President Roh announces that South Korea "will use nuclear energy strictly for peaceful purposes, and will not manufacture, possess, store, deploy, or use nuclear weapons" and will not develop a reprocessing or uranium enrichment capability.

DECEMBER 13 North and South Korea sign the Nonaggression and Reconciliation Agreement.

DECEMBER 18 President Roh states that there are no nuclear weapons in South Korea; President Bush modifies the traditional U.S. "neither confirm nor deny" policy and states that he is "not about to argue" with Roh's statement.

DECEMBER 31 North and South Korea agree to make the Korean peninsula free of nuclear weapons and of reprocessing and enrichment facilities, signing the Joint Denuclearization Declaration.

JANUARY 7, 1992 Seoul cancels the Team Spirit '92 military exercise.

JANUARY 22 Under Secretary of State Arnold Kanter meets with senior Korean Workers Party official Kim Yong Sun in New York City in the first high-level meeting between the United States and the DPRK.

JANUARY 30 North Korea signs an IAEA safeguards agreement, which its Supreme People's Assembly ratifies on April 9.

FEBRUARY 19 North and South Korea ratify the denuclearization accords signed on December 31, 1991.

MARCH North and South Korea establish a Joint Nuclear Control Commission (JNCC) and agree to conduct bilateral inspections by June.

May IAEA Director General Hans Blix visits the DPRK and tours the "radiochemical laboratory."

August 24 China and South Korea establish diplomatic relations.

February 9, 1993 Blix formally asks Pyongyang if the IAEA can perform special inspections at two suspected nuclear waste sites; Pyongyang refuses four days later.

February 23 The IAEA's Board of Governors gives North Korea one month to comply with the special inspection request.

March 9 Team Spirit '93 begins.

March 12 North Korea announces it is withdrawing from the NPT, effective in ninety days under Article 10(1).

June The first round of direct U.S.-DPRK talks ends with North Korea agreeing to "suspend" its withdrawal from the NPT.

July The second round of U.S.-DPRK talks begins.

September A third round of U.S.-DPRK talks is postponed; Blix warns that the "continuity of safeguards" in North Korea is threatened.

November 7 On NBC's *Meet the Press* U.S. President Bill Clinton announces: "North Korea cannot be allowed to develop a nuclear bomb. We have to be very firm about it."

November 23 Presidents Clinton and Kim Young Sam announce a new "broad and thorough" approach to the DPRK, although Clinton administration officials cannot explain what this means.

December Blix states that safeguards in the DPRK cannot provide any "meaningful assurance" that diversion of nuclear material is not taking place.

U.S. Defense Secretary Les Aspin states that North Korea has probably assembled a nuclear bomb; a Special National Intelligence Estimate states that it "is more likely than not" that North Korea already has one or two nuclear weapons.

February 1994 The IAEA and the DPRK agree on inspections of the North's declared facilities; the United States and the DPRK agree on four preconditions for a third round of talks on March 21.

MARCH The North-South talks go badly, and Pyongyang obstructs IAEA inspections; Washington cancels the third round of talks.

MAY The DPRK starts to unload its nuclear fuel without IAEA supervision; the DPRK allows the IAEA to complete its March inspection; the United States immediately offers to go to a third round of talks but is rebuffed; by early June the North's nuclear history is lost.

JUNE The Clinton administration tries to forge a UN sanctions strategy and now adopts Moscow's idea for an international conference on Korea, a proposal that it had rejected in March.

As tensions rise on the Korean peninsula, former U.S. President Jimmy Carter travels to Pyongyang and meets with President Kim Il Sung; Kim offers three "concessions," and Carter wrongly states that the Clinton administration has halted its UN sanctions activity; within a day, the United States reverses its policy, dropping its demand that Pyongyang permit the IAEA to verify, by analyzing the fuel rods, that no diversion has occurred at the Yongbyon reactor.

JULY Kim Il Sung dies during the third round of U.S.-DPRK talks in Geneva; power is apparently transferred smoothly to his son, Kim Jong Il.

AUGUST 5 The new third round of U.S.-DPRK talks occurs; the DPRK agrees not to reprocess spent fuel and to halt nuclear construction in return for U.S. assurances that it will receive LWR technology.

SEPTEMBER 23 The fourth round of U.S.-DPRK talks begins, after discussions earlier in the month on LWR technology, safe storage of the fuel rods, and setting up liaison offices.

OCTOBER 21 An Agreed Framework between the United States and the DPRK is officially signed in Geneva; the day before, Clinton sends a letter reassuring Kim Jong Il of the U.S. intention to facilitate the pledges contained in the framework agreement.

Notes

[1]Trying to decipher the motives behind North Korea's behavior recalls Winston Churchill's characterization of Joseph Stalin's Soviet Union: "a riddle wrapped in a mystery inside an enigma." For a spectrum of the possible motivations for North

Korea's nuclear activities, see Andrew Mack, "The Nuclear Crisis on the Korean Peninsula," *Asian Survey* 33, no. 4 (April 1993): 341–44; Burrus Carnahan, James Tomashoff, and Joseph Yager, "Nuclear Nonproliferation Policy and the Korean Peninsula," SAIC, prepared for the U.S. Department of Energy, Contract No. DE-AC01-90DP30414, April 29, 1991; Andrew Mack, "Nuclear Dilemmas: Korean Security in the 1990s" (paper presented at Korean Institute for Defense Analyses/Center for Strategic International Studies Conference, Seoul, October 13–14, 1992).

[2]For details on North Korea's nuclear development, see Leonard S. Spector and Jacqueline R. Smith, "North Korea: The Next Nuclear Nightmare?" *Arms Control Today* 21, no. 2 (March 1991): 8–13; Joseph S. Bermudez, "North Korea's Nuclear Program," *Jane's Intelligence Review* (September 1991), pp. 404–11; Larry A. Niksch, "North Korea's Nuclear Weapons Program," *CRS Issue Brief* IB91141 (December 17, 1992).

[3]All nuclear reactors can be described in terms of either their thermal (t) or their electrical (e) capacity. The Yongbyon reactor has been characterized as either a 30MW(t) or a 5MW(e) reactor; this has sometimes given rise to confusion. Since its main purpose was not to generate electrical power, it will be referred to as a 30MW reactor in this chapter.

[4]See Michael R. Gordon, "North Korea Joins Pact to Prevent the Spread of Nuclear Weapons," *New York Times*, December 27, 1985. The DPRK did not announce to its own people that it had signed the NPT until June 1986.

In the mid-1980s, Soviet-DPRK relations were at a high point. Also, North Korea thought that signing the NPT would lead to the U.S. withdrawal of nuclear weapons from South Korea. See Li Yong Ho, "The Nuclear Problem in Korea and Its Prospects" (paper presented at the Conference on the Prevention of Nuclear Proliferation Risks, Stockholm, November 19–21, 1992). At the time, Li was a member of the DPRK's Disarmament and Peace Institute.

[5]This starting date was provided by North Korean officials to IAEA Director General Hans Blix during his trip to North Korea in May 1992. Other sources state that the reactor began operations in 1987. The length of time the reactor had operated would directly influence the amount of spent fuel produced and the amount of plutonium that could be extracted.

[6]See Spector and Smith, "North Korea: The Next Nuclear Nightmare?" p. 9. Design information for the Calder Hall reactor had previously been declassified.

[7]According to a State Department official interviewed in September 1994, the U.S. intelligence community has not uncovered any credible evidence of a uranium enrichment capability in North Korea. The Soviet Union had earlier supplied a 4MW(t) research reactor, which started operating in the mid-1960s. Located at Yongbyon, this reactor has been under IAEA safeguards since 1977.

[8]U.S. government official, personal interview, Washington, D.C., January 6, 1994. In early 1993, the DPRK reportedly agreed not to hire Russian nuclear scientists after the Russian deputy foreign minister threatened to break off diplomatic relations. "North Korea to Cease Hiring Russian Scientists," *Radio Free Europe/Radio Liberty Daily Report*, no. 32 (February 17, 1993), p. 2; "North Koreans Give In to Russia on Scientists," *International Herald Tribune*, February 18, 1993.

[9]See testimony of Deputy Assistant Secretary of State Desaix Anderson, in House Subcommittee on Asian and Pacific Affairs, *Hearing on Korea: North-South Nuclear Issues*, 101st Cong., 2d sess., July 25, 1990 (Washington, D.C.: USGPO,

1991), p. 19. Interestingly, halting the sale of ballistic missiles was not on this list. According to a State Department official, the United States "didn't care" that North Korea was exporting Scuds to Iran. With the end of the Iran-Iraq war and the increasing volume of ballistic missile sales during the next few years, stopping the North's missile transfers emerged as a more important policy concern for Washington.

[10]The DPRK has refrained from any terrorist acts since November 1987, when two of its agents blew up a South Korean jetliner as it flew from Bahrain to Bangkok; 115 passengers were killed. In 1983, a bomb planted by North Korean agents almost succeeded in killing the entire South Korean cabinet during an official ceremony in Rangoon.

[11]See Peter Maass, "North Korean Arrives in South for Historic Talks," *Washington Post,* September 4, 1990. North Korea dropped its traditional demand that all U.S. troops would have to be withdrawn from South Korea before it would sit down with Seoul to discuss unification matters. Its position shifted to having U.S. forces withdrawn at the end of the unification process. Some observers have speculated that the North may see a continued U.S. presence as a beneficial restraining influence on the ROK military. State Department official, personal interview, Washington, D.C., January 6, 1994.

[12]Don Oberdorfer and T. R. Reid, "North Korea Issues Demand for Mutual Nuclear Inspections," *Washington Post,* June 21, 1991; see also Robert Carlin, "North Korea," in Mitchell Reiss and Robert S. Litwak, eds., *Nuclear Proliferation after the Cold War* (Washington, D.C.: Woodrow Wilson Center Press, 1994), p. 133.

In June 1978, the United States had issued a "negative security assurance" (NSA) that applied to NPT members "or any comparable internationally binding commitment not to acquire nuclear explosive devices," for example, an IAEA full-scope safeguards agreement. But the NSA carved out an exception designed to cover the Warsaw Pact countries and the DPRK. The assurance would not apply if the United States or its allies were attacked by a nonnuclear weapon state that was allied to or associated with a nuclear weapon state at the time of such attack. See U.S. Arms Control and Disarmament Agency, *Arms Control and Disarmament Agreements: Texts and Histories of the Negotiations* (Washington, D.C.: U.S. ACDA, 1990), p. 94.

[13]See Don Oberdorfer, "North Koreans Pursue Nuclear Arms," *Washington Post,* July 29, 1989. In response to the Oberdorfer article, on August 4, 1989, North Korea for the first time explicitly denied that it was developing nuclear weapons. A 1994 *Wall Street Journal* article stated, "The Yongbyon reactor was shut down for 71 days in 1989, for 30-odd days in 1990, and for 50 or so days in 1991." Albert Wohlstetter and Gregory S. Jones, "'Breakthrough' in North Korea?" *Wall Street Journal,* November 4, 1994.

[14]Roh met Gorbachev at the end of the Soviet leader's U.S. tour. Jane Gross, "Gorbachev, Ending U.S. Trip, Meets South Korea Leader, Who Seeks a Renewal of Ties," *New York Times,* June 5, 1990. Closer Soviet–South Korean ties reflected increased trade between the two countries, trade that totaled an estimated $1 billion in 1990.

[15]See "Moscow, Seoul Link Spurs N. Korea Threat," *Washington Times,* January 2, 1991; *Jane's Defense Weekly,* January 12, 1991, p. 46.

[16]See, for example, "Soviets Warn N. Korea on A-Controls," *Washington Post,* April 16, 1991. Moscow had withheld delivery of the four 440MW VVER nuclear power stations it had promised North Korea in 1985 for joining the NPT.

¹⁷See David E. Sanger, "Japan Says Talks with Korea Stall," *New York Times*, May 26, 1991.

In 1990, North Korea had surprised Tokyo by suggesting that the two countries normalize relations. This contradicted the DPRK's long-standing policy of opposing dual recognition (Japan already recognized South Korea) for fear of legitimizing the division of the Korean peninsula and reflected Pyongyang's need for hard currency and perhaps as well its desire to gain some diplomatic maneuvering room with Seoul and Washington by playing Japan off against its two allies.

In Japan, Shin Kanemaru, the vice chairman of the ruling Liberal Democratic Party, was the main advocate of improving relations with the DPRK. Many of Shin's constituents were members of Chosen Soren, an organization of pro-DPRK Koreans in Japan. This constituency bankrolled Shin's political operations, largely from their involvement in the pachinko parlor business. During Shin's visit to Pyongyang in September 1990, he embarrassed Japan by suggesting compensation to North Korea not only for the period of Japanese colonial occupation, 1910–45, but also for the post–World War II era. Nonetheless, formal talks on recognition were held in January and March 1991. At one point, Japan had suggested that it was prepared to extend billions of yen in reparations payments and loans and credits to North Korea, although it balked at compensation for the postwar period. But after Washington briefed Tokyo on the Yongbyon nuclear complex, Tokyo informed Pyongyang that it would not normalize relations without full IAEA inspections. See Mark Hibbs, "Japan May Condition Aid on North Korean Safeguards Deal," *Nucleonics Week*, November 22, 1990, pp. 6–7; see also "A Knock on the Nuclear Door," *Newsweek*, April 29, 1991, pp. 38–40. Later that year, Washington persuaded Tokyo to raise the bar further. On November 13, after meeting with Secretary of State James Baker, Japanese Prime Minister Kiichi Miyazawa stated that North Korea not only must allow IAEA inspections but also must dismantle its reprocessing facility. David E. Sanger, "Tokyo's Atom-Site Stance," *New York Times*, November 14, 1991. Pyongyang lost an influential friend when Shin was forced to resign in disgrace because of a political scandal in 1992. In February 1992, a senior Bush administration official affirmed, "This tough stance by Tokyo has been a major factor in sending North Korea a clear and unmistakable message on nuclear proliferation." Testimony of Under Secretary of State Arnold L. Kanter, in Senate Subcommittee on East Asian and Pacific Affairs, *Hearings on the Threat of North Korean Nuclear Proliferation*, 102d Cong., 1st and 2d sess., February 6, 1992 (Washington, D.C.: USGPO, 1992) (hereafter cited as Kanter testimony, 1992), p. 101.

¹⁸Don Oberdorfer, "U.S. Decides to Withdraw A-Weapons from S. Korea; North Korea to Be Pressed to Halt Program," *Washington Post*, October 19, 1991. The mid-October announcement was also a reply to Gorbachev's more sweeping arms control response on October 5 to Bush's September 27 announcement. In 1990, the American ambassador in Seoul, Donald P. Gregg, had told Washington that it was in America's self-interest to remove all its nuclear weapons from the ROK.

¹⁹State Department official, personal interview, Washington, D.C., December 31, 1992. A final component of the Bush administration's strategy toward the DPRK was Baker's "2 plus 4" formula for talks between the two Koreas, the United States, the Soviet Union, China, and Japan. See James A. Baker III, "America in Asia: Emerging Architecture for a Pacific Community," *Foreign Affairs* 70, no. 5 (Winter 1991–92): 13. The idea, which had been cooked up by a small group of Baker aides and was not circulated for comment within the State Department,

went nowhere. It had not been aired in advance with the countries concerned, and it particularly annoyed Seoul.

[20]See T. R. Reid, "S. Korean Leader Pledges Policy of No Nuclear Arms," *Washington Post*, November 8, 1991.

[21]David E. Sanger, "Cheney, in Korea, Orders Halt to U.S. Pullout," *New York Times*, November 22, 1991. In 1990, the Bush administration decided to downsize U.S. forces in Korea from a leading to a supporting role in three phases over ten years. For a description of this strategy and the timing of the three-phase withdrawal, see U.S. Department of Defense, *A Strategic Framework for the Asian Pacific Rim: Report to Congress, 1990*, pp. 9–10. This report devoted a single sentence to the North Korean nuclear program. Two years later, the Defense Department's assessment had changed dramatically; the 1992 version of this report stated, "North Korea's quest for a nuclear weapons capability continues to be the most urgent threat to security in Northeast Asia." U.S. Department of Defense, *A Strategic Framework for the Asian Pacific Rim: Report to Congress, 1992*, p. 10.

[22]See David E. Sanger, "Seoul to Permit Nuclear Inspections," *New York Times*, December 12, 1991.

[23]The full text of this agreement can be found in Foreign Broadcast Information Service, East Asia (hereafter cited as FBIS-EAS) 91-240 (December 13, 1991), pp. 11–13. The agreement entered into force on February 19, 1992. The two countries could not sign a peace agreement because there was never officially a state of war between them. The ROK was not a party to the 1953 Armistice Agreement, which had been signed by China and the DPRK and the United Nations.

[24]Quoted in FBIS-EAS-91-243 (December 18, 1991), p. 14. In Seoul in the following month, Bush declared, "To any who doubted [President Roh's] declaration, South Korea, with the full support of the United States, has offered to open to inspection all of its civilian and military installations, including U.S. facilities."

[25]The text of this agreement can be found in National Unification Board, *Intra-Korean Agreements* (Seoul: National Unification Board, 1992), pp. 49–50. For press coverage of this accord, see Robin Bulman, "Koreas Sign Declaration Banning Nuclear Arms," *Washington Post*, January 1, 1992; "2 Koreas Agree on Nuclear Ban, But Not on Method of Inspections," *New York Times*, January 1, 1992. The agreement was formally signed on January 20, 1992, and entered into force on February 19, 1992. There is a loophole in the agreement: it does not prevent either party from importing HEU or weapons-grade plutonium.

North Korea could hardly resist South Korea's request for a nuclear-weapon-free Korean peninsula, since its Korean Workers Party had issued an appeal for this with the Japan Socialist Party in 1983. This had been enshrined in an official DPRK statement on June 23, 1986, and North Korea had recently requested it at the 1990 NPT Review Conference. The two December agreements were the first formal agreements between North and South since each state was founded.

Neither the 1967 Treaty of Tlatelolco for Latin America nor the 1985 Treaty of Rarotonga for the South Pacific contained a provision banning reprocessing and uranium enrichment facilities.

[26]The DPRK later alleged that in return for signing the safeguards agreement, it had been promised that there would be no more Team Spirit exercises, ever. Some American commentators also held to this view. In fact, however, Pyongyang stated in January 1992 in an authoritative article in the party daily, *Nodong Sinmun*, that

the ROK and the United States would not conduct "joint military maneuvers this year," indicating that it clearly understood that the suspension was for a single year. See FBIS-EAS-92-011 (January 16, 1992), p. 10.

[27]FBIS-EAS-92-004 (January 7, 1992), p. 9.

[28]Some members of the U.S. government thought that the messages Washington delivered at the working level in Beijing did not reach the highest levels of the DPRK government. Kanter's meeting was designed to rectify this. Aside from resolving the nuclear issue, Kanter identified six other preconditions, stating that North Korea should (1) end all ballistic missile exports, (2) place its chemical and biological weapons programs under international controls, that is, by adhering to the Chemical Weapons Convention (then under negotiation) and the Biological and Toxin Weapons Convention, (3) regularize the return of the remains of MIAs, (4) declare unequivocally that it would not engage in or support terrorism, (5) make "substantial progress" in the North-South talks, and (6) improve human rights conditions, for example by helping to unite divided families. State Department official, personal interview, Washington, D.C., November 2, 1994.

[29]State Department official, personal interview, Washington, D.C., January 6, 1993.

[30]See Jon B. Wolfsthal, "North Korean Signs Safeguards Pact," *Arms Control Today* 22, no. 1 (January–February 1992): 42; Michael Z. Wise, "North Korea Signs Agreement for Inspection of Nuclear Sites," *Washington Post,* January 31, 1992.

[31]State Department officials, personal interviews, Washington, D.C., January 6, 1993, September 7, 1994, November 4, 1994. For an insightful South Korean critique of establishing bilateral inspections as a precondition to discussing other North-South issues, see Taewoo Kim, *Korea and World Affairs* (Summer 1992), pp. 271–74.

[32]Kim Chong-whi, personal interview, Seoul, January 28, 1993. Kim was national security adviser to President Roh at this time and was one of the main architects of Roh's Nordpolitik policy. See also Damon Darlin, "Economics Underpins Agreement on North Korean Nuclear Sites," *Wall Street Journal,* January 2, 1992; John Merrill, "North Korea in 1992: Steering away from the Shoals," *Asian Survey* 33, no. 1 (January 1993): 47.

[33]Personal interview, Seoul, January 25, 1993.

[34]Robert Gates, director of the CIA, testified in February 1992 that Pyongyang might be "within a few months" of acquiring nuclear bombs. Elaine Sciolino, "C.I.A. Chief Says North Koreans Plan to Make Secret Atom Arms," *New York Times,* February 26, 1992. The Gates assessment was reportedly informed by Russian intelligence that North Korea was developing nuclear weapons.

The CIA had been publicly embarrassed for reportedly not knowing more about Iraq's covert nuclear weapons program, and this embarrassment was widely thought to have influenced the intelligence community's subsequent analysis of the North Korean nuclear weapons program. In what would become a regular occurrence during the next few years, State Department analysts at the Bureau of Intelligence and Research strongly objected to the CIA's assessment. One official called Gates's testimony "the absolute worst-case analysis." This official added, "The more reasonable, middle-of-the-road assessment is that you're still talking about several years." Elaine Sciolino, "U.S. Agencies Split over North Korea," *New York Times,* March 10, 1992. A few weeks later, Under Secretary of State Kanter testified, "I am unaware of any information that North Korea has a nuclear device." Kanter testimony, 1992, p. 101.

[35]Ad hoc, routine, and special inspections are standard provisions of the IAEA's model safeguards agreement, INFCIRC/153. They can be found in Articles 71, 72, and 73 and 77, respectively, of the safeguards agreement that the DPRK signed with the IAEA. See "Agreement of 30 January 1992 between the Government of the Democratic People's Republic of Korea and the International Atomic Energy Agency for the Application of Safeguards in Connection with the Treaty on the Nonproliferation of Nuclear Weapons," INFCIRC/403, May 1992.

When issuing a request for a special inspection, the IAEA secretariat is obligated to consult first with the state concerned, which cannot legally refuse such a request. If the state disagrees with the need for such an inspection, the state and the secretariat can bring the matter to the IAEA's Board of Governors.

[36]Hans Blix, answers to questions posed by the House Committee on Foreign Affairs, *Joint Briefing on the North Korean Nuclear Program*, 102d Cong., 2d sess., July 22, 1992 (Washington, D.C.: USGPO, 1992), p. 31. See also Blix's Beijing press conference, May 16, 1992, in Annex 6, "IAEA Travel Report: Visit to the Democratic People's Republic of Korea, May 11–16, 1992."

In February 1992, the *Washington Post* reported that North Korea had backed up trucks to the Yongbyon reprocessing facility and hauled away equipment. See R. Jeffrey Smith, "N. Koreans Accused of Arms Ploy," *Washington Post*, February 28, 1992. This story came from a U.S. embassy official in Singapore; according to a State Department official who closely followed North Korea's nuclear activities, it was "nonsense." Personal interview, Washington, D.C., January 6, 1993.

[37]See House Committee on Foreign Affairs, *Joint Briefing*, pp. 9, 31.

[38]See ibid., pp. 9, 22–23.

[39]See Gerald F. Seib, "U.S. Analysts Worry North Korea May Be Hiding Nuclear Potential," *Wall Street Journal*, June 11, 1992; David E. Sanger, "North Korea Plan on Fueling A-Bomb May Be Confirmed," *New York Times*, June 15, 1992. The DPRK's not listing its hot cells in its initial declaration to the IAEA implied that the North might well be hiding other aspects of its nuclear weapons program. The IAEA asked to inspect the hot cells, a request the DPRK permitted.

[40]State Department official, personal interview, Washington, D.C., January 6, 1993. At the time, this seemed a more useful precedent than it later proved to be.

[41]"IAEA Director General Completes Official Visit to the Democratic People's Republic of Korea," IAEA Press Release 92/25, May 15, 1992. Blix also suggested to DPRK officials that although the IAEA could not publicly disclose certain information from its inspections, North Korea could always voluntarily share this information to ease international anxieties.

[42]The White House, Office of the Press Secretary, *Joint Statement on Korean Nuclear Nonproliferation*, June 17, 1992.

[43]JPRS-TND-92-019 (June 10, 1992), pp. 8–9.

[44]*Yonhap* (Seoul), July 24, 1992, reported in FBIS-EAS-92-143 (July 24, 1992), p. 2.

[45]*Chungang Ilbo* (Seoul), August 26, 1992, reported in FBIS-EAS-92-166 (August 26, 1992), p. 11. China was clearly moving in the direction of recognizing the ROK when Taiwan "bought" relations with Niger in June 1992. China, reluctant to enter into a bidding war with Taiwan, responded by establishing relations with the ROK, one of Taiwan's few allies in the world. State Department official, personal interview, Washington, D.C., January 6, 1993. The DPRK refrained from any public criticism of the China-ROK link but responded in turn by opening a trading company office in Taiwan.

In December 1992, China ended most of its barter trade with North Korea (temporarily) and insisted on cash payment for goods. See Nicholas D. Kristof, "Cash Only, No Bartering, China Tells North Koreans," *New York Times*, December 30, 1992. An indication of testy PRC-DPRK relations had been revealed during Senator Bob Smith's visit to Pyongyang earlier that month. Smith requested information on American POWs/MIAs from the Korean War. Pyongyang told him to check with Beijing because China had run the POW camps.

46*Yonhap* (Seoul), November 19, 1992, reported in JPRS-TND-92-045 (December 7, 1992), pp. 7–8; *ITAR-TASS* (Moscow), November 20, 1992, reported in JPRS-TND-92-046 (December 11, 1992), p. 19; see also Andrew Pollack, "Yeltsin Promises Roh to 'Pressure' North Korea," *International Herald Tribune*, November 21–22, 1992. Russia had first indicated that it wanted to revise the 1961 defense agreement in December 1991. See FBIS-EAS-91-250 (December 30, 1991), p. 31. In August 1992, Moscow clarified its interpretation of the defense agreement by stating that it would support the DPRK in case of an unprovoked aggression, implying that it would not support the DPRK if North Korea initiated hostilities. *ITAR-TASS* (Moscow), August 11, 1992, reported in FBIS-SOV-92-156 (August 12, 1992), p. 9. In 1993, Russia added insult to injury by offering to repay its $1.5-billion debt to South Korea with military equipment. See *Korea Herald*, August 25, 1993, reported in JPRS-TND-93-027 (September 3, 1993), p. 8.

47*Korean Central News Agency (KCNA)* (Pyongyang), November 23, 1992, reported in FBIS-EAS-92-226 (November 23, 1992), p. 10.

48David E. Sanger, "2 Koreas Agree to A-Inspection by June," *New York Times*, March 15, 1992; "2 Koreas Agree on Inspections," *Washington Post*, March 15, 1992. The text of the "Agreement to Establish a South-North Joint Nuclear Control Commission" can be found in National Unification Board, *Intra-Korean Agreements*, pp. 51–54.

49The South initially insisted on three elements for an effective bilateral regime: (1) an equal number of inspections; (2) no sanctuaries, which meant that it could gain access to the North's military bases; and (3) "challenge" inspections, which could take place on twenty-four-hour notice. South Korea submitted a draft inspection regime that called for fifty-four inspections, comprising fourteen routine inspections and forty "challenge" inspections. Chung Tae Ick, personal interview, Seoul, January 26, 1993. Chung was director general of the American Affairs Bureau in the ROK Foreign Ministry. This constituted the most sweeping, intrusive verification scheme in the history of arms control.

The North responded to the South's proposal by stating that inspections should be limited to verifying that no nuclear weapons existed on the peninsula. The North argued that it had a legitimate right to visit all military bases in the ROK to verify that there were no nuclear weapons, consistent with President Roh's December 18 announcement. The South, on the other hand, did not have a similar right to inspect the North's military bases, according to Pyongyang, because the North had never possessed any nuclear weapons. Regarding challenge inspections, North Korea pointed out that the Joint Denuclearization Declaration stated that inspections had to be "agreed upon by the two sides," which gave each party a veto over any site selected by the other. Regarding the North's unilateral right to inspect military bases in the South, Article 2(2) of the JNCC Agreement could be interpreted to support the North's claim. The language in the Joint Denuclearization Declaration that permitted each state to veto the inspection of sites selected by the other party had been suggested by North Korea. The South

Korean negotiators had mistakenly agreed to it. Gong Ro-myung, personal interview, Seoul, January 27, 1993. The Joint Denuclearization Declaration contained another drafting error. It used the conjunction "and" when it should have used the word "or" in connection with prohibiting the possession of reprocessing and uranium enrichment facilities.

For the DPRK's view of the JNCC talks, see Li Yong Ho, "The Nuclear Problem in Korea and Its Prospects"; see also the news conference by Choe U-chin, chairman of the DPRK delegation to the JNCC, in JPRS-TND-93-001 (January 7, 1993), pp. 6–7. Legally, Pyongyang had every right to reject challenge inspections.

The North itself proposed a regime that called for "one" inspection per year but that consisted of many inspections conducted simultaneously. The South refused, and the two sides failed to meet their June inspection deadline.

[50]Quoted in David E. Sanger, "North Korea's A-Bomb Plans Seem Less Perilous," *New York Times*, September 18, 1992.

[51]Inside the Bush administration at this time, midlevel officers at the State Department proposed that the United States take affirmative steps to encourage North Korea. The month before, the United States and the ROK had conducted a joint military exercise named "Ulchi Focus Lens." This exercise had previously been primarily a desktop and limited training exercise but was now converted into a proxy for the Team Spirit exercises that had been canceled earlier in the year; it actually involved more personnel than had been planned for Team Spirit. Still, North Korea did not halt or obstruct the IAEA inspections. To "reward" this behavior and encourage further cooperation, these midlevel officers proposed that the DPRK ambassador to the United Nations, Ho Jong, be invited to Washington to give a talk at the Library of Congress. This recommendation was turned down by higher-level officials at the State Department. (Ho Jong was invited a few months later and spoke at the Library of Congress in mid-November 1992.)

In September, the State Department also quietly authorized a policy review to examine under what conditions the United States would consider extending formal diplomatic recognition to the DPRK. The resulting report recommended that the North first meet four conditions: (1) cooperation in the nuclear area, including IAEA inspections and a North-South inspection regime; (2) no more exports of ballistic missiles and associated technology; (3) a freeze (but not the elimination) of its chemical and biological weapons programs; and (4) improvement in human rights. State Department officials, personal interviews, Washington, D.C., December 8, 1992, November 2, 1994.

During the summer of 1992, the DPRK's Kang had repeatedly written to Arnold Kanter asking for another high-level meeting. Kanter replied that "one meeting meant one meeting" and that there would not be a second meeting until the North addressed the concerns he had outlined during the January 1992 meeting in New York. Arnold Kanter, personal interview, Washington, D.C., November 14, 1992.

[52]See FBIS-EAS-92-198 (October 13, 1992), pp. 22–23, 46–47; FBIS-EAS-93-199 (October 14, 1993), p. 21.

[53]The United States made this decision with the ROK without consulting its embassy in Seoul, which opposed the announcement. Ambassador Donald P. Gregg, telephone interview, September 27, 1994.

Interestingly, the SCM communiqué had little to do with an assessment of North Korea's nuclear activities at this time. At the end of the month, the director of the U.S. Arms Control and Disarmament Agency, Ronald Lehman, effectively retracted Gates's alarming assessment of February 1992. See Don Oberdorfer, "North Korean A-Arms Danger Is Downgraded," *Washington Post,* November 1, 1992.

[54]U.S. Defense Department, State Department, and National Security Council officials, personal interviews, Washington, D.C., December 29, 1992, December 8, 1992, and January 8, 1993, respectively. To be sure, these officials all thought that the bilateral regime was an unparalleled confidence-building measure because implementation would be a litmus test of the North's intentions.

It was highly unlikely that U.S. inspectors would participate in a bilateral inspection regime, due to *South* Korea's strong objections. North Korea had accepted U.S. participation. See *Mainichi Shimbun* (Tokyo), August 3, 1992, reported in JPRS-TND-92-006-L (August 4, 1992), pp. 9–10.

[55]See "Report by the Director General of the International Atomic Energy Agency on Behalf of the Board of Governors to the Security Council and to the General Assembly of the United Nations on the Non-Compliance of the Democratic People's Republic of Korea with the Agreement between the IAEA and the Democratic People's Republic of Korea for the Application of Safeguards in Connection with the Treaty on the Nonproliferation of Nuclear Weapons (INFCIRC/403) and on the Agency's Inability to Verify the Non-Diversion of Materials Required to Be Safeguarded," April 6, 1993, copy in author's possession.

[56]R. Jeffrey Smith, "N. Korea and the Bomb: High-Tech Hide-and-Seek," *Washington Post,* April 27, 1993. North Korea planted the trees and shrubs so quickly at the older storage site that they all died within days.

[57]An April 1993 report by Blix to the UN Security Council and General Assembly explained: "(a) The characteristics of the declared and presented plutonium product are not consistent with the irradiation history of the fuel declared by the DPRK to have been processed during a single reprocessing campaign; (b) The characteristics of the presented plutonium product and waste and the declared irradiation history of the reprocessed fuel are mutually inconsistent and inconsistent with the declaration that they resulted from the single campaign." A/48/133, S/25556, April 12, 1993, p. 5, copy in author's possession.

[58]See David Albright, in *Arms Control Today* (May 1993), pp. 8–9; Smith, "N. Korea and the Bomb." Richard Hooper, a U.S. national who had worked for the U.S. Department of Energy before joining the IAEA, is credited with suggesting that the IAEA perform a comparative analysis of the separated plutonium and the nuclear waste products.

[59]See Michael R. Gordon, "North Korea Rebuffs Nuclear Inspectors, Reviving U.S. Nervousness," *New York Times,* February 1, 1993; David E. Sanger, "In Reversal, North Korea Bars Nuclear Inspectors," *New York Times,* February 9, 1993. The visit to Pyongyang in late January by Russian Deputy Foreign Minister Georgy Kunadze did nothing to make the DPRK feel more secure; he stated that Moscow wanted to strike the article in their 1961 defense pact that required automatic military intervention in case of a war. See *Korea Herald,* January 30, 1993; JPRS-TND-93-005 (February 12, 1993), p. 14.

[60]Molding the views of the North Korean leadership was a videotape, which many of them had seen, showing the death of Rumanian dictator Nicholae Ceausescu, who was chased through the presidential residence and executed along with his wife, Elena, during a violent uprising against his regime in late 1989.

[61]On DPRK decision making, see Alexandre Y. Mansourov, "North Korean Decision Making Processes Regarding the Nuclear Issue," *Northeast Asia Peace and Security Network* (April 1994). Mansourov served in the Soviet Embassy in Pyongyang for three years. See also Rinn-Sup Shinn, "North Korea: Policy Determinants, Alternative Outcomes, U.S. Policy Approaches," *CRS Report* 93-612F (June 24, 1993); Carlin, "North Korea," pp. 143–44.

[62]See Lee Sung-yul, "Korea, U.S. to Hold Team Spirit Exercises in March," *Korea Herald,* January 27, 1993. Seoul called the exercise a "defensive training event" and invited North Korean observers to attend, as it had in the past.

[63]Chung Tae Ick and Gong Ro-myung, personal interviews, Seoul, January 26 and 27, 1993, respectively. Team Spirit had not been announced at the end of December or the beginning of January, as was traditional practice, because Washington and Seoul wanted to wait until the last possible minute in case Pyongyang changed its mind on inspections. (They did this despite great pressure from the U.S. and ROK militaries not to suspend the Team Spirit exercise two years in a row, both because of the degradation in training and because of the fear that a more-than-one-year suspension might become permanent.)

Also, a December roundtable discussion of U.S. policy toward Korea, chaired by the former chairman of the Joint Chiefs, William Crowe, had urged a policy of greater engagement with the North. The Summit Council for World Peace, roundtable discussion on "American Foreign Policy and the Future of the Two Koreas," Washington, D.C., December 17, 1992. The Council's proceedings received no attention in Washington, D.C., but were publicized by the South Korean press and then picked up by the North. Both Koreas mistakenly thought that the "Crowe report" would have wide influence after Crowe was named in January to the largely ceremonial position of chairman of the President's Intelligence Oversight Board. Finally, the DPRK thought that the incoming Clinton administration, with a number of former Carter administration officials in senior positions, would take a new approach to the situation.

Not for the first or last time, the DPRK had misread the situation or simply miscalculated. A cleverer policy would have been to agree to almost any type of weak bilateral inspection regime in 1992, because this would then have forced the United States and the ROK to live up to their pledge not to conduct Team Spirit '93; indeed, many ROK and American officials were very concerned at the time that Pyongyang would do precisely that.

[64]On October 6, 1992, Assistant Secretary of State William Clark, Jr., testified before Congress that the United States wanted the DPRK, in addition to resolving the nuclear dispute, to stop exporting missiles and to stop developing chemical and biological weapons. Pyongyang denounced these demands as "unreasonable preconditions." *KCNA* (Pyongyang), October 7, 1992, reported in JPRS-TND-92-037 (October 9, 1992), pp. 4–5. See also William Clark, Jr., "What Does North Korea Ultimately Want?" *International Herald Tribune,* November 3, 1993 ("Perhaps North Korea has reason to believe that the United States shifts the goalposts").

[65]Information on the Blix presentation comes from personal interviews with IAEA officials present at the meeting, Vienna, November 4, 1993. Also, see David E. Sanger, "West Knew of North Korea Nuclear Development," *New York Times,* March 13, 1993; David Albright, "North Korea Drops Out," *Bulletin of the Atomic Scientists* 49, no. 4 (May 1993): 9–11; Smith, "N. Korea and the Bomb."

The presentation of this type of intelligence information was unprecedented. Fortunately, Blix did not ask the board for its permission, since the Indian governor had reportedly received instructions from New Delhi to formally object to the introduction of this material—if the board was asked.

Blix presented the DPRK dispute to the board despite North Korea's attempts to intimidate the IAEA. In the weeks preceding the board meeting, Pyongyang said that the board was bowing to U.S. pressure to conduct special inspections and that the IAEA was relying on "information and satellite data offered by a third country." If the IAEA insisted on special inspections, "it would result in plunging the whole land of the North and the South into the holocaust of a war." Quoted in "North Korea, Blaming U.S., Rebuffs Inspectors," *International Herald Tribune*, February 23, 1993. See also *KCNA* (Pyongyang), February 13, 1993, reported in JPRS-TND-93-006 (March 5, 1993), p. 3 (North Korea would take "proper countermeasures for self-defense" if the United States insisted on special inspections).

[66]As the board was deliberating over what step it should take, on February 24, 1993, the new CIA director, R. James Woolsey, gave some unsettling Senate testimony: "We have every indication that the North Koreans are hiding evidence of some nuclear weapons-related activities from the international community. . . . [There] is the real possibility that North Korea has already manufactured enough fissile material for at least one nuclear weapon." North Korea's nuclear program, Woolsey added, was the CIA's "most grave current concern." Senate Committee on Governmental Affairs, *Hearing on Proliferation Threats of the 1990s* (Washington, D.C.: USGPO, 1993), p. 14. See also the Gates interview in Don Oberdorfer, "Gates Remains Suspicious of N. Korea," *Washington Post*, January 13, 1993. After the revelations about Iraq's nuclear program, the U.S. intelligence community compared what it knew before the war with what it learned after the war and then applied this "before" and "after" template to North Korea to see what nuclear activities it might have missed.

[67]"Report of the Implementation of the Agreement between the Agency and the Democratic People's Republic of Korea for the Application of Safeguards in Connection with the Treaty on the Nonproliferation of Nuclear Weapons," IAEA document GOV/2636, February 26, 1993; see also R. Jeffrey Smith, "North Korea Gets More Time to Accept Nuclear Inspections," *Washington Post*, February 26, 1993.

[68]The initial U.S. position at the Board of Governors meeting was to set the date for DPRK compliance at March 15. This date was before the start of Team Spirit '93; the United States wanted to avoid the suggestion that there was any connection between the two events. But U.S. allies on the board did not think that this gave the DPRK enough time, so the date then slipped to March 17. In what should have been a tip-off to future behavior, China wanted a much later date, measured in months. The compromise was thirty days, which would end after the Team Spirit field exercise and permit the DPRK a face-saving way out, if it wanted one. U.S. State Department official, telephone interview, March 9, 1993. The board later pushed this date to March 31.

[69]"North Koreans Reject Atomic Inspections," *New York Times*, February 27, 1993.

[70]On Kim Young Sam's political background and electoral triumph, see David E. Sanger, "South Korea Elects Ex-Dissident, Ending 30 Years of Military Rule," *New York Times*, December 19, 1992; David E. Sanger, "Korea's Pick: A Pragmatist," *New York Times*, December 20, 1992. Kim's personal background suggested that he would

be far harder on North Korea than his critics thought. In the early 1960s, a DPRK agent had murdered Kim's mother after she found him rummaging in her house.

[71]The DPRK's military and general mobilization efforts in response to Team Spirit consume roughly enough energy to power Pyongyang for six months. They were also a drag on the economy, since workers were pulled from factories for military service. Daniel Russel, personal interview, Seoul, January 26, 1993. Russel was a political counselor at the American Embassy in Seoul at this time.

[72]"Statement of DPRK Government Declaring Withdrawal from NPT," March 12, 1993, copy in author's possession; see also letter from Kim Yong Nam, minister for foreign affairs of the Democratic People's Republic of Korea, to the president of the Security Council of the United Nations, March 12, 1993.

[73]Article 10(1) of the NPT states that each party shall have the right to withdraw from the NPT "if it decides that extraordinary events, related to the subject matter of this treaty, have jeopardized the supreme interests of its country." The DPRK withdrawal statement reprised this language.

The North's announcement set off a frantic investigation by lawyers at the State Department and the U.S. Arms Control and Disarmament Agency (ACDA), who hoped to find that the North had not complied with standard practice concerning proper notice for withdrawal. Was a public announcement sufficient, or did the North have to inform each NPT member separately? The lawyers did not reach a legal conclusion.

The DPRK probably thought that withdrawing from the NPT would have removed any legal basis for special inspections. Article 26 of the DPRK's safeguards agreement stated that the agreement would remain in force as long as it was "party to the Treaty." However, as a purely legal matter, North Korea would still have been responsible for any violations of the safeguards agreement while it was an NPT member. See Douglas Jehl, "U.S. Pressing Plan on Arms Pact to Force North Korea to Comply," *New York Times,* March 13, 1993.

The DPRK had previously hinted in February 1990 that it might withdraw from the NPT.

[74]Nicholas D. Kristof, "A North Korean Warning," *New York Times,* March 13, 1993. The DPRK ambassador did not explain what was meant by this phrase.

[75]David E. Sanger, "South Korea Puts Troops on Alert as 'Precaution,'" *New York Times,* March 14, 1993; see also Michael Breen, "S. Korea Worried U.S. May Pull Back," *Washington Times,* June 22, 1993.

On March 24, President Clinton was interviewed on CBS's *48 Hours,* where he said that he hoped and prayed that North Korea would rethink its withdrawal from the NPT. The following day, Secretary Christopher testified before the House of Representatives, "There seem to be a number of ways in which pressure can be put on [North Korea], and perhaps we won't have to get to that point because they'll realize earlier on that they made a mistake in withdrawing from this convention." On the importance of continued close U.S.-ROK ties, both Clinton and Christopher were silent.

[76] In addition to its concerns that the North might acquire a nuclear arsenal, South Korea alternately worried about what might be termed the "explosion" and "implosion" scenarios. It was worried that UN sanctions would provoke Pyongyang either to lash out militarily or to disintegrate internally, with the unwelcome prospect of massive refugee flows to the South.

On the reunification issue, see Lawrence H. Summers, "The Unified German Economy and Its Implications on a Unified Korean Economy," *RINU Newsletter* 1, no. 4 (December 1992): 5–10 (reunification sooner rather than later would be less costly); "Seoul Estimating Unification's Cost," *New York Times*, January 31, 1993 (reunification by the year 2000 would cost $980 billion).

[77]Quoted in Nicholas D. Kristof, "China Opposes U.N. Over North Korea," *New York Times*, March 24, 1993. U.S. officials were also concerned that even if China could be persuaded not to veto economic sanctions, it could easily subvert such sanctions at multiple points along its one-thousand-mile border with North Korea. The Clinton administration would not officially delink trade and China's human rights practices until late May 1994.

[78]Don Oberdorfer, "South Korean: U.S. Agrees to Plan to Pressure North," *Washington Post*, March 30, 1993; see also Patricia M. Lewis, "A Little Carrot Could Go a Long Way," *International Herald Tribune*, March 31, 1993; see also Douglas Jehl, "U.S. May Bargain with Korea on Atom Issue," *New York Times*, May 27, 1993. For a more resolute approach, see Mitchell Reiss, "Bring North Korea Back from the Nuclear Brink," *International Herald Tribune*, March 31, 1993.

[79]IAEA Press Release 93/8, April 1, 1993. See also David E. Sanger, "Atomic Energy Agency Asks U.N. to Move against North Koreans," *New York Times*, April 2, 1993; R. Jeffrey Smith, "Nuclear Agency Says N. Korea Violates Rule," *Washington Post*, April 2, 1993. The IAEA had the authority to report the matter to the UN Security Council under Article 12.C of its statute and Article 19 of the safeguards agreement with the DPRK.

The reason for the timing of the April 1 board resolution was that on March 18, 1993, the board had extended the deadline for the North's compliance with the February 25 resolution from March 25 to March 31. See GOV/2639, March 19, 1993.

At this time, the DPRK repeatedly accused the IAEA of not being "impartial"; it circulated letters to the board and the United Nations, explaining that the IAEA could demonstrate its impartiality by (1) getting the board to reverse its resolutions on North Korea, (2) having the director general issue an apology, and (3) removing certain unnamed IAEA personnel. Senior IAEA official, personal interview, Vienna, November 4, 1993.

[80]See Senate Committee on Foreign Relations, Subcommittee on East Asian and Pacific Affairs, *North Korea's Withdrawal from the NPT: Implications for U.S. Policy*, May 26, 1993 (transcript available at Senate Committee on Foreign Relations). See also R. Jeffrey Smith, "U.S. Outlines Compromise On Korea Talks," *Washington Post*, May 27, 1993; R. Jeffrey Smith, "U.S., North Korea Set High-Level Meeting on Nuclear Program," *Washington Post*, May 25, 1993; Douglas Jehl, "U.S. May Bargain with Korea on Atom Issue," *New York Times*, May 27, 1993.

[81]"Keynote Statement by First Vice Minister of Foreign Affairs, Kang Sok Ju, Head of the Delegation of the Democratic People's Republic of Korea," New York, June 1993, p. 5, copy in author's possession.

[82]"Joint Statement of the Democratic People's Republic of Korea and the United States of America," New York, June 11, 1993, copy in author's possession. State Department officials in New York who drafted the initial text of the joint U.S.-DPRK statement included boilerplate language on mutual respect for sovereignty and noninterference in each other's internal affairs. The draft was faxed to Washington, where NSC officials objected until they were told that the language came from the

UN Charter. State Department official, personal interview, Washington, D.C., June 22, 1993.

[83]See R. Jeffrey Smith, "N. Korea Won't Quit Nuclear Ban Treaty," *Washington Post*, June 12, 1993. North Korean officials thought that the statement marked a new and more positive chapter in U.S.-DPRK relations. Ambassador Kim Jong Su, personal interview, New York, June 23, 1993.

[84]Ambassador Kim Jong Su, personal interview, New York, June 23, 1993.

[85]Before the second round of U.S.-DPRK talks took place, ROK President Kim Young Sam publicly chided Washington not to let North Korea manipulate the nuclear talks to its advantage. "Time is running short," he cautioned. "By early next year, they will be able to produce plutonium [for a stockpile of nuclear weapons]." David E. Sanger, "Seoul's Leader Says North Is Manipulating U.S. on Nuclear Issue," *New York Times*, July 2, 1993.

North Korea's nuclear weapons program apparently rekindled a latent ROK interest in acquiring nuclear weapons via reprocessing. See Mark Hibbs, "South Korea Renews Quest for Plutonium Separation Ability," *Nucleonics Week*, October 29, 1992, p. 7; Martin Sieff, "Domino Effect Triggers Seoul, Tokyo Nuke Plans," *Washington Times*, March 23, 1994; Paul Shin, "U.S. Said to Stop South Korea's Nuke Bomb Plans," *Washington Times*, March 29, 1994. It would not be surprising if the ROK had been conducting research on (1) how to separate plutonium from MOX fuel and (2) how to build implosion devices, with a view toward shortening the time it would take to build a plutonium bomb after Seoul seized plutonium that had been stored in South Korea under IAEA safeguards. (On November 27, 1991, the ROK and Britain had signed a nuclear cooperation agreement that allowed British firms to reprocess spent fuel from the ROK's nuclear reactors. As noted earlier, the December 1991 Joint Denuclearization Declaration did not prohibit weapons-grade material from being introduced to the peninsula.)

In response to written questions following Woolsey's February 24, 1993, testimony before the Senate Committee on Governmental Affairs, the CIA refused to comment in an unclassified manner on whether South Korea was seeking a nuclear weapons option and whether it was developing any missile systems that would exceed the guidelines of the Missile Technology Control Regime.

Washington tried to assuage Seoul's anxieties in July 1993. During Clinton's trip to Asia in early July, the president warned North Korea against engaging in "endless discussions." White House officials suggested that the United States would move quickly to the United Nations and pursue sanctions if the second round of talks was unsuccessful. David E. Sanger, "Clinton, in Seoul, Tells North Korea to Drop Arms Plan," *New York Times*, July 11, 1993. During his visit to South Korea, Clinton stood near the demilitarized zone and warned the North Koreans that if they ever developed and used nuclear weapons, it would "be the end of their country as they [knew] it." See Ruth Marcus, "Clinton Threatens Annihilation If N. Korea Uses Nuclear Arms," *Washington Post*, July 12, 1993; Michael Kranish, "Clinton Warns N. Korea," *Boston Globe*, July 11, 1993. The DPRK Foreign Ministry complained of the president's "violent remarks," which had "severely irritate[d]" the North Koreans. JPRS-TND-93-023 (July 19, 1993), p. 6.

[86]The text of the joint statement can be found in FBIS-EAS-93-137 (July 20, 1993), p. 20.

[87]For press coverage of the second round, see Richard W. Stevenson, "U.S.–North Korea Meeting Yields Some Gains on Arms," *New York Times*, July 20,

1993; William Drozdiak, "U.S., N. Korea Reach Compromise on Nuclear-Arms Inspection Crisis," *Washington Post*, July 20, 1993.

As early as June 1992, the DPRK had asked the United States for assistance in building an LWR. At the time, the United States replied that it would consider the request if the North allowed bilateral nuclear inspections and abandoned its reprocessing activities. In July 1993, the United States offered help with LWRs without first insisting on bilateral inspections.

[88]State Department official, personal interview, Washington, D.C., September 20, 1993.

[89]The North Koreans told the inspectors that there was a temporary power outage and that they could inspect the sites once the electricity was turned back on. The IAEA refused to wait and demanded to see the sites immediately, which they were allowed to do. In addition, the broken seal on a door to the hot cell area was one of three seals on this door; the other two seals remained intact. The IAEA and the Clinton administration chose not to accurately report these facts for their own reasons. State Department officials, personal interviews, Washington, D.C., September 20, 1993, September 23, 1994. IAEA spokesman David Kyd was later quoted as saying: "Our August inspection was not a good one. It was something we launched unwisely." John J. Fialka, "Check of North Korea Nuclear Sites Won't Provide Comfort Clinton Wants," *Wall Street Journal*, January 31, 1994. See also "Report by the Director General," IAEA document GC/1084, September 26, 1993, pp. 5–6; R. Jeffrey Smith, "North Korea Said to Harm U.N. Ability to Verify Nuclear Compliance," *Washington Post*, October 28, 1993.

[90]See comments of DPRK Foreign Ministry spokesman, *KCNA* (Pyongyang), September 8, 1993, reported in JPRS-TND-93-029 (September 17, 1993), p. 14; "Report by the Director General," IAEA document GC/1084, September 26, 1993, p. 6. Technically, these discussions involved both ad hoc inspections to verify the DPRK's initial declaration and routine inspections of the 4MW IRT reactor that had been placed under safeguards in 1977.

[91]"Report by the Director General," IAEA document GC/1084, September 26, 1993, pp. 7–8.

[92]State Department official, personal interview, Washington, D.C., September 20, 1993; senior IAEA official, personal interview, Vienna, November 4, 1993.

[93]Hans Blix, "Statement to the Thirty-Seventh Session of the General Conference of the International Atomic Energy Agency," September 27, 1993, copy in author's possession.

[94]IAEA document GC(37)/1090, September 30, 1993. The vote was 72–2; China was one of eleven members to abstain. The members at the general conference also reappointed Blix for a fourth four-year term, which was an endorsement of his stewardship of the agency.

[95]Emphasis added. *Yonhap* (Seoul), October 19, 1993, reported in JPRS-TND-93-035 (November 10, 1993), p. 15; "UN Atomic Agency Suspects N. Korea," *International Herald Tribune*, October 20, 1993; also, David E. Sanger, "U.S. Warns North Koreans of U.N. Action on Nuclear Inspections," *New York Times*, October 15, 1993.

[96]See John J. Fialka, "IAEA Declares North Korea in Violation of Nuclear Treaty," *Wall Street Journal*, October 4, 1993.

[97]State Department officials, personal interviews, Washington, D.C., September 23, 1994, November 2, 1994. The Pentagon and the National Security Council sus-

pected that the North Korean proposal had actually been drafted by the foreign service officer, a suspicion that contributed to their wariness in pursuing the proposal.

[98]*Yonhap* (Seoul), October 13, 1993, reported in JPRS-TND-93-034 (October 27, 1993), p. 6.

[99]*KCNA* (Pyongyang), October 14, 16, 1993, reported in JPRS-TND-93-034 (October 27, 1993), pp. 7–8.

[100]State Department official, personal interview, Washington, D.C., September 23, 1994; see also Tim Weiner, "U.S. in Quiet Talks with North Korea," *New York Times,* October 27, 1993; Jim Mann, "U.S. Gains Support of South Korea for Overtures to North," *Washington Post,* October 28, 1993.

[101]*Chungang Ilbo* (Seoul), *Choson Ilbo* (Seoul), *Yonhap* (Seoul), October 23, 1993, reported in JPRS-TND-93-035 (November 10, 1993), pp. 9, 17, 18–19, respectively.

[102]See *Kyodo* (Tokyo), October 27, 1993, reported in JPRS-TND-93-035 (November 10, 1993), p. 2.

[103]"Telex Message Sent to the Director General of the IAEA," DPRK Mission to the United Nations Press Release, no. 36, October 29, 1993; see also Tim Weiner, "Shift on Cameras by North Koreans," *New York Times,* October 30, 1993.

[104]Personal interview, Vienna, November 4, 1993.

[105]"Statement by the Director General of the IAEA, Hans Blix, to the United Nations General Assembly," New York, November 1, 1993, p. 8, copy in author's possession.

[106]U.N. document GA/8375, November 1, 1993.

[107]Former Bush administration official Peter Rodman and journalists Lally Weymouth and Charles Krauthammer all wrote articles recommending a preemptive military strike during the second half of 1993. Reportedly, Defense Secretary Richard Cheney and JCS Chairman General Colin Powell had discussed in November 1991 with their South Korean counterparts the possibility of a preemptive military strike against North Korea's nuclear facilities, but it is unclear who first raised the subject. See Leslie Helm and Jim Mann, "2 Koreas Move toward Accord to Bar A-Arms," *Los Angeles Times,* December 12, 1991.

[108]Lee first privately made these remarks to journalists on April 12, 1991, but repudiated his own comments after they were reported in the local press. See David E. Sanger, "Furor in Seoul over North's Atom Plant," *New York Times,* April 16, 1991. He repeated this suggestion on September 27, 1991. See *Yonhap* (Seoul), September 27, 1991, reported in FBIS-EAS-91-188 (September 27, 1991), pp. 23–24. Seoul was embarrassed by the defense minister's comments, but he was not immediately dismissed because the ROK thought that the DPRK might interpret this move as a repudiation of this option. In November 1993, Lee was sentenced to three years in jail for accepting bribes while serving as defense minister.

In February 1992, it was reported that North Korea had earlier installed a ring of antiaircraft guns around Yongbyon. See Bill Gertz, "North Korea Digs Tunnels for Nuclear Arms," *Washington Times,* February 21, 1992. The DPRK also reportedly increased security at Yongbyon in February 1994. See "Seoul Says North Korea Steps Up Nuclear Security," *Washington Post,* February 9, 1994.

[109]"An Israeli Lesson for North Korea?" *Foreign Report,* April 22, 1993, pp. 1–2.

[110]James Adams and Jon Swain, "U.S. Targets Cruise Missiles at Korea," *Sunday Times*, November 7, 1993. The former U.S. ambassador to South Korea, Donald P. Gregg, cautioned the Clinton administration against engaging in "compensatory toughness" with North Korea to make up for U.S. foreign policy shortfalls elsewhere. See *Wall Street Journal*, December 9, 1993.

[111]Kongdan Oh, "Background and Options for Nuclear Arms Control on the Korean Peninsula," *RAND Note* N-3475-USDP (1992), p. 25. For a recent assessment of the Korean military balance, see John M. Collins, "Korean Crisis, 1994: Military Geography, Military Balance, Military Options," *CRS Issue Brief* 94-311S (April 11, 1994); see also Michael R. Gordon and David E. Sanger, "North Korea's Huge Military Spurs New Strategy in South," *New York Times*, February 6, 1994.

[112]R. Jeffrey Smith, "North Korea Deal Urged by State Dept.," *Washington Post*, November 15, 1993. *Newsweek* reported at this time that the Pentagon's computer simulations of a new Korean war showed North Korea prevailing. Bill Powell and John Barry, "Public Enemy Number One," *Newsweek*, November 29, 1993, p. 45. See also Michael R. Gordon, "Pentagon Studies Plans to Bolster U.S.-Korea Forces," *New York Times*, December 2, 1993; Barton Gellman, "Trepidation at Root of U.S. Korea Policy," *Washington Post*, December 12, 1993.

[113]For a discussion of the limitations of the military option, see Taewoo Kim, "South Korea's Nuclear Dilemmas," *Korea and World Affairs* 16, no. 2 (Summer 1992): 267–71. For the consequences of DPRK strikes against nuclear power stations in the ROK, see Nuclear Control Institute, "Backgrounder: Potential Nuclear Consequences of a Conventional Korean War," March 25, 1994; more generally, Bennett Ramberg, *Nuclear Power Plants as Weapons for the Enemy: An Unrecognized Military Peril* (Berkeley: University of California Press, 1984).

In December 1993, Secretary of Defense Aspin unveiled a "U.S. Counterproliferation Initiative," which included the option of preemptively destroying the nuclear facilities of other countries. See "Remarks by Secretary of Defense Les Aspin," National Academy of Sciences, Washington, D.C., December 7, 1993. The draft as delivered by Aspin contained no reference to North Korea, but this was only because the State Department had reviewed an earlier draft and insisted that all such references be deleted. State Department official, personal interview, Washington, D.C., December 7, 1993. For an analysis of counterproliferation, see Zachary S. Davis and Mitchell Reiss, "U.S. Counterproliferation Doctrine: Issues for Congress," *CRS Report* 94-734 (September 21, 1994); see also Mitchell Reiss and Harald Müller, eds., "International Perspectives on Counterproliferation," Woodrow Wilson Center Working Paper No. 99 (January 1995).

[114]"There's a lot of questions in connection with sanctions . . . are they appropriate, would they work, would they result in the desired outcome?" "Transcript of News Conference by Les Aspin, Secretary of Defense," American Embassy, Tokyo, November 3, 1993, p. 5, copy in author's possession.

Japan was reluctant to support UN sanctions for fear of angering China, provoking North Korea (which had tested a nuclear-capable Rodong 1 ballistic missile in late May that could reach almost anywhere in Japan), and stirring unrest among ethnic Koreans in Japan, who contributed an estimated $600 million annually in remittances to North Korea. See David E. Sanger, "North Korea Is Collecting Millions from Koreans Who Live in Japan," *New York Times*, November 1, 1993; David E. Sanger, "U.S. Delay Urged on Korea Sanction," *New York Times*, November 4, 1993.

[115]T. R. Reid, "Aspin Prods, Warns North Korea," *Washington Post*, November 5, 1993.

[116]According to Elizabeth Drew, Clinton misspoke because he "had got his briefing notes wrong." She attributed this to "carelessness, stemming from inexperience and inattention." See *On the Edge: The Clinton Presidency* (New York: Simon and Schuster, 1994), p. 364.

Clinton's statement evoked memories of President Jimmy Carter's declaration in late 1979 that a Soviet brigade in Cuba was "unacceptable." It became acceptable after Moscow refused to withdraw it. A press release from the DPRK Mission to the United Nations again commented that President Clinton's remarks were "seriously getting on [their] nerves." Press Release no. 42, November 10, 1993.

[117]As the war of words heated up in the fall, the DPRK repeatedly stated that economic sanctions would be considered an "act of war." It would have been useful to research if the DPRK had ever used this phrase before and, if so, what actions had followed. In particular, it would have been instructive to review exactly what Pyongyang had said in the months, weeks, and days leading up to the start of the Korean War in June 1950.

[118]"The Nuclear Problem of the Korean Peninsula Can Never Be Solved by Pressure, but Can Be Solved Only by Means of Dialogue and Negotiation," DPRK Press Release, no. 43, November 12, 1993, reprinted in *KCNA* (Pyongyang), November 12, 1993, reported in JPRS-TND-93-037 (December 8, 1993), p. 19. Kang's public proposal vindicated the foreign service officer by closely matching the private proposal that had been relayed from Pyongyang during the Ackerman trip. In other words, it showed that the foreign service officer had *not* drafted the earlier proposal and then sold it as a North Korean initiative.

[119]See two articles by R. Jeffrey Smith: "North Korea Deal Urged by State Dept.," and "U.S. Weighs N. Korean Incentives," *Washington Post*, November 15 and 17, 1993; David E. Sanger, "U.S. Revising North Korea Strategy," *New York Times*, November 22, 1993; Douglas Jehl, "U.S. May Dilute Earlier Threats to North Korea," *New York Times*, November 23, 1993; Patrick E. Tyler, "China Chooses Not to Prod North Korea," *New York Times*, November 28, 1993.

[120]The White House, Office of the Press Secretary, "Remarks by President Clinton and President Kim Young-sam of South Korea," November 23, 1993. See also Ruth Marcus and R. Jeffrey Smith, "U.S., South Korea Shift Strategy on North," *Washington Post*, November 24, 1993; Thomas L. Friedman, "U.S. and Seoul Differ on Offer to North," *New York Times*, November 24, 1993.

The ROK was less than thrilled with the Clinton administration's new strategy (even though Seoul had been nervous about seeking UN sanctions). It now saw itself further marginalized as the United States took center stage with the North. On the morning of the Clinton-Kim announcement, Kim had objected to the phrase "package deal," which had been originally suggested by the North. So Clinton agreed to use Kim's phrase, "broad and thorough," to characterize the new approach. (The Clinton administration could be petty over language too. Because the Bush administration had used the word "carrots" in relation to its North Korea policy, the Clinton NSC banned the use of this word; "carrots" reportedly does not appear on any interagency memo. Instead, the Clinton administration favored "inducements.")

Adding to the confusion from the Kim-Clinton meeting was that there was no written record of the discussion that morning. No one from the White House or the

NSC took notes; no one from the State Department had been invited. The conversation between the two presidents had to be reconstructed later.

[121]The White House, Office of the Press Secretary, "Background Briefing by Senior Administration Officials," November 23, 1993. Although this was a background briefing, the White House disclosed the names of the "senior administration officials" in the first paragraph of the press release.

[122]Thomas L. Friedman, "U.S. and Seoul Differ on Offer to North," *New York Times*, November 24, 1993.

[123]State Department official, personal interview, Washington, D.C., September 23, 1994. The Kim Young Sam government insisted that Seoul announce any cancellation of Team Spirit to provide it with some political cover from conservatives who advocated a tougher approach to the North.

[124]IAEA Press Release 93/25, December 2, 1993. See also David E. Sanger, "U.N. Agency Finds No Assurance North Korea Bars Nuclear Arms," *New York Times*, December 3, 1993.

[125]R. Jeffrey Smith, "U.S. Analysts Are Pessimistic on Korean Nuclear Inspection," *Washington Post*, December 3, 1993. Smith reported that the Bureau of Intelligence and Research at the State Department strongly dissented from this view.

[126]See R. Jeffrey Smith, "West Watching Reactor for Sign of N. Korea's Nuclear Intentions," *Washington Post*, December 12, 1993; Eric Schmitt, "Koreans May Hold a Nuclear Device," *New York Times*, December 13, 1993; Michael R. Gordon, "U.S. Sees Progress on Nuclear Talks with North Korea," *New York Times*, December 31, 1993.

In March 1993, a senior U.S. official reportedly said that the consensus of the intelligence community was that the DPRK had amassed enough fissile material for one or two weapons but that it was "a couple of years away, at least," from having the ability to manufacture an actual device. Don Oberdorfer, "South Korean: U.S. Agrees to Plan to Pressure North," *Washington Post*, March 30, 1993. In December 1994, Robert Gallucci testified, "U.S. intelligence believes that the maximum amount of plutonium [in North Korea] is less than ten kilograms." Testimony of Robert Gallucci, Senate Foreign Relations Committee, Subcommittee on East Asian and Pacific Affairs, December 1, 1994, author's personal notes.

Any DPRK nuclear device had not been tested, although the South Korean media had reported that Pyongyang had conducted over seventy high-explosive tests at the Yongbyon site to develop the nonnuclear components of a nuclear bomb. In January 1993, a State Department official said, "There has been no high-explosive testing [by North Korea] for a long time." Personal interview, Washington, D.C., January 6, 1993.

[127]State Department official, personal interview, Washington, D.C., September 23, 1994.

[128]Ibid. See also Michael R. Gordon, "U.S. Sees Progress on Nuclear Talks with North Korea," *New York Times*, December 31, 1993.

[129]On January 7, Charles Krauthammer's *Washington Post* article, entitled "Capitulation in Korea," accused the administration of "unconditional surrender" and suggested that the U.S.-DPRK agreement be signed "on the deck of the battleship Missouri." His article set off alarm bells on the seventh floor of the State Department, but it took the administration almost three weeks to draft, clear, and publish a rebuttal. See Lynn Davis, "Korea: No Capitulation," *Washington Post*, January 26,

1993. Moreover, Davis's article revealed the Clinton administration's inability to set foreign policy priorities by reviving other concerns—North Korea's "support for terrorism, violation of human rights, export of ballistic missiles and hostile foreign policy"—at a particularly delicate stage of the negotiations.

Finally, there was some confusion at this time over whether or not the United States and the DPRK had agreed to "one-time" inspections. At her January 5 press conference, Davis never used this phrase; in her January 26 *Washington Post* article, she also explicitly disavowed that this was part of the bargain. In fact, Washington thought that after a one-time inspection of the seven declared facilities, the United States and DPRK would then go to the third round, where the ad hoc, routine, and special inspection issues could be settled.

[130]State Department official, personal interview, Washington, D.C., November 2, 1994.

[131]See David Brunnstrom, "Seoul, U.S. Tighten Vise for N. Korean Inspections," *Washington Times,* February 1, 1994; see also R. Jeffrey Smith, "N. Korea Denounces U.S. Plan to Install Missile Interceptors," *Washington Post,* February 2, 1994.

[132]See Smith, "N. Korea Denounces U.S. Plan to Install Missile Interceptors." The North Korean announcement touched off a furious exchange of notes between the State Department and the DPRK's Permanent Mission to the United Nations. During this exchange, U.S. diplomatic letters were drafted in English and translated into Korean but then were sent without checking the Korean-language version against the English-language original to ensure accuracy. State Department official, telephone interview, March 28, 1994.

[133]See R. Jeffrey Smith, "North Korea Faces Inspection Deadline," *Washington Post,* February 7, 1994.

[134]See IAEA Press Release 94/4, February 15, 1994; R. Jeffrey Smith, "North Korea Agrees to Inspections," *Washington Post,* February 16, 1994; David E. Sanger, "North Koreans Agree to Survey of Atomic Sites," *New York Times,* February 16, 1994; Warren Strobel, "N. Korea Agrees to Inspections, Averts Sanctions," *Washington Times,* February 16, 1994.

[135]Under the IAEA's version of events, there was no backtracking on its opposition to inspections à la carte. Blix preferred to describe the IAEA's proposed activities at Yongbyon as a "technical visit," not an inspection, and he was upset when the IAEA press release of February 15, 1994, used the word "inspection." Pierre Villaros, personal interview, Dallas, Texas, November 19, 1994. Villaros, recently retired from the IAEA at the time of the interview, had assisted Demetrius Perricos in these safeguard negotiations with the North Koreans. By not advertising the nature of this "inspection," Blix and the IAEA were betting that the United States could resolve the inspection issue with the DPRK at the third round. This may also have been the best deal that the IAEA could achieve at the time, since Pyongyang continued to state that it was not a full member of the NPT and therefore was not subject to the full obligations of membership.

[136]The key sticking point had been Team Spirit, which neither the Joint Chiefs of Staff nor the Department of Defense wanted to cancel. They were finally persuaded after it was arranged that President Kim Young Sam would announce the decision, since this would preserve their relationship with the ROK military. State Department official, personal interview, Washington, D.C., November 2, 1994. See testimony of Under Secretary of State Lynn Davis before the Senate Foreign Relations Committee, Senate Subcommittee on East Asian and Pacific Affairs, March 3,

1994; see also Julia Preston, "N. Korea Issues Visas to U.N. Inspectors," *Washington Post,* February 27, 1994; "Statement of Head of DPRK Delegation to DPRK-USA Talks," DPRK Permanent Mission to the United Nations, Press Release no. 13, March 5, 1994.

In late February 1994, a special working group convened by the U.S. Institute of Peace drafted a report on U.S. policy toward North Korea. Entitled "North Korea's Nuclear Program: Challenge and Opportunity for American Policy," the report recommended that Washington appoint a "senior coordinator" to present a "package deal" to Pyongyang. See also Donald P. Gregg, "Offer Korea a Carrot," *New York Times,* May 19, 1994.

[137]The first problem arose with Seoul's tardy invitation to Pyongyang to resume the North-South dialogue; North Korea retaliated by delaying the start of the IAEA inspections. State Department officials, personal interviews, Washington, D.C., November 2 and 4, 1994. See also David Briscoe, "U.S. Rewards N. Korea with Talks, Canceled Exercises," *Washington Times,* March 4, 1994; Thomas W. Lippman and T. R. Reid, "N. Korea Nuclear Inspection Begins," *Washington Post,* March 4, 1994; David E. Sanger, "Atom Inspectors in North Korea, Easing Rift," *New York Times,* March 2, 1994.

For press coverage of the IAEA's March inspection visit, see R. Jeffrey Smith, "N. Korean Conduct in Inspections Draws Criticism of U.S. Officials," *Washington Post,* March 10, 1994; David E. Sanger, "North Korea Said to Block Taking of Radioactive Samples from Site," *New York Times,* March 16, 1994; JPRS-TND-94-006 (March 16, 1994), pp. 48–52.

[138]Sanger, "North Korea Said to Block Taking of Radioactive Samples from Site"; *Nucleonics Week,* March 24, 1994, pp. 1–2; R. Jeffrey Smith, "N. Korea Adds Arms Capacity," *Washington Post,* April 2, 1994; Michael R. Gordon, "North Korea May Be Expanding Atom Site," *New York Times,* April 3, 1994. The second reprocessing line reportedly used high-quality steel imported from Japan. On the use of Japanese technology in North Korea's nuclear weapons program, see Katsumi Sato, "Japanese Components and Yen-Produced North Korean Nuclear Weapons," Modern Korea Institute, Tokyo, December 1993, copy in author's possession.

[139]State Department officials, personal interviews, Washington, D.C., September 7, 23, 1994.

[140]See IAEA Press Release 94/9, March 21, 1994. For a DPRK perspective on the March inspections, see DPRK Permanent Mission to the United Nations, "Memorandum of the General Department of the Atomic Energy of the Democratic People's Republic of Korea," no. 17 (March 21, 1994), copy in author's possession. China abstained on the board's resolution.

[141]Quoted in Robert S. Greenberger and Thomas E. Ricks, "Korean Move Puts U.S. Talks in Doubt," *Wall Street Journal,* March 17, 1994. Two other news events at this time compounded the Clinton administration's political troubles. First, CIA Director R. James Woolsey revealed on March 17 that North Korea was developing two types of long-range ballistic missiles, with ranges of over one thousand and two thousand miles. See R. Jeffrey Smith, "CIA Confirms North Korea's New Missiles," *Washington Post,* March 18, 1994. Second, in an embarrassing rebuke, the Singapore government rejected a personal appeal from President Clinton not to cane an American teenager, Michael Faye, who had been convicted of vandalism.

[142]R. Jeffrey Smith and Ann Devroy, "Clinton Orders Patriot Missiles to South Korea," *Washington Post,* March 22, 1994. The Clinton administration had favored the transfer since at least January 1994 but had not made a formal decision because

of South Korea's fear that such a move would provoke North Korea and upset negotiations with the IAEA. See John Lancaster and Ann Devroy, "U.S. Weighs Deployment of Patriots to S. Korea," *Washington Post*, January 27, 1993; David E. Sanger, "North Korea Warns U.S. on Patriot Missiles," *New York Times*, January 30, 1994; Lee Su-wan, "North Korea Denounces U.S. Missiles," *Washington Post*, January 29, 1994. These Patriots were upgraded from the ones used in the Persian Gulf war against Scuds similar to those possessed by the DPRK. It is interesting to note that during the Gulf war the Patriots played a politically reassuring role but that during the first few months of 1994 they had the reverse effect on Seoul.

[143]Stephen Barr and Lena H. Sun, "China's Cooperation on N. Korea Seen," *Washington Post*, March 21, 1994. It might be argued that China never blocked any UN or IAEA resolution, but this would be slightly misleading. These resolutions were watered down to gain China's support. Also, once developments reached this stage, the United States became more flexible because it had shown its "toughness" just by getting there.

[144]Quoted in Michael R. Gordon, "U.S. Will Urge U.N. to Plan Sanctions for North Korea," *New York Times*, March 20, 1994. This formulation left the door open to a Chinese abstention.

[145]Quoted in Steven Greenhouse, "Christopher Says U.S. Stays Firm on Korea, but Pledges Diplomacy," *New York Times*, March 23, 1994.

[146]On May 11, 1993, the UN Security Council passed resolution 825 urging the DPRK to open sites to IAEA inspections and reconsider its decision to withdraw from the NPT. China and Pakistan had abstained. The day after this resolution, the DPRK rejected its demands.

[147]The statement requested that the IAEA report back to the UN Security Council in six weeks. See Julia Preston, "U.N. Bows to China, Issues Mild Call to N. Korea to Permit Nuclear Checks," *Washington Post*, April 1, 1994; see also Paul Lewis, "China Shields North Korea on Atom Issue," *New York Times*, March 30, 1994; Ann Devroy and Daniel Williams, "China Resists U.N. Resolution on North Korea, U.S. Aides Say," *Washington Post*, March 30, 1994.

In late March, Kim Young Sam had visited Japan and China to persuade them to pressure the United States not to force the issue by seeking a sanctions resolution. State Department official, personal interview, Washington, D.C., September 7, 1994.

[148]Quoted in Mark Thompson, "Well, Maybe a Nuke or Two," *Time*, April 11, 1994, p. 58 (emphasis added). Peter Grier was the first to report this shift in the thinking of the Clinton administration. See Peter Grier, "North Korea Bends a Bit on Opening Nuclear Sites," *Christian Science Monitor*, February 17, 1994; see also Michael Kramer, "Playing Nuclear Poker," *Time*, February 28, 1994, p. 45; Jim Hoagland, "Containing North Korea," *Washington Post*, March 10, 1994.

On March 24, Perry had stated that the DPRK already "might have one or two nuclear devices." Quoted in Rowan Scarborough, "Pentagon Official Tells Panel N. Korean Threat Is Bluster," *Washington Times*, March 25, 1994. These comments appeared to contradict Clinton's unequivocal declaration in early November 1993 that the DPRK could not be permitted to have a bomb.

[149]See R. Jeffrey Smith, "S. Korea Offers Gesture to North," *Washington Post*, April 16, 1994; *Yonhap* (Seoul), April 15, 1994, reported in JPRS-TND-94-010 (May 5, 1994), p. 2. Seoul had telegraphed this policy change ten days earlier. See R. Jeffrey Smith, "U.S. Tough Talk Rattles Nerves in Asia," *Washington Post*, April 5, 1994. The Patriots arrived on April 8, 1994.

[150]R. Jeffrey Smith, "U.S. South Korean Exercise Put Off as Gesture to North," *Washington Post*, April 21, 1993. Some State Department officials had jokingly asked: "What do you call Team Spirit if South Korea does not grant permission? Answer: an invasion."

[151]See David E. Sanger, "North Korea Will Remove Nuclear Fuel," *New York Times*, April 22, 1994; R. Jeffrey Smith, "N. Korea Refuses Demand to Inspect Reactor Fuel," *Washington Post*, April 28, 1994; Joan Biskupic and R. Jeffrey Smith, "N. Korea Keeps Nuclear Inspectors at Bay," *Washington Post*, May 1, 1994. In light of subsequent events, it is interesting to speculate whether IAEA inspectors, even if they had only observed and counted the fuel rods, could have preserved the DPRK's nuclear history.

[152]"Letter from the Director General of the IAEA to the Secretary General of the United Nations," May 19, 1994, copy in author's possession; see also *Nodong Sinmun* (Pyongyang), May 21, 1994, reported in JPRS-TND-94-013 (June 24, 1994), pp. 46–47. North Korea had told the IAEA in early 1993 that it would pull the core from this reactor in April 1993. At the time, and in subsequent communications, it had agreed to let the IAEA conduct an isotopic examination of the fuel rods and then compare the results with the plant's operating records to see if any diversion had taken place. State Department official, personal interview, Washington, D.C., January 6, 1994.

[153]The administration justified this decision by claiming that both preconditions from the February 25, 1994, agreement with North Korea had now technically been "met": (1) IAEA inspections at the seven declared sites; (2) the North-South exchange of special envoys. Seoul had unilaterally removed the second as a precondition in mid-April. The administration also noted that the DPRK had not yet withdrawn any of the three hundred or so fuel rods that the IAEA considered crucial to its technical analysis.

[154]Unknown to the IAEA and the United States, North Korea was working around the clock with a new and faster unloading machine; it had originally been estimated that the unloading would take two to three months. See Stewart Stogel, "Continued North Korean Militancy," *Washington Times*, June 1, 1994; David Albright, "North Korean Plutonium Production," *ISIS Monograph*, June 3, 1994.

[155]Quoted in David E. Sanger, "North Korea Foils Efforts to Halt Its Nuclear Plans," *New York Times*, May 29, 1994; see also Michael R. Gordon, "Korea Speeds Nuclear Fuel Removal, Impeding Inspection," *New York Times*, May 28, 1994; R. Jeffrey Smith and Julia Preston, "Nuclear Watchdog Says N. Korea Steps Up Fuel Rod Withdrawal," *Washington Post*, May 28, 1994.

The obvious question is, why did North Korea pull the fuel at this time? None of the U.S. government officials whom I interviewed, including members of the U.S. negotiating team, felt that they really understood the motivation(s) behind this action.

However, in the fall of 1993, Kang Sok Ju, the chief North Korean nuclear negotiator, had told U.S. officials that if there was no progress on U.S.-DPRK talks, Pyongyang would unload the fuel. One State Department analyst thought that in spring 1994 Kang may have lost control of the situation to those in Pyongyang who feared that the United States was stringing the talks along in response to South Korean pressure. Unloading the fuel would break this U.S.-ROK connection. Personal interview, Washington, D.C., November 4, 1994.

An alternative theory, one that I favor, is that pulling the fuel satisfied the agendas of both the "soft-liners" and the "hard-liners" in North Korea at the time. The soft-liners hoped that this action would get Washington's attention and force them back to the negotiating table. The hard-liners could support this action because it would move the North one step closer to acquiring material for nuclear weapons.

[156]This letter is reproduced in the annex to UN document S/1994/656, June 2, 1994; see also Paul Lewis, "U.N. Told North Korea's Nuclear Record Can't Be Retrieved," *New York Times*, June 4, 1994. The United States did not share the IAEA's technical assessment of the situation. Gallucci stated that the agency's ability to determine that fuel had not been diverted had been "seriously eroded." He added, "That does not mean destroyed." Quoted in Thomas W. Lippman, "Nudging North Korea to Negotiate," *Washington Post*, June 4, 1994; see also Warren Strobel and Stewart Stogel, "Nuclear Clues Are Gone, Say Experts," *Washington Times*, June 7, 1994. Technically, this was correct. If North Korea had given the IAEA unfettered access to the spent fuel rods and graphite tubing in the reactor, had shared the reactor's operating records, and had otherwise extended full cooperation, the agency may have been able to reconstruct some of the North's nuclear history. Needless to say, Pyongyang had never previously extended this type of cooperation to the IAEA.

[157]In late March, after the third round of U.S.-DPRK talks had been canceled, Moscow had blindsided Washington by suggesting this conference without giving Washington any advance notice. Concerned about rising tensions on the peninsula, seeking a way to reassert its influence, and perhaps trying to diminish U.S. standing in Northeast Asia, Moscow had proposed this idea after a meeting between Russian Foreign Minister Kozyrev and Japanese Foreign Minister Tsutomu Hata. It was a reflection of Russia's diminished position in world affairs that it needed a multilateral forum to have influence in Korea. See Fred Hiatt, "Moscow Proposes Conference to Deal with North Korea," *Washington Post*, March 25, 1994; Don Oberdorfer, "The Remilitarized Zone," *Washington Post*, May 1, 1994.

[158]Personal interview, Washington, D.C., July 15, 1994; see also Julia Preston, "U.S. Unveils Proposal for Sanctions," *Washington Post*, June 16, 1994; Paul Lewis, "U.S. Offers a Plan, for U.N. Sanctions on North Koreans," *New York Times*, June 16, 1994. To gain bargaining leverage in the UN Security Council, Washington had signaled that it would ask Japan and South Korea to impose sanctions if the United Nations did not take action. See David E. Sanger, "North Korea Threatens Japan over Backing U.S.-Led Sanctions," *New York Times*, June 10, 1994.

Observers thought that China might have been quietly pressuring North Korea, especially after Clinton announced on May 29 that the United States would renew China's MFN status without any link to human rights. An indication was soon provided by Chinese President Jiang Zemin, when he greeted North Korea's chief of army staff in Beijing by hailing the "blood-bound friendship" between China and the DPRK, a friendship as close as "lips and teeth." See Patrick E. Tyler, "Japanese Hears China Oppose Korea Sanctions," *New York Times*, June 13, 1994. See also Jim Mann, "China Assisted U.S. Efforts on N. Korea, Officials Say," *Los Angeles Times*, June 29, 1994.

[159]The safeguards agreement remained in force. See David E. Sanger, "North Korea Quits Atom Agency in Wider Rift with U.S. and U.N.," *New York Times*, June 14, 1994; R. Jeffrey Smith and T. R. Reid, "North Korea Quits U.N. Nuclear Body," *Washington Post*, June 14, 1994.

[160]State Department official, personal interview, Washington, D.C., September 7, 1994. Another State Department official corroborated this account of DPRK military maneuvers. Personal interview, Washington, D.C., September 23, 1994.

[161]For press coverage of the Carter visit, see David E. Sanger, "Carter Visit to

North Korea: Whose Trip Was It Really?" *New York Times,* June 18, 1994; R. Jeffrey Smith and Bradley Graham, "White House Disputes Carter on North Korea," *Washington Post,* June 18, 1994; Michael R. Gordon, "U.S. Shift on Korea," *New York Times,* June 18, 1994; *Yonhap* (Seoul), June 17, 1994, reported in FBIS-EAS-94-117 (June 17, 1994), p. 22; R. Jeffrey Smith and Ann Devroy, "Carter's Call from N. Korea Looms Large," *Washington Post,* June 26, 1994.

Carter later apologized for his comment that the United States had stopped the sanctions process, admitting that he had failed to make clear that this was his personal preference and not administration policy. R. Jeffrey Smith and Ruth Marcus, "Carter Trip May Offer 'Opening,'" *Washington Post,* June 20, 1994.

[162]Quoted in David E. Sanger, "Two Koreas Agree to Summit Meeting on Nuclear Issue," *New York Times,* June 19, 1994; see also T. R. Reid, "Leaders of 2 Koreas Seek First Summit," *Washington Post,* June 19, 1994. At the same time that Carter was chiding the Clinton administration for being too tough on the DPRK, Republican lawmakers were criticizing it for being too soft.

[163]Michael R. Gordon, "Back from Korea, Carter Declares the Crisis Is Over," *New York Times,* June 20, 1994. There is little doubt that the Clinton administration's "subcontracting" U.S. foreign policy to Jimmy Carter further damaged its domestic standing at the time. The obvious question is why the White House authorized Carter to visit Pyongyang. A State Department official answered: "As a private citizen, Carter is free to travel as he wishes, so long as he does not engage in negotiations. He claimed to go [to North Korea] only to collect information, but while there decided he had best intervene." Personal interview, Washington, D.C., November 2, 1994. President Carter declined to be interviewed for this book.

[164]Gordon, "Back from Korea, Carter Declares the Crisis Is Over." Special inspections, almost forgotten in the flurry of activity, would be discussed at the third round, as the United States had originally intended back in November 1993. Critics pointed out that the spent fuel needed a few months to cool before the North could reprocess it in any case.

When asked why the United States included the condition of no refueling (which was really a second-order issue), a State Department official remarked that since this reactor had "started" the recent problem, the DPRK should not be allowed to reload it. He also doubted that the North Koreans would accept this condition, since they would argue that they needed the reactor for energy production. Was torpedoing the deal the real purpose of the condition? "No, we're not that smart." When it was mentioned that this condition might look to Pyongyang like the United States was leaving open the option of striking the Yongbyon nuclear complex, the response was that the State Department had not considered this point. Telephone interview, June 16, 1994.

[165]Quoted in Douglas Jehl, "Clinton Is Hopeful yet Cautious about Carter's North Korea Trip," *New York Times,* June 21, 1994. One State Department official commented that by undermining the sanctions approach, "Carter did [the administration] a favor, because it wasn't going to fly." Telephone interview, June 16, 1994. Another State Department official disagreed, stating that the North capitulated because it was afraid that Washington *would* succeed in getting UN sanctions. Personal interview, Washington, D.C., July 15, 1994.

[166]Quoted in Douglas Jehl, "Clinton Finds North Koreans Really May Be Ready to Talk," *New York Times,* June 23, 1994; see also Ruth Marcus and R. Jeffrey Smith, "North Korea Confirms Freeze; U.S. Agrees to Resume Talks," *Washington Post,* June 23, 1994.

167For a somewhat dated but still good examination of the leadership question, see Kong Dan Oh, "Leadership Change in North Korean Politics: The Succession to Kim Il Sung," RAND/R-3697-RC, October 1988; see also R. Jeffrey Smith, "N. Korean Strongman: 'Crazy' or Canny?" *Washington Post*, September 26, 1993. For an ROK history of Kim Jong Il, including salacious tales of his sexual predilections, see Institute for South-North Korea Studies, *The True Story of Kim Jong-il* (Seoul: Korea Herald, 1993).

Kim Il Sung's funeral took place on July 19, attended by an estimated two million North Koreans. The ROK prohibited any of its citizens from accepting the North's offer to attend the funeral. *Yonhap* (Seoul), July 14, 1994, reported in FBIS-EAS-94-135 (July 14, 1994), p. 27. North Korea indefinitely postponed the planned presidential summit that had been set for July 25–27, 1994.

For Kim Il Sung's obituary, see David E. Sanger, "Kim Il Sung, North Korea's 'Great Leader' Who Puzzled Outsiders, Dies at 82," *New York Times*, July 10, 1994. President Clinton offered his condolences on Kim Il Sung's death to North Korea on behalf of the American people; Republican Senator Robert Dole, a World War II veteran, criticized the president's gesture.

168R. Jeffrey Smith, "U.S. Reassured on North Korean Nuclear Policy," *Washington Post*, July 11, 1994.

169See "Agreed Statement between the Democratic People's Republic of Korea and the United States of America," Geneva, August 12, 1994; Office of Public Affairs, United States Mission, "Assistant Secretary Robert Gallucci's Press Conference," Geneva, August 12, 1994, copies of both documents in author's possession.

Kang had told the U.S. delegation that Pyongyang understood that being an NPT member included allowing special inspections, although he refused to state this publicly after the agreed statement was released to the press. Special inspections would take place before any LWR technology was transferred to the North. State Department official, comments at the Carnegie Endowment for International Peace, Washington, D.C., September 8, 1994.

170The spent fuel was North Korea's "ace in the hole," observed a member of the U.S. delegation. "They will not let it leave their country." Personal interview, Washington, D.C., August 31, 1994.

171Quoted in Andrew Pollack, "Seoul Is Offering Nuclear Plants to North Korea," *New York Times*, August 15, 1994.

172In early September, ROK Foreign Minister Han Sung Joo visited Washington to request that Washington once again link the exchange of special envoys between North and South with the U.S.-DPRK talks, a position Seoul had abandoned in mid-April after the tumultuous end of North-South talks in March 1994. Washington said no. But to reassure South Korea, Christopher promised to visit Seoul later in the year and to urge the DPRK to restart talks with the ROK. See R. Jeffrey Smith, "U.S. Soothes South Korea on Dialogue with North," *Washington Post*, September 8, 1994; T. R. Reid, "U.S.–North Korea Ties Worry Seoul," *Washington Post*, September 6, 1994.

173See James Sterngold, "Korea Talks: Hint of Thaw," *New York Times*, September 18, 1994; Sang-hun Choe, "N. Korea Not Free to Choose Reactors," *Washington Times*, September 17, 1994. Gallucci described the DPRK demands as "ludicrous."

The Clinton administration had originally hoped that Japan would finance the construction of the reactor project and had proposed the idea to Tokyo in June

1994. The Japanese Foreign Ministry favored the idea, but the Ministry of International Trade and Industry (MITI) opposed it. After the third round in August 1994, Japan waited to see what offer Seoul would make. Seoul then announced that it would provide the technology and much of the financing for the two LWRs. State Department official, personal interview, Washington, D.C., November 2, 1994.

After the third round, U.S. and North Korean officials continued their low-level discussions in New York through August. By the end of the month, they had agreed to hold technical discussions in Pyongyang on setting up a liaison office and in Berlin on light-water reactor technology and the safe disposition of the fuel rods. Martin Sieff, "United States, North Korea Agree on Talks," *Washington Times*, September 2, 1994; "U.S. to Talk with North Korea about Opening Diplomatic Ties," *Washington Post*, September 2, 1994. The U.S. team that visited Pyongyang on September 10 was the first U.S. diplomatic mission to the North since the end of the Korean War.

The North Koreans reportedly selected the Berlin site because of the DPRK's large diplomatic presence there. At the Berlin talks in mid-September, the North Koreans insisted on receiving Westinghouse AB600 model reactors. When the U.S. side told them that this reactor model had not yet been formally approved and that U.S. domestic laws prohibited the direct transfer of any U.S. technology, the head of the DPRK delegation said that this was a U.S. problem, not a North Korean one. State Department official, personal interview, Washington, D.C., September 23, 1994. A State Department official later chided a member of the DPRK delegation for acting in an "imperialist" manner and interfering in U.S. domestic affairs. The North Korean apologized.

[174]State Department official, personal interview, Washington, D.C., November 21, 1994. The day before this round of the Geneva talks began, the negotiating atmosphere was not helped by a statement made by the U.S. commander-in-chief of the Pacific Fleet, who noted that a carrier battle group had been deployed to the Sea of Japan in a show of gunboat diplomacy to intimidate the North Koreans. See "U.S. Warships Sail off North Korea," *Washington Times*, September 23, 1994.

[175]See R. Jeffrey Smith, "U.S.–N. Korea Talks Snag on Pyongyang Demands," *Washington Post*, September 30, 1994; Alan Riding, "U.S. and North Korea Announce Pause in Talks, but No Progress," *New York Times*, September 30, 1994; R. Jeffrey Smith, "Stalemate in North Korea Talks May Strain Relations, Officials Say," *Washington Post*, October 2, 1994.

[176]See R. Jeffrey Smith and Ann Devroy, "U.S. to Hold Its Course in North Korea Dealings," *Washington Post*, October 5, 1994; Robert Evans, ""What's the Rush? Kim Asks the U.S.," *Washington Times*, October 12, 1994; "U.S. Makes Offer in N. Korea Talks," *Washington Times*, October 13, 1994.

[177]China also publicly backed the agreement. See Thomas W. Lippman, "China Backs U.S.–N. Korea Nuclear Accord," *Washington Post*, November 14, 1994. On the IAEA, see U.S. Department of State, "Remarks by Secretary of State Warren Christopher and Director General of the IAEA Hans Blix," Washington, D.C., October 19, 1994, copy in author's possession; Robert Burns, "U.N. Agency Praises U.S.-Korean Nuclear Deal; Dole Critical," *Associated Press*, October 20, 1994; IAEA Press Releases 94/45 and 94/47, October 20 and November 11, 1994, respectively. Regarding the ROK, Foreign Minister Han Sung Joo stated, "The Government evaluates the just-concluded accord as having laid a major cornerstone for fundamentally resolving the North Korean nuclear issue and also for maintaining stabil-

ity and peace on the Korean peninsula." Korean Overseas Information Service Press Release, no. 94-168, October 18, 1994. On Japan, see Martin Sieff, "Clinton Lauds Nuclear Pact with N. Korea," *Washington Times,* October 19, 1994.

[178]A more creative approach to the LWR offer might have recommended that the North and the South share the same power grid, in a Korean equivalent of the Schuman Plan proposed by the French foreign minister in 1950 to promote Franco-German rapprochement. Like the Schuman Plan, a common energy source would have given each side one more reason to cooperate and one less reason to fight each other. In fact, before the Korean War, "north" Korea had supplied "south" Korea with electricity. (In a historical curiosity, near the end of World War II, Japan had actually moved its small nuclear weapons program to northern Korea to take advantage of the region's energy resources.)

[179]Testimony of Robert Gallucci, Senate Foreign Relations Committee, Subcommittee on East Asian and Pacific Affairs, December 1, 1994, author's personal notes (hereafter cited as Gallucci oral testimony). This was the most explicit statement by a Clinton administration official on what would occur if discrepancies remained *after* the special inspections took place. On this point, see also the testimony of Mitchell Reiss, in Senate Committee on Foreign Relations, Subcommittee on East Asian and Pacific Affairs, *Hearing, Implications of the U.S.–North Korea Nuclear Agreement,* 103d Cong., 2d sess., December 1, 1994 (Washington, D.C.: USGPO, 1995) (hereafter cited as *Nuclear Agreement*).

[180]United States Mission, Geneva, "Press Conference Given by Ambassador at Large Robert L. Gallucci," October 21, 1994; Gallucci oral testimony. Four countries had told the United States that they were willing, in principle, to accept the spent fuel rods. State Department official, presentation at the Woodrow Wilson International Center for Scholars, Washington, D.C., October 24, 1994. As of January 1995, none of these states had yet been publicly identified.

[181]North Korean performance under the agreement and confidential minute was not tied to any hard dates but to the status of LWR construction. The United States did not want to place hard dates in the agreement or the confidential minute because of the commercial uncertainty of meeting a firm delivery schedule for the LWRs and because of its desire not to risk breaching its obligations.

On November 4, 1994, the UN Security Council granted the IAEA additional authority to perform its new and unprecedented safeguard responsibilities of monitoring the DPRK's freeze and the dismantlement of its nuclear facilities.

[182]KEDO would deliver 50,000 metric tons of oil during the first year, 100,000 the second year, and 500,000 annually thereafter. It was not certain how much of this oil the United States and/or other countries would pay for, although the first shipment of oil (50,000 metric tons), which would be delivered by January 21, 1995, would cost approximately $5.5 million and come from funds already allocated to the Defense Department.

As calculated by the U.S. Department of Energy, the total amount of oil was equivalent to the amount needed to produce 255 megawatts of electricity (a figure that was derived from the amount of electricity that would supposedly have been generated by the 5MW(e), 50MW(e), and 200MW(e) reactors in operation or under construction in North Korea). Gallucci oral testimony. U.S. officials claimed that this heavy oil could not be used to fuel the North Korean military machine. State Department official, presentation at the Woodrow Wilson International Center for Scholars, Washington, D.C., October 24, 1994. To purify the pond water containing the spent fuel rods, the United States would also spend roughly

$200,000, which would come from funds already appropriated to the Energy Department.

[183]Senior State Department official, Washington, D.C., December 12, 1994. On possible South Korean and Japanese reluctance to foot their share of the bill, see "Who Will Pay North Korea's Bills?" *Foreign Report*, no. 2331 (December 8, 1994). North Korean suspicion that South Korea might back out of the deal prompted the DPRK to request, and President Clinton to send, a letter, dated October 20, 1994, to reassure Pyongyang: "In the event that this reactor project is not completed for reasons beyond the control of the DPRK, I will use the full powers of my office to provide . . . such a project from the United States, subject to the approval of the U.S. Congress." Copy of letter in author's possession. See Steven Greenhouse, "Clinton, in Letter, Assures North Koreans on Nuclear Reactors," *New York Times*, October 27, 1994. The South Koreans were furious when they learned that Clinton's letter referred to Kim Jong Il as "His Excellency." Perhaps to compensate, the letter was simply signed "Bill Clinton" and did not use his official title.

[184]Testimony of Warren Christopher, reported in Steven Greenhouse, "Administration Defends North Korea Pact," *New York Times*, January 25, 1995; Thomas W. Lippman, "U.S. Considered Attacks on N. Korea, Perry Tells Panel," *Washington Post*, January 25, 1995.

[185]Written testimony of Robert Gallucci, in *Nuclear Agreement*. In the wake of the framework agreement, on October 21, 1994, Seoul announced that the 1994 Team Spirit joint military exercise would be canceled.

[186]See also the testimony of Henry Sokolski and Gary Milhollin, in *Nuclear Agreement*. The DPRK could avoid the stigma of special inspections by amending its initial declaration at any time to include the two waste sites; the IAEA could then conduct ad hoc inspections there. In fact, Blix had repeatedly suggested that Pyongyang do just this.

[187]Gallucci oral testimony. "[Special inspections] are not a nuclear Rosetta stone that will unlock the past mysteries of the North's nuclear program. It is likely that laboratory analysis of the nuclear waste . . . will simply confirm what the United States and the IAEA already strongly suspect: that North Korea conducted multiple reprocessing campaigns that might have resulted in the separation of 6–12 kilograms of weapons-grade plutonium." Testimony of Mitchell Reiss, in *Nuclear Agreement*.

[188]"The agreed framework suggests a fundamental shift away from a long-standing U.S. policy of ensuring nuclear deterrence by sanction and penalty. Rather than using pressure tactics against countries attempting to build an indigenous nuclear weapons program, the Administration leaves itself vulnerable to being forced to buy them off, one by one." Written statement by Senator Charles S. Robb, Committee on Foreign Relations, Subcommittee on East Asian and Pacific Affairs, December 1, 1994, copy in author's possession.

[189]Gallucci oral testimony.

[190]See George Perkovich, "The Korea Precedent," *Washington Post*, September 28, 1994; see also R. Jeffrey Smith, "N. Korea Accord: A Troubling Precedent?" *Washington Post*, October 20, 1994.

[191]See "Agreed Framework between the United States of America and the Democratic People's Republic of Korea," Geneva, October 21, 1994, copy in author's possession (emphasis added).

[192]Other key phrases were spelled out in the U.S.-DPRK negotiating history from the third and fourth rounds. State Department official, telephone interview, December 13, 1994.

[193]See Robert Manning, "The North Korean Nuclear Deal: Mistrust—and Verify," *Los Angeles Times*, October 23, 1994.

[194]Three other criticisms of the agreement deserve mention. First, the proposed transfer of the two LWRs did not aid nonproliferation, because these reactors would actually produce *more plutonium* than the three reactors they would replace. But without a reprocessing capability, North Korea would be unable to extract plutonium from the spent fuel. The timing of the steps in the deal diminished this proliferation risk. If the North reneged on the deal after the completion of the first LWR, there would not immediately be any plutonium to separate, since the spent fuel rods would already have been shipped out of the country. If the North reneged on the deal after the construction of both LWRs, it would have to construct another reprocessing plant, because construction of the second LWR would be finished only when the reprocessing plant was dismantled. In both cases, Pyongyang's dependence on foreign suppliers for LEU limited the amount of spent fuel it could produce and hence the amount of plutonium it could extract should it violate the agreement.

Second, the agreement did not address the disposition of the spent fuel from the two LWRs, a point that Deputy Secretary of Defense John Deutch publicly criticized after the agreement had been finalized. See R. Jeffrey Smith, "North Korea Pact Contains U.S. Concessions," *Washington Post*, October 19, 1994; Elaine Sciolino, "Clinton's High Roll," *New York Times*, October 20, 1994. The question over how to dispose of the spent fuel from the two LWRs had been raised only one time—in an interagency meeting in the spring of 1994. Gallucci had not received any negotiating instructions on this point for either the third or the fourth rounds. State Department official, personal interview, Washington, D.C., November 21, 1994. In any case, disposition of the spent fuel from the two LWRs could be handled in the KEDO-DPRK agreement on the LWR project (to be negotiated by April 1995), in the fuel supply contract, or in the U.S.-DPRK agreement on nuclear cooperation. Andrew Mack has recommended that KEDO lend the LEU fuel rods to the North, which would have to return them when they were removed from the reactor. See "Nuclear Endgame on the Korean Peninsula" (paper provided to the author by Andrew Mack, November 1994).

Another question concerned whether the agreement was a legally binding document under international law. The author believes that the agreement legally binds the United States to use its best efforts to fulfill its obligations therein, although this point is debated by other legal scholars. See *Nuclear Agreement*.

What is not in question is that if U.S. nuclear technology is provided to the DPRK, the United States and the DPRK must first sign an agreement for nuclear cooperation, which would have to be approved by Congress. Under the Nuclear Nonproliferation Act of 1978, the United States would be unable to enter into such an agreement if the DPRK was not in full compliance with its IAEA safeguards obligations—unless the president invoked the "national security" exception, an action that would likely trigger a clash between the executive and the legislative branches. See Zachary S. Davis et al., "Korea: Procedural and Jurisdictional Questions Regarding Possible Normalization of Relations with North Korea," *CRS Report* 94-933S (November 29, 1994).

[195]See David Albright, "North Korea's Corroding Fuel," *ISIS Occasional Report*, August 2, 1994. In July 1994, the U.S. side had offered technical assistance to en-

sure the safe storage of the fuel rods—by filtering and adjusting the water quality in the pond, by preserving the fuel in special canisters, or by transferring the rods overseas for reprocessing. The two delegations revisited the issue at the third round in August, with the United States declaring again that *any* reprocessing would end the negotiations and force it to return to the United Nations.

[196]State Department officials, personal interviews, Washington, D.C., November 2, 4, 1994. One disgruntled Defense Department official complained, "The White House would have accepted *any* deal that Gallucci brought back from Geneva." Personal interview, Washington, D.C., November 4, 1994.

In the November 8, 1994, midterm elections, the Republicans won a majority of Senate seats, and captured the House for the first time since 1954. As of March 1995, some Republican lawmakers have criticized the framework agreement, but it appears unlikely that they will overturn it.

[197]Just how bumpy this road might be was demonstrated when a U.S. Army helicopter strayed into North Korean territory and was shot down on December 17, 1994. One soldier was killed, and the other soldier, Chief Warrant Officer Bobby Hall, was captured. After unsuccessfully demanding that the DPRK immediately release Hall, the United States sent a State Department official, Thomas Hubbard, to North Korea to defuse the tense situation. Washington then expressed "sincere regret" for the incident and assured Pyongyang that it would discuss ways to avoid a similar incident in the future. Hall was returned on December 30.

[198]Personal interview, Washington, D.C., November 3, 1994.

[199]State Department official, personal interview, Washington, D.C., November 21, 1994.

[200]Ibid.

[201]Ibid.

[202]Although the Clinton administration delinked human rights and MFN in late May, it aggravated relations with China in September 1994 by upgrading U.S. relations with Taiwan. This decision satisfied no one—not those in Congress who were unhappy with the MFN decision and wanted the president to go further, not the Taiwanese, who did not request the diplomatic upgrade, and certainly not the Chinese, who protested loudly. See Steven Mufson, "China Decries New U.S. Tie with Taiwan," *Washington Post*, September 11, 1994; Patrick E. Tyler, "China Warns U.S. on Relations with Taiwan," *New York Times*, September 11, 1994.

[203]Robert Manning has stated, "Most troubling is not the substance of the agreed framework itself, but the apparent lack of a larger strategy for reducing the conflict on the Korean peninsula and fostering a genuine inter-Korean reconciliation process." See *Nuclear Agreement*.

[204]In February 1992, CIA Director Robert Gates testified before the House Foreign Affairs Committee. He said that North Korea was "within a few months to . . . a couple of years" of acquiring nuclear bombs. Evidence suggested that North Korea had "a deception plan for hiding their nuclear activities." Elaine Sciolino, "C.I.A. Chief Says North Koreans Plan to Make Secret Atom Arms," *New York Times*, February 26, 1992. The Gates assessment was reportedly informed by Russian intelligence that North Korea was developing nuclear weapons. See Nayan Chanda, "Atomic Ambivalence," *Far Eastern Economic Review*, October 1, 1992, p. 9.

[205]Myron Kratzer, "IAEA Safeguards in North Korea: The Case for Interim Arrangements," *Atlantic Council Bulletin* 5, no. 6 (July 20, 1994).

Chapter 7

Conclusion

In 1969, the clinical oncologist Elisabeth Kübler-Ross published a slim volume called *On Death and Dying* that soon became a minor classic. Seeking to help patients, their families, and their doctors better understand the emotional travails and transformations of a terminally ill cancer sufferer, Kübler-Ross identified five distinct stages that such patients pass through: denial, anger, bargaining, depression, and eventually, acceptance.[1]

It is not too much to say that the world community goes through a similar series of reactions each time it learns that another country is developing nuclear weapons. First, the United States and other leading members of the international nonproliferation regime—hoping to prevent countries from acquiring nuclear weapons—oppose, obstruct, and negotiate. If these efforts are unsuccessful, gradually they come to tolerate and then, finally, to accept the existence of a new nuclear power.

Yet just as not all cancers are terminal, nuclear status is not immutable. With the proper treatment (and a dose of good luck), a serious illness can go into remission. Sometimes, it can even be reversed. As the nine cases examined in this book have shown, so too can nuclear weapons programs be slowed, stopped, and sometimes even reversed.

Each of the nine countries had varied and sometimes contradictory reasons for slowing, stopping, or reversing the growth of nuclear capabilities. All, or almost all, of these, however, were influenced by five factors: changes in the international system after the cold war and their influence on "new thinking" about the value of nuclear weapons; a new kind of "dollar diplomacy"; U.S. nonproliferation efforts; the quality of political leadership; and the global nonproliferation regime.

The New Strategic Situation after the Cold War

The end of the global political, military, and ideological contest between the Soviet Union and the United States fundamentally changed the international system. Although in many cases the precise nature of these changes and their implications remains uncertain, the end of the superpower rivalry has clearly reawakened long-dormant local feuds and regional antagonisms, while generally increasing the significance of economic strength in world affairs.

The thaw in Soviet-American relations during the 1980s and the end of the cold war also accelerated steps to reduce the nuclear arsenals of the United States and the Soviet Union/Russia. The 1987 Intermediate-range Nuclear Forces (INF) treaty eliminated a complete category of ballistic missiles. The Strategic Arms Reduction Treaties (START I and II) will reduce the American and Soviet/Russian stockpiles by two-thirds, to 3,000–3,500 nuclear weapons each, and will require the abolition of all land-based multiple, independently targetable reentry vehicles (MIRVs). Four nuclear weapon states (the United States, Russia, Britain, and France) took another helpful step by issuing unilateral declarations that each would suspend nuclear testing. In September 1993, President Clinton committed the United States to achieving a comprehensive test ban treaty as soon as possible. These steps suggested a world in which nuclear weapons would no longer be the measure of a state's international power and influence.

Further doubt about the value of nuclear weapons has been sown by the huge and largely unexpected bills that have started to fall due from four and a half decades of nuclear arms racing. The "back-end" costs of repairing the environmental damage caused by the superpowers' nuclear complexes are a bitter nuclear legacy of the cold war. Cleanup costs for the United States are expected to amount to at least $30 billion and perhaps as much as $100 billion; in the former Soviet Union, the bill could reach $300 billion, although it is unlikely that a sum of money anywhere close to this amount will ever be found. In addition, the opportunity costs incurred by having a generation of skilled scientists, engineers, and technicians devote their careers to building bombs instead of the gross national product cannot be estimated.

Perhaps the most startling contribution to any new thinking, however, is the recognition that an awesome collection of thirty thousand nuclear weapons—the world's largest arsenal—could not preserve the Soviet empire or, indeed, even prevent the collapse of the Soviet Union itself. Moreover, nuclear weapons are completely irrelevant to resolving the host of problems that today increasingly afflict countries and undermine regional and international stability: civil war, ethnic and tribal conflict, mass migration, AIDs, economic weakness, and international terrorism. In the efforts to confront these daunting challenges, nuclear weapons are elaborate and expensive anachronisms.

All of the encouraging developments would have had a greater impact in shaping "new thinking" about the illegitimacy of nuclear weapons but for two countervailing influences. First, much of the promise of recent nuclear disarmament efforts remains unfulfilled. The deep reductions in the nuclear arsenals of the United States and the Soviet Union/Russia called for by START I and II have not yet been implemented fully, and Washington appears reluctant to contemplate further cuts at this time. Although four nuclear weapon states have suspended nuclear testing, China has not, and a comprehensive test ban treaty has not yet been concluded. In addition, the Clinton administration has not expanded the traditional U.S. "negative security assurance" for all NPT parties to include a formal renunciation of the first use of nuclear weapons in a conflict, even though many doubt that the United States would ever use nuclear weapons first. In the absence of fundamental changes in the nuclear behavior of the five leading nuclear powers, the legitimacy of nuclear weapons cannot be very much diminished. To those whose decisions about nuclear weapons are influenced by a desire for status and prestige, the actions of the nuclear weapon states have sent a mixed message.

A second factor also influenced perceptions about the value of nuclear weapons: a generalized apprehension with the end of the bipolar international system and the absence of any solid security architecture to adequately replace it. The threat of nuclear Armageddon has diminished, but regional instabilities and local disorder have increased in many parts of the world. Ancient antagonisms, ethnic strife, and religious hatreds have all resurfaced, literally with a vengeance in some cases. Life in all too many places appears at least as solitary, poor, nasty, brutish, and short as it was during the previous five decades. In retrospect, the first major post–cold war conflict—the 1991 Persian Gulf war—is better viewed not as a model of future UN-sanctioned multilateral cooperation to defeat aggression but as a harbinger of a more anarchic international system. The real "lesson" of that war was that it occurred at all.

Although the global environment has changed in important ways during the past few years, it has not changed as much as some observers predicted and many others would have liked. To the extent that security concerns motivate states to acquire nuclear weapons and expand their arsenals, the uncertainty and unrest ushered in by the end of the cold war have probably made such weapons appear more attractive to some countries. It may thus be more than a coincidence that the three states that most radically changed their nuclear posture—South Africa, Argentina, and Brazil—were located in regions not only where there were no nuclear threats but also where the risk of conventional armed conflict was virtually nonexistent. In countries where the local security environment either remained unchanged or deteriorated after the cold war—India, Pakistan, Ukraine, Belarus, Kazakhstan, and North Korea—nonproliferation achievements proved much harder to obtain.

In South Africa, the end of the cold war played an indirect role in the decision to dismantle the country's stockpile of nuclear weapons. The decline of Soviet influence in southern Africa (and the removal of Moscow's Cuban proxies from the region) helped de Klerk gain the support of his fellow cabinet officials and senior military officers for a decision he had already made: that Pretoria could—indeed, should—give up the bomb.

South America had largely been sheltered from the chill of the cold war, which had not directly influenced the nuclear programs in Argentina and Brazil. But with the end of the cold war, officials in both countries, starting with Presidents Menem and Collor, realized the need to more closely integrate their countries into the global economy to ensure future prosperity. Their signing of the Quadripartite Agreement in December 1991 was the key step along this path.

The Soviet Union had served as India's primary source of military equipment (at concessionary rates) and as a diplomatic counterweight to the United States. When New Delhi could no longer play its "Soviet card" after the cold war, it sought a new relationship with Washington, emphasizing commercial interaction and financial investment. This has made India more susceptible to appeals by the United States (as well as by Europe and Japan) to limit the country's nuclear and ballistic missile programs, but it is still unclear how, or if, New Delhi will revise the country's policies in favor of nuclear restraint.

Pakistan is far more vulnerable than India to outside nonproliferation pressures. The removal of Soviet forces from Afghanistan in early 1989 greatly reduced Pakistan's strategic value to the West and therefore lowered the consequences to Washington of invoking the Pressler amendment because of Islamabad's nuclear activities. Pakistan's ongoing failure to meet the Pressler standard indicates that it too is currently unwilling to reverse its nuclear stance, at least unilaterally.

The demise of the Soviet Union actually "created" a new set of proliferation problems: the tactical and strategic nuclear weapons stationed on the territories of Ukraine, Belarus, and Kazakhstan. At the same time, though, close cooperation between the United States and

Russia helped to win denuclearization commitments from these three newly independent countries, as well as to persuade them to join the NPT and accept full-scope IAEA safeguards.

It is likely that the end of the cold war had a paradoxical effect on the DPRK. On the one hand, the disintegration of the Soviet Union, the ignominious collapse of North Korea's fraternal allies in Eastern Europe, Pyongyang's inability to obtain reparations and financial assistance from Tokyo, and the normalization of relations between Seoul and Moscow and between Seoul and Beijing all intensified the DPRK's international isolation. The North Korean regime may have thought that nuclear weapons offered a measure of security in an increasingly inhospitable environment and, if needed, a last-gasp way to preserve the regime. On the other hand, all of the above factors, coupled with the withdrawal of U.S. nuclear weapons from South Korea in late 1991 and the severe strain imposed by the North's rapidly contracting economy, may have convinced Pyongyang that it should barter its nuclear weapons program in exchange for a supply of heavy oil and two light-water reactors, a limited (and tightly controlled) economic opening to the outside world, and a new diplomatic relationship with the United States. The October 1994 U.S.-DPRK Agreed Framework suggests that these arguments were ascendant in North Korea. There may have been times, however, when both sets of factors were shaping Pyongyang's nuclear policies.

Judging the contribution that the end of the cold war made to "new thinking" about nuclear weapons in each of the nine countries thus leads to a hung jury. Although much was done, it is possible that more new thinking, and new policies, by the nuclear weapon states could have produced correspondingly greater international cooperation and stronger nonproliferation commitments by the nonnuclear weapon states.[2] By shedding their cold war mental armor and seizing the moment with greater imagination and bolder leadership, the nuclear weapon states might have consolidated individual nonproliferation accomplishments and, with sufficient momentum, converted these efforts into a trend. Nuclear programs that had been slowed down might have been frozen, and those that had been frozen might have been rolled back. The currency of nuclear weapons might have been devalued further.

Nevertheless, officials in the nine countries realized that nuclear arsenals and their boundless expansion were unnecessary, even counterproductive, to larger economic and political objectives. This restraint may be only temporary in some countries; in others, it appears to be permanent. At the very least, these actions suggest that more nuclear weapons may not be better. And, under some circumstances, none may be best of all.

"Dollar Nonproliferation Diplomacy"

The use of economic incentives to promote nonproliferation behavior dates at least from "Atoms for Peace," which President Dwight Eisenhower announced in December 1953.[3] Under this initiative, the United States offered nuclear technology at concessionary rates in return for pledges by the recipient countries to use such technology only for peaceful purposes. This incentive was later formalized in the NPT, which enshrined, in Article 4, the "inalienable right" of all states to share in the peaceful benefits of nuclear energy. Yet Atoms for Peace actually accelerated the spread of nuclear weapon capabilities around the globe, a fact forcefully brought home by India's self-proclaimed peaceful nuclear explosion in May 1974.

Even before this time, however, the careful calibration of economic incentives to promote nonproliferation goals proved difficult to implement for two reasons. First, the United States and other donor countries found themselves reluctant in some cases to withhold much-needed humanitarian relief and developmental assistance, regardless of a country's nuclear behavior; withholding such aid would harm the least fortunate members of these societies and might not alter a nuclear stance in any case. Second, during the cold war, agendas and interests driven by the Soviet-American competition often vied with, and frequently superseded, nonproliferation objectives. Regardless of a country's nuclear ambitions, Washington's fears that a strategic partner might switch sides on the diplomatic chess board effectively foreclosed the option of ending U.S. assistance (which in many cases was largely in the form of military rather than financial credits).

The end of the cold war permitted the resurrection and application of this "old" nonproliferation tool in new ways. A new kind of "dollar diplomacy"—using financial and commercial levers to influence nuclear behavior—has invigorated recent nonproliferation efforts.[4] To be sure, this diplomacy is not solely, and in some cases, not even primarily, based on American dollars. Japan, South Korea, Russia, and Europe have also used economic assistance to promote nonproliferation objectives.

Benefactors have largely avoided the moral dilemma of ending programs designed to help the developing world. With a few exceptions, this dollar diplomacy has focused not on cutting off existing financial and commercial assistance but rather on providing additional assistance; in other words, the United States and other countries have offered the "carrot" instead of wielding the "stick."

The offer of financial and commercial inducements to obtain nonproliferation commitments also has succeeded because the end of the cold war eliminated the perceived need to tolerate proliferation in the name of recruiting and keeping friends and allies. Without the zero-sum superpower competition, there now is a greater willingness by the leading members of the world community to relegate many states to the margins of international economic life by denying them the benefits of foreign trade and commerce unless they undertake nonproliferation commitments. This approach will be more effective on weaker and less powerful states, which can most easily be marginalized.

Among the nine countries in this study, North Korea was by far the biggest winner in the nuclear nonproliferation sweepstakes; it is set to receive, from a multinational consortium, an energy package worth an estimated $4 billion in return for undertaking a number of measures that are expected to resolve past mysteries of its nuclear program and eliminate its future capability to build nuclear weapons.

Financial inducements also played an important role in the denuclearization of Ukraine, Belarus, and Kazakhstan, in their accession to the NPT, and in their acceptance of comprehensive IAEA safeguards. The United States pledged to Ukraine a total of $900 million in Nunn-Lugar funds and other U.S. assistance. Russia also forgave over $2 billion of Ukrainian oil and gas indebtedness. Kazakhstan and Belarus received lesser, but nonetheless substantial, sums from Washington to return the strategic nuclear weapons stationed on their territories. The European Union and individual European states collectively contributed hundreds of millions of dollars in nuclear assistance to the former Soviet Union.

U.S. dollar diplomacy attempted to influence the nuclear policies in South Asia. Washington's threat to withdraw $5 billion of OPIC insurance from U.S. private-sector investment in India influenced New Delhi's decision to keep IAEA safeguards on its two Tarapur nuclear reactors. The inability of the Bush administration to certify Pakistan under the Pressler amendment has meant a cutoff of American economic and military assistance since 1990. To date, although Islamabad has not rolled back its nuclear weapons program, it remains hopeful of resuscitating its relationship with Washington and has reportedly frozen its nuclear program at the level attained in 1990.

Economic incentives were not directly offered to influence the nuclear decisions in South Africa, Argentina, and Brazil. At best, there was in these countries a generalized belief that tempering or eliminating their nuclear programs would accelerate and expand commercial interaction with other regional actors and with the industrialized West. They also hoped that changes in their nuclear programs would attract foreign investment and lift multinational restrictions on sensitive technologies that could be used for economic development.

It is unclear whether the aggressive use of dollar diplomacy as a nonproliferation instrument will encourage a "let's make a deal" mentality among other countries (whether or not they harbor serious nuclear ambitions). If recent developments are part of a nonproliferation endgame in which the United States and others are using "buy-outs" to deal with the last, tough proliferation challenges, then it is unlikely that other countries will try to use their nuclear weapons capability as a means of extortion. If, however, the international nonproliferation regime is damaged by uncertainty over the future of the NPT, then many more countries may try to hedge their bets against the possibility of the regime's eventual demise, increase their nuclear competence, and narrow the time between a political decision to build nuclear weapons and actual acquisition of a nuclear stockpile. Even if this hedging took place under IAEA safeguards, it would erode confidence in the NPT regime. Efforts by some countries to acquire a nuclear option would increase suspicion and mistrust among others, who in turn would feel compelled to undertake similar efforts. An element of self-fulfilling prophecy would take place as countries that were initially motivated by caution would end up being driven by fear. Under such a scenario, dollar diplomacy as a nonproliferation instrument could get very expensive, very fast.

U.S. Nonproliferation Efforts

The role of the United States in halting nuclear proliferation cannot be evaluated simply on the basis of its policies toward these nine countries during the past few years. Rather, it should be seen against the backdrop of a half century of work to prevent the spread of nuclear weapons. U.S. leadership has been essential in actively dissuading countries from acquiring nuclear weapons and in establishing and strengthening the international nonproliferation regime.

If the spread of nuclear weapons is indeed the greatest threat to international peace and stability, then it is imperative that the United States continue to take a leading role in preventing proliferation. To be sure, in all but a few cases the United States by itself will not be able to stop nuclear proliferation. Yet without the United States, nonproliferation efforts will be unlikely to succeed. As the world's most influential country, with unequaled political, economic, and military assets, the United States is best positioned to direct the diplomatic charge against the rise of new nuclear powers.

In practice, this means presidential leadership and, when necessary, the president's ongoing, active involvement. The threats posed by nuclear weapons, and even attempts to acquire nuclear weapons, are not just another foreign policy issue, wedged somewhere on the daily briefing schedule between smuggling in Albania and unrest in Zaire. They involve grave issues of war and peace affecting not only important U.S. national security interests but also the security of millions of people around the world. Many of these decisions demand tough trade-offs between competing objectives and the choice of a single policy among many unsatisfactory and often messy options. When a choice needs to be made, only the president can break the impasse.

The Quality of Leadership

Of all the factors influencing the behavior of countries in this study, by far the single most significant one is the *quality* of political leadership. Good leaders can, and do, help make their states more secure and more prosperous. Poor leaders, on the other hand, bring adversity and hardship. They miss opportunities, aggravate relations with neighbors and key allies, and can even blunder into war.[5] The implications of inadequate leadership for nonproliferation efforts are troubling: no matter how attractively assembled a package of denuclearization incentives, and no matter how well a country's strategic objectives are promoted by nonnuclear status, a single decision at the top can frustrate regional and global efforts to halt the spread of nuclear weapons.

Choosing the right goal is only the first element of good leadership. The real challenge is in finding the means to achieve desired ends. How close a country comes to actually achieving its objectives is the final measure of leadership. By this standard, de Klerk (South Africa), Menem (Argentina), Collor (Brazil), and Nazarbayev (Kazakhstan) scored well. To be fair, they were not good leaders because they chose to codify their countries' nonproliferation obligations but rather because they realized that their countries' nuclear ambitions impeded the achievement of political and economic goals that they valued more highly.

The clearest example of visionary political leadership was in South Africa. Jettisoning the lessons of his conservative Afrikaner upbringing and political affiliation, de Klerk decided to chart a different future for his party and his country. A nuclear arsenal had no place in de Klerk's vision of a multiracial democracy and South Africa's status as a respected member of the international community. In September 1989, he alone decided it had to go. Menem of Argentina and Collor of Brazil were both committed to introducing domestic market reforms and to creating larger roles for their countries internationally. To move forward in this direction, they were willing to pay the price of admission imposed by the international nonproliferation regime—comprehensive IAEA safeguards. Kazakhstan's leader, Nazarbayev, generally played a weak hand well. He had a keen appreciation of just how far he could push the United States and Russia to extract economic, political, and security benefits. In contrast to his counterpart in Ukraine, Nazarbayev astutely never forced Moscow or Washington to seriously doubt that Almaty would ultimately return the SS-18 ICBMs and strategic bombers.

The record of political leadership in South Asia is mixed. India and Pakistan managed to avoid war in 1990 and have wisely refrained from deploying nuclear weapons or ballistic missiles (so far). But serious questions about the caliber of political leadership in each country have lingered, spurring U.S. concerns in the spring of 1990 that the crisis might flare into a conventional war and then escalate to the nuclear level. In the hothouse political environment of the subcontinent, it is far too easy for officials to reap domestic political profits by denigrating the other country. Further, in Pakistan the rivalry between Sharif and Bhutto, a rivalry that is closer to a blood feud than to a political disagreement, stifles debate on security issues and frustrates any accommodation with India on nuclear matters. All of these developments cast doubt on the *joint* ability of Islamabad and New Delhi to manage and defuse the next crisis.

Ukraine's Kravchuk scored poorly on the leadership scale. Too much a prisoner of his years of service to the Communist Party, he failed to comprehend his country's fundamentally weak position. On the domestic front, Kravchuk refused to dismantle the old command economy, thereby driving his country toward financial ruin. Internationally, his posturing over nuclear weapons that he could not control aggravated relations with Russia and alienated the United States and those European countries that wanted to provide much-needed economic and military assistance. In the end, for transferring the nuclear warheads to Russia, Kravchuk obtained for his country not much more in foreign financial assistance or security assurances than he could have won years earlier. The election of Kuchma as president in

July 1994 brought the nuclear matter in Ukraine to a close. He saw far more clearly than Kravchuk the harmful impact that the country's fitful and irresolute handling of the NPT had on solidifying a strategic relationship with the West. Kuchma actively and effectively prodded the Rada to ratify the NPT in mid-November 1994. Clinton promptly rewarded this action with an additional $200 million in U.S. assistance.

A full assessment of Kim Il Sung's nuclear diplomacy, and that of his son and presumptive heir, Kim Jong Il, must wait until Pyongyang's true motivations and objectives are revealed, if they ever are. The Great Leader, who portrayed himself as a North Korean combination of Moses and George Washington, initiated the nuclear weapons program but also pledged in June 1994 to freeze it. But at the very least, through its nuclear brinkmanship, the North Korean leadership skillfully maneuvered the country into a position where it now stands poised to receive unprecedented economic and diplomatic benefits in return for dismantling its capability to build nuclear weapons.

The NPT and the International Nonproliferation Regime

The nuclear Nonproliferation Treaty is the centerpiece of a network of interlocking, overlapping, and mutually reinforcing mechanisms and arrangements that are commonly referred to as the international nonproliferation regime. These domestic, regional, and global measures form an important benchmark against which nuclear behavior can be measured. In particular, membership in the NPT by a nonnuclear weapon state and the associated safeguards agreement with the IAEA legally codify a prior political decision not to acquire nuclear weapons. By providing confidence that neighbors, adversaries, and even allies are not developing nuclear weapons, the NPT has dampened some countries' incentives to acquire nuclear weapons.

That said, the international nonproliferation regime did not directly compel any of the nine countries in this study to reverse, stop, or slow down their nuclear ambitions. But there is little doubt that the regime played a useful *indirect* role in the nuclear decisions of all nine countries. For four of these countries—South Africa, Ukraine, Belarus, and Kazakhstan—joining the NPT was the nonproliferation equivalent of obtaining the good housekeeping seal of approval; indeed, the NPT is the "gold standard" for advertising a country's commitment not to acquire nuclear weapons. NPT membership, in turn, helped clear the way for improved diplomatic and commercial relations with the international community. For two other countries—Argentina and Brazil—a full-scope safeguards agreement with the IAEA (the real backbone of the NPT) largely performed the same function.

It is more difficult to evaluate the influence of the international nonproliferation regime on the recent nuclear behavior of India, Pakistan, and North Korea, but it is likely that the regime had some limited persuasive power. New Delhi and Islamabad refrained from openly testing or deploying nuclear weapons; neither exported sensitive nuclear technologies to third parties. Any of these actions would have contravened regime norms and codes of conduct, although fears of jeopardizing relations with the United States, other Western powers, and international financial lenders were arguably much more important reasons for this restraint.

North Korea's nuclear program demonstrated both the strengths and the shortcomings of the international nonproliferation regime. The United States was able to use Pyongyang's violation of IAEA safeguards obligations to turn a bilateral (or regional) dispute into a matter of global concern because it could persuasively argue that the North's action was a threat to the integrity of the NPT and the nonproliferation regime. At the same time, however, the inability of the UN Security Council to apply tough sanctions against the DPRK highlighted the lack of a lawful and effective international mechanism to enforce compliance with the regime. Although North Korea's flouting of its IAEA obligations evidenced a contempt for the regime, Pyongyang ultimately did not leave the NPT and never halted all IAEA safeguards activities. The full story may never be known, but it is likely that the international nonproliferation regime did influence North Korea's nuclear calculations to some degree.

In sum, the NPT and the international nonproliferation regime generally played a modest but useful role in shaping the nuclear behavior of these nine countries. When viewed over the course of the past five decades, the NPT regime has achieved remarkable success. The NPT regime must continue to play this role for another five decades, and beyond, if future efforts to halt the spread of nuclear weapons are to be successful.

By abandoning, constraining, or pulling back from an actual or contemplated nuclear weapons program, the countries in this study have entered into an unwritten global compact with the nuclear powers. This compact calls on the nuclear weapon states to reduce the number and role of nuclear weapons to ensure that these weapons remain unnecessary and largely irrelevant in world affairs—to ensure, in other words, that nuclear weapons no longer are the coin of the realm.

Will this informal understanding be honored? Do these success stories herald a fundamental transformation to a world that places less emphasis on nuclear arms? Or are they only short-lived aberrations? Will prestige and power in the twenty-first century turn more on a state's economic strength than on its ability to build nuclear bombs? At this time, it is simply too early to tell.

Nonetheless, the countries in this study have performed an invaluable service. They remind us that nuclear weapons are not always essential or even particularly useful for promoting national security, enhancing prestige, or attaining larger economic and political objectives. By their actions, these countries have pointed the way to a more secure future for themselves and for the world.

Notes

[1] Elisabeth Kübler-Ross, *On Death and Dying* (New York: Macmillan, 1969).

[2] See the policy recommendations of an independent task force sponsored by the Council on Foreign Relations, in "Nuclear Proliferation: Confronting the New Challenges" (January 1995), which outlines a "revitalized nonproliferation approach" in which both the nuclear and the nonnuclear weapon states that are parties to the NPT assume new responsibilities and obligations.

[3] The text of Eisenhower's speech can be found in *Public Papers of the Presidents of the United States: Dwight D. Eisenhower, 1953* (Washington, D.C.: USGPO, 1960), pp. 813–22.

[4] The phrase "dollar diplomacy" originated during the administration of William Howard Taft (1909–13) to characterize a policy that enlisted the resources of the U.S. government to expand and protect U.S. commercial and financial interests in the Far East and Latin America. See Dana G. Munro, *Intervention and Dollar Diplomacy in the Caribbean, 1900–1921* (Princeton, N.J.: Princeton University Press, 1964); Herbert Feis, *The Diplomacy of the Dollar* (Hamden, Conn.: Archon, 1965); Joseph S. Tulchin, *The Aftermath of War: World War I and U.S. Policy toward Latin America* (New York: New York University Press, 1971). For a radical critique, see Scott Nearing and Joseph Freeman, *Dollar Diplomacy: A Study in American Imperialism* (New York: Arno Press, 1970).

[5] Unfortunately, the literature on "leadership" does not provide a very satisfying definition of the term. See, for example, James MacGregor Burns, *Leadership* (New York: Harper and Row, 1978); John Gardner, *On Leadership* (New York: Free Press, 1990); Garry Wills, *Certain Trumpet: The Call of Leaders* (New York: Simon and Schuster, 1994). Good leadership is more easily recognized than explained.

Acknowledgments

During the past two years, I have visited a dozen countries on five continents to gather information for this book. A great many people have helped me, and more than a few have been indispensable. It may be an exaggeration, but only a small one, to say that never has one person owed so much to so many. Every author should be as fortunate.

Three people deserve special mention for believing not only in the merits of the original research proposal but also in my ability to perform the work. Hilary Palmer helped shape my initial thinking about this project and provided continuous guidance and support from its inception. Scott Thompson championed this work when it was still just an idea and recommended that I include a study of Kazakhstan, Ukraine, and Belarus. Thomas Graham also supported my work and was especially helpful with the chapter on South Africa. Quite simply, without these individuals this book would not have been possible.

Financial support came from the Rockefeller Brothers Fund, the United States Institute of Peace, and the Rockefeller Foundation. The Ford Foundation's grant to the Woodrow Wilson International Center for Scholars underwrote a conference on nuclear proliferation after the cold war and a series of "Nonproliferation Working Group" seminars, both of which greatly assisted my thinking on the subject.

The Wilson Center is a model for how an institution devoted to scholarship should be organized and administered. I am indebted to the Director, Charles Blitzer, the Deputy Director, Sam Wells, and the Director of the Division of International Studies, Rob Litwak. Blair Ruble, Director of the Kennan Institute for Advanced Russian Studies, repeatedly took time from his own work to explain Russian politics and their implications for the denuclearization process in Russia and the former Soviet republics. His colleagues Mark Teeter and Dan Abele were also helpful. Kristin Hunter, of the East European Studies Program, thoughtfully ensured that I received the latest information published by Radio Free Europe/Radio Liberty. Joseph Brinley, Carolee Belkin Walker, and Cheryl Anderson at the Woodrow Wilson

335

Center Press were a pleasure to work with and somehow were able to turn a manuscript into a finished book in only three months. The people at Johns Hopkins University Press also did an outstanding job on very short notice, especially Douglas Armato, Robert Oeste, and Inger Forland. The staff of the Wilson Center, especially Michele Carus-Christian, Bonnie Terrell, Leslie Robinson, and Bruce Napper, generally made my life easier so that I could devote more time to my research. Steve Lagerfeld supported this project in untold ways. Catherine Fellows did an outstanding job in proofreading and patiently tracking down source material. Maria Farnon was an excellent research assistant. Tinh Nguyen performed well the thankless task of cite-checking for the final draft.

A number of people, in the United States and overseas, accepted some personal and professional risk in talking with me and providing information. I regret that I cannot name those who spoke with me off the record, but my gratitude to them is no less than to those who are named below.

My understanding of the subjects covered in this book benefited greatly from frequent and often lengthy conversations with U.S. government officials in Washington, D.C. Robert Carlin, Robert Gallucci, Jon Gundersen, Mary Elizabeth Hoinkes, Michael Lemmon, Robert Oakley, Kenneth Quinones, and David Webster deserve special mention. Gary Samore demonstrated his expertise and friendship in many ways and always had time to talk with me. Randy Rydell, of the Senate Committee on Governmental Affairs, allowed me access to his files. Zachary Davis, of the Congressional Research Service, gave unstintingly of his time and was a superb source of information. Kurt Campbell constantly offered support and friendly encouragement.

Desley Parker and Michael Saks, of the United States Information Agency (USIA), scheduled me to present lectures in five of the countries I examined, giving me the chance to become acquainted with a much broader spectrum of these societies than I would have obtained simply through meetings in government office buildings. Elehie Natalie Skoczylas provided me with USIA's public opinion polling data from Ukraine.

At the International Atomic Energy Agency (IAEA), I met with Mohammed el-Baredi, Sven Thorstensen, Thomas Canada, and Berhan Andemichael of the New York office. Hans-Friedrich Meyer, in the Public Relations Office, made sure that I received all pertinent agency publications. Michael Lawrence, of the U.S. Mission to the IAEA, organized many of these meetings and shared his thoughts with me on the agency's operations.

The following people took the time to talk with me about my work and/or to provide documents I had difficulty obtaining: James Adams, David Albright, Walter Andersen, James Baker, Richard Barlow, Bruce Blair, Susan Clark, William Clark, Thomas Cochran, Chester Crocker, Thérèse Delpech, James Doyle, Jonathan Eyal, Rodney Fisk, David Fite, Harold Flashman, Virginia Foran, Sumit Ganguly, Robert Gates, Rose Gottemoeller, Richard Haass, Stephen Hadley, Seymour Hersh, Mark Hibbs, Ioanna Iliopulos, Neil Joeck, Richard Kennedy, Richard Kerr, Michael Krepon, Roman Laba, Ronald Lehman, Paul Leventhal, James Lilley, Dunbar Lockwood, Andrew Mack, Evgeni Maslin, Igor Maslov, Michael Mazarr, James McNally, Sally Newman, George Perkovich, Steven Pifer, William Potter, John Redick, Joan Rohlfing, Dennis Ross, Edward Rowny, Matthew Rudolph, Monica Serrano, Nadia Shadlow, Nelson Sievering, Sharon Squassoni, James Timbie, Anita Vasquez, Paul Wolfowitz, and Jon Wolfsthal. I also benefited immeasurably from my conversations and correspondence with David Fischer and Joseph Pilat, who each offered many insightful comments on the entire manuscript.

In South Africa, J. W. de Villiers and Waldo Stumpf, of the Atomic Energy Corporation, generously devoted an entire morning to discussing with me the history of the nuclear weapons program. Both also repeatedly made themselves available to answer further questions. Nic Ligthelm gave me a personal tour of the Pelindaba facility; over lunch Anthony Jackson, Director of the Y Plant, diagrammed on a cocktail napkin how South Africa's enrichment process worked. At the Foreign Ministry, I met with Jeremy Shearer, Peter Goosen, and Dieter Petzsch. At Armscor, I met with G. J. Smith and Don Henning, who provided useful information on the actual manufacture of the nuclear devices and diligently answered repeated inquiries. Over dinner in Johannesburg, Wynand Mouton explained his role as auditor in the dismantlement process.

I also met with Roger Jardine, of the African National Congress, Ambassador Donald Sole, George Barrie, Helmoed-Romer Heitman, General H. D. E. V. Du Toit, General Tienie Groenewald, Richard Ellis, Renfrew Christie, and at the American Embassy, Mark Bellamy and William Pope. John Barrett, the National Director of the South African Institute of International Affairs, kindly hosted a luncheon in my honor at Jan Smuts House, and Deon Fourie patiently explained aspects of the South African military. Dan Mozena, of the State Department, and Errol de Montille, of the South African Embassy in Washington, helped me with my trip preparations; Valerie Thomas, the embassy's Librarian, located a copy of Donald Sole's unpublished autobiography for me.

In Argentina, the Science Counsellor at the American Embassy, Kenneth Cohen, offered his assistance. Cohen's deputy, John Rubio, shared with me his extensive knowledge of the Argentine nuclear program. Ambassador Julio Carasales and Enrique de la Torre, of the Foreign Ministry, provided their thoughts on the history of and motivations for the nuclear rapprochement between Argentina and Brazil. Ambassador Carlos Ortiz de Rozas kindly hosted me for lunch at the Buenos Aires Jockey Club, where he furnished a unique perspective on Argentina's nuclear ambitions. Richard Kessler offered his insights into the Argentine nuclear program. I am grateful to Ambassador James Cheek for his hospitality when I was in Buenos Aires. Eduardo Acevedo Diaz and Pablo Tettamanti, at the Argentine Embassy in Washington, helpfully identified those officials I needed to meet in Buenos Aires.

In Brazil, Rex Nazaré Alves, the former Director of the National Commission on Nuclear Energy (CNEN), and his colleagues at the Military Institute of Engineering spent a Friday afternoon discussing the Brazilian nuclear program, including the "parallel program." Laercio Antonio Vinhas and Roberto Fulfaro, of CNEN, answered questions relating to Brazil's nuclear activities and international inspections. The Secretary of the Brazilian-Argentine Agency for Accounting and Control of Nuclear Materials (ABACC), Jorgé Coll, and his assistant, Ana Claudia Raffo, patiently explained how ABACC evolved and how it currently operates. Oskar Klingl, of the Ministry of Science and Technology, Stelson Ponce de Azevedo, Legislative Assistant to Senator Dirceu Carneiro, and Fernando de Souza Barros also met with me while I was in Brazil. Finally, Paulo Wrobel not only provided me with a copy of his dissertation on Brazil's nonproliferation policy but also took time from his busy schedule to discuss the finer points of Brazil's nuclear policy. Beyond the call of duty, Paulo and his wife, Wilma, were also gracious hosts during my stay in Rio de Janeiro.

In both Argentina and Brazil, I benefited enormously from the expertise of my traveling companion, John Redick, who generously shared his knowledge of the nuclear programs and politics of both countries. I am also indebted to Ed Fei and Beth Lisann, of the U.S. Department of Energy, who invited me to the Conference on the Peaceful Uses of Nuclear Energy and Nonproliferation, which was held at San Carlos de Bariloché from April 18 to 21, 1994. This conference was a type of "one-stop shopping" for my research, since it was attended by leading nuclear officials from both Argentina and Brazil. Virginia Gamba recommended individuals to meet and offered valuable insights from her own scholarly work on Argentina and her knowledge of the region. Monica Serrano provided me with a copy of her doctoral dissertation on the Treaty of Tlatelolco and with other writings pertinent for my research. Jean Krasno also provided me with a copy of her doctoral dissertation on Brazil's nuclear program and kindly included me in meetings she arranged with Brazilian legislators and their staffs, where she doubled as an expert translator. José Goldemberg met with me during one of his visits to Princeton University, where we discussed Brazil's nuclear policies and his own experiences in the Collor government.

In Belarus, I met with General Mecheslav Grib, Vyachaslau Paznyak, and Georgiy Tarazevich, of the Foreign Ministry, and at the American Embassy with Ambassador David Swartz and Deputy Chief of Mission George Krol. The State Department's Desk Officer for Belarus, Michael Snowden, helped with my trip preparations.

In Ukraine, I owe a great debt to John and Margarita Hewko, with whom I stayed and who arranged many of my meetings in Kiev. I would like to thank Boris Tarasiuk, of the Foreign Ministry, Parliamentarians Serhiy Holovaty, Dmytro Pavlychko, and Ihor Derkach; and Borys Bazilewsky, Ihor Fedorowycz, Bohdan Mysko, Dmitriy Vydrin, Markian Bilynskyj, Irene Jarosewich, and Mary Mycio. Special thanks are due to the Kiev office of Baker & McKenzie, especially to Eugene Kazantsev and Olena Khomenko, for their skill in translating highly technical discussions with Ukrainian officials. Valeriy Kuchinsky, of the Ukrainian Embassy in Washington, recommended individuals I should meet in Kiev.

In Kazakhstan, Oumirserik Kasenov was a gracious host while I was in Almaty, arranging meetings with Kazakh officials and providing his view of Kazakhstan's denuclearization efforts; he also offered valuable insights on the Kazakhstan chapter of this book. Tulegen Zhukeyev, National Security Adviser, took time from a very busy schedule to meet with me, as did Deputy Prime Minister Galym Abylseitov; at the Foreign Ministry, Bolat Nurgaliev spent the better part of a morning explaining Kazakhstan's nuclear diplomacy from 1991 to 1993. At the American Embassy, I talked with William Courtney and Richard Lankford, who broke away from preparing for Secretary of State Warren Christopher's visit. Almaz Khamzaev, of the Kazakhstan Embassy in Washington, and Jason Hyland, of the State Department, provided the names of Kazakh officials with whom I should meet; they also offered generally useful advice before my visit.

The renewed American emphasis on South Asian affairs in the past few years provided me with numerous opportunities to discuss nuclear matters with a wide array of experts both in India and in the United States. These included Neelam Deo, Raja Mohan, Inder Malhotra, General K. Sundarji, Rakesh Sood, K. Subrahmanyam, Brahma Chellaney, P. R. Chari, A. G. Noorani, Raja Ramanna, and V. S.

Arunachalam. Stephen Cohen's hospitality when I was in Delhi in February 1993 was greatly appreciated, as was his subsequent advice and guidance. Sumit Ganguly, my colleague at the Wilson Center during 1993–94, shared his voluminous knowledge of South Asia with me. At the American Embassy in Delhi, Peter Heydemann and Dundas McCullough were very helpful, and Kenneth Brill went out of his way to ensure that my visit to India was a success.

The chapter on Pakistan profited by meetings with Ambassador Niaz Naik, General K. M. Arif, Sarwar Naqvi, Munir Ahmad Khan, Abdul Sattar, and Munir Akram. At the American Embassy in Islamabad, John Monjo, Edward Abington, and William Stanton helped my understanding of Pakistan's nuclear policies.

Unfortunately, I was unable to obtain a visa to visit Pyongyang but was able to meet on two occasions in New York City with Dong Kyong Choi and Kim Jong Su, of the Democratic People's Republic of Korea (DPRK) Mission to the United Nations. The DPRK Mission also provided me with all its official statements during 1993 and 1994.

My visit to South Korea provided a good deal of new information and sensitized me to some of the government's concerns about North Korea's nuclear program. Ambassador and Mrs. Donald Gregg graciously let me stay with them (and included me in their dinner parties). The ambassador also helped arrange meetings for me with senior South Korean officials, and his subsequent insights on Korea always proved useful. I would also like to thank James Pierce, Daniel Russel, Kenneth Cohen (who served in Seoul before being posted to Buenos Aires), Bruce Donahue, and Nicholas Rasmussen, all at the U.S. Embassy, and Stephen Bradner, Gong Ro-Myung, Kim Chong-whi, Seongwhun Cheon, Yinhay Ahn, Jeong Woo Kil, Dalchoong Kim, Woo Joo Chang, Tae Ik Chung, Bon-tae Koo, Bongkil Shin, Kim Taewoo, Bon-Tae Koo, and Chung Tae-Ick for taking the time to meet with me.

Needless to say, any errors of fact or interpretation are solely mine.

All this travel and time away from home would not have been possible without the love and support of my family, especially my mother, Rhea Reiss, and my mother-in-law, Bobbie Anselmi. But the person who has sacrificed most and without whom this book could not have been written is my wife, Elisabeth, who has had to care for our two young children, Mathew and Michael, for long stretches of time by herself. I hope that it is some small compensation that this book is dedicated to her.

Washington, D.C.
March 1995

Index

SSH
BOOK FOR LOAN